D0574931

INVESTIGATING COMMUNICATION

An Introduction to Research Methods

LAWRENCE R. FREY

Loyola University of Chicago

CARL H. BOTAN

Rutgers University

PAUL G. FRIEDMAN

University of Kansas

GARY L. KREPS

Northern Illinois University

 PRENTICE HALL
Englewood Cliffs, New Jersey 07632

Library of Congress Cataloging-in-Publication Data

Investigating communication : an introduction to research methods /
  Lawrence R. Frey . . . [et al.].
     p.   cm.
  Includes bibliographical references.
  ISBN 0-13-503426-4
    1. Communication—Research—Methodology. I. Frey, Lawrence R.
P91.I58   1991   90–30320
302.2′072—dc20   CIP

Editorial/production supervision and
   interior design: Bayani Mendoza de Leon
Cover design: Patricia Kelly
Manufacturing buyer: Ed O'Dougherty

 © 1991 by Prentice-Hall, Inc.
A Division of Simon & Schuster
Englewood Cliffs, New Jersey 07632

Printed in the United States of America
10 9 8 7 6 5 4 3

ISBN   0-13-503426-4

Prentice-Hall International (UK) Limited, *London*
Prentice-Hall Australia Pty. Limited, *Sydney*
Prentice-Hall Canada, Inc., *Toronto*
Prentice-Hall Hispanoamericana, S.A., *Mexico*
Prentice-Hall of India Private Limited, *New Delhi*
Prentice-Hall of Japan, Inc., *Tokyo*
Simon & Schuster Asia Pte. Ltd., *Singapore*
Editora Prentice-Hall do Brasil Ltda., *Rio de Janeiro*

Contents

Preface

On March 23, 1989, two respected chemists, B. Stanley Pons, chair of the chemistry department at the University of Utah, and Martin Fleischmann of England's University of Southampton, called a press conference to announce several "table-top" experiments that had generated fusion, the nuclear reaction that powers the sun. Their discovery held the promise of solving the world's energy problems for all time.

Since then, unfortunately, efforts to replicate their discovery have proved futile, and general scientific opinion holds that they were mistaken. Their intentions were good, and their reasoning was promising—but their research methods were faulty.

Pons and Fleischmann inferred that fusion had taken place because they measured its "symptoms"—additional neutrons and heat produced when an electric current was sent through a palladium rod immersed in heavy water. Their critics question this conclusion. They maintain that the two indicators of fusion are more likely outcomes of other processes, and the two researchers could have determined this if they had conducted controlled experiments, such as using other chemicals under the same conditions to learn whether the same results would occur. But they did not. Concerned that their work would leak out and be usurped by others, they rushed to report their findings, thereby creating enormous excitement about the promise of their "discovery" and enormous disappointment when its significance was deflated.

This scientific argument, carried out on the front pages of newspapers all over the world, reflects the potential and the limitations of research. If we understand what makes essential processes work, such as fusion—or in our own discipline, communication—we can harness them to meet the needs of humanity. Yet these processes, which we observe around us naturally every day, contain elements that remain mysterious and elusive. *Time* magazine, when reporting the fusion controversy, pulled from its files reports of purported breakthroughs in fusion research from 1926, 1951, 1956, and 1958. All proved to be false alarms because the research methods used were insufficient to the task.

Today, scholars all over the world are conducting research to improve our understanding of the complex, profoundly important process called communication. Research on communication is somewhat analogous to that on fusion. Conventional methods for achieving fusion have not yet put out more energy than must be put in to conduct the experiment. Yet Harold Furth, director of Princeton's effort, says, "We are essentially within a factor of two of break-even now. Seeing that it used to be a factor of a million, we feel optimistic" (Elmer–De Witt, 1989, p. 72). Likewise, great progress has been achieved in communication research, and there is also a long way to go. We know a lot about communication, and we have a lot yet to learn.

Like fusion, whenever progress has been made toward understanding communication, it has involved rigorous research methodologies. False leads have emerged from research using invalid methods. In this book we will share with you the excitement of research, the discipline required for rigorous research, and common errors that impede researchers' progress. You will learn characteristics of high-quality research and what it takes to achieve them. You will learn shortcomings in research and what it takes to avoid them.

We have tried to write a text that encourages you to become excited about studying research methods. We start by equating learning about research methods with learning about a new culture. Like a foreign culture, research methods have their own language, rules, and social customs. Learning about a foreign culture takes time and patience. As professors, we must remember what our entry period into the culture of research was like; we must start at the very beginning and proceed slowly, making sure that everyone is with us along the way. Learning about a foreign culture is also helped by actual experience with it. You need to be exposed to many examples of research and gain experience in conducting your own research.

We also begin by equating the individual researcher with a detective. The social detective starts with a topic worth studying, poses research questions that need asking, and then attempts to find the answers in a systematic manner. Research methods are thus the strategies that researchers use to solve puzzling questions asked about communication. Like a detective, a researcher searches for evidence as carefully and systematically as possible, sorts the meaningful from the trivial, and offers the best solution.

Although a number of research methods textbooks are available, our approach is unique. First, we aim at students with little or no familiarity with primary research in communication. We seek to provide you with an understanding of this culture by demystifying the research process, making it accessible instead of esoteric. This does not mean that we do not deal with important, substantive, and at times difficult material; we do, but we never forget that you are an introductory student. Instead of throwing you into the deep end of the pool where you must swim or drown, we prefer to take you into the water slowly, allowing you to get your feet wet first and then to immerse yourself into the pool at a comfortable rate.

Second, this text is not designed to train professional researchers. Though some limited production of research may be appropriate, we believe that an introductory research methods course should aim primarily at enabling students to become knowledgeable and critical consumers of research. Only secondarily should the course aim at enabling you to do original research. You may not have to conduct research in future jobs, but certainly you will have to be able to find, read, understand, and evaluate research related to your work. Doing research in this course should improve your understanding of the research you read.

Third, we have written this textbook explicitly for students who wish to understand how research methods are used to study communication. Most research methods textbooks are written for psychology and sociology classes. A general knowledge of research methods and how they cut across disciplines is certainly desirable. This approach, however, ignores the particular characteristics of communication as a discipline. It does not prepare communication majors to study, research, and analyze the real-world communication problems they encounter in the various careers they pursue. For this reason, we have chosen to focus on how research methods apply directly to the study of communication behavior. To help accomplish this goal, we provide a thorough grounding in the nature of communication and current communication research in two chapters before discussing how to design and conduct communication research.

Fourth, in a national survey about the teaching of undergraduate communication research methods, Frey and Botan (1988) found that most professors require students to read and report on communication research published in scholarly journals. If you are to remain current and make use of primary source material in this field, you must find and understand the information generated by scholars. Doing so, however, is far more difficult than merely obtaining the leading journals and reading them. Students often feel bewildered by what they encounter in these scholarly academic journals and vow to avoid all further contact with them. To combat these feelings, we try to provide you with the "code" in which scholarly research articles are written. Once you know the purpose and the meaning of each section in research articles, the internal logic of an article emerges more clearly. This textbook thus follows the format of a traditional journal article by proceeding in a logical sequence:

1. Introducing you to the research process
2. Exposing you to topics that communication scholars consider worth studying and how research questions are posed

3. Showing you how to find and read previous research
4. Examining how researchers plan and design their studies
5. Explaining how researchers conduct their studies using appropriate methodologies
6. Understanding how the information collected is analyzed
7. Discussing how these results are interpreted in a meaningful manner

Finally, the field of communication is fragmented into many subspecialties. Differences in method and levels of analysis sometimes result in a lack of convergence. Diversity, though rich, also means the possibility of losing sight of what others in the field are doing. Too often textbooks aim at one particular subspecialty of the discipline (such as mass communication) or promote one kind of research method (such as experimental) while giving only lip service to some of the other research methods.

We believe firmly that understanding research methods fosters the complementary integration of these subspecialties. Each of the four authors in this project has extensive experience in both teaching introductory communication research methods courses and conducting research. Our various research efforts have spanned the three major areas of the communication discipline (speech communication, journalism, and mass communication), the four methodologies we examine (experimental, survey, textual analysis, and ethnography), and the two major types of data analyses (quantitative and qualitative). We believe that this diversity of interest and experience has resulted in a balanced approach to this textbook that could not possibly have been achieved had any one of us written it alone. We try to maintain consistency in how we present the material while at the same time respecting differences among the methodologies used to conduct communication research.

In the final analysis, we encourage you to approach this textbook and this course with an open mind. Too often preexisting attitudes obstruct learning new ones, and certainly this is the case with the introductory communication research methods course. So expose yourself to research; as the saying goes, "Try it, you might like it!"

ACKNOWLEDGMENTS

Writing this textbook on communication research methods was a grand endeavor that spanned three years of hard work. We are indebted to many people whose time, energy, and knowledge have shaped this text. We would like to express our sincere thanks to these colleagues and friends.

We would like to thank Steve Dalphin, executive editor at Prentice Hall, for his faith in this project from the very start, and Sandra Johnson, editorial assistant at Prentice Hall, for being so responsive to our many requests for advice and information. We also thank the superb team of reviewers selected by Prentice Hall—Marshall Scott Poole, University of Minnesota; Robert D. McPhee, University of

Wisconsin at Milwaukee; and Michael E. Mayer, Arizona State University—whose insightful comments, criticisms, and suggestions guided our rewrites.

We are also indebted to a number of colleagues who wrote research overviews of some areas covered in this text and allowed us liberal use of their material: Richard Johannesen, Northern Illinois University, for his help with rhetorical criticism; Kathleen Kendall, State University of New York at Albany, for her help with political communication; Leah Lievrouw, Rutgers University, for her help with bibliometrics; Tom Socha, Old Dominion University, for his help with conversation analysis; and Myoung Chung Wilson, Rutgers University Library, for her help with online databases and CD-ROM.

We want to thank Steve Spear, Loyola University of Chicago, and Charles Larson, Northern Illinois University, for pretesting an earlier draft of this book in their communication research methods course, and all the students at Loyola University of Chicago, Northern Illinois University, and Rutgers University who offered comments. We also are deeply indebted to JoAnn Fricke of Loyola University of Chicago for all of her secretarial help.

The authors extend special acknowledgment to Sandra Metts of Illinois State University. Sandra's only formal commitment was to write the instructor's manual, but she went over each draft of the manuscript with a fine-toothed comb, literally rewrote much of the material, and offered important suggestions. Thanks for your rigor, enthusiasm, and professionalism, Sandra.

We would like to dedicate this text to the 390 colleagues throughout the United States who completed Frey and Botan's lengthy questionnaire on teaching undergraduate communication research methods. The information you provided was extremely valuable, and we sincerely hope that this text meets your needs.

Finally, each of us would like to thank the following people:

I want to thank Elaine Bruggemeier, chair of the Department of Communication of Loyola University of Chicago, for her continual support of me and my work. I couldn't ask for a better chairperson, colleague, and friend. I also want to thank my family for their love and support, especially my father, Harvey H. Frey, who has always been there for me. Thanks to all my friends (especially Betsy, Bill, Bruce, Gary, Ken, Kerstin, Mark, Mike, and Stephanie in Chicago) for putting up with me during this project. Most of all, this book is dedicated to the one I love, Marni Cameron.

L.R.F.

A number of colleagues and students have provided me with ideas and encouragement over the past several years. Particularly helpful were Sandra Metts, William Cupach, and Mark Comadena of the Illinois State University Department of Communication, who welcomed and helped a freshly graduated assistant professor when he wanted to teach research methods. Syllabi, a test item bank, classroom exercises, and handouts were offered freely, and many hours were spent thrashing out some of the finer points of course content. In the same vein, I also want to acknowledge the role of my coauthor, Larry Frey of the Department of Communication at Loyola University of Chicago, for the hundreds of hours we have spent in conversation refining each other's grasp of research methods in communication. My current colleagues in the Department of Communication at Rutgers University, including Bob Kubey and Leah Lievrouw, have provided helpful contributions to this effort, as has Myoung Chung Wilson of the Rutgers University Library.

C.H.B.

I wish to thank the students at the University of Kansas for their inspiration and input as we learned together about the research process, and my wife, Reva, and children, Jeremy, Joy, and Glen, for being the loving core of everything I do.

P.G.F.

My sincerest thanks to my wife, Stephanie; my daughter, Becky; and my son, David for their love and support.

G.L.K.

part 1

CONCEPTUALIZING COMMUNICATION
RESEARCH

chapter **1**

Introduction
to the Research Culture

Research methods! To some people these words are intimidating, conjuring up pictures of scientists in white coats studying mice in a laboratory. Indeed, we asked a group of college students to write the first thought that came to mind in response to the words *research methods*. They said such things as "Time-consuming," "Difficult," "Worth the crap?" "Boring," and "Grade:C." In contrast, faculty members, when asked the same question, responded with "The pursuit of truth," "Planned investigation," and "Proof."

To quote the title character of the movie *Cool Hand Luke,* "What we have here is a failure to communicate." Students don't understand the full value of learning research methods. They see research as the province of the elite, as difficult or even impossible to master. This attitude is often validated, unfortunately, by how research methods are taught. The research methods course becomes a battleground or a proving ground, students wishing merely to survive it and then forgetting what they learned as soon as possible thereafter.

In short, the gap between teachers' and students' attitudes is an obstacle to learning about research methods. In this chapter we try to convey the excitement of research. We first examine the difference between everyday ways of knowing and research methods and then explore in more depth the key characteristics of the research methods culture.

EVERYDAY WAYS OF KNOWING

It would surely be impossible to question and test every piece of knowledge we possess. **Everyday ways of knowing** are based on faith, accepting things at face value. When we rely on knowledge that we have not questioned or tested, we are using everyday ways of knowing.

One everyday way of knowing is relying on **authority,** believing something because of our faith in the person who said it. Numerous persuasion studies about source credibility, the characteristics that make a person believable, report that who says something may be as important as or even more important than what is said. Take the statement "Communication courses are worthwhile" and attribute it to four different sources: a high school student, a college senior, a college communication professor, and the president of a large corporation. Which source do you think knows best what he or she is talking about?

A second everyday way of knowing is **personal experience and introspection.** We believe that what's in our own minds and social encounters is generally true. If I fear public speaking, I may assume that most people are judging my performance critically. If I have been hurt by an unfaithful spouse, I may believe that most marriages are not monogamous. Many police officers who deal frequently with criminals believe that most people are dishonest. Many psychologists who deal primarily with mentally ill patients believe that most people are neurotic. Their opinions are influenced by their own personal experiences.

Opinions acquired from personal experiences guide our behavior. Many of us learned as children, for example, that touching a hot stove burns, a personal experience that still guides our behavior toward stoves today.

A third everyday way of knowing is **intuition,** believing that something is true or false simply because it "makes sense." We generally accept love and friendship as valuable goals of communication because people simply sense their value intuitively. Intuition also refers to leaps of insight that we can't explain rationally. When you suspect that someone is lying but can't explain why, you're using intuition.

A fourth everyday way of knowing is **custom,** believing something simply because most people in our society assume it to be true. Some beliefs held on the basis of custom are racist or sexist stereotypes, such as "Women are less capable top managers than men." When pressed about why they hold this belief, prejudiced people might respond, "Because it's always been that way." Other habits based on custom are less problematic but still reflect unquestioned beliefs. Should school vacations be scheduled in the summer? Should people touch glasses when making a toast? Most people hold these opinions, but they can't necessarily say why.

A final everyday way of knowing is **magic** or **superstition,** as when we use the word *mystery* to explain an otherwise unexplainable event. Fortunetellers rely on crystal balls or tarot cards to predict the future. Even Nancy Reagan consulted her astrologer before making important decisions about President Reagan's speaking schedule! A 1984 Gallup poll, in fact, found that 55 percent of American teenagers believe in astrology, far more than the number of teenagers who understand the rudimentary physical science of how a lever works (Petersen, 1989).

The Value of Everyday Ways of Knowing

These everyday ways of knowing can certainly lead to valid and reliable knowledge. Relying on authorities, for example, serves an important purpose. We assume that doctors know how to diagnose diseases, mechanics know how to fix cars, and pilots know how to fly airplanes.

Personal experience can also be a starting point for gaining valid knowledge. Archimedes, a Greek mathematician, physicist, and inventor regarded by some historians as the father of experimental science, for example, was asked by King Hiero of Syracuse, Sicily, to determine whether his crown was made of pure gold or, as he suspected, a mixture of gold and silver. Just when he was about to give up, Archimedes stepped into the bathtub and noticed that the water ran over the edge. He reasoned that the spilled water equaled the volume of his own body. At that moment he realized that he could submerge both the crown and a piece of pure gold that weighed the same and observe whether both objects displaced the same amount of water. Legend has it that he was so excited about his discovery that he ran down the street naked shouting, "Eureka [I have found it]!" Archimedes found that the crown did indeed displace more water than the same weight of pure gold. This proved that the crown was not made of pure gold, an observation confirmed later by the goldsmith's confession.

Intuitive hunches also pay off in useful ideas. Campbell, Daft, and Hulin (1982), for example, asked well-known scholars in organizational behavior to trace the origins of their most successful projects. Several attributed their ideas to thinking intuitively about promising ideas. The investigators summed up one scholar's comments this way: "I threw out an idea in [a] doctoral seminar to which a student responded. Sense of great excitement—continuous interaction to test ideas against one another—couldn't let go" (p. 98). From this and subsequent exchanges a pioneering research project was born.

Some customary beliefs we now know make very good sense, such as cuddling babies and playing word games with them. Finally, many things remain a mystery. An example is fire-walking, walking across beds of burning coals that register over 1300 degrees Fahrenheit (Grosvernor & Grosvernor, 1966). Scientists can explain the lack of pain felt as mind over matter, but they can't explain why people don't burn their feet.

The Problems with Everyday Ways of Knowing

The problem with everyday ways of knowing is not questioning what is assumed to be true, accepting things simply at face value or because someone says so. In effect, this cuts off the inquiry process, making people passive receivers of apparent truths instead of active pursuers of kowledge. After all, don't "inquiring minds want to know"?

Everyday ways of knowing also lead to conflict and miscommunication. If I never examine my assumed knowledge and you never examine yours, we make claims as though they were facts or observable conclusions, forgetting their subjective nature.

Knowledge gained by everyday means is thus difficult to evaluate and trust. Determining who is an authority and who isn't, for example, can be quite problematic. Not all certified physicians are equally informed or trustworthy. Who is an expert in interpersonal communication? People whose relationships are problem-free? (Many of us "interpersonal communication experts" have been accused by our significant others at one time or another of leaving our work at the office!) In addition, some people claim expertise simply because they hold positions of power. Is what the boss says true? Does might make right?

Some research also indicates that we form inaccurate opinions about everyday events because we are limited in our ability to think about the information available to us. We need to simplify the complexities of life in order to cope with all the information to which we're exposed. One way we do this is jumping to conclusions on the basis of very limited knowledge. Nisbett and Ross (1980) found that when making judgments, most people ignore sound generalizations (e.g., what's reported in research based on studies of large numbers of people) and give preference to vivid personal experiences. For example, although research on a large cross-section of people indicates that college graduates earn a higher income than nongraduates, someone is likely to argue, "Yes, but *I know someone* who dropped out of school in the tenth grade, and he's a millionaire." People tend to trust firsthand, concrete, and vivid experiences more than abstract generalizations. Although information based on many people's lives is more trustworthy, it is also remote and pallid and therefore easily ignored.

Research by Kahneman and Tversky (1982) also shows that people's judgments are influenced by how a question is posed. One factor influencing thinking about solutions to problems, for example, is whether "gains" or "losses" are emphasized. Here's a decision for you to make:

A television production firm has been hit hard by an economic downturn. Three series must be cancelled, and 60 people must be laid off. Two plans exist for avoiding this crisis.

- Plan A will save one of the three shows and 20 jobs.
- Plan B has a ⅓ chance of saving all three shows and all 60 jobs, but it has a ⅔ chance of saving no shows and no jobs.

Would you consider Plan A or Plan B?

Now reconsider the problem, replacing the original choices with these:

- Plan C will result in the loss of two of the three shows and 40 jobs.
- Plan D has a ⅔ chance of losing all three shows and all 60 jobs but a ⅓ chance of losing no shows and no jobs.

Would you choose Plan C or Plan D?

Most people faced with the first two choices, emphasizing gain, pick A over B. Most faced with the second set of choices, emphasizing loss, pick D over C. Notice that Plans A and C are essentially the same, as are B and D. When a decision is placed in a framework or context of gain (Plans A and B), people are less likely to take a risk than when the decision is couched in terms of loss (Plans C and D).

This type of comparison is used to illustrate a tendency to distort information apparently inherent in people's "common sense." (Albert Einstein once said, "Common sense is the collection of prejudices acquired by age eighteen.")

Moreover, for several reasons we tend to hold on to conclusions we reach even when presented with contradictory evidence—a proclivity called *cognitive conservatism* (Schenkler, 1985). First, we identify with our ideas—to accept that our ideas have been inadequate is to admit, in a sense, that we ourselves have been inadequate. We want to feel good about ourselves, so we resist and tend to deny indications that we might be wrong. It's threatening to our self-esteem to acknowledge that we've been misguided, even when evidence suggests that.

Second, social interaction reinforces cognitive conservatism. People prefer us to be consistent in thought and deed, so they can predict how we will respond to them. Frequently changing our mind or actions makes others uncomfortable; people flexible in thought are often accused of being unstable, wishy-washy, or fickle.

Third, we use our ideas to guide our actions. Since action choices about communication must often be made instantaneously, we prefer to keep our ideas about communication simple and consistent. We have little time to think in everyday interactions. So we tend to avert or deny information that contradicts what we already believe to avoid confusion and uncertainty. To preserve consistency we sometimes perpetuate fallacious beliefs.

Cognitive conservatism ultimately cuts off the inquiry process and subsequent growth of knowledge, leading us to cling tenaciously to the beliefs we hold. Consider how cognitive conservatism affected the reaction to Galileo's work on astronomy. Aristotle argued that one should be a "passive observer" in learning about the world because he believed that people's preconceptions distort what is learned (Wolf, 1981). Two thousand years later, when Galileo invited his inquisitors (professors at the nearby university!) to look through his telescope at the moon, they "refused to do so, arguing that whatever might be visible through the telescope would be a product not of nature but of the instrument" (Lincoln & Guba, 1985, p. 45).

RESEARCH

Authority, personal experience, intuition, custom, and magic may be good starting points for the systematic pursuit of knowledge, but they don't necessarily lead to valid knowledge about the world. When we go beyond these particular ways of knowing to question and test what we know and don't know, we engage in research. Archimedes, for example, went beyond his personal bathtub experience to design research to test whether the king's crown was made of pure gold. **Research** is thus based on *disciplined* inquiry, studying something in a planned manner and reporting it so that other inquirers can replicate the process if they choose.

Research certainly is all around us: "The latest research shows that . . . ," "Four out of five doctors recommend that. . . ." We have become a research-dominated society; the word *research* serves as a stamp of approval.

Yet the public must often accept or reject research findings on faith because it knows little about the research process. People are bewildered when confronted with contradictory findings from research, as often is the case. How can one decide which to believe and which to reject? Before one can judge the quality of the product (the research findings) adequately, one must first understand the process (the methods) by which it was produced.

Characteristics of Research

Research is founded on the belief that we must question and test what we know as well as what we don't know. The purpose of communication research is understanding the underlying organizing principles guiding social behavior. Examples of organizing principles include how one thing causes another to occur and how people organize their social behavior, including how they accomplish communicating with one another.

Research can be differentiated into two types: *proprietary research* and *scholarly research*. **Proprietary research** is conducted for a specific audience and is not shared beyond that audience. For example, an auto insurance company might conduct research to determine the relative theft rates of various makes and models of cars in a local area. **Scholarly research,** by contrast, is conducted to promote public access to knowledge, as when researchers investigate and publish articles about the effectiveness of various means of persuasion or new vaccines for treating diseases. Although the research methods examined in this test certainly apply to proprietary research, we are interested primarily in scholarly research.

The scholarly research process, or scholarship, has the following characteristics:

1. *Scholarship is question-oriented.* Scholarly research is directed by questions posed at various levels of abstraction, such as asking what people do, why they do it, or what effect behavior has on them. These questions might spring from observed theoretical inconsistencies or gaps in what's reported in scholarly literature or from a practical concern, such as the effects of television on children or how women function as leaders. At the heart of all scholarly research is a question worth answering.

2. *Scholarship is methodological.* Scholarly research depends on a planned, systematic process of investigation. Research proceeds in a careful step-by-step manner, employing an ordered system of inquiry. Scholarship is not for the purpose of proving the preconceptions of researchers. Objective procedures are used to ensure that researchers find and report what is accurate.

3. *Scholarship is creative.* Scholarly research is a creative act that reveals underlying order in the world and among its inhabitants. It brings into being concepts not articulated before, and it assesses ideas created previously. Scholarship begins with inventive ingenuity, a leap of the imagination, and leads to breakthroughs that extend the frontiers of knowledge.

4. *Scholarship is replicable.* Because scholarly research follows a systematic plan, other scholars can replicate, or reproduce, the entire inquiry process. Scholarly research leads to reliable conclusions precisely because it can be replicated. Replication ensures that the idiosyncrasies in the context of any one study, producing distorted results, don't lead to inappropriate generalizations. For example, only after repeated testing is a new drug allowed to be released on the market.

5. *Scholarship is self-critical.* Scholarly research is reflexive; it explicitly examines itself to discover and report flaws or threats to its own validity or accuracy. Scholarly researchers evaluate the strengths and weaknesses of their own and others' research studies.

6. *Scholarship is public.* Scholarly research serves a societal purpose, so it's everyone's business. Because the findings from scholarly inquiry may be used to make important decisions that affect people, scholarship must be reported thoroughly and must be open to examination, questioning, and criticism by the public and other scholars. Scholarship is public, not private, information. Every association of scholars publishes journals in which recent research is described in detail.

7. *Scholarship is cumulative and self-correcting.* Scholarly research, by being open to one and all, creates a shared history. The accumulation of information from scholarly research allows for knowledge to evolve and grow. Old beliefs are discarded when they no longer hold true, and new beliefs emerge from the process, only to be challenged once again. Scholarship thus leads to more scholarship. Not only is scholarship part of the broader community, but it also creates a community of inquirers. Scholars meet regularly at conferences to share, discuss, and critique one another's work.

8. *Scholarship is cyclical.* Scholarly research proceeds in stages and ends up back where it started. A researcher begins with a topic worth studying, asks questions and/or makes predictions, plans research carefully, carries out the planned research, analyzes the data to provide tentative answers, and starts all over again by posing new topics and questions worth studying. Scholars thus provide feedback to themselves; new questions emerge from answers to previous questions.

Research as Culture

These characteristics make research methods fundamentally different from the everyday ways of knowing of authority, personal experience, intuition, custom, and magic. Indeed, it is helpful to think about the research community as a discrete culture. Like any culture, research has its own language, rules, and social customs.

Learning about any new culture takes time and patience. When we first enter a new culture, we feel awkward because we do not know what the natives are saying or how to engage in appropriate behavior. We must start by becoming familiar with the language used. Barnlund (1988) notes that "every culture attempts to create a 'universe of discourse' for its members, a way in which people can interpret their experience and convey it to one another" (p. 11). Once we know the code and the ropes, we feel more comfortable and competent within that culture. By giving you a feel for the culture of research, we hope you will become excited about it, understand its value, and, most important, learn to live comfortably and profitably within it.

The communication research culture.   Even though scholarly researchers are all guided by eight characteristics of scholarship, they do not necessarily all share the same view of the world or the same assumptions about how people and communication should be studied. Just as there are different subcultures in any society, there are different scholarly research cultures. For example, we might distinguish three general research cultures: the **physical sciences,** which study the physical and natural world, as represented by the disciplines of physics, chemistry, and biology; the **humanities,** which study the achievements of creative people, such as music, art, and literature; and the **human** or **social sciences,** which apply scientific methods to the study of human behavior.

Communication overlaps in part of each of these three scholarly research cultures. Biologists, for example, sometimes talk about cells "communicating" with one another. The speech sciences, such as audiology (the study of hearing), are also tied to biology. Communication is also associated with the humanities, since art, music, and literature are forms of communication. Finally, communication is a human or social science since researchers, like their colleagues in psychology, sociology, and anthropology, use scientific methods to study human communication.

Communication research is influenced by two basic scholarly research processes: *behaviorism* and *phenomenology.* Cahn and Hanford (1984) identify some important differences between these two research cultures (see Figure 1.1).

Behaviorism is based on the belief that objective knowledge is obtained through the careful and systematic *observation* and *measurement* of what people do. Behavioral research methods rely on *operationalism,* transforming abstract con-

Figure 1.1 Behaviorism, phenomenology, and an integrated approach to human communication research

Metatheoretical Concerns	Behaviorism	Phenomenology	Integrated Approach
1. Subject matter	Behavior	+ Meanings	= Human action
2. Method	Operationalism	+ Interpretation	= Operationalism of inter-subjective experience
3. Major concern	Method	+ Subject Matter	= Subject matter's fit to the method
4. Goal	Explanation, prediction, and control	+ Understanding	= Prediction through explanation and understanding

Source: Dudley D. Cahn and Jack T. Hanford, "Perspectives on Human Communication Research: Behaviorism, Phenomenology, and an Integrated View," *Western Journal of Speech Communication,* 48(3), p. 281, copyright © 1984 by the Western Speech Communication Association. Reprinted by permission of the Western Speech Communication Association.

cepts into behaviors that can be precisely quantified. For example, the abstract concept of stage fright might be operationalized into quantifiable behaviors by measuring the number of speech disfluencies ("ah," "um") a person exhibits while giving a public speech. Behaviorists also seek to learn what occurs before (antecedents) and after (consequences) the behaviors they study. They believe that physical objects and human beings react to environmental forces, so the goal of behavioral research is to identify and test laws that can *explain, predict,* and lead to the *control* of behavior.

Phenomenology, by contrast, is based on the belief that what people do depends on what they perceive, what goes on in their minds. Phenomenologists thus focus on how internal, psychological meanings guide behavior. Phenomenological methods of research rely on discovering how individuals construct meaning, believing that objective observation is not sufficient. Cahn and Hanford (1984) explain that "one of the most important points in phenomenology is its attempt to do justice to the uniqueness of the individual and the uniqueness of the individual's world view" (p. 279). Phenomenologists, therefore, give priority to the subjective aspect of human life. The goal of phenomenological research is to describe how people *understand* their lived experience.

Both behaviorism and phenomenology inform the study of communication. Communication certainly is a behavior that can be studied using behavioral methods, as evidenced by many of the research methods examined in this textbook. In fact, early communication research was dominated by the appeal of behavioral methods. Fisher (1978) explains:

Most of the general populace is in awe of science and scientists. We fear science. We respect science. We worship science. We endow the very word with a mystique all its own and, fundamentally, don't understand it. But above all else, we do know that science is methodical with a method that pretentiously bears its own name—*the* scientific [behavioral] method. (p. 65)

In their attempt to understand communication, many scholars adopted the behavioral methods of the physical sciences. Indeed, Freud would have had a field day with this "physics envy"!

Communication, however, also depends on meaning and thus can be studied using phenomenological methods. We can't fully understand important human events, such as romantic love or political power, without understanding how people think and feel about them.

Because communication takes into account both behavior and meaning, Cahn and Hanford (1984) argue for an integrated approach to communication research (see Figure 1.1). Behaviorism and phenomenology can be seen as making complementary contributions to understanding human communication, as two sides of the same coin. A full explanation of human action demands accounting for both behavior and meanings. There is a physical, objective world, but there is also the subjective world of the individual. Knowledge about communication is a result of agreements between subjective individuals about what appears objectively to be true. Communication, of course, is the key to creating this knowledge. The end result of integrating behaviorism and phenomenology is the ability to explain, understand, predict, and control human communication.

Communication scholars celebrate the contributions of behaviorism and phenomenology and use both types of research to study human beings and the complex process called communication. You thus will be exposed in this textbook to some research methods grounded in behaviorism, some in phenomenology, and some in a combination of these two research cultures comprising the comprehensive study of communication.

THE RESEARCHER AS DETECTIVE

Too often researchers are portrayed as dispassionate scientists in white coats handling test tubes in the laboratory. This image omits the creativity and excitement of research. A more apt metaphor might be a detective searching for clues to a crime. Poole and McPhee (1985) explain:

> Like a good detective, the researcher is confronted by a confusing pattern of clues that is meaningful in both an immediate and a deeper, sometimes hidden sense. To get at this deeper meaning and unravel the mystery, the detective (researcher) must probe and order this "reality," often relying on improvisation, inspiration and luck. Once things fall into place there is the possibility of true understanding and insight, but there is also the danger of misinterpreting the multitude of available signs. . . . [Research] requires the capacity to ask the right questions as well as a sense of what form the answer should take. Detective novels are replete with devices and strategies for attacking a mystery, and this is no less true of social scientific writing. (p. 100)

Research methods may therefore be viewed as the strategies researchers use to solve puzzling mysteries about the world. Like any good detective, researchers want to make sense of what's unknown, and their methods are the substance of the research culture. This text, then, explains the culture-specific detectives who use their research methods to answer important questions.

The Detective at Work: Explanation and Evidence

Being a detective involves constructing a possible explanation for an event and seeking evidence to test the explanation. Both behavioral and phenomenological researchers engage in two interrelated research activities: building theories and collecting evidence.

Theory building.   Many people misinterpret the word *theory*. They contrast it with practical knowledge. Have you heard the cliché, "It may work in theory but certainly not in practice"? And as that wise sage Charlie Chan once said, "Theories are like a mist on the eyeglasses: They tend to obscure one's vision."

To researchers, theories are eminently practical. They represent tentative solutions to a problem. Kaplan (1964) explains that "a theory is a way of making sense of a disturbing situation" (p. 295). A **theory** is a generalization about a phenomenon, an explanation of how or why something occurs. Indeed, any statements that *explain* what is measured or described—any general statements about cause or effect—are theory-based, as least implicitly.

The power of a theory is its ability to connect events into a unified web. Hawes (1975) explains:

> What gives a theory its power is not the declarative statements it consists of but rather the relationship among those statements. It is the form of the relationship among statements rather than the individual statements themselves that distinguish between theory and description. (p. 29)

The usefulness of any theory can be judged by the extent to which it meets a number of important functions (see Figure 1.2). A theory is thus a useful explanation to the extent that it excites us about inquiry, organizes our knowledge, leads us to expect certain outcomes to occur, and focuses research efforts. There often are trade-offs, however, among these criteria. Sometimes a theorist has to sacrifice one criterion, such as simplicity, to achieve a higher degree of another one, such as validity.

One traditional debate among scholars concerns how theory is built and how it should guide research. Generally speaking, behavioral research tends to be **theory-driven,** or **deductive.** The researcher starts with a theory and then seeks to learn whether empirical (observable) data support it. Phenomenological research, by contrast, tends to be **theory-generated,** or **inductive.** The researcher first gathers data, then develops a theory from them.

Figure 1.2   Evaluating theories

The following is a synthesis of some of the most important functions that theory serves, functions that can be used to evaluate any theory. This synthesis is based on work by Barnlund (1968), Bross (1953), Dance (1982), Hall and Lindzey (1970), Hawes (1975), Kaplan (1964), Kuhn (1970), Littlejohn (1983), and Poole (1988).

1. **EXPLANATION:** Theories clarify, make sense of, and account for a subject matter. Theories help us understand what something involves by organizing and summarizing knowledge into a system. To the extent that a theory explains something, it is considered to have explanatory power.

   a. *Theoretical Scope:* The explanatory power of any theory is limited by its boundary, the behavior, people, or context it covers. A theory might explain many things or something specific.

   b. *Validity:* A theory must be valid internally, or consistent, being free from contradiction. A theory also needs to be valid externally, being consistent with observed facts and common everyday experiences.

   c. *Simplicity:* A theory should be as simple, or parsimonious, as possible. The fewer the number of propositions, the better the theory.

2. **PREDICTION:** Theories offer a way of foretelling what will happen beforehand. They provide informed guesses about what will occur and when. To the extent that a theory provides testable predictions about something, it is considered precise.

   a. *Focusing:* A theory focuses attention on the most important variables and their expected outcomes.

   b. *Observational Aid:* A theory tells us what to look for in observing and measuring the important variables and their effects.

   c. *Open to Falsification:* A theory is open to falsification, or corroboration. It must be able to be tested in order to determine the extent to which it is true or false.

3. **CONTROL:** To the extent that a theory explains and predicts the occurrence of a process, we can gain some measure of control over that process. Such control allows us to produce the object of inquiry and direct it in meaningful ways, by setting up the necessary conditions for causing or inhibiting its occurrence.

4. **HEURISTIC:** A theory should generate scholarly research. Theory serves as an impetus for testing its concepts and predictions. Scholars usually devote their energies to testing the most promising theories. Thus theories that have been examined widely are usually deemed most worthwhile.

5. **COMMUNICATIVE:** A theory serves as an important focus for discussion and debate. It is a public message about a phenomenon that scholars argue for and against.

6. **INSPIRATION:** A theory ought to be exciting, catch our imagination, and teach us something. It ought to solve important puzzles and intriguing mysteries and should address important and meaningful concerns.

This is a false dichotomy, however. Theory building can take place both inductively and deductively. Sometimes researchers engage in deductive research—they start with a tentative conclusion and conduct an investigation to test its accuracy. At other times researchers engage in inductive research—they start with only a question and gather evidence upon which they can build a conclusion. Thus it is helpful to think of induction as the process of developing theories and deduction as the process of testing them (see Figure 1.3).

Theory-building and research methods, therefore, are cyclical; each one feeds the other. Theory and research are not separate; both are sides of the same coin. Poole and McPhee (1985) argue that we need to think of "theory-method complexes as the driving force in the research process" (p. 101).

Collecting evidence: research methods. Regardless of whether scholars look for evidence to test theories or whether evidence is used to build theories, all scholarly research at some point involves collecting evidence, or data. **Research methods** are the particular strategies researchers use to collect the evidence necessary for building and testing theories.

A traditional debate concerns the appropriate nature of evidence and the man-

Figure 1.3   The theory-building-research cycle (After Wallace, 1971)

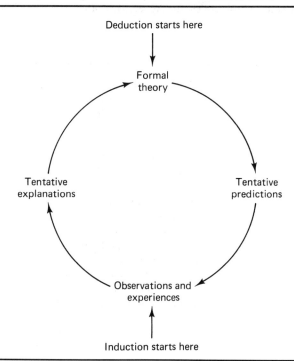

ner in which it is to be collected. Generally speaking, behaviorists collect atomistic (small) quantitative (numerical) units of analysis (behavior) under controlled conditions (in a research laboratory). Phenomenologists typically collect holistic (meaningful) qualitative (symbolic) units of analysis (concepts) under naturalistic conditions (in the field).

Understanding complex phenomena, such as communication, however, often demands combining both approaches. *Triangulation* is a term that in surveying refers to locating a point in terms of two other fixed positions. In the context of communication research, **triangulation** means that different research techniques producing consistent results provide a more effective base for describing, explaining, understanding, interpreting, predicting, controlling, and critiquing a communication process or event than a single research technique producing a single result. Answering important questions about complex subject matter by using different but ultimately complementary research methods allows Humpty Dumpty to be put back together again.

The importance of triangulation is well put by John Godfrey Saxe in his famous poem, "The Blind Men and the Elephant" (see Figure 1.4). Feeling only one part of the animal leads to some erroneous conclusions about what the whole animal is like. The same is true for studying communication. Any single research method is a one-dimensional approach to a three-dimensional phenomenon. Only through the use of multiple research methods can the research community hope to achieve complete understanding of the aspect of communication being studied.

Figure 1.4

THE BLIND MEN AND THE ELEPHANT
by
John Godfrey Saxe

It was six men of Indostan
To learning much inclined,
Who went to see the Elephant,
(Though all of them were blind),
That each by observation
Might satisfy his mind.
The *First* approached the Elephant,
And happening to fall
Against his broad and sturdy side,
At once began to bawl:
"God bless me! but the Elephant
is very like a wall!"
The *Second*, feeling of the tusk,
Cried, "Ho! what have we here
So very round and smooth and sharp?

To me 'tis mightly clear
This wonder of an Elephant
is very like a spear!"
The *Third* approached the animal,
And happening to take
The squirming trunk within his hands,
Thus boldly up he spake:
"I see," quoth he, "the Elephant
Is very like a snake!"
The *Fourth* reached out an eager hand,
And felt about the knee
"What most this wonderous beast is like
Is might'ly plain," quoth he;
" 'Tis clear enough the Elephant
is very like a tree!"
The *Fifth* who chanced to touch the ear,
Said: "E'en the blindest man
Can tell what this resembles most;
Deny the fact who can,
This marvel of an Elephant
Is very like a fan!"
The *Sixth* no sooner had begun
About the beast to grope,
Then seizing on the swinging tail
That fell within his scope,
"I see," quoth he, "the Elephant
Is very like a rope!"
And so these men of Indostan
Disputed loud and long,
Each in his own opinion
Exceeding stiff and strong,
Though each was partly in the right,
And all were in the wrong!

Let us consider an example. Suppose that the editors of a magazine want to know how well the articles in their magazine appeal to readers. One way they could do this is to count how many copies of each issue are sold. The more issues sold, the more appealing the magazine must be. Another way they could do this is to ask a group of readers to express their feelings about the magazine. From the readers' comments, they learn which articles are most appealing and *why*. Obviously, some combination of the number of issues sold (behavioral or quantitative data) and the specific comments of readers (phenomenological or qualitative data) would be most effective for assessing the magazine's appeal.

Understanding how human beings act and interact therefore necessitates acquiring both quantitative and qualitative data. Research requires studying people's behavior and meanings, both in laboratories and in natural settings, using many research methods. The choice of any particular method at any particular time is determined by the method that seems to provide the best way of answering the research question posed. As scholars argue, one always fits the method to the problem, not the other way around.

A WORKING MODEL OF COMMUNICATION RESEARCH

To begin the rigorous process of scholarship, let's divide the communication research process into concrete stages that form the basis for the sections of this textbook, stages that involve both conceptual concerns and practical decisions (see Figure 1.5). The communication research process can be viewed as an ongoing cycle of five interrelated phases of research activities: (1) conceptualization, (2) planning and designing research, (3) methodologies for conducting research, (4) analyzing and interpreting data, and (5) reconceptualization.

Stage 1: Conceptualizing Communication Research

Conceptualization, the first phase of research, involves forming an idea about what needs to be studied. Researchers begin communication inquiry by engaging in such conceptualizing activities as identifying a topic worth studying, defining the primary concepts relevant to the topic, reviewing the relevant literature to learn what is already known about the topic, and phrasing the topic as a formal research question or hypothesis.

Researchers establish a field of inquiry by narrowing their focus to a particular

Figure 1.5   The research process cycle model

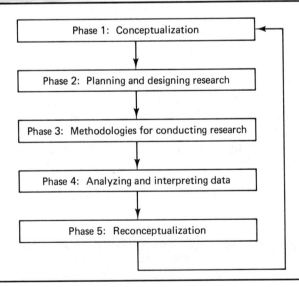

topic worth studying. That topic may result from a practical problem that needs solving, an experience that needs explaining, or a theoretical proposition that needs testing. At the broadest level, that field of inquiry is grounded in assumptions about the research process, as all scholarly research is founded on assumptions about philosophy. We have tried to explain in this chapter some of the philosophical assumptions underlying communication research.

The best way to establish a focal point for research is to choose a topic worth studying and a specific question worth asking. To do this, the appropriate boundaries for communication research must be established. Chapter 2 explains some of the fundamental principles that help define the concept of communication.

These principles of communication then can be used to pose a formal research question or hypothesis (prediction). Chapter 3 examines how researchers ask research questions and pose hypotheses. We also provide an overview of how some general questions have guided communication research.

Research topics do not exist in isolation. To understand fully and accurately any particular research topic, concept, or research question or hypothesis, it is necessary to know what scholars in the discipline have found by reviewing primary source materials. Reviewing the literature demands a working knowledge of where such sources exist, how to find them with a minimum of effort, and how to read them. The nature of documentary or library research is discussed in Chapter 4.

Stage 2: Planning and Designing Communication Research

Good research projects are thought out carefully in advance. One important step is selecting a topic worth studying. Once a topic has been selected, the available information on it has been found, and a formal research question or hypothesis has been posed, researchers need a systematic plan for conducting their study.

Moving from the conceptualization phase to planning and designing research demands that researchers transform abstract concepts into operational, or measurable, terms. **Operationalization** involves determining the observable attributes, or characteristics, of the concepts of interest. Researchers must then develop strategies for measuring those observable concepts. Communication researchers usually rely on three general techniques for measuring research concepts: questionnaires, interviews, and observations. These three measurement techniques, however, produce different types of information. Chapter 5 examines the nature of operationalization and measurement and how questionnaires, interviews, and observations are used in communication research.

Measurement techniques, of course, need to be valid, or accurate. Validity, however, is not just important for the purposes of measurement; it affects the entire research plan and design. The internal validity of a study has to do with whether the procedures researchers use to answer a research question are accurate. As we shall see, researchers must control a number of important threats to designing internally valid research. The external validity of a study is concerned with the extent to which researchers can generalize findings to people not involved directly in the research. Since researchers usually cannot include everyone they might wish to study, they typically rely on a limited number of people, called a sample, from a targeted population. External validity is thus tied to the nature of the sample and how it was obtained. Being able to generalize also depends on the realism of the procedures that were used, as well as replication of research findings. Chapter 6 examines the process of designing internally and externally valid research.

Planning and designing communication research involves a number of ethical decisions. Ethics affects each stage of the research process: how researchers choose research topics and frame research questions, how the literature is reviewed, how research is designed and conducted, how data are analyzed, and how the findings are interpreted and used. Chapter 7 explores some important ethical decisions confronting communication researchers.

Stage 3: Methodologies for Conducting Communication Research

Once the topic has been chosen, the research question has been determined, the review of the literature has been conducted, and the research has been designed, researchers are ready to conduct their studies. Conducting careful research demands understanding and adhering to the specific assumptions and requirements of the methodology chosen. These methods tell researchers what evidence to look for and how to look for it. Chapters 8 through 11 examine four major methodologies available to communication researchers.

Chapter 8 explains the nature of experimental research. Experimental research applies principles about causation developed from the physical sciences to the study of human beings. Because of its emphasis on prediction and control, the experimental method is a powerful technique for examining how one variable produces changes in another variable.

Chapter 9 explains the nature of survey research. Survey research is used to discover the self-reported characteristics of a relatively small number of people for the purpose of generalizing those characteristics to the population from which they were drawn. The use of the survey method in communication research sacrifices some of the need for control and prediction from the experimental method in order to describe how people perceive communication behavior and its effects.

Chapter 10 explains the nature of textual analysis, which is how researchers analyze spoken, written, electronic, and visual texts, or documents. One form of textual analysis is rhetorical criticism, which researchers use to understand and critique a text. Textual analysis also includes identifying patterns in the communication content of written, electronic, and visual documents, called content analysis, as well as the analysis of messages exchanged during conversation, called conversation analysis. Textual analysis also includes the study of unobtrusive measures, texts that are collected without people's knowledge, as through examining archival records, bibliographical citations, or the physical traces people have left behind. Textual analysis is thus an important methodology for communication scholars because it focuses directly on the content and structure of communication.

Chapter 11 explains the nature of ethnography, or naturalistic research. Ethnographers study people in particular natural settings, attempting to capture the way people use symbols to make sense of their world. Researchers use this method to probe for people's interpretations of the world and how they see themselves making choices, particularly with regard to their communication behavior.

Try to keep in mind throughout our discussions of these four methodologies that no one methodology is inherently better than another. The use of a particular methodology must always be guided by the nature of the topic chosen and the research question asked. Fitting the method to the topic and the question rather than the other way around avoids the "law of the hammer," the tendency to hit everything in sight with a favorite tool or research method. Researchers must thus ask themselves whether the topic and question are addressed best by the experimental, survey, textual, or ethnographic method. We also believe firmly that answering complex questions about communication often demands using these different methodologies in a complementary manner.

Stage 4: Analyzing and Interpreting Data

Once data, or evidence, have been gathered through the use of the methodologies discussed in stage 3, they need to be analyzed and interpreted. For some methods, particularly experimental and survey and sometimes textual analysis, this means processing quantitative (numerical) data through the use of appropriate statistical procedures. For that reason, Chapters 12 through 14 examine how quantitative data are analyzed and interpreted.

Chapter 12 explains the theory underlying the use of statistics, which are powerful tools for describing the nature of quantitative data and for inferring important consequences from them. The use of statistics, just like any other tool or procedure, rests on a set of fundamental assumptions. Before discussing specific statistical procedures, we examine the reasons for engaging in this type of analysis and what the results will mean once the analyses are complete.

One type of statistical analysis examines whether and how groups of people (or texts) differ with regard to one or more variables of interest. For example, do men and women differ in their willingness to reveal personal information, or do liars and nonliars use different nonverbal gestures? Chapter 13 explains the underlying assumptions and specific techniques for determining whether and the extent to which groups of people differ.

A second type of statistical analysis examines whether and how variables are related. Are age and listening ability related positively, such that as one goes up, the other goes up? Are they related negatively, such that as one goes up, the other goes down? Are they related in an even more complex manner? Or are they not related at all, such that as one goes up or down, the other remains unchanged? Chapter 14 explains the underlying assumptions and specific techniques for analyzing whether and how variables are related.

Stage 5: Reconceptualizing Communication Research

Reconceptualization occurs when researchers rethink the topic of inquiry as a result of the systematic processes associated with conceptualization, planning and designing research, using methodologies to conduct research, and analyzing the data acquired by research. Once data have been collected and analyzed, the findings need to be interpreted within the broader context of the research process.

Reconceptualization involves explaining the significance of the findings. Researchers try to explain how the findings answer the research questions posed, confirm or disconfirm the predictions made, and support or refute previous theory and research. Researchers also identify any problems with the research and how these problems may limit the validity and use of the findings. Finally, researchers address the implications of their findings for future reseach and policy decisions. Identifying implications from research for future communication theory, research, and practice completes the full cycle of the research process. Chapter 15 examines this important concluding phase of the research process.

CONCLUSION

We are confronted by research findings every day. If we are to be knowledgeable and critical consumers of research, we must understand the processes used to conduct it. Researchers constitute an important subculture, complete with their own assumptions about how the world works, terminology, and rules of conduct. They may be viewed as detectives looking for explanations of important processes and events. Our goal in this textbook is to acquaint you with the research process and the detection methods used to carry it out.

chapter 2

The Nature of Communication

As you've probably discovered, when you tell people that you are studying communication, many images come to mind. People may assume that you're studying broadcasting or public speaking or telephone systems or letter writing or something else entirely. The term *communication* is used in various contexts to refer to many different things.

As a sign, therefore, communication isn't very useful, since there's little agreement as to its meaning. It functions well, however, as an umbrella term because it covers and clusters numerous apparently disparate activities that actually have important elements in common. Also, communication is commonly recognized as essential to successful human living. For these reasons, the term is used widely in academia to refer to the kinds of behavior studied and practiced by professionals who accept communication as their common ground.

But you can't point to, dissect, or measure a "communication" as you can a microphone or a speech transcript. Because *communication* is a broad, abstract term imposed on a large collection of processes, little can be said about "communication in general." In fact, the first step most researchers take is carving out and defining the precise piece of the big communication pie they will investigate. What they learn enables them to say with some certainty a few specific things about their own slice. They are also able to compare and contrast what they've learned about their own slice with what's known about the slices studied by other researchers.

Over time, as researchers describe more and more small pieces, the whole realm of communication gradually takes on new meaning.

The process of communication and the slices of human life it covers were created and named by people. Since our knowledge of these processes is growing, and with it our thinking about them, the meanings of terms in this field are evolving. In this chapter we will examine the overall concept of communication, what researchers have understood it to mean over time, and how they have subdivided it into its component slices. In doing so, we will explain the need for communication research, define communication, and identify some implications of our definition for conducting communication research.

HISTORY OF COMMUNICATION INQUIRY

Communication is an important topic of study in the modern world. We depend on our communication with others to gather relevant information, develop relationships, and exert professional and interpersonal influence. The effectiveness of our communication is related directly to our level of success in interpreting our world and accomplishing our goals.

Yet communication is deceivingly complex, and ineffective communication is all too common. We are often surprised and confused when our communication strategies are unsuccessful, when we are misinterpreted, or when we fail to accomplish our intended communication goals. Communication research is conducted to demystify the communication process, to help us understand why communication does or does not work as it is intended, to identify and explore the many interrelated elements that comprise the communication process, and to help us develop strategies for using communication more effectively and appropriately.

Communication is not a new topic of research; it has intrigued and been studied for centuries. The earliest study of communication can be traced back to the fifth century B.C., during the *classical period* of communication inquiry. Philosophers like Plato and his student Aristotle studied the public-speaking strategies of Greek orators, naming this area of inquiry *rhetoric* (Paulson, 1980). Later, during the Roman Empire, statesmen like Cicero and Quintillian studied the role of public communication in Roman society (Ruben, 1988). The classical period of communication inquiry thus emphasized the central role of public communication in developing and maintaining government and society and firmly established the importance of the *oral tradition* in communication inquiry.

The oral tradition dominated communication inquiry for many years and led to the study of public speaking and elocution. In 1882 the National Association of Elocutionists was formed to promote the study of speaking style, articulation, and gestures in public address, followed by the formation of the National Association of Academic Teachers of Public Speaking in 1914 (Anderson, 1987; Ruben, 1988). Establishing these professional associations marked the first steps in the early development of the communication discipline. These associations helped legitimize communication inquiry and provided communication researchers with a forum for sharing their scholarship.

Development of the Communication Discipline

In the 1800s, colleges moved from a liberal tradition of education that emphasized generalized knowledge to a disciplinary model of education that emphasized specialized knowledge within specific academic disciplines. Specialized departments were established in colleges to represent such different academic disciplines as English, history, and biology. Until the early 1900s, there were no departments of communication within colleges because communication was not yet an established discipline. Instead, communication was viewed as an important part of many different disciplines rather than as a separate field of inquiry. Most teachers and researchers of communication (covering such areas as public speaking, rhetoric, forensics, journalism, and literature) were in college departments of English. These communication scholars gradually developed their own professional associations and found themselves and their work increasingly distinct from English and out of place in English departments.

In the early 1900s, speech and journalism scholars began breaking away to form their own departments. To legitimize their right to establish separate departments, speech and journalism faculty members had to justify the status of their specialties as academic disciplines. Speech and journalism, however, developed separate strategies for asserting disciplinary status. Speech faculty members adopted from the physical and human sciences a primarily scientific justification for disciplinary status, often referring to their new discipline as "speech science" (Woolbert, 1916). Journalism faculty members, by contrast, used a primarily professional justification for disciplinary status, claiming that their mission was to train professional journalists. These justifications separated speech and journalism from English, which had a strong literary tradition but neither a scientific nor a professional orientation (Anderson, 1987).

Role of Research in the Development
of the Communication Discipline

The use of a scientific justification for the establishment of speech as a separate department had important implications for the development of communication research. Speech scientists emulated the more established human sciences, such as psychology and sociology, which had emulated such physical sciences as biology and physics. Speech scientists adopted their research methodologies, as well as many interdisciplinary concepts and perspectives for studying communication phenomena, from the physical and other human sciences.

Communication inquiry began to broaden beyond its traditional focus on presentational communication to examine such communication events and processes as the relationship between communication and attitude formation, communication and relationship development, communication and group decision making, and communication flow within organizations. This broadening of communication research led to changing the name of the professional association from the National Association of Academic Teachers of Public Speaking to the Speech Association of America and, more recently, to the Speech Communication Association. The human scientific perspective of speech expanded from focusing on the areas of public speaking and rhetoric to exploring the broader study of communication in all walks of life.

Meanwhile, the introduction of radio, television, and film as important communication media in the 1900s expanded the boundaries of journalism study beyond the professional training of print journalists to the examination of the social impact of the media. As mass communication theories were developed and as research explored the production, use, and influence of the mass media, the justification for journalism as a unique discipline changed from journalism as professional training to journalism as an applied human science devoted to the pragmatic analysis of the role of the media in society (Anderson, 1987; Weaver & Gray, 1980). This applied human scientific research orientation expanded the area of journalism into the broader study of all forms of mediated communication.

Structure of the Communication Discipline

Human scientific developments within speech and journalism led toward a reintegration of the two disciplines, which had separated after breaking away from English. Speech and journalism represented complementary perspectives for studying communication, combining to form the more comprehensive communication discipline. Many modern college departments and schools of communication now incorporate both face-to-face human communication and mediated communication perspectives. In fact, it is not uncommon for schools of communication to include departments of journalism, mass communication (sometimes called mass media or communications), and speech communication (sometimes called communication, speech, or rhetoric), as well as theater and film studies programs. Research methods, in turn, are now used to study both face-to-face and mediated aspects of communication.

Today many major professional associations represent both the human and mediated communication orientations. The Speech Communication Association (SCA) and the International Communication Association (ICA), for example, serve as major associations for speech and mass communication scholars, while the Association for Educational Journalism and Mass Communication (AEJMC) serves as a major association for mass communication and journalism scholars. There also are four regional and many state communication associations as well as other associations representing more specific communication topics.

The major areas of inquiry within the communication discipline are defined by the interest groups established within these professional associations (see the representative examples in Figure 2.1). Most communication scholars identify them-

Figure 2.1   Interest groups in SCA, ICA, and AEJMC

Applied communication
Argumentation and debate (forensics)
Communication and aging
Ethics and communication
Feminist scholarship
Health communication
Human communication technology
Information systems
Instructional communication
International and intercultural communication
Interpersonal and group communication
Interpretation (oral interpretation of literature)
Intrapersonal communication
Mass communication (mass media)
Newspaper
Organizational communication
Philosophy of communication
Political communication (communication and the law)
Popular communication
Public address
Public relations
Rhetorical and communication theory
Speech and language sciences
Theater

selves and their primary areas of inquiry somewhere within this disciplinary framework, and some of the research conducted within these areas of communication will be examined in Chapter 3.

THE NEED FOR COMMUNICATION RESEARCH

Research is conducted to help people understand complex and challenging communication phenomena as well as the mundane and apparently simple everyday routines like ordinary conversation. The many topic areas of communication inquiry demonstrate the complex, multifaceted nature of communication. Further, the centrality of communication in modern life makes knowledge about communication processes crucially important.

Systematic and rigorous inquiry means that researchers study worthwhile topics, ask relevant questions, build on previous theory and research, design and conduct careful research, analyze data appropriately, and discuss the significance of the findings. Systematic communication inquiry adds to the body of communication knowledge by providing meaningful descriptions and trustworthy explanations about complex communication phenomena. Research about communication is thus needed for two reasons: to extend the growth of the communication discipline and to apply what we know.

Systematic Inquiry and the Growth of Knowledge

Systematic inquiry is necessary for the growth and development of any academic discipline. Littlejohn (1987) explains that research helps a discipline grow in three ways: by *extension, intension,* and *revolution.* First, research helps a discipline grow because every new piece of research extends our knowledge about the subject matter being studied. Second, research helps a discipline grow by developing increasingly precise knowledge about specific concepts and processes, which is known as intension. Third, research leads to revolutionary changes in what we know as old theories die and are replaced by new theories.

Due to the youth of communication as a human scientific discipline, people still argue about whether communication is a distinct and coherent discipline or just a field of study that is connected loosely. Perhaps this argument exists because our current research-based knowledge about communication is somewhat limited and fragmented. Many studies need replication and extension. The results of communication research conducted with narrow research populations, such as the widespread use of college student samples, need to be extended to other audiences and contexts.

Remember that any one communication study is limited in the amount of information it can provide. Our epistemology, or warehouse of knowledge, is developed through the accumulation of findings from many individual research studies. The more the results of individual communication studies identify common patterns, the more confidence we have in our knowledge about communication and our ability to apply that knowledge.

We still need to know much about the nature and effects of communication. Future research will help test and extend current theories of communication. In the process, we will increase our base of communication knowledge and solidify our stand as a discipline.

Communication Research Applications

What constitutes effective communication within different situations? How can communication be used to promote intrapersonal growth? How can communication be used strategically to accomplish organizational goals or world peace? These important questions about practical communication problems deserve answers.

Valid and reliable communication research allows us to make communication even more effective. Such information helps demystify the communication process and helps us describe, explain, understand, predict, and control certain outcomes of communication phenomena, which ultimately helps us to develop effective communication strategies. A primary purpose of communication inquiry is helping people understand communication phenomena and direct their communication toward accomplishing individual and organizational goals.

It is very likely that you will use research as a tool to help you accomplish your goals as a student in conducting class projects, writing papers, participating in discussions, evaluating your performance, and making informed decisions about the options available to you. Using research, however, is not limited to universities. It is also likely that you will use research to help you in your chosen profession. Communication practitioners in organizations, for example, have to understand and evaluate research reports about the effectiveness of communication training programs or a public relations campaign. Mass media producers have to understand and make policy decisions based on readership or viewership studies or ratings research. As a former student put it, "I didn't realize how valuable communication research methods would be until I had to deal with the results from research almost every day." Who knows, you may even find yourself conducting research someday!

To apply communication research effectively, researchers have to draw trustworthy conclusions from research. This means developing sound theories that explain communication events. The theory-building-research cycle model (see Figure 1.1 in Chapter 1) described how theories sometimes develop out of accumulated observations while at other times theories are used to guide communication inquiry. Theories direct enlightened communication practice because they represent communication knowledge generated through scholarship. In the following pages we examine some of our current knowledge and theoretical positions about the nature of communication. We will see that the very complexity of the communication process provides communication researchers with significant challenges and constraints for studying communication phenomena effectively.

DEFINING COMMUNICATION

Defining the term *communication* is like trying to define the purpose of life itself— there are an enormous number of interpretations and points of view. Dance and Larson (1976), in fact, found in a survey of the literature that there were 126 definitions for the word *communication!*

Definitions of communication tend to emphasize one of two different concerns (see Figure 2.2). The earliest definitions originated from the scientific study of how information could be transferred from one place to another, thus representing an *information-based* view. Because it was derived from a behavioral perspective, communication was seen as a behavior, the intentional act of getting information from one person (a source) to another person (a receiver). In contrast, later definitions originated from the phenomenological study of how communication produces meaning and leads to developing effective interpersonal relationships, thus representing a *meaning-based* view. Though proponents of the meaning-based view did not deny the characteristics of communication advocated by the information-based

Figure 2.2 Two perspectives on communication

Information-based View	Meaning-based View
Representative definition: "Communication means that information is passed from one place to another." (Miller, 1951, p. 6)	*Representative definition:* "Communication occurs whenever an individual assigns significance or meaning to an internal or external stimulus." (Thayer, 1981, p. 43)
This view tends to stress the following characteristics:	This view tends to stress the following characteristics:
1. Communication is a *message:* It is something that one person attempts to get across to another person.	1. Communication is a *meaning:* It is something that one attributes to behavior.
2. Communication is an *act:* It is a behavior that one engages in to influence another person.	2. Communication is *processual:* It is an ongoing, ever-evolving interaction between people.
3. Communication is *intentional:* A person makes a conscious choice to send a message to another person.	3. Communication is *unintentional:* It occurs whenever we attribute meaning to behavior, whether intended or not.
4. Researchers typically study *verbal communication* and *intentional nonverbal communication.*	4. Researchers study *unintentional nonverbal communication* in addition to verbal and intentional nonverbal communication.
5. Communication is *optional:* One can choose whether or not to engage in the act of sending a message to another person.	5. Communication is *unavoidable:* One cannot choose to not communicate since it occurs whenever people attribute meaning to behavior.
6. Communication is *source-oriented:* Because it is the intentional act of sending a message, communication starts with the source, the person encoding the message.	6. Communication is *receiver-oriented:* Because it occurs whenever a person assigns meaning to behavior, communication is located in the receiver, the person decoding the behavior.
7. The goals of communication are to *exchange information* and to *persuade* others. Communication is thus the *content* we wish to get across to others for a specific purpose.	7. The goals of communication are to *attribute meaning* and to *understand one another.* Communication creates the *relationship* between ourselves and another person.

view, they argued that communication was more than the intentional attempt to get a message from a source to a receiver. Communication was also seen as a process of attributing meaning to people's actions and developing a relationship between people.

In this text we use the following definition for the term *communication: Communication is the management of messages for the purpose of creating meaning.* That is, communication occurs whenever a person attempts to send a message or whenever a person perceives and assigns meaning to behavior.

Key Characteristics of Communication

Our definition captures key elements of both the behavioral, information-based and the phenomenological, meaning-based perspectives. By combining the following key elements from both perspectives, the human scientific study of communication recognizes the complex nature of communication. Furthermore, combining these perspectives leads to some important implications for conducting communication research.

Messages and meanings.   Our definition of communication recognizes both a message and its meaning. Messages are symbols and signs that people attend to consciously and for which they create meanings. They can be intentionally spoken or written words exchanged between people or messages we send to ourselves about other people's unintentional facial expressions and other displays of feelings.

Basically, there are two groups of messages: **internal messages,** those we send to ourselves, and **external messages,** those we react to from other people. External messages are relatively easy to study using behavioral research methods since they are observable and recordable. Internal messages are more problematic for communication researchers because they are largely invisible.

Meanings are mental images we create in order to interpret and understand stimuli. People respond to messages (emanating both internally and externally) and create meanings for these messages. Communication researchers often infer meanings based on messages they observe or rely on self-reports from people about their meanings. These self-report measures of meaning, however, may not always be accurate, a problem we examine in later chapters.

Communication acts and processes.   Our definition of communication recognizes that human communication is composed of individual acts that combine to form a dynamic, ongoing process. The individual acts of communication represent attempts on the part of communicators to send and receive specific messages, while the processual nature of communication recognizes the ongoing, ever-evolving quality of communication. When we first meet someone, we exchange messages, but those acts are clearly a reflection of the entire process of how each of us has interacted with people in the past. The specific interaction and subsequent acts are new, but they take place within the context of a developing and ongoing process.

Communication, therefore, is **transactional,** a process containing many interrelated components. Some of these key components are the messages to which people react; the meanings people create; the context of the interaction; the relationship established between communicators; the personalities, dispositions, and past experiences of the communicators; the purposes people have for communicating; and the effects of human communication on people and situations.

Communication researchers often examine specific communication acts without taking into account the processual nature of human communication. Since they cannot possibly explore all pertinent elements of communication, communication researchers must study key communication variables (which may well be specific acts), aware of the fact that they are framing or putting boundaries on the ongoing communication processes. The processual nature of communication also encourages communication researchers to engage in longitudinal research (involving numerous points of analysis over time) rather than cross-sectional research (an analysis at one point in time). By studying both acts and processes, researchers broaden the scope of communication research and move closer to capturing the complex nature of communication.

Intentional and unintentional communication.   Our definition of communication recognizes both the intentional act of choosing to send a message and the conscious internal messages we send to ourselves about other people's unintentional behavior. Human communication is obviously directed toward accomplishing individual goals. At the same time, however, we also provide unintentional cues that allow others to construct internal messages about us. For example, it is difficult to hide the joy of drawing a full house when playing poker, although it is certainly in your best interest as a gambler to withhold your emotions until after you have won the hand. Another gambler, however, may pick up on the unintended nonverbal cues of joy and consciously decide to fold. In such cases, a person has constructed an internal message based on another person's unintentional behavior.

Communication researchers also recognize that there is an important relationship between unintentional behavior and intentional messages. People assign meaning to other people's unintended behaviors and then use that meaning to construct intended messages. For example, your best friend may not want you to know that she is angry, but her unintentional nonverbal behaviors lead you to ask, "Is there anything wrong?" Communication is thus both *source-oriented,* since we send intentional messages, and *receiver-oriented,* since we also construct internal and external messages from other people's unintentional behaviors.

Verbal and nonverbal message systems.   Our definition of communication recognizes both verbal and nonverbal messages. Earlier we explained that messages may be generated internally or externally. There are two kinds of external message systems: verbal and nonverbal.

Verbal message systems include the use of words and language, both spoken and written. The study of word meanings (semantics) recognizes that people assign two types of meanings to words: denotations and connotations. **Denotations** are the accepted public meanings assigned to words, as found in a dictionary. The denotative meaning of *doctor,* for example, is "a person licensed to practice medicine or some branch of medicine." **Connotations** are the more personal, subjective meanings people create and assign to words, which usually result from accumulated personal experiences. The word *doctor,* for example, might mean connotatively "helper" or "avoid at all costs," depending on one's personal experiences with doctors.

A culture assigns only a limited number of denotative meanings, usually 10 or fewer, to a given term, but there can be many individual connotative meanings.

Communication researchers, therefore, are careful when developing questionnaires and interview guides to avoid using terms that are denotatively ambiguous or evoke strong connotative meanings for certain respondents. We will examine in Chapters 5 and 9 how researchers construct effective questionnaire and interview guides.

Nonverbal message systems include the wide range of messages in addition to the use of words (verbal communication) to which people assign meaning. Nonverbal communication makes use of many message systems, ranging from intentional body movements to internal messages derived from environmental cues. It is important to realize, however, that verbal and nonverbal communication work together closely. In fact, there is no way to use verbal communication (words) without using some form of nonverbal communication. Communication researchers thus recognize the interdependence of verbal and nonverbal message systems for understanding the complex nature of human communication.

Information and meaning. Our definition of communication recognizes both the message, which contains information, and the meaning we attach to that information. Intentional communication is designed to convey substantive information about objects, events, and specific arrangements. Communication, in this sense, has a physical property and serves as an external message.

Human beings also have an insatiable appetite for creating meanings and making sense of information they receive. We strive to know what isn't being said explicitly about what is going on around us, to understand the people with whom we interact, and to comprehend the situations in which we find ourselves. Human communication is the means by which we make inferences about these concerns. We read a lot into messages available to us and interpret these messages to help us cope more effectively with the complex situations of modern life.

Accordingly, while some information is contained in the message, meanings are in people (Korzybski, 1948; Hayakawa, 1972). No object has inherent meaning; no word is imbued with unambiguous meaning. Human beings create meanings for words and objects for the purpose of relating to one another. This intersubjectivity of meaning, however, is far from perfect. People are bound to assign different meanings to the messages they receive and thus derive different information from them. Because individuals perceive and create meaning selectively, communication researchers must take great care in generalizing the responses from one set of respondents to any other population. We will show in Chapter 6 how the people researchers study influence the ability to generalize research findings.

Content and relationship dimensions. Finally, our definition of communication recognizes that messages provide communicators with two kinds of information: information about the content of a message and information about the relationship between the communicators. The content dimension of human communication refers to the substantive information present in any message. The primary subject, topic, and theme of what is being said constitute the content level of communication. The content of communication helps people understand the world around them by reducing the uncertainty they have about people and things.

The relationship dimension of communication, by contrast, provides information about how the message content should be interpreted, such as whether a message is a command, a request, a confirmation, or a sarcastic remark. Interpreting the content of the message depends on the nature of the relationship established between the communicators. A put-down between friends, for example, means something different from a put-down of an employee by an employer. Every time a message is exchanged between people, therefore, it communicates something about how the communicators perceive the nature of their relationship.

Content and relationship information are expressed simultaneously in every interpersonal communication message sent and received. Every time you say something, you are not merely sending someone a message about the specific topic being discussed (the content information); you also are defining the relationship you have established or are establishing with your communication partner (the relationship information). Researchers, in fact, are aware that the relational implications of the messages they exchange with the people they study may influence their cooperation and responses.

THE CONTEXT OF COMMUNICATION

Human communication is an extremely complex and encompassing social process. In addition to the defining characteristics just described, communication is influenced by the context in which it occurs. **Context** refers to the environment in which human communication takes place.

One important contextual aspect of communication is the point in time at which it takes place. When communication occurs and how people feel about the timing of the communication have a major effect on human interaction. It is a far different communication situation when someone phones you at 8 in the evening, for example, than at 3 in the morning!

A second important contextual aspect of communication is the setting in which it takes place. You communicate differently with people in a class, at a party, in an office, or in a court of law. Even if you say exactly the same thing in different situations to the same people, the changes in the context inevitably affect the communication that takes place. In fact, if one says the same thing to the same people in different contexts, it is no longer the same thing. As the saying goes, "One cannot step in the same river twice."

Though the number of contexts is infinite, there are some distinct social and institutional settings in which communication plays a crucial role. We will see in Chapter 3 how researchers study communication in such significant contexts as educational and health settings. An important goal for communication research is to explain not only how communication occurs within particular settings but also how communication differs across settings. We know from intercultural communication research, for example, that communication competence involves different communication skills and strategies in different cultural settings.

Levels of Communication

A third important contextual aspect of communication is the level at which it takes place. There are five basic levels of human communication: intrapersonal, interpersonal, group, organizational, and societal communication.

Intrapersonal communication. **Intrapersonal communication** is an internal communication process that occurs when we send messages to ourselves and develop messages to send to others. In essence, it is communication with ourselves. Intrapersonal communication is the most basic level of human communication, since the individual communicator is the starting point for any communication. The intrapersonal process for creating messages is called **encoding,** and the intrapersonal process of interpreting others' messages is called **decoding.**

Intrapersonal communication poses several challenges for communication inquiry, the most serious of which is the difficulty of observing internal message behavior. Intrapersonal communication has been studied traditionally through self-report measures or through physiological measures (such as pulse rate or body temperature) that can be related to intrapersonal communication variables. We will see in later chapters how the relative invisibility of intrapersonal communication makes it problematic for communication inquiry.

Interpersonal communication. **Interpersonal communication** is communication between two people (a dyad), either face to face or through mediated forms (such as a telephone), characterized by the mutual awareness of the individuality of the other. Interpersonal communication is one of the most important and popular topics in communication research because it leads to one of our most treasured outcomes, the development of human relationships.

Interpersonal communication builds on intrapersonal communication because each communicator decodes the messages sent by other people and encodes the messages he or she sends to them. Communication researchers are thus often interested in the relationship between intrapersonal and interpersonal communication, showing how differences between people's intrapersonal communication processing relate to differences in the communication behavior used to develop interpersonal relationships.

Group communication. **Group communication** occurs among three or more people interacting in an attempt to achieve commonly recognized goals. These goals may be task-oriented, such as a group making a decision within an organization, or socioemotional in nature, such as a family outing or a social gathering of friends. Patton, Giffin, and Patton (1989) claim that group communication is important to study if only because there are far more groups in this world than individuals, since we are each part of many groups.

Just as intrapersonal communication facilitates interpersonal communication, interpersonal communication enables people to communicate at the group level of human communication. Group communication, however, involves numerous interpersonal communication relationships. The size of a group, generally limited to the number of people who can participate together actively in a group conversation (about 15), also creates the potential for the development of subgroups and opposing coalitions among a group's members. These coalitions often complicate communication and the relationships between group members and can have a strong impact on the interactions within a group.

Organizational communication. Organizational communication occurs within a particular social system composed of interdependent groups attempting to achieve commonly recognized goals. Organizational communication is thus made possible by the prior levels of communication—intrapersonal, interpersonal, and group. Organizational communication is also a unique and important level of analysis for communication researchers because we spend a significant portion of our lives working and communicating within organizations.

Organizational communication includes both formal channels of communication (such as an organizational chart of who reports to whom) as well as informal channels of communication (such as the office grapevine). Organizational communication is also concerned with both internal communication within an organization and external communication among members and representatives of various organizations.

Societal communication. Societal communication is the broadest level of communication (often called the macrosocial level) and occurs within and between social systems composed of interdependent organizations attempting to achieve commonly recognized goals. It thus encompasses all of the prior levels of communication—intrapersonal, interpersonal, group, and organizational.

Societal communication not only focuses on communication within a particular culture (such as the United States) but also on communication between people from different cultures (such as the United States and Japan). Communication researchers studying societal communication are thus interested in both intracultural and intercultural communication.

Two special forms of communication are discussed most appropriately at the societal communication level: public communication and mass communication. **Public communication** occurs when a small number of people (usually one person) address a larger group of people. Speeches, lectures, oral reports, and dramatic performances are all forms of public communication. Although the speaker takes the major responsibility for the public communication and sends the preponderance of verbal messages, that person is not the only one engaging in communication. The audience sends messages to the speaker, primarily via the nonverbal message system.

Mass communication occurs when a small number of people send messages to a large, anonymous, and usually heterogeneous audience through the use of specialized communication media. Because of the size and complexity of most social systems, it is virtually impossible to have face-to-face communication between members of the various publics, necessitating the use of mediated communication technologies. Mass communication uses such diverse media as film, television, radio, newspapers, books, and magazines. Mass communication is similar to public communication in that the source of the messages takes primary responsibility for the communication. Mass communication, however, also has the potential for reaching larger audiences than face-to-face public communication and provides less opportunity for audience feedback.

Both public communication and mass communication have the advantage of being able to reach large audiences, thereby communicating with many people in a short amount of time. But both forms of communication also have the disadvantage of limited shared communication with the audience and often seem like one-way communication situations.

The hierarchical nature of communication.   In summary, the five levels of human communication build on one another and increase according to the number of people involved, from intrapersonal communication to interpersonal communication to group communication to organizational communication to societal communication (see Figure 2.3). As you can see, intrapersonal communication is the largest and most basic form of human communication. It is at the intrapersonal level that we think and process information and create meaning. Interpersonal communication builds on the intrapersonal level, adding another person to the communication situation and introducing the interpersonal relationship. Group communication in turn builds on interpersonal interaction, involving several communicators and adding the new dimension of multiple interpersonal relationships to the communication situation. Organizational communication exists through the combination of the three previous levels of communication to coordinate large numbers of people in the shared accomplishment of a particular organization's complex goals. Societal communication exists when organizations establish interdependent relationships for the accomplishment of the public's goals.

It is thus important to recognize how each level of communication is informed by its higher and lower levels. Group communication, for example, is affected by group members' intrapersonal communication, but a person's intrapersonal communication is also affected by important referent groups, such as family and friendship groups, to which the person belongs. Communication researchers, however, often focus only on one particular level to the exclusion of others. Chaffee and Berger (1987) lament, "Specialists in these different levels rarely consult with one another; frequently they are housed in different departments at many universities and present their research to separate academic bodies" (p. 143). Communication researchers, therefore, are aware of the "embedded" nature of communication; that is, that different levels of communication influence the particular phenomena they

Figure 2.3　Hierarchical levels of human communication

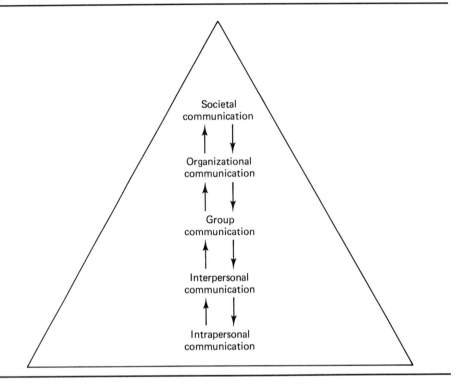

are studying. Sophisticated inquiry provides "layered" or multilevel analyses of communication. At the very least, communication researchers identify the level of communication they are examining and are aware of the influences of the other levels of communication.

THE NATURE OF COMMUNICATION RESEARCH

In this chapter we have explored the historical development of communication inquiry, defined the nature of communication, identified some key principles of communication, and recognized the importance of studying the context of communication. After reading about the multifaceted nature of communication, you may feel somewhat bewildered about what exactly constitutes communication research. In Chapter 3 we will examine how communication researchers choose topics, define concepts, select variables, and pose formal research questions. Here, however, we want to explain how our definition puts a particular boundary on what constitutes communication research. We then provide a summary of some important implications for conducting communication research.

What Constitutes Communication Research?

As broadly as we may define the concept of communication, not all research fits within it. A traditional model of communication helps illustrate the appropriate boundaries that demarcate communication research: People exchange messages through channels within contexts. Thus there are four important components of the model: people, messages, channels, and contexts.

Our definition of communication as "the management of messages for the purpose of creating meaning" places important boundaries on communication research. The key term is *messages*—the central focus for communication research must be on the exchange of messages between (or within) people. Accordingly, only the study of message behavior constitutes communication research per se.

The other three components become relevant to communication research when studied in relation to message behavior. Studying how people's self-esteem changes as they get older, for example, may be appropriate for psychology researchers, but it does not constitute communication research because it does not focus on message behavior. Studying how self-esteem or age affects the encoding or decoding of messages, however, is a communication study because it links these variables to message behavior. Similarly, studying how electronic signals (as a channel) travel through a television cable is appropriate for physicists, but that question lies outside communication research. Studying whether people acquire more information from messages received via mass-mediated or face-to-face channels, however, is communication research because it relates that channel to message behavior. Finally, studying how much organizations (a context) spend on computers is appropriate research for accountants or computer consultants but not for communication researchers. Studying how messages exchanged within organizations influence computer purchasing decisions, however, is communication research.

Communication research thus focuses on message behavior, regardless of whether that message behavior occurs intrapersonally, interpersonally, or within and between groups, organizations, and societies. In the final analysis, communication researchers study messages directly or how message behavior is related to people, channels, and/or contexts.

Implications for Research

Our contention that communication researchers study message behavior leads to the following important implications for the conduct of communication research.

1. Communication researchers realize that it is just as important to examine meanings attributed to messages as it is to study the nature of the messages themselves. Studying meanings often necessitates that communication researchers use self-report measures.

2. Communication researchers must select particular communication variables they wish to examine, since they cannot possibly explore all pertinent elements of any communication event. They are aware, however, of the ongoing, multifaceted processual nature of communication and the fact that their research temporarily "frames" (puts artificial boundaries on) communication behavior.

3. Acknowledging the processual nature of communication encourages communication researchers to engage in longitudinal research (involving numerous points of analysis over time) rather than cross-sectional research (analysis at one point in time).

4. Traditionally, communication researchers have focused on messages intentionally designed. Some, however, also assess how people construct internal messages about others' unintentional behavior, thereby rendering it communicative.

5. Communication researchers recognize that although verbal and nonverbal message systems may be studied separately, these message systems are interdependent. Nonverbal cues, for example, always accompany and influence the interpretation of verbal messages.

6. Because of the connotative characteristics of language, communication researchers usually develop questionnaires and interview guides that carefully avoid using ambiguous terms or terms that have strong, distracting implications for certain respondents.

7. Because of differences in the way individuals manage and create meanings for messages, communication researchers take great care when generalizing findings from one set of people to another.

8. Communication researchers realize that although the content and relationship dimensions of messages may be studied separately, in practice they interact to influence message exchanges and personal relationships.

9. Communication researchers consider the effects of the context on communication. They recognize the "embedded" nature of communication, that different social rules apply in different environments. Context-sensitive analyses of communication are encouraged, and communication researchers, at the very least, identify the context in which their communication research is done and are aware of how it might influence the communication behavior being studied.

10. In the final analysis, communication is not just one thing. It is a complex process by which people manage messages and create meaning. Capturing the complexity of communication demands ultimately that research results be triangulated; that is, comparable findings must be obtained from multiple methods of inquiry. Only through triangulation will communication behavior be described, understood, explained, predicted, and controlled effectively.

CONCLUSION

We said at the start that *communication* is a term invented by people to cover an important dimension of human behavior. We've discovered in this chapter that this canopy term for our field is remarkably elastic. People have stretched it in so many directions that it now covers a wide range of events and the variables that influence those events. We have also taken our own stab at defining communication in a way that keeps the purposes of research in mind: "Communication is the management of messages for the purpose of creating meaning."

Now that you've read this chapter, you won't fall into the same linguistic trap of the young observer who said to an astronomer, "Oh, I see how astronomers figure out the distance of the stars and their sizes and temperatures and all that. What really amazes me, though, is how they find out what their names are." Obviously, the youth is confusing two processes related to research: naming phenomena and studying them. Defining or naming communication and its parts is a vital first or preresearch process. It gives us terms to use when we talk about the communication activities researchers will measure and describe. Now that we understand what we mean when we use *communication* and its related terms, we can proceed to discussing how researchers operate when studying them.

chapter 3

Asking Questions

Research begins with curiosity. Researchers notice something about communication in the world around them and wish to learn more about it. That moment might occur in the midst of the give-and-take of social interaction in a family, business, or community, or it might occur while perusing the published literature in communication.

They move from that sense of curiosity to formulating a question that lends itself well to being answered in a research project. Question articulation is a primary and critical step in the research process. The saying from the world of computers applies: "Garbage in, garbage out." Phrasing worthwhile questions is an early turning point in the research process. If expressed well, the research question outlines the framework upon which the entire research project will be built. Research methods are designed to answer the particular questions posed by investigators. We discuss here four important steps associated with articulating questions: choosing research topics, defining the central research concepts, identifying variables, and posing formal research questions and hypotheses. We then provide an overview of how some general research questions have guided communication research.

CHOOSING RESEARCH TOPICS

The first part of the research process involves identifying **research topics**, the ideas that communication researchers consider worth studying. Research topics are generally derived from two sources: the need to test and refine theory, referred to as **basic** or **pure research,** and the need to solve a practical problem, referred to as **applied research.**

Basic communication research examines topics derived from a theoretical base. Numerous theories attempt to explain a wide array of communication events and processes, far too many for us to catalog in this chapter. You might consult Littlejohn's (1987) text on theories of human communication for specific examples. In fact, if you pick up almost any issue of an academic communication journal, most of the articles are designed to test the validity or increase the precision and scope of particular theories.

Yet no theory is ever complete; no theory reaches its goal of describing, explaining, understanding, predicting, and controlling any particular communication phenomenon fully. Theories, like communication, are ongoing and ever-changing. Theories can always benefit from further refinement and elaboration.

Weick (1969), for example, developed a model of organizing that has received a great deal of attention from communication researchers. The model asserts that the more complex the problems an organization faces, the more the organization depends on interaction to resolve them. The less complex the problems, the more the organization depends on preset rules for solutions. Bantz and Smith (1977) conducted a laboratory experiment to test Weick's model and found that varying levels of complexity did not necessitate the use of different interactive strategies. Kreps (1980) argued, however, that the results of Bantz and Smith's experiment were due to the poor representativeness of the laboratory environment. So he conducted a field experimental study of organizational decision making to retest the central tenets of Weick's model of organizing. His results supported and validated Weick's model. Later research by Putnam and Sorenson (1982) supported and broadened Kreps's findings, thus validating and adding a few refinements to Weick's original model of organizing. Research that tests, refines, and elaborates theories helps increase knowledge about important communication phenomena.

Applied communication research, by contrast, uses theory and method to solve practical communication problems (O'Hair, Kreps, & Frey, 1990). Cissna (1982), editor of the *Journal of Applied Communication Research,* explains:

> *Applied* research sets out to contribute to knowledge by answering a real, pragmatic, social question or by solving a real, pragmatic, social problem. Applied *communication* research involves such a question or problem of human communication or examines human communication in order to provide an answer or solution to the question or problem. The intent or goal of the inquiry (as manifest in the research report itself) is the hallmark of applied communication research. Applied communication research involves the development of knowledge regarding a real human communication problem or question. (Editor's note)

Since there are an unlimited number of potential communication problems in the world, there also are an unlimited number of contexts for conducting applied communication research. Certain contexts, however, have received particular attention from communication researchers (see Figure 3.1). Applied communication re-

Figure 3.1   Some important contexts for applied communication research

These are some of the contexts (both places and particular populations) in which communication plays an important role.

COMMUNICATION AND THE AGED: The study of how communication affects the elderly. Researchers are interested in the communication abilities of the elderly and whether their communication needs are being met.

COMMUNICATION AND CHILDREN: The study of how communication affects children. Researchers are interested in how children acquire language; how they develop communication competence; how they communicate with their parents, teachers, friends; and how the media influence children.

COMMUNICATION CAMPAIGNS: The study of how communication is used by change agents to influence audience behavior. Researchers are interested in political, informational, and preventive (health, safety) communication campaigns.

COMMUNICATION EDUCATION: The study of communication within the educational system. Researchers are interested in teacher-student communication patterns and the use of communication strategies to influence learning.

CONSUMER BEHAVIOR: The study of communication between sellers, or ''marketers,'' and consumers, or ''buyers.'' Researchers are interested in how mass-mediated communication influences consumers' information processing and buying behavior.

FAMILY COMMUNICATION: The study of communication within families. Researchers are interested in how communication is used within the spouse, parenting and sibling subsystems to affect such outcomes as role relationships and satisfaction.

HEALTH COMMUNICATION: The study of communication within the health care system. Researchers are interested in how patients talk about their illnesses, communication between physicians and patients, message flow within health care organizations, and health care public campaigns.

INTIMATE COMMUNICATION: The study of how people in close romantic relationships (both heterosexual and homosexual) express and maintain their intimacy. The study of sexual communication is representative of research in this context.

LEGAL COMMUNICATION: The study of communication within the criminal and civil justice system. Researchers are interested in communication between lawyers and clients, argumentation in the courtroom setting, and the jury deliberation process.

PUBLIC OPINION PROCESSES: The study of how public opinion is influenced by communication. Researchers are interested in the formation of public opinion, its measurement, and strategies for changing it.

search thus seeks to demonstrate the relevance of communication knowledge to everyday life.

In actual practice, however, the distinction between basic and applied research is not always clear. Eddy and Patridge (1978) explain:

> There is no genuine theoretical or methodological distinction between ''pure'' and ''applied'' science. In popular thought, scientists engaged in pure research have little con-

cern with practical uses of the results of their labor, and applied scientists are not concerned with making theoretical contributions. Yet, as any physician or biologist will testify, this neat distinction does not exist in actual scientific work. Physicians use theory daily in order to diagnose and treat clinical cases, and the results they obtain alter both theory and clinical practice. If this were not the case, they would still be using unicorn horn, leeches, and extract of human skull. Similarly, biologists utilize theory to develop pesticides permitting the control of fruit flies, and modify theory when fruit flies multiply in the laboratory. (p. 4)

Theory and practice are thus interrelated. Lewin (1951) argues that "there is nothing so practical as a good theory" (p. 169); Levy-Leboyer (1988) adds that "there is nothing so theoretical as a good application" (p. 785). For example, researchers study the effects of television violence on children's behavior for both theoretical and practical reasons. This research is important theoretically because it builds on an existing body of theory and research about the ability of the mass media to influence receivers. The topic is also important practically because it answers crucial questions being asked by parents, educators, government, and media representatives about the effects of television on children's behavior.

Regardless of whether a topic emerges from basic or applied research, perhaps the most important criterion for selecting a topic is whether it investigates something important. Tucker, Weaver, and Berryman-Fink (1981) argue that research that does not investigate important topics and questions is subject to the reactions "So what?" and "Who cares?" What differences does this research make? What does it have to offer? If research is not relevant theoretically or practically, of what value is it? To answer these questions, researchers need to develop a clear rationale for why the research is being conducted.

Answering the questions "So what?" and "Who cares?" however, is not as easy as it might appear. For many years, United States Senator William Proxmire of Wisconsin presented a dubious achievement award called the "Golden Fleece" to what he thought were the most wasteful federally funded research projects. Senator Proxmire, quick to point out a lack of practical value in the research receiving his award, assumed that there is no valid standard for evaluating research but commonsense, practical value. However, many breakthroughs in science result from studying phenomena that do not seem immediately relevant to the person on the street. In fact, the more developed a science is, the less a layperson can make decent judgments about what is or isn't important. Dr. Watson's commonsense ideas of what was important for Sherlock Holmes to investigate, for example, were nearly always wrong.

Finally, research topics have to be of sufficient scope and depth to enable researchers to investigate them. But overly broad or complex topics have to be narrowed to bring them within the constraints of available time and resources. Topics often are narrowed by limiting their investigation to specific conditions, such as certain groups, times, or contexts.

For example, a researcher might be interested in studying the role of communication in providing social support (the feeling of being aided or assisted by others).

This topic is important both theoretically and practically, yet it is too broad to study as phrased. The researcher might narrow the topic by examining how a specific demographic group of communicators (such as the elderly, children, health care providers, teachers, or students) use communication to express social support. The researcher might also narrow the range of contextual settings by studying how social support is communicated within families, nursing homes, schools, self-help groups, or sports teams. Identifying specific demographic groups or contexts allows researchers to narrow the scope of their research to a realistic piece of the larger research topic they seek to investigate. Several narrow pieces of research can then be used to build a body of theory and research that provides valuable information about the larger topic of interest.

CONCEPTUAL DEFINITIONS

The topics that researchers consider worth studying are made up of specific concepts, abstract ideas, that need to be defined precisely. **Conceptual definitions** describe what a concept means by relating it to similar concepts. Just as a dictionary defines a word by relating it to other words, researchers define a concept by relating it to other concepts.

A communication researcher interested in studying the topic of how social support is expressed between members of intimate relationships, for example, has to define two primary concepts: "expression of social support" and "intimate relationships." The researcher must specify the major characteristics of these concepts in order to operationalize and measure the concepts effectively. Otherwise, it will be impossible to study this research topic competently.

How might a researcher go about defining these two concepts? A first step would be to review the relevant literature to see how similar concepts have been defined conceptually in the past. In many cases, researchers can simply adopt widely accepted conceptual definitions for the concepts they investigate. Building on existing communication theory and research also helps add to the knowledge developed in the past.

For example, a review of the relevant literature would show that the concept "social support" has been defined conceptually as "verbal and nonverbal communication between recipients and providers which reduces uncertainty about the situation, the self, the other, or the relationship, and functions to enhance a perception of control in one's life experience" (Albrecht & Adelman, 1987, p. 19). The concept "intimate relationships" has been defined conceptually as "the degree of emotional attachment between dyadic partners and knowledge dyadic partners have about one another" (Cody & McLaughlin, 1985, p. 289).

But what if researchers cannot find any acceptable conceptual definitions for concepts in past research? In that case, they might have to modify conceptual definitions that have been developed previously for related concepts, or they might have to create new conceptual definitions for these concepts.

Good conceptual definitions enable researchers to design their research, select research methods, and employ data-analytic strategies in accordance with their theoretical and practical research goals. Good conceptual definitions describe clearly the primary elements of the research topics being investigated and help researchers make certain that the concepts they observe and measure in their study match the conceptual components of the research topic. Just as a house is built on a solid foundation to meet construction standards, communication inquiry is built on a solid conceptual foundation to meet research standards.

IDENTIFYING VARIABLES

Researchers study concepts that take on different values. For example, they might be interested in whether people with high and low levels of communication apprehension (fear of communicating) use different compliance-gaining strategies (how we get others to follow our requests). In this instance, the concept "communication apprehension" takes on two different values, high and low.

A **variable** is any concept that takes on two or more values. A single object, therefore, is not a variable; it becomes a variable only when it varies by existing in different types or different amounts. A particular make of car, such as a Ford or a Honda, for example, is not a variable, but the categories of American and foreign cars are variables. In the study of how social support is communicated within intimate relationships, the primary concepts ("social support" and "relational intimacy") are variables because they vary from time to time and from person to person. These variables can be operationalized and measured so as to ascertain different values of the attributes they represent.

Researchers study many variables in communication research. Several *kinds* of variables are important: ordered versus nominal variables, independent versus dependent variables, and confounding variables.

Ordered and Nominal Variables

Two types of variables depend on the values researchers assign to them. **Ordered variables** can be assigned meaningful numerical values that indicate how much of the concept is present. Variables such as class rank, age, weight, temperature, or income are ordered variables since they provide researchers with meaningful numbers. Being 10 years old, for example, is less than being 20 years old, which is less than being 30 years old. The numerical value, in this case, indicates how much age a person possesses.

Nominal variables, by contrast, can be differentiated only on the basis of type. Variables such as gender (male, female), race (black, white, Hispanic, Native American), and political affiliation (Democrat, Republican, independent) are nominal variables since they identify different types. Nominal variables usually do not indicate how much of a concept is present; they simply indicate whether an attribute is present or absent (such as whether one is a male or a female). In some cases, nominal variables indicate extent along an ascending or descending range (such as low, medium, or high in communication apprehension).

Our example of the communication of social support in intimate relationships can be used to illustrate the difference between ordered and nominal variables. Suppose that a researcher measured the communication of social support on a scale ranging from 0, indicating no social support, to 100, indicating the highest possible level of social support. In this case, social support would be an ordered variable, since 0 is less than 10, which is less than 20, and so on. If intimacy in dyadic relationships is measured either as being high or low, however, it would be a nominal variable since it only assesses two types of intimacy conditions.

Any ordered variable can easily be transformed into a nominal variable. The ordered measurement of social support on a 0–100 scale, for example, can be changed into a nominal measurement by calling social support scores from 50 to 100 "high" and those below 50 "low." Nominal variables can also be turned into ordered variables sometimes. Gender, for example, has been studied as an ordered variable by using numerical values to describe the psychological orientations of men and women toward femininity and masculinity, called "psychological gender orientation" (Bem, 1979). People indicate on a 5-point ordered scale their agreement with statements representing masculine and feminine traits and are then given a score for each type of trait that ranges just like the ordered scale we used to measure social support. Biological gender, however, can only be treated as a nominal variable.

Independent and Dependent Variables

Another important way of classifying variables is by identifying whether they function as independent or dependent variables. An **independent variable** is thought to influence changes in another variable, whereas a **dependent variable** is thought to be changed by another variable. This classification thus identifies the relationship between research variables by distinguishing which variables influence other variables (independent variables) and which variables are influenced by other variables (dependent variables).

The use of independent and dependent variables is an important part of much communication research, particularly experimental research (see Chapter 8) that is concerned with establishing causal relationships between variables—how one variable causes changes in another variable. Independent and dependent variables, however, are also used often in survey research, textual analysis, and even in ethnomethodology.

In our hypothetical study about how social support is communicated within intimate relationships, we may, for example, be interested in knowing whether more social support is expressed within relationships characterized either by high or low intimacy. If so, we are interested in determining how increases or decreases in relational intimacy influence the expression of social support. Relational intimacy is therefore the independent variable that is thought to cause changes in the dependent variable, social support.

Whether a variable is assumed to be independent or dependent depends on the bounds of the particular study and on theory. No variable functions intrinsically as an independent or dependent variable. For example, in another study, a researcher might be interested in how personality (the independent variable) affects the expression of social support (the dependent variable).

Confounding Variables

Establishing a relationship between independent and dependent variables is often difficult because other variables may in reality account more for the changes in the dependent variable. Variables that explain the changes in the dependent variable better than the independent variable are referred to as **confounding variables.**

In our hypothetical study of how social support is communicated in intimate relationships, level of intimacy might not influence the amount of social support communicated. Perhaps the amount of social support communicated depends more on how openly the partners communicate. Regardless of intimacy level, the more open they are, the more they may communicate social support. Openness thus might explain communication of social support better than intimacy level.

Researchers often try to account somehow for the effects of confounding variables on the dependent variable. One way they do this is by treating a potential confounding variable as another independent variable. It is then possible to measure the relative effects of each independent variable on the dependent variable. For example, a researcher could make communication openness an additional independent variable and see whether it affects the communication of social support more than intimacy level. Of course, there could also be a positive relationship between openness and intimacy level of the dyadic relationship, and the study could now assess this as well.

Another possible way to control for confounding variables is to hold them constant. For example, if we thought that communication openness was a confounding variable in this study, we could control for it by studying only very open or very closed couples. Finally, there are ways to remove the effects of a confounding variable through particular statistical procedures. In each case, an attempt is made to control for the effects produced by a confounding variable.

RESEARCH QUESTIONS AND HYPOTHESES

After researchers have selected topics, defined the central concepts, and identified variables, they express a formal question or statement to guide their research. Researchers either pose a formal research question or state an hypothesis (a prediction).

Research Questions

Research questions are the explicit questions researchers ask about the variables that interest them. Two general questions researchers ask about communication are "What is the nature of communication?" and "How is communication related to other variables?"

    Describing communication behavior.   One important direction for research is describing and understanding the nature and characteristics of a particular communication behavior or sequence of communication behaviors that have theoretical or practical significance. The behavior studied most often is strategic communication, communication designed to accomplish a particular goal.

    When researchers seek to describe a communication variable, the general research question is "What is the nature of communication?" The actual research question, of course, specifies the communication variable of interest. Consider the following research questions asked about communication behavior:

> ▷   What cues do actors rely on to recognize the presence of bias in a message? (Doelger, Hewes, & Graham, 1986, p. 307)
>
> ▷   What patterns of deceptive communication characterize close relationship? (Metts, 1989, p. 163)
>
> ▷   What are the perceived dimensions of giving feedback in a task-oriented small group? (Ogilvie & Haslett, 1985, p. 63)
>
> ▷   In employment screening interviews, what purposes (seeking information, eliciting interviewer options, or clarifying interviewer statements) do the majority of interviewee questions fulfill? (Babbitt & Jablin, 1985, p. 513)
>
> ▷   What types of power strategies do subordinates perceive themselves using in interactions with their supervisors? (Richmond, Davis, Saylor, & McCroskey, 1984, p. 90)
>
> ▷   In what ways do members of the college taste culture organize music genres; how do they "map" the music world? (Christenson & Peterson, 1988, p. 289)

Each of these questions seeks to describe fully the communication behavior being studied. Before researchers examine the relationship between a particular communication behavior and other important variables, they must first describe that communication behavior carefully. Many scholars have argued that in the past researchers rushed into predicting the effects of communication behavior before describing adequately the nature and characteristics of that behavior. The call for more descriptive research has led to a renewed interest in describing and classifying various forms of communication behavior.

    Relating communication behavior to other variables.   A second direction for communication research is to understand how communication is related to other important variables of interest. When researchers go beyond description, they are interested in answering the general research question "How is communication related to other variables?" In such cases, the research question asks about the nature of the relationship between the independent and dependent variables being studied. Consider the following research questions:

▷ Will the demographic variables of age, gender, education level, and household size be related to interpersonal communication motives? (Rubin, Perse, & Barbato, 1988, p. 610)

▷ Do men and women report significantly different levels of satisfaction with conflict interaction? (Papa & Natalle, 1989, p. 263)

▷ Is organizational identification (as an outcome) associated with the presence or absence of specific types of turning points? (Bullis & Bach, 1989, p. 277)

▷ How does family mediation of television affect children's comprehension of specific programs and of television in general? (Desmond, Singer, Singer, Calam, & Colimore, 1985, p. 467)

▷ Does attorney gender, disfluency, or delivery style affect or interact to affect juror perceptions of defendant's credibility and guilt? (Barge, Schlueter, & Pritchard, 1989, p. 335)

▷ What is the association between how patients communicate about their illness, other patient illness-related behavior, and utilization factors of medical treatment? (Pettegrew & Turkat, 1986, p. 379)

Each of these questions asks about the relationship between communication behavior and other variables. Sometimes researchers assume a *noncausal relationship* between variables, meaning that variables are associated, or occur together, without one necessarily causing changes in the other. For example, how does self-disclosure (sharing information about ourselves) relate to how much we like another person? It could be that liking a person leads to self-disclosure, but it could also be that disclosing ourselves to a person leads to liking. It is a chicken-and-egg question; which comes first, the self-disclosure or the liking? We know that these two variables are related, but we cannot necessarily say that one is the cause and one is the effect.

At other times researchers assume a *causal relationship* between variables, believing that communication produces predictable *outcomes,* meaning that communication is produced by important preceding, or *input,* variables. The causal analysis of communication thus focuses on how communication leads to outcomes and how input variables lead to communication.

When researchers examine the effects of communication on outcomes, communication functions as the independent variable that is thought to cause changes in the outcome variable. When researchers ask which types of communication behaviors lead to effective listening, which types of communication strategies lead to the most amount of persuasion, or whether the type of arguments a person uses within a small group lead to that person's emergence as a leader, for example, they are asking how communication functions as an independent variable that produces change in a dependent variable.

When researchers examine the effects of input variables on communication, they realize that communication does not just lead to important outcomes; it is itself an important outcome that results from other variables that precede it. Researchers might ask, for example, how self-esteem influences public speaking ability, how status differences affect the type of persuasive strategies used, or how loneliness affects television viewing behavior. Questions of this type ask how communication functions as a dependent variable that is changed by an independent variable.

How a formal research question about the relationship between variables is phrased depends on whether the independent variable is measured on an ordered or a nominal scale and whether the research question is nondirectional or directional. Let's use a hypothetical study about how the intimacy level of a relationship relates to the amount of social support communicated to illustrate how formal research questions about relationships between variables are phrased (see Figure 3.2).

When the independent variable is treated as ordered, measured in meaningful numbers, the research question asks directly about the nature of the relationship between the independent and the dependent variable. Independent variables may be related to dependent variables in one of three ways: (1) a *positive relationship,* in which increases in the independent variable are associated with increases in the dependent variable; (2) a *negative relationship,* in which increases in the independent variable are associated with decreases in the dependent variable; and (3) *no relationship,* in which changes in the independent variable are not associated with any systematic changes in the dependent variable.

When the independent variable in a study is treated as nominal, measured in categories, the research question asks whether there is a significant difference between the independent variable categories with respect to the dependent variable. In our hypothetical study, if intimacy is measured as high or low, the research question asks whether there is a significant difference between high and low intimate relationships with respect to the amount of social support that is communicated.

Asking how groups differ with regard to communication is simply an extension of a question about the relationship between variables. When researchers examine differences between groups, they are essentially asking whether the relationship between one group (such as high intimate relationships) and a dependent variable (such as the amount of social support communicated) is different from the relationship between another group (such as low intimate relationships) and the same dependent variable.

Research questions are also either nondirectional or directional (see Figure 3.2). Most research questions are **nondirectional,** which means that an open-ended question is asked. Some research questions, however, are **directional,** which means that a closed-ended question is asked. The choice of an open-ended or closed-ended research question depends on how much researchers know about the relationships between the variables based on the available literature. If researchers know nothing about the relationships, as in exploratory research, they usually advance an open-

Figure 3.2   Research questions and hypotheses

The following research questions and hypotheses could be posed for our hypothetical study on the effects of intimacy of a dyadic relationship (the independent variable) on the amount of social support communicated (the dependent variable).

RESEARCH QUESTIONS

A. Ordered Independent Variable (intimacy measured on a 10-point scale)
  1. Nondirectional (open-ended) research question
     RQ_1: What is the relationship between intimacy and the amount of social support communicated?
  2. Directional (closed-ended) research question
     RQ_1: Is there a positive (or a negative) relationship between intimacy and the amount of social support communicated?

B. Nominal Independent Variable (intimacy measured as high or low)
  1. Nondirectional (open-ended) research question
     RQ_1: Is there a significant difference between the amount of social support communicated within high and low intimate relationships?
  2. Directional (closed-ended) research question
     RQ_1: Is more social support communicated within high than low intimate relationships?

HYPOTHESES

A. Ordered Independent Variable
  1. Two-tailed (nondirectional) research hypothesis
     H_1: There is a relationship between intimacy and the amount of social support communicated.
  2. One-tailed (directional) research hypothesis
     H_1: There is a positive (or negative) relationship between intimacy and the amount of social support communicated.
  3. Null hypothesis
     H_0: There is no relationship between intimacy and the amount of social support communicated.

B. Nominal Independent Variable
  1. Two-tailed (nondirectional) research hypothesis
     H_1: There is a difference in the amount of social support communicated within relationships of high and low intimacy.
  2. One-tailed (directional) research hypothesis
     H_1: More social support is communicated within relationships of high than low intimacy.
  3. Null hypothesis
     H_0: There is no difference in the amount of social support communicated within high and low intimate relationships.

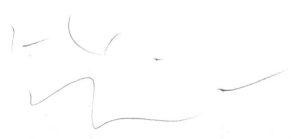

ended question, whereas if they know something about the relationships, they usually advance a closed-ended research question.

Hypotheses

Researchers often have a more concrete idea, or a tentative answer, about the nature of the relationship between an independent variable and a dependent variable. This tentative answer may be derived from the available body of theory and research about the variables, general observations made about them in the everyday world, and logic.

When researchers feel confident enough to make a prediction, they advance a **research hypothesis,** a tentative statement about the relationship between the independent and dependent variables. Wimmer and Dominick (1983) argue that a good research hypothesis should meet four criteria: "(1) It should be compatible with current knowledge in the area; (2) it should follow logical consistency; (3) it should be in its most parsimonious [simplest] form; and (4) it should be testable" (p. 195).

Research hypotheses have a number of important characteristics (see Figure 3.2). First, a research hypothesis is phrased as a declarative sentence, whereas a research question is phrased as a question. This means that research hypotheses always are directional, since they assert an answer to an implied question. Second, research hypotheses have an implied, and often explicit, "if–then" format: "If the independent variable does *X,* then the dependent variable will do *Y.*" Finally, research hypotheses, like research questions, are phrased in one of two ways. A **two-tailed research hypothesis** predicts that there is a significant relationship between variables or a significant difference between groups but does not indicate the specific nature of that relationship or difference. A **one-tailed research hypothesis** predicts the specific nature of the relationship or the difference. Choosing a two-tailed or a one-tailed research hypothesis depends on how confident researchers are about their predictions.

The null hypothesis. A research hypothesis always is contrasted against a null hypothesis. A **null hypothesis** (H_0) states that there is no relationship between an independent and dependent variable (for an ordered independent variable) or no significant difference between the independent variable categories with respect to a dependent variable (for a nominal independent variable).

Researchers can never actually prove a research hypothesis to be true because of the potential error involved in the measurement and selection of research subjects (see Chapter 12). Instead, a researcher tests whether the null hypothesis is probably true or probably false. If the null hypothesis is determined to be false, a researcher accepts the research hypothesis as the logical alternative.

Erickson and Nosanchuck (1977) and Bowers and Courtright (1984) argue that testing the null hypothesis is similar to a courtroom trial. The defendant is assumed to be not guilty, and the prosecutor must show that this claim is false. Similarly, a researcher assumes that the null hypothesis of no relationship or no significant difference is true and tries to disprove this claim.

OVERVIEW OF COMMUNICATION RESEARCH

Because communication is a vast field that encompasses many points of view, it is impossible to discuss all the directions in which communication research has gone in the past and where it is headed currently. In later chapters we will review specific communication research studies. In this section we paint a picture of how the general questions researchers ask about communication have guided research on verbal and nonverbal communication message systems and the various levels of communication.

Research on Communication Message Systems

Much communication research cuts across the five levels of communication to study the two different message systems of verbal and nonverbal communication. While almost all communication research is concerned in one way or another with these message systems, some research focuses directly on them.

Verbal communication.   Research on verbal communication focuses on the study of language, a field known as linguistics. There are four historical approaches to the study of verbal message systems: phonology, syntactics, semantics, and pragmatics.

Phonology.   **Phonology** is the study of the sounds a language finds meaningful. Every infant makes every sound for every language in the world during the babbling phase. Since only some of these are meaningful to a given language community and hence produce a reaction from caretakers, nonmeaningful ones fall out of the repertoire. Every language thus has a certain number of phonemes, or meaningful sounds, from which words are constructed. For example, English has both an \l\ and an \r\ sound, whereas Japanese does not; English speakers pronounce \r\ with the lips, Spanish speakers trill it on the tongue, and the French trill it on the uvula. One reason that foreign languages sound so fast to a nonnative is because nonnatives do not know what sounds constitute a phoneme or what sets of phonemes go together logically. Nonnative listeners therefore have trouble separating one word from another because speakers do not pause between words as a rule, so the speech just sounds fast.

One interesting line of research on phonemes is the role they play in speech errors. Research tells us that we make speech errors and other slips of the tongue when we blend sounds in ways that violate the phonetic rules of our language. One of us has friends named Chuck and Sue—guess how often they are called Suck and

Chew! Phonology has traditionally been examined in what is called the speech and hearing sciences, such as speech pathology and audiology.

Syntactics.   **Syntactics** is the study of meaning derived from word order and emphasizes the grammar of verbal messages. Two leading theoretical positions concerning the description and production of language, according to Littlejohn (1987), are structural linguistics, the study of the component parts of language (such as words and phrases; Bloomfield, 1933; Harris, 1951; Fries, 1952), and Chomsky's (1957, 1966) generative grammar, the study of implicit rules for generating and interpreting sentences. An important offshoot of syntactics is the study of how children acquire language and how language use grows during different stages of development.

Semantics.   **Semantics** is the study of word meanings. For example, there is a big difference between the words *died, killed,* and *assassinated.* They all mean that someone no longer is alive, but the mental images and associations with other concepts (such as political office) illustrate clearly how important word choice is in conveying meaning efficiently.

Research on semantics seeks to understand how we create shared meaning and the effects of shared meaning with regard to a variety of outcomes, including relationship formation and the development of culture. Sapir (1964) and Whorf (1956), for example, advanced an hypothesis (known as the Sapir-Whorf hypothesis) that asserts that not only does language reflect the way you talk about the world, but, more important, it also determines what you look for and how you think about what you see. Accordingly, the limits of one's language tend to be the limits of one's world. What we cannot conceive, we cannot perceive. Most of us, for example, have trouble thinking about a fourth dimension, but mathematicians do so all the time.

Pragmatics.   **Pragmatics** is the study of the effects, both intended and unintended, of language use by people in different situations. Pragmatic communication serves particular functions. McQuail (1987) explains, "A function is a purposeful communication activity as it might seem to the acting unit or agent, such as a person, group, or organization" (p. 329). Both verbal and nonverbal communication serve many important functions (see Figure 3.3).

Nonverbal communication.   The study of the nature and effects of nonverbal comunication is one of the most popular and diverse areas for research. Nonverbal communication refers to two general sets of variables: nonverbal message systems and contextual nonverbal messages.

Nonverbal Message Systems.   Research on nonverbal message systems concerns four things: artifacts, kinesics, paralanguage, and tactiles. These are interrelated nonverbal systems, but each has been studied separately as well.

Artifacts refer to physical appearance (such as body shape), personal appearance (such as makeup and hairstyle), objects that people carry, and objects that people use to decorate their environment. Artifacts, in particular, have a strong effect on initial perceptions and impression formation.

Figure 3.3   Communication functions

One important area of communication research concerns how communication is used pragmatically or functionally. The following represent some of the most important functions that cut across all five levels of communication.

ADAPTATION: The study of how communication is used to maintain stability in a changing environment.

AFFILIATION (LINKING/BINDING):   The study of how communication produces and reflects feelings of liking and attachment, as well as how communication produces and reflects feelings of disliking and disassociation.

BEING: The study of how communication is used to create and maintain a person's sense of identity, as well as to promote growth and change in one's identity.

CONFLICT: The study of how communication produces conflict (which occurs whenever incompatible desires exist), can be symptomatic of conflict, and can be used to manage conflict.

INFORMATION AND INFORMATION PROCESSING: The study of how information is transferred from one person to another and the nature and effects of an individual's encoding and decoding processes, including the study of listening.

MANAGEMENT OF INTERACTION: The study of how communication is used to coordinate and regulate conversation or group interaction.

MEANING AND UNDERSTANDING: The study of how communication creates shared meaning and understanding.

MENTATION: The study of how communication relates to the development of cognitive activities and processes.

PERSUASION: The study of how communication is used purposefully to influence people's beliefs, attitudes, and behavior.

POWER: The study of how communication is used to create power and status differences and the effects of power differences on communication behavior.

SOCIALIZATION (REGULATION):   The study of how communication is used to integrate individuals into social structures. Socialization is "the process by which individuals acquire the knowledge, skills, and dispositions . . . that make them more or less able members of society" (Brim, 1966, p. 3).

Kinesics refer to the way people move their bodies and position themselves, such as posture, gestures, head nods, and leg movements, as well as facial expressions and eye behavior, sometimes referred to as **oculesics.** Much of the research has been concerned with developing systems for describing the different types of body movements and gestures. Researchers are also interested in how facial expressions convey emotions as well as how eye behavior regulates the flow of conversation.

Paralanguage is the nonverbal aspect of verbal communication. Much of the research on paralanguage examines the effects of such paralinguistic features as speech rate, pauses and silence sequences, vocal intensity, vocal pitch, talk duration, breathiness, throatiness, nasality, flatness, and disfluent speech on how communicators are perceived.

Tactiles is the study of touching behavior, which fulfills important physiological and social needs for people. Touch certainly communicates our emotional feelings toward one another, and much of the research has been concerned with discovering the rules associated with who touches whom, where, and how touch is interpreted.

Contextual Nonverbal Messages. Research on contextual nonverbal messages examines the nature and effects of the setting on behavior. **Proxemics** is the study of the nature and effects of space or distance between people as a communication variable, and **chronemics** is the study of the nature and effects of time as a communication variable. The variables of time and space serve as cues about how to behave in specific contexts and are often referred to as the "hidden dimension" of communication (Hall, 1966). Researchers are particularly interested in how these nonverbal context messages differ among cultures.

Research on Levels of Communication

Communication research can also be discussed in terms of the level of communication at which it is directed. The following discussion provides an overview of some of the research in each of the five levels of communication.

Intrapersonal communication. Intrapersonal communication refers to the internal messages we send to ourselves. McQuail (1987) explains that "at this level of analysis we are concerned mainly with the seeking out, reception, interpretation, and further processing of messages or signals from an environment of objects, events, and other people" (p. 334). One direction for intrapersonal communication research has thus been on information processing, the nature and effects of how individuals encode and decode messages.

Encoding means putting thoughts into symbols that can be transmitted to another person, and decoding means attributing meaning to the symbols received. Researchers interested in informational decoding have focused on how information is learned and recalled and how information is processed according to one's psychological makeup. Researchers interested in informational encoding have focused on how individuals prepare and edit communication prior to actual transmission.

Research on information processing has inevitably led intrapersonal communication scholars to study listening, particularly behaviors associated with active, effective listening. Listening is an important area of research since we spend more time listening than performing any other communication behavior. Yet Nichols and Stevens (1957) point out that we miss about half of what others tell us.

One of the most important directions for intrapersonal communication research concerns the effects of individual differences on communication behavior. This research investigates the unique characteristics of individual communicators, who are clearly the starting point of the communication transaction.

One important research tradition has been to examine how differences on soci-odemographic variables, such as gender, age, socioeconomic status, and race, influence communication behavior. Research on individual differences also seeks to identify and relate personality traits, or dispositional tendencies, to communication behavior. A personality trait is defined as "any distinguishable, relatively enduring way in which one individual differs from others" (Guilford, 1959, p. 6). Daly (1987) argues that "personality and communication are inherently intertwined. Traits are correlated with communication-related variables in meaningful ways. At the same time, communication plays a role in the development and maintenance of dispositional tendencies" (p. 29).

A number of personality characteristics have been related to communication behavior. Self-esteem (one's overall positive or negative view of oneself), authoritarianism (the desire to dominate and to be dominated), dogmatism (the extent to which one's mind is open or closed), rigidity (the degree of resistance to a change in personal beliefs), intolerance of ambiguity, Machiavellianism (the extent to which one is focused on one's own goals and not on other persons as worthwhile individuals), extroversion-introversion, dominance-submissiveness, locus of control (the extent to which one perceives responsibility for actions as located in the environment or in people), loneliness, depression, the need for affiliation and approval, emotional stability, exhibitionism and impulsivity, schizophrenia, and psychological gender orientation (the degree to which one possesses masculine, feminine, and androgenous traits) have each been related to differences in communication behavior.

The most important intrapersonal communication research, for our purposes, concerns the study of communication-based personality predispositions. These are traits that relate directly to a person's tendencies toward communication behavior and can be labeled "communication predispositions" (Figure 3.4 presents some of the most important communication predispositions that have been studied).

Let's take just one example. McCroskey and Richmond (1987) devised a questionnaire to measure the willingness to communicate in four different situations (public, meeting, group and dyad) and with three different partners (stranger, acquaintance, and friend). Please take a moment to fill out this instrument (see Figure 3.5). Compare your scores to the mean scores of 428 college students who completed the questionnaire. Are you more or less willing to communicate than most college students? Are there some contexts in which you are more hesitant to communicate than others?

McCroskey and Richmond (1987) found from many studies that this communication predisposition has some important effects on communication behavior:

> The general conclusion that can be drawn from this immense body of research is that reduced willingness to communicate results in an individual being less effective in communication and generating negative perceptions of himself or herself in the minds of others involved in the communication. (p. 152)

Interpersonal communication.   Interpersonal communication research seeks to understand the communication behavior that occurs in the context of a dyad

Figure 3.4   Some important communication predispositions

The following are some of the most important personality predispositions that relate directly to individual differences in communication behavior.

COMMUNICATOR STYLE: "The way one verbally, nonverbally, and paraverbally interacts to signal how literal meaning should be taken, interpreted, filtered, or understood" (Norton, 1978, p. 99). Communicator style is composed of 10 attribute variables: animated, attentive, contentious/argumentative, dominant, dramatic, friendly, impression-leaving, precise, open, and relaxed.

INTERACTION INVOLVEMENT: "The extent to which an individual partakes in a social environment" (Cegala, 1981, p. 112). This personality predisposition represents a person's willingness and tendency to become involved in interpersonal communication situations.

RHETORICAL SENSITIVITY: Possessed by a person who characterizes himself or herself willingly as an undulating, fluctuating entity, always unsure, always guessing, and continually weighing potential communicative decisions (Hart, Carlson, & Eadie 1980). The rhetorically sensitive person displays five characteristics: acceptance of personal complexity, avoidance of communicative rigidity, interaction consciousness, appreciation of the communicability of ideas, and tolerance for inventional searching. Rhetorically sensitive individuals are contrasted with *noble selves,* who "see any variation from their personal norms as hypocritical, as a denial of integrity, as a cardinal sin," and *rhetorical reflectors,* who "have no selves to call their own. For each person and for each situation they present a new self" (Darnell & Brockriede, 1976, pp. 176, 178).

SELF-MONITORING: The degree to which an individual pays attention to his or her verbal and nonverbal behaviors and adapts them to the requirements of social situations (Snyder, 1974, 1979). Bell (1987) explains that "self-monitoring individuals carefully, deliberately, and strategically construct images consistent with and appropriate to the contexts in which they find themselves" (p. 206).

VERBAL AGGRESSIVENESS: A person's predisposition toward being aggressive in his or her communication. Types of verbal aggressiveness that are seen as constructive are assertiveness and argumentativeness. Infante (1987) explains that "assertiveness may be viewed as a general tendency to be interpersonally dominant, ascendant, and forceful" and that "argumentativeness is the tendency to recognize controversial issues in communication situations, to present and defend positions on the issues, and to attack the positions that other people take" (p. 164). The destructive types of symbolic aggressiveness include hostility (the use of symbols to irritate others) and verbal aggressiveness (the tendency to attack others instead of, or in addition to, their position).

WILLINGNESS TO COMMUNICATE: The degree to which one is oriented psychologically toward talking, determined by a person's unwillingness to communicate, predispositions toward verbal behavior, and shyness (McCroskey & Richmond, 1987). Some people are more inclined to verbalize than others, and the best predictor of one's willingness to communicate is communication apprehension, "an individual's level of fear or anxiety associated with either real or anticipated communication with another person or persons" (McCroskey, 1977, p. 79).

Figure 3.5   The willingness-to-communicate scale

Directions: Below are 20 situations in which a person might choose to communicate or not to communicate. Presume that you have *completely free choice*. Indicate the percentage of the time you would choose *to communicate* in each type of situation (0 = never, 100 = always).

_____ 1. Talk with a service station attendant.
_____ 2. Talk with a physician.
_____ 3. Present a talk to a group of strangers.
_____ 4. Talk with an acquaintance while standing in line.
_____ 5. Talk with a salesperson in a store.
_____ 6. Talk in a large meeting of friends.
_____ 7. Talk with a police officer.
_____ 8. Talk in a small group of strangers.
_____ 9. Talk with a friend, while standing in line.
_____ 10. Talk with a waiter or waitress in a restaurant.
_____ 11. Talk in a large meeting of acquaintances.
_____ 12. Talk with a stranger while standing in line.
_____ 13. Talk with a secretary.
_____ 14. Present a talk to a group of friends.
_____ 15. Talk in a small group of acquaintances.
_____ 16. Talk with a garbage collector.
_____ 17. Talk in a large meeting of strangers.
_____ 18. Talk with a spouse or sweetheart.
_____ 19. Talk in a small group of friends.
_____ 20. Present a talk to a group of acquaintances.

Scoring: To compute the subscores, add the percentages for the items indicated and divide the total by the number indicated below. The mean scores based on a sample of 428 college students are also provided.

	Items	**Divide by**	
PUBLIC:	3 + 14 + 20	3	(mean = 56.1; SD = 22.2)
MEETING:	6 + 11 + 17	3	(mean = 60.0; SD = 20.9)
GROUP:	8 + 15 + 19	3	(mean = 73.4; SD = 15.8)
DYAD:	4 + 9 + 12	3	(mean = 79.5; SD = 15.0)
STRANGER:	3 + 8 + 12 + 17	4	(mean = 41.3; SD = 22.5)
ACQUAINTANCE:	4 + 11 + 15 + 20	4	(mean = 75.0; SD = 17.9)
FRIEND:	6 + 9 + 14 + 19	4	(mean = 85.0; SD = 13.8)

To compute the total score, add the subscores for Stranger, Acquaintance, and Friend. Then divide that total by 3. (mean = 67.3; SD = 15.2)

Source: Adapted from James C. McCroskey & Virginia P. Richmond, "Willingness to Communicate," in James C. McCroskey and John A. Daly (Eds.), *Personality and Interpersonal Behavior*, pp. 135–136, copyright © 1987 by Sage Publications, Inc. Used by permission of Sage Publications, Inc.

Figure 3.6   Some important interpersonal communication behavior and strategies

Researchers have been interested in the following interpersonal communication behavior and strategies. This research involves constructing descriptive category systems and analyzing the effects of these behaviors on communicators and their interactions. For each behavior or strategy we identify some relevant research.

ACCOUNTING BEHAVIOR: Communication designed to manage failure episodes in interpersonal relationships (McLaughlin, Cody, & O'Hair, 1983; McLaughlin, Cody, & Rosenstein, 1983; Schonbach, 1980).

AFFINITY-SEEKING STRATEGIES: Communication designed to get others to like a person (Bell & Daly, 1986; Bell, Tremblay, & Buerkel-Rothfuss, 1987; Richmond, Gorham, & Furio, 1987).

COMFORTING STRATEGIES: Communication designed to provide a relational partner with emotional support or help (Burleson, 1984; Samter & Burleson, 1984).

COMPLIANCE-GAINING OR COMPLIANCE-RESISTING STRATEGIES: Communication designed to get others to behave in accordance with one's request (Boster & Stiff, 1984; Marwell & Schmitt, 1967; Wiseman & Schenck-Hamlin, 1981) or to refuse such compliance (McLaughlin, Cody, & Robey, 1981; McQuillen, 1986).

CONFLICT STRATEGIES: Communication designed to manage dyadic disagreements (Millar, Rogers, & Bavelas, 1984; Sillars, 1980; Sillars, Coletti, Parry, & Rogers, 1982).

DECEPTION STRATEGIES: Communication designed to lie or be deceitful (deTurk & Miller, 1985; Greene, O'Hair, Cody, & Yen, 1985; Knapp, Hart, & Dennis, 1974; Zuckerman, De Paulo, & Rosenthal, 1981).

DISENGAGEMENT STRATEGIES: Communication designed to terminate interpersonal relationships (Baxter, 1979, 1982; Cody, 1982; Cupach & Metts, 1986; Wilmot, Carbaugh, & Baxter, 1985).

DISQUALIFICATION OR EQUIVOCATION STRATEGIES: Communication designed to answer questions in an evasive manner (Bavelas & Chovil, 1986; Bavelas & Smith, 1982; Williams and Goss, 1975).

EMBARRASSMENT-REDUCING STRATEGIES: Communication designed to reduce the discomfort associated with embarrassment (Brown, 1970; Cupach, Metts, & Hazelton, 1986; Petronio, 1984).

INTERRUPTION AND SILENCE: Communication designed to interrupt another person or to produce silence (Markel, Long, & Saine, 1976; Capella, 1979, 1980; Capella & Planalp, 1981; Kennedy & Camden, 1983; McLaughlin & Cody, 1982; Zimmerman & West, 1975).

POLITENESS STRATEGIES: Communication designed to be courteous toward others (Baxter, 1984; Brown & Levinson, 1978; Craig, Tracy, & Spisak, 1986).

"SECRET TESTS": Communication designed to acquire knowledge about the state of a person's opposite-gender relationship (Baxter & Wilmot, 1984).

SELF-DISCLOSURE: Communication designed to share information about oneself with others (Cozby, 1973; Jourard, 1971; Wheeless, 1976; Wheeless & Grotz, 1976).

STORYTELLING: Communication designed to tell a story (McLaughlin, Cody, Kane, & Robey, 1981).

(two-person interaction) and the role of communication in the formation, maintenance, adaptation, and termination of dyadic relationships. Researchers are also interested in how the individual differences just discussed relate to these two things.

One direction for intepersonal communication research is understanding the nature and efects of intentional message strategies and unintentional behaviors used in a two-person interaction. The nature of this two-person interaction is not relevant; rather, the focus is on studying the communication behaviors used, and the most useful context for doing so is the dyad. Many specific interpersonal communication behaviors and strategies have been studied (see Figure 3.6).

Let's look at one of these communication strategies, compliance-gaining strategies—how we get others to follow our requests. Marwell and Schmitt (1967) proposed a taxonomy of 16 compliance-gaining strategies that might be used by a parent to get his or her son (Dick, a high school student) to increase his studying (see Figure 3.7). Which particular compliance-gaining strategy do you believe would be most effective in getting the son to comply? Which would be least effective? Which strategies do most parents use? Is there a difference between the strategies mothers use and those that fathers use? Would it make a difference if the child was a girl? How would using some of these strategies affect other aspects of the relationship,

Figure 3.7 Sixteen compliance-gaining strategies

1. PROMISE	("If you comply, I will reward you.") You offer to increase Dick's allowance if he increases his studying.
2. THREAT	("If you do not comply, I will punish you.") You threaten to forbid Dick the use of the car if he does not increase his studying.
3. EXPERTISE (POSITIVE)	("If you comply, you will be rewarded because of 'the nature of things.'") You point out to Dick that if he gets good grades, he will be able to get into a good college and get a good job.
4. EXPERTISE (NEGATIVE)	("If you do not comply, you will be punished because of 'the nature of things.'") You point out to Dick that if he does not get good grades, he will not be able to get into a good college or get a good job.
5. LIKING	(Actor is friendly and helpful to get target in a "good frame of mind" so that he will comply with the request.) You try to be as friendly and pleasant as possible to get Dick in the right frame of mind before asking him to study.
6. PREGIVING	(Actor rewards the target before requesting compliance.) You raise Dick's allowance and tell him you now expect him to study.
7. AVERSIVE STIMULATION	(Actor continuously punishes the target, making cessation contingent on compliance.) You forbid Dick the use of the car and tell him he will not be allowed to drive until he studies more.
8. DEBT	("You owe me compliance because of past favors.") You point out that you have sacrificed and saved to pay for Dick's

(continued)

Figure 3.7   Sixteen compliance-gaining strategies (continued)

	education and that he owes it to you to get good enough grades to get into a good college.
9. MORAL APPEAL	("You are immoral if you do not comply.") You tell Dick that it is morally wrong for anyone not to get as good grades as he can and that he should study more.
10. SELF-FEELING (POSITIVE)	("You will feel better about yourself if you comply.") You tell Dick he will feel proud if he gets himself to study more.
11. SELF-FEELING (NEGATIVE)	("You will feel worse about yourself if you do not comply.") You tell Dick he will feel ashamed if he gets bad grades.
12. ALTERCASTING (POSITIVE)	("A person with 'good' qualities would comply.") You tell Dick that since he is a mature and intelligent boy, he will naturally want to study more and get good grades.
13. ALTERCASTING (NEGATIVE)	("Only a person with 'bad' qualities would not comply.") You tell Dick that only someone very childish does not study as he should.
14. ALTRUISM	("I need your compliance very badly, so do it for me.") You tell Dick that you really want very badly for him to get into a good college and that you wish he would study more as a personal favor to you.
15. ESTEEM (POSITIVE)	("People you value will think better of you if you comply.") You tell Dick that the whole family will be very proud of him if he gets good grades.
16. ESTEEM (NEGATIVE)	("People you value will think worse of you if you do not comply.") You tell Dick that the whole family will be very disappointed in him if he gets poor grades.

Source: Adapted from Gerald Marwell and David R. Schmitt, "Dimensions of Compliance-gaining Behavior: An Empirical Analysis," *Sociometry, 30,* pp. 357–358, copyright © 1967 by the American Sociological Association. Reprinted by permission of the American Sociological Association.

such as maintaining positive feelings between the parent and the son? This gives you a feel for some of the research questions that can guide the study of interpersonal communication behavior and strategies.

A second direction for interpersonal communication research is the study of how communication is used to develop important dyadic relationships that are characterized by mutual awareness of the individuality of the other. Researchers are interested in how communication behavior and strategies affect the formation, development, maintenance, and termination of intimate interpersonal relationships.

Both types of interpersonal communication research describe the nature of the communication and its effects on important outcomes. These outcomes include not only the acomplishment of the intended strategies, such as gaining someone's compliance, but also impression formation, perceptions of communicator credibility and competence, satisfaction with the relationship, and trust in one's partner, to name a few.

Group communication.   Group communication research focuses primarily on decision-making group interaction, although some researchers have studied groups concerned with personal growth (such as encounter and therapy groups). One direction for group research is to examine the characteristics of communication associated with group decision making. Many researchers, among them Bales (1950, 1970), Fisher and Hawes (1971), and Hirokawa (1980, 1982, 1983), developed schemes for classifying individuals' communication behavior in a group decision-making context (see Figure 3.8).

A second direction for group research focuses on how communication affects important group outcomes. The primary outcome, of course, is decision-making effectiveness. What, for example, is the ideal ratio of task to socioemotional (relational) communication for good decision making? What types of group discussion techniques or decision-making procedures (such as majority rule versus consensus) lead to effective decision making? Other important outcomes include the development of leadership within the group, the tendency for groups to conform (groupthink) or to polarize and make more extreme judgments than their individual members would make (known as choice shifts), members' satisfaction with the group, and how communication affects the development of the group itself.

A third direction for group research focuses on how input variables affect group communication and group outcomes. Does the nature of the task, the physical environment, or group members' personalities and communication predispositions affect the communication behavior characterizing small groups as well as group outcomes?

The need for group communication research is often tied to social trends. In times of international stress (as when countries are at war), group communication research seems to flourish. When society is at peace, communication research focuses more on individuals and institutions. Group communication since the late 1970s has therefore been somewhat limited. It is also important to understand that studying groups of people is much more difficult than studying two individuals. The number of people involved makes it difficult even to describe group communication.

Organizational communication.   Organizational communication became one of the most popular areas of the communication field during the 1970s and 1980s. Given the amount of time we spend working and the importance of the decisions made within organizations, the study of organizational communication is a significant area for research.

At the most general level possible, organizational communication researchers are interested in how symbols are used to motivate and direct people's efforts. Communication is not just something that occurs within organizations; it is also the means by which organization occurs. Researchers study how communication creates organizational identity among members, such as how stories told to new employees socialize them into the culture of an organization.

A second direction for organizational research concerns the use of communication to accomplish particular purposes. Downs, Clampitt, and Pfeiffer (1988) see

Figure 3.8   A group communication coding scheme

GENERAL FUNCTIONS
  1. Analyze the Group Problem
     Definition: Any statement or question which helps the group (a) identify the nature
     of the problem; (b) identify symptoms or signs of the problems; (c) determine the
     extent or seriousness of the problem; (d) identify existing problems with present
     solutions; or (e) identify possible causes of the problem.
  2. Establish Evaluation Criteria
     Definition: Any statement or question which helps the group decide (a) what qual-
     ities or characteristics a "good" solution must contain; (b) what specific aspects of
     the problem must the solution remedy; or (c) what things need to be done to alle-
     viate or remedy the problem without creating additional problems.
  3. Generate Alternative Solution
     Definition: Any statement or question which helps the group identify an alternative
     solution to solving the problem.
  4. Evaluate Alternative Solution
     Definition: Any statement or question which helps the group evaluate, weigh or as-
     sess the desirability of a given alternative; or any statement or question which helps
     the group identify implications and consequences of accepting or not accepting a
     particular alternative solution.
  5. Establish Operating Procedures
     Definition: Any statement or question which helps the group (a) decide what needs
     to be done; (b) how they should go about approaching/solving the task or problem;
     or (c) how they should structure and organize the discussion to meet their goals and
     objectives.
  6. Positive Socioemotional
     Definition: Any statement or question which is non-task-related and appears to be
     an attempt to establish and maintain cooperative interpersonal relationships, friend-
     ships, cohesiveness or goodwill.
  7. Negative Socioemotional
     Definition: Any statement or question which is non-task-related and appears to be
     an attempt to break down cooperative interpersonal relationships, friendships, co-
     hesiveness or goodwill; or any statement or question which reflects an attempt, on
     the part of one member, to undermine the integrity or intelligence of another mem-
     ber.

Source: Randy Y. Hirokawa, "Group Communication and Problem-solving Effectiveness: An Investigation of Group Phases," *Human Communication Research, 9*(4), p. 296, copyright © 1983 by Sage
Publications, Inc. Reprinted by permission of Sage Publications, Inc.

communication as accomplishing five general purposes in an organization: (1) instruction, (2) information, (3) persuasion, (4) integration, and (5) innovation. More
specific purposes include increasing productivity, establishing effective supervisor-
subordinate links, and promoting job satisfaction. These functions thus identify
the outcomes that communication is intended to accomplish in an organizational
setting.

Organizational communication research can also be classified with regard to whether it focuses on internal or external communication. Internal organizational communication occurs within an organization among its members. Greenbaum, Hellweg, and Falcione (1988) identify four directions for research on internal organizational communication: (1) information flow studies, studying the channels and networks of communication within an organization; (2) message content studies, studying the meaning, purpose, and accuracy of messages within an organization; (3) communication climate studies, studying the relationship between communication processes and job satisfaction; and (4) individual training and organizational development studies, studying the assessment of organizations' communication needs. The International Communication Association's Communication Audit, for example (see Figure 3.9), assesses communication needs within an organization with respect to two categories: the amount of actual information versus needed information received and sent. Training programs can then be developed to help solve any communication needs that exist.

External organizational communication occurs across the boundaries of the organization between organizational members and outsiders (e.g., customers and suppliers). External organization communication research focuses primarily on public relations, the "management of communication between an organization and its publics" (Grunig & Hunt, 1984, p. 6). Velmans (1984) argues that public relations allow organizations to create and maintain organizational identity, ensure organizational survival, and increase organizations' effectiveness and productivity. External organizational communication research also includes marketing and advertising, lobbying, recruitment, public opinion and market research, and long-range planning.

Societal communication.   There are three types of societal communication research: public communication, cultural communication, and mass communication.

Public Communication Research.   Public communication research tends to be rhetorical, focusing on how communicators create messages to influence their audiences. We will save our review of one important type of public communication research, rhetorical criticism, for our discussion of textual analysis in Chapter 10. Here we examine what is perhaps the epitome of public communication, political communication.

Political communication is defined as the process of using communication to negotiate the allocation of limited resources (especially money) among a group of people. Kendall (1988) explains that political communication researchers study six things: (1) political news (the sources people use to get political information), (2) voter decision making (how people use information to reach a voting decision), (3) the political statements made by presidents, (4) political discourse (the content, organization, style, delivery, and effects of political messages), (5) the fantasy element in mass-mediated politics, or how the media create pictures or images in the minds of political audiences, and (6) political advertising. Kendall also identi-

Figure 3.9 The ICA Communication Audit

RECEIVING INFORMATION FROM OTHERS

Instructions for Questions 1 through 10: You can receive information about various topics in your organization. For each topic listed . . . mark your response on the answer sheet that best indicates: (1) the amount of information you *are* receiving on that topic and (2) the amount of information you *need* to receive on that topic, that is, the amount you have to have in order to do your job.

| Topic Area | | This is the amount of information I receive now. | | | | | | This is the amount of information I need to receive. | | | | |
		Very little	Little	Some	Great	Very great		Very little	Little	Some	Great	Very great
How well I am doing in my job.	**1.**	1	2	3	4	5	**2.**	1	2	3	4	5
My job duties.	**3.**	1	2	3	4	5	**4.**	1	2	3	4	5
How organization decisions are made that affect my job.	**5.**	1	2	3	4	5	**6.**	1	2	3	4	5
Important new product, service or program developments in my organization.	**7.**	1	2	3	4	5	**8.**	1	2	3	4	5
How my job relates to the total operation of my organization.	**9.**	1	2	3	4	5	**10.**	1	2	3	4	5

SENDING INFORMATION TO OTHERS

Instructions for Questions 11 through 16: In addition to receiving information, there are topics on which you can send information to others. For each topic listed . . . mark your responses on the answer sheet that best indicates: (1) the amount of information you *are* sending on that topic and (2) the amount of information you *need* to send on that topic in order to do your job.

| Topic Area | | This is the amount of information I send now. | | | | | | This is the amount of information I need to send now. | | | | |
		Very little	Little	Some	Great	Very great		Very little	Little	Some	Great	Very great
Reporting what I am doing in my job.	**11.**	1	2	3	4	5	**12.**	1	2	3	4	5
Reporting what I think my job requires me to do.	**13.**	1	2	3	4	5	**14.**	1	2	3	4	5
Requesting information necessary to do my job.	**15.**	1	2	3	4	5	**16.**	1	2	3	4	5

Source: Goldhaber, G. and Rogers, D. (1979) *Auditing Organizational Communication Systems: The ICA Communications Audit.* Dubuque, IA: Kendall-Hunt.

fies two promising directions for future research: the perception of politicians' inter-personal communication and the comparative study of political communication in different nations.

Cultural Communication.   There can be little doubt that culture influences everything we know about. Porter and Samovar (1988) explain:

> Culture is the deposit of knowledge, experiences, beliefs, values, attitudes, meanings, hierarchies, religion, timing, roles, spatial relations, concepts of the universe, and material objects and possessions acquired by a large group of people in the course of generations through individual and group striving. (p. 19)

Two forms of cultural communication are of particular interest to researchers: intercultural and intracultural communication. Intercultural communication refers to "the communication phenomena in which participants, different in cultural backgrounds, come into direct or indirect contact with one another" (Kim, 1984, p. 16). Researchers study how members of different cultures communicate in similar and different ways and the effects of such differences on all of the outcome variables discussed in this chapter. Researchers also look at some important outcomes that are unique to intercultural interactions, such as how people are socialized or assimilated into a new culture or how communication can reduce ethnocentrism and create closer international ties.

Intracultural communication, also called interethnic communication, is "the type of communication that takes place between members of the same dominant culture, but with slightly different values" (Sitaram & Cogdell, 1979, p. 28). Different groups within the same culture are called subcultures, each of which is "a racial, ethnic, regional, economic, or social community exhibiting characteristic patterns of behavior sufficient to distinguish it from others within an embracing culture or society" (Porter & Samovar, 1988, p. 20). Researchers are interested in how members of various subcultures within a culture (such as blacks, whites, and Hispanics in the United States) communicate within their subcultures and with others.

Mass Communication.   Wimmer and Dominick (1987) identify four directions for mass communication research: (1) mass media effects, (2) the print media, (3) the electronic media, and (4) advertising and public relations. The study of mass media effects is theory-based, whereas the other research directions have a more applied focus, are usually initiated within the private sector, and attempt to solve problems within a particular mass-mediated context.

One important direction for the study of mass media effects is "uses and gratifications research," which focuses on how audiences use the mass media to meet particular needs. Sometimes people use television as a way to escape reality; at other times they use it to learn more about reality. Rubin (1979) identifies six primary reasons young people gave for watching television (see Figure 3.10).

A second direction for mass media effects research concerns the positive and negative effects of media content. In particular, researchers examine the effects of

Figure 3.10 Television use by children and adolescents

The reasons that children and adolescents in the fourth, eighth, eleventh, and twelfth grade in public schools gave for watching television fell into six broad categories.

Learning
1. So I can learn about things happening in the world.
2. So I can learn how to do things I haven't done before.
3. Because it teaches me things I don't learn in school.
4. Because it helps me learn things about myself.
5. So I could learn about what could happen to me.
6. Because it shows how other people deal with the same problems I have.

Pastime, Habit
1. When I have nothing better to do.
2. Because it passes the time away.
3. Because it gives me something to do.
4. Because it's a habit.
5. Because I just like to watch.
6. Because I just enjoy watching.

Companionship
1. So I won't be alone.
2. When there's no one to talk to or play with.
3. Because it makes me feel less lonely.

Distraction
1. So I can forget about school and homework.
2. So I can get away from the rest of the family.
3. So I can get away from what I'm doing.

Arousal
1. Because it's thrilling.
2. Because it excites me.

Relaxation
1. Because it relaxes me.
2. Because it's a pleasant rest.

Source: Adapted from Alan M. Rubin, "Television Use by Children and Adolescents," *Human Communication Research, 5*(2), pp. 112–113, copyright © 1979 by Sage Publications, Inc. Reprinted by permission of Sage Publications, Inc.

television on children's learning and development of prosocial (positive) and antisocial (or aggressive) tendencies. A third direction is the study of agenda setting, or the media's ability to structure our thinking. Cohen (1963) observed that the media are usually quite successful in telling people what is important. How likely is it, for example, that a special televised report on terrorism leads people to perceive this as a significant problem in our society? A final direction for mass media effects research, which is related to agenda setting, is called cultivation research and examines how viewers' beliefs about social reality are based on the mass-mediated images to which they are exposed. Specifically, the cultivation hypothesis presupposes that television is a mass ritual that serves as a source of information about everyday rules and reality (Gerbner, Gross, Morgan, & Signorielli, 1986). How likely is it, for example, that repeated exposure to soap operas leads people to overestimate the incidence of illegitimate births, divorces, and suicides in society?

Stone (1987) identifies four directions for research on newspapers. First, researchers study the process of information gathering, particularly with regard to the reporter-source relationship and the accuracy of news stories. Second, researchers analyze the nature of writing and editing, which includes readability studies (how difficult it is to read newspapers), graphic design, and packaging, as well as newswriting style and decision making by editors about what to keep in and what to leave out. Third, a recent focus for research concerns the study of newsroom personnel and management, such as the demographics of newsroom personnel, the hiring and training of new employees, and the nature and influence of media chains. Fourth, researchers study important characteristics of the audience, such as how demographics and psychographics (readers' psychological lifestyles) influence reading habits.

Research on the electronic media (broadcasting) is concerned primarily with ratings research. The Nielsen Company and the Arbitron Ratings Company, for example, provide ratings for television and radio, respectively, and much of the debate in this area concerns the methods appropriate for attaining accurate ratings. Nonratings research is concerned with such things as program testing, music preferences, and audience perceptions of various performers and entertainers.

Research on advertising and public relations focuses on how the mass media industry uses communication to influence its various publics. Research is used to determine the effectiveness of types of advertisements (such as reward and fear appeals) and other mass-mediated campaigns as well as the effectiveness of the mass media in reaching their intended audiences.

CONCLUSION

In every area of communication, some things we can describe with precision, some we can predict with confidence, and some we can control. This knowledge comprises the material you read in textbooks assigned in other courses. Many more aspects of communication, however, we still don't understand, can't make dependable predictions about, and can't control. To bring these aspects within our circle of understanding, researchers must first phrase meaningful, researchable questions.

We started this chapter by saying that research begins with curiosity. We hope that you now undertand the distinction Robert Lynd made when he said:

> There are two sorts of curiosity—the momentary and the permanent. The momentary is concerned with the odd appearance on the surface of things. The permanent is attracted by the amazing and consecutive life that flows on beneath the surface of things. (Murphy, 1978, pp. 198–199)

The best research questions reflect the latter kind of curiosity.

The communication field is a broad and complex discipline. Research in communication has proceeded in many directions, from using theory to guide research to solving practical communication problems, from verbal to nonverbal communication, from the intrapersonal to the social communication levels. We cannot possibly examine every topic studied, every theory used, every problem selected, every research question asked, or every research direction pursued. Instead, we have examined the general steps associated with the conceptualization phase of research and have given you a flavor of some of the research done in the communication discipline. We encourage you to find our more about what is being done. Of course, to study the relevant research, you need to know where to find it and how to read it, as explained in Chapter 4.

chapter 4

Finding, Reading, and Using Research

For some people, going to the library is like going to the dentist—a real pain. For others, it's like shopping in a great department store of ideas, an absorbing search for products to enrich their minds. Most libraries, especially those at colleges and universities, contain many more items than even the largest of shopping malls. To enjoy perusing the library's resources—rather than wandering around in confusion or searching futilely down blind alleys—you need to know where to find what you're there to obtain.

It's likely that your library contains information about research conducted previously on *any* communication topic that interests you. In fact, as you pore through references to research reports, you're likely to be amazed at the breadth and variety of topics communication scholars explore. This prior work provides a foundation for aspiring researchers to build on. Anyone interested in a communication process, either as a consumer or as a producer of research, should access what's already been done and learned about the topic of interest. The major purpose of library research is to avoid "reinventing the wheel." The trick lies in conducting that search efficiently.

When you walk into a large, unfamiliar shopping mall with a specific purpose in mind, you usually stop in front of a directory to learn where you're likely to find what you're looking for. In this chapter we will offer a sort of directory to the research literature available in most libraries. Once you master these basic library procedures, you'll be able to go directly to the places where you're most likely to find whatever you want to know. From then on, your library visits will be rewarded swiftly and amply with the best ideas and information the human mind has produced.

THE SEARCH

The actual search begins by understanding what informational resources exist and what form they take (see Figure 4.1). Once appropriate informational resources have been found, you need to understand the information contained therein. Doing so, however, requires understanding the standard way it is reported. Once relevant research has been found and understood, its usefulness must be evaluated. Finding, reading, and evaluating research undoubtedly causes researchers to rethink the original topic they considered worth studying, and this probably makes it necessary to find additional, and more focused, research. This cyclical process of finding, reading, and evaluating research enables researchers to select and review the most appropriate research. Once a topic worth studying has been refined, an appropriate review

Figure 4.1   A library search model

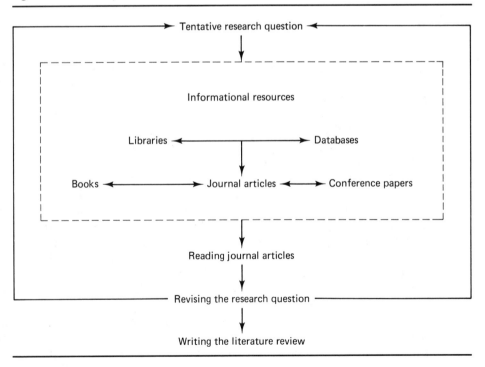

of the literature has been conducted and written, and the research question has been formalized, it becomes possible to plan and design a communication study.

Locating Relevant Research

Relevant research may be found in many places and in many forms. Here we identify two primary places: libraries and electronic information services.

Libraries. **Libraries,** as we all know, are locations set aside specifically to store knowledge in an organized fashion. This knowledge can take the traditional form of printed books and journals on shelves or an "electronic form" whereby research is stored and transmitted in nonprint form.

There are three basic kinds of libraries: *public* or *general-use libraries, research libraries,* and *special-use libraries.* These three kinds of libraries differ in content and organization. If your high school was small, the library probably contained a few thousand books, perhaps bound volumes of a few magazines, and current magazines and newspapers. Even if you went to a large high school, the chances are good that your library contained mostly general-interest and reference books. This type of library, called a **public** or **general-use library,** stocks a broad range of materials to serve its community, including novels, adventure stories, children's books, how-to manuals, popular periodicals (such as *Time* and *Newsweek*), and newspapers. These informational resources can be quite helpful in the early stages of the research process for choosing a topic to study and asking a tentative research question. Public libraries, however, do not stock formal research documents, which means that they are of limited use to scholars.

Research libraries, such as those on most university campuses, try to collect a wide selection of books, of course, but include a narrower range of materials than public or general-use libraries. This is because they do not attempt to meet all the entertainment and training needs of a given community. Many of the library materials researchers use will not be books because books are typically the product of research, not the basis of it. The primary form in which actual research is reported is the scholarly journal. The principal survival skill for any researcher is learning how to use research libraries and read scholarly journals.

Special-use libraries take several forms. One important form is an **archive,** which provides permanent storage of original records and documents and can be useful in conducting historical research (see Chapter 10). Other types of special-use libraries include corporate and legal libraries and those of historical societies, museums, religious societies, and the like.

Electronic information services. Although libraries are the primary place to find relevant research, researchers also have at their disposal a bewildering array of potentially useful electronic information services. Most of these services are specialized to meet the needs of researchers in particular fields, including communication. Two primary kinds of electronic information services are important to communication researchers: *online databases* and *CD-ROM*.

Online Databases.   A **database** is a place where large amounts of data, usually on a specific topic, are stored. An **online database** is one that can be accessed through a computer via a modem.

Online databases are often very large but, unfortunately, quite expensive to use, for two reasons. First, the cost of "connect time," the time during which the computer is accessing the database, can be high and is paid by researchers. For example, the CLAIMS/UNITERM database on chemical patents available through Dialog costs $300 per hour. Second, online searches can be quite complex, often requiring researchers to cover the cost of help from a librarian trained in the particular software and terminology of the database being used. When these problems are overcome, however, an online database search can help researchers find the most up-to-date references.

Many online databases are available, three of which are used frequently by communication researchers: *ERIC, Dialogue,* and *Comserve.* **ERIC** (for Educational Resources Information Center) is an online database started by the U.S. Department of Education in 1966 that specializes in education-related references. With 660,868 records, it is one of the most complete databases for materials relevant to the human sciences, including communication. ERIC is also available on CD-ROM (to be discussed shortly) and in printed and microfiche form in many research libraries.

Dialog, founded in 1972, is one of the largest and most popular scholarly online databases. Dialog is referred to more accurately as a vendor because it is not a single database but rather an umbrella organization with over 320 separate databases and more than 175 million records (Dialog, 1989). According to its 1989 catalog, Dialog offers material relevant to science, business, technology, chemistry, law, medicine, engineering, social sciences, business, economics, and current events. Dialog spans 32 human science databases, including *Dissertation Abstracts Online,* which has 988,740 records including virtually every Ph.D. dissertation submitted in the United States since 1861.

Comserve is particularly useful to communication researchers because it is an online communication database sponsored by the Rensselaer Polytechnic Institute's Department of Language, Literature, and Communication. Comserve is an excellent source of up-to-date information on communication research, including grants, and even provides a job-advertising service called COMJOBS (Stephen & Harrison, 1989). Comserve also is available through *Bitnet,* the worldwide computer message network. Best of all, Comserve is free and operates 24 hours a day.

CD-ROM.   **CD-ROM** stands for "compact disk, read-only memory." Such disks are similar to the audio compact disks with which you are probably familiar.

One 5¼-inch CD-ROM disk is capable of storing about 275,000 printed pages, or about 1,500 floppy disks' worth of information (Taylor, 1989).

More and more databases are becoming available on CD-ROM, and these disks appear to be the wave of the future in electronic information services. Taylor (1989) reports, for example, that the University of North Carolina at Chapel Hill first installed a CD-ROM in 1985 when it provided about 2,000 online database searches. By 1989 the UNC library expects over 11,000 CD-ROM searches but only a few hundred online database searches. The burgeoning interest in CD-ROM services may reach a new peak with the conversion of INFO-TRAC (a large database that may be thought of as an electronic reader's guide to periodicals and newspapers) from large laser disks to CD-ROM in 1989.

The shift to CD-ROM reference services seems to stem from two factors. First, although expensive to buy initially—Taylor (1989) reports that *Dissertation Abstracts International* costs $1695 for just the current file and $5495 for the backfile), CD-ROMs become very economical when used by many people. Second, CD-ROM databases are usually made available at terminals on the library floor where computer-literate users can help themselves. Even computer illiterates can usually be taught how to use CD-ROM-databased systems in a matter of minutes. CD-ROM databases are also often available to researchers at no charge, which will probably ensure their ascendancy over online systems.

Finding Relevant Research

To find any research, you must understand how research libraries are organized. You probably know much of the following information, and your library probably has handouts on it, but we want to be as thorough as possible in explaining a library search.

Libraries adopt what is known as a **cataloging system** that is used to decide where any given piece of research can be found. There are many types of cataloging systems, particularly in special-use libraries. The two systems used most commonly, however, are the Dewey Decimal System and the Library of Congress system. The **Dewey Decimal System** is used most frequently in public libraries. It employs 10 numbered categories as general headings (see Figure 4.2). Each of these headings is subdivided as many times as necessary to assign a unique **call number** to each book. The **Library of Congress** cataloging system, by contrast, uses letters to designate its major categories and a combination of numbers and letters to subdivide each category so that each book is assigned a unique call number.

Card catalog.   Libraries have a centralized file called a **card catalog** that lists all of their holdings. This card catalog is cross-referenced in three ways: by author, by title of work, and by subject area. This means that each book may have three cards explaining where to find it. A sample card contains some valuable information that makes a search easier (see Figure 4.3).

Figure 4.2 Library cataloging systems

Dewey Decimal System

000	General works	500	Natural sciences
100	Philosophy	600	Applied science
200	Religion	700	The arts
300	Social science	800	Literature
400	Language	900	History, geography

Library of Congress System

A	General works	M	Music
B	Philosophy, religion, psychology	N	Fine arts
C	History, auxiliary sciences (genealogy, archaeology, etc.)	P	Language and literature
		Q	Science
D	General and Old World history	R	Medicine
E, F	History: America	S	Agriculture
G	Geography, anthropology, recreation	T	Technology
		U	Military science
H	Social sciences	V	Naval science
J	Political science	Z	Bibliography, library science
L	Law		

Many libraries now use electronic card files that are accessible to library users through computer terminals. These electronic card files, like card catalog files, reference works by author, title, and subject. Electronic card files make it easy for libraries to keep their files current and provide fairly exhaustive information about the reference material, sometimes even indicating whether the book is checked out.

Electronic card files are here to stay, but like many other advances, they are not without their drawbacks. A graduate student once ran into a library patron who was looking up a book in the card file of a library several miles from his home. When the patron was asked why he didn't use the library closer to his home, he responded, "Oh! I will, but they don't have a real card catalog file, just computers. So I come over here, look up the call number, and then go home and get the book off the shelf." This is an extreme case of computer apprehension, but it illustrates an important problem with the new electronic technologies: If people are not comfortable using them, they can become expensive toys for an elite few. If large numbers of people use them, they can be a boon to scholarly research. Thus it is important to learn how to use electronic card files.

Books. Books can provide a good introduction to a topic. Their authors have done the work of finding relevant journal articles and summarizing the results. Books, however, take a long time to write and are not as current as journal articles. In addition, many books are fairly general to meet the needs of a relatively large

Figure 4.3 Sample catalog card

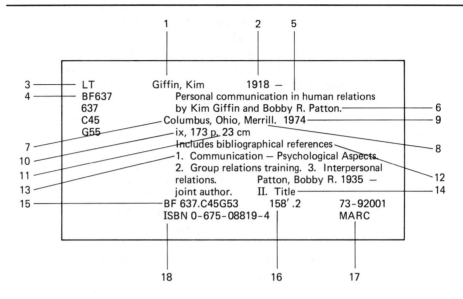

1. Author's name
2. Year author was born
3. Shelving location
4. Library of Congress call number
5. Title of book
6. Coauthor's name
7. City and state of publication
8. Publishing company
9. Year of publication
10. Number of book pages; Roman numerals indicate frontmatter (table of contents and preface)
11. Height of the book in centimeters
12. Bibliographical references included
13. Subject matter headings under which book is cataloged
14. The book is also cataloged under its title
15. Library of Congress call number
16. Dewey Decimal System call number
17. A computer call number, which all books have
18. Book publication serial number

audience and may therefore lack information about the specific research question that is being asked.

Researchers thus use books primarily as orienting material to help guide a review of the research literature. Communication researchers might begin, for example, by consulting an encyclopedia, such as the *International Encyclopedia of Communications* (1989). There also are a variety of handbooks that provide overviews of communication research, such as Pool, Frey, Schramm, Maccoby, and Parker's (1973) *Handbook of Communication,* Berger and Chaffee's (1987a) *Handbook of Communication Science,* Knapp and Miller's (1985) *Handbook of Interpersonal Communication,* Goldhaber and Barnett's (1988) *Handbook of Organizational Communication,* Jablin, Putnam, Roberts, and Porter's (1987) *Handbook of Organizational Communication: An Interdisciplinary Perspective,* Nimmo and Sanders's (1981) *Handbook of Political Communication,* or Asante and Gudykunst's (1989) *Handbook of International and Intercultural Communication.* Once a general area of communication is identified, researchers often consult recent textbooks to see what research has been conducted in that area.

Some books also include original research articles. For example, the *Communication Yearbook* and the *Mass Communication Review Yearbook* series, published annually by Sage Publications, include original research as well as overviews of various areas of the communication discipline. Books are thus quite useful for getting a feel for a topic, but they do not substitute for the most current research, which is found in the leading scholarly journals.

Library reference materials.   Some libraries have such large collections that it could take a long time to locate a single piece of research unless you know how to do it efficiently. Fortunately, libraries have a number of **reference aids** to help locate any piece needed in a matter of minutes. Learning to use these reference aids is one of the most important steps because it saves researchers a tremendous amount of time and energy. Many types of general reference aids are used to locate materials, including abstract services, bibliographies, directories, guides to the literature, indexes, and legal reference sources (see Figure 4.4).

Scholarly journals.   Researchers' primary reference source is the scholarly journal. A **scholarly journal** is a regular publication, often quarterly, that prints scholarly essays and book reviews. Research results reported in journals, thanks to their frequent publication and shorter production deadlines, tend to be more current than results reported in books. Furthermore, unlike most other informational sources, the importance and accuracy of the results published in scholarly journals have been reviewed by experts in the field before being printed. Articles printed in

Figure 4.4   General library reference aids

The following are examples of the reference aids available in research libraries.

Abstract Service
A. *Communication Abstracts*
B. *Library and Information Science Abstracts*
C. *Psychological Abstracts*
D. *Sage Family Studies Abstracts*
E. *Sociological Abstracts*
F. *Women's Studies Abstracts*

Guides to the Literature

A. Sheehy, E. P. (1976). *Guide to reference books* (9th ed.). Chicago: American Library Association.
B. White, C. (1973). *Sources of information in the social sciences* (2nd ed.). Chicago: American Library Association.
C. Rivers, W. L., Thompson, W., & Nyhan, M. J. (1977). *Aspen handbook of the media, 1977–79 edition: A selective guide to research, organization and publications in communication.* New York: Aspen Institute for Humanistic Studies/Praeger.

Bibliographies

A. *Bibliographic Index*
B. Blum, E. (1980). *Basic books in mass media* (2nd ed.). Urbana: University of Illinois Press.
C. Sterling, C. H. (Ed.). (1969–). *Communication booknotes.* Washington, DC: George Washington University Press.
D. *Subject catalogue: A cumulative list of works represented by Library of Congress printed cards.* (1950–). Washington, DC: U.S. Library of Congress.

Directories

A. *IMS Ayer directory of publications.* (1880–). Philadelphia: IMS Press.
B. *Educational film locator* (2nd ed.). (1980). New York: Bowker.
C. *Media review digest.* (1973–). Ann Arbor, MI: Pierian.
D. Brooks, T., & Marsh, E. (1981). *The complete directory to prime time network TV shows, 1946–present* (2nd rev. ed.). New York: Ballantine.

Indexes

A. Periodical Indexes
    1. *The Reader's Guide to Periodical Literature*
    2. Matlon, R. J. (1987). *Index to journals in communication studies through 1985.* Annandale, VA: Speech Communication Association.
    3. *Social Science Index*
    4. *Applied Science and Technology Index*
    5. *Art Index*
    6. *Biological and Agricultural Index*
    7. *Business Periodicals Index*
    8. *Education Index*
    9. *General Science Index*
    10. *Humanities Index*
    11. *Index to Legal Periodicals*
B. Newspaper Indexes
    1. *New York Times Index*
    2. *Wall Street Journal Index*
C. Broadcast News Indexes
    1. *CBS News Index*
    2. *The MacNeil/Lehrer Report*
D. Biographical Indexes
    1. *Biography and Genealogy Master Index*
    2. *Index to Artistic Biography*
E. Indexes to Other Information
    1. *Book Review Index*
    2. *Book Review Digest*
    3. *Current Book Review Citations*

the leading journals are typically reviewed by a panel of experts to make sure that they are of unassailable quality. Journal editors usually conduct **blind reviews** by asking experts in the field who are not told the name or reputation of the researchers to determine whether the piece should be published or not and what changes should be made. Some leading journals reject over 90 percent of the manuscripts submitted to them. This review process tries to ensure that only the highest-quality research in an area is published.

Scholary communication journals can be classified as to their primary intended audience. Communication journals are intended primarily for speech communication, mass communication, journalism, or speech science researchers (see Figure 4.5).

Useful articles also appear in journals from related disciplines. Journals in disciplines such as business and management, political science, psychology, and sociology frequently publish articles that relate directly to communication (see Figure 4.6). Many of these journals also are interdisciplinary, meaning that they publish articles of interest beyond their field of primary focus.

Figure 4.5   Scholarly communication journals

Speech Communication

Argument Studies Quarterly
Association for Communication Administration Bulletin
Communication
Communication and Cognition
Communication Education
Communication Quarterly
Communication Monographs
Communication Research: An International Quarterly
Communication Research Reports
Communication Studies
Communication Theory
Communication Yearbook
European Journal of Communication
Health Communication
Human Communication Research
Information and Behavior
Journal of Applied Communication Research
Management Communication Quarterly
National Forensic Journal
Philosophy and Rhetoric
Political Communication and Persuasion
Quarterly Journal of Speech
Rhetoric Society Quarterly
Southern Communication Journal
Text and Performance Quarterly
Western Journal of Speech Communication
Women's Studies in Communication

World Communication
Written Communication

Mass Communication

Broadcasting
Cinema Journal
Comm/Ent: A Journal of Communication and Entertainment Law
Communication and the Law
Critical Studies in Mass Communication
Cutting Edge
Educational Communication and Technology
Feedback
Feedback Communications Law Journal
Film Comment
Film Journal
Film Quarterly
International Journal of Advertising
Journal of Broadcasting & Electronic Media
Journal of Communication
Journal of Popular Culture
Journal of Popular Film
Jump Cut
Marketing and Media Decisions
Mass Comm Review
Media & Methods
Media & Values
Media Culture & Society
Quarterly Review of Film Studies
Telecommunications Policy

Journalism

Columbia Journalism Review
Journalism Educator
Journalism History
Journalism Monographs
Journalism Quarterly
Newspaper Research Journal
Public Opinion Quarterly
Public Relations Quarterly
Public Relations Review

Speech and Language

American Speech
Et Cetera
Human Development
Journal of Communication Disorders
Journal of Speech and Hearing Disorders
Journal of Speech and Hearing Research
Journal of Verbal Learning and Verbal Behavior
Language & Communication

Figure 4.6   Selected scholarly journals in other disciplines

Business and Management

Academy Management Journal
Academy of Management Review
Administrative Science Quarterly
Industrial and Labor Relations Review
Journal of Advertising
Journal of Advertising Research
Journal of Business
Journal of Consumer Research
Journal of Management Systems
Journal of Marketing
Journal of Marketing Research
Journal of the Market Research Society
Labor Studies Journal
Management Review
Organizational Behavior and Human Performance
Personnel Journal

Language and Linguistics

American Speech
Anthropological Linguistics
International Journal of American Linguistics
International Journal of Psycholinguistics
Journal of Linguistics
Language
Language and Social Psychology
Language and Speech
Linguistics
Theoretical Linguistics

Library and Information Science

Behavioral and Social Science Librarian
Cataloguing and Classification Quarterly
Information Technology and Libraries
International Journal of Computer and Information Science
International Library Review
Journal of Documentation
Journal of Library History
Library Journal
Library Quarterly
Quarterly Journal of the Library of Congress

Political Science

American Journal of Political Science
American Political Science Review
American Politics Quarterly
Comparative Political Studies
Comparative Politics

    Conflict Studies
    International Studies
    Journal of Conflict Resolution
    Journal of Politics
    Political Quarterly
    Political Science Quarterly
    Political Studies

Psychology

    American Behavioral Scientist
    American Journal of Psychology
    Cognitive Psychology
    Developmental Psychology
    Family Processes
    Group & Organization Studies
    Human Organization
    International Journal of Psychology
    Journal of Abnormal Psychology
    Journal of Applied Social Psychology
    Journal of Experimental Social Psychology
    Journal of Human Relations
    Journal of Humanistic Psychology
    Journal of Intergroup Relations
    Journal of Marriage and the Family
    Journal of Nonverbal Behavior
    Journal of Personality
    Journal of Personality and Social Psychology
    Journal of Sex Research
    Personality and Social Psychology Bulletin
    Small Group Behavior
    Social Psychology Quarterly

Social Science

    International Social Science Journal
    Journal of Divorce
    Journal of Homosexuality
    Journal of Social and Behavioral Sciences
    Journal of Social and Personal Relationships
    Philosophy of the Social Sciences
    Sex Roles: A Journal of Research
    Social Research
    Social Science Quarterly

Social Work

    Aging
    Child and Family
    Community Development Journal
    Family Processes
    Family Relations

(continued)

Figure 4.6   Selected scholarly journals in other disciplines (continued)

Health and Social Work
International Journal of Group Psychotherapy
International Social Work
Journal of Gerontology
Journal of Marriage and Family
Journal of Youth and Adolescence
Marriage and Family Review
Social Work

Sociology

American Journal of Sociology
American Sociological Review
International Journal of Sociology
Journal of Popular Culture
Journal of Social Issues
Public Opinion Quarterly
Qualitative Sociology
Social Forces
Sociological Methods and Research
Sociological Quarterly
Sociology

Journal indexes and abstracts.   Scholarly communication journal articles are referenced in *Communication Abstracts* and Matlon's (1987) *Index to Journals in Communication Studies through 1985. Communication Abstracts* is a quarterly publication that prints one- or two-paragraph summaries of communication-related articles published in the previous 90 days.

Matlon's index, by contrast, is a reference book that indexes and classifies every article published in the major communication journals since the first issue of *Quarterly Journal of Speech* in 1915. Unlike *Communication Abstracts,* which prints summaries of articles, Matlon's index lists articles published by their title and indexes them by author and by subject. Matlon's index therefore covers many years in a single book, whereas *Communication Abstracts* gives more information about fewer articles over a shorter period of time. This is a common difference between works that abstract and works that index research findings.

There are many reference works for other disciplines. Researchers consult, for example, *Psychology Abstracts, Business-related Abstracts, Sociological Abstracts,* and the *Social Science Citation Index* to find relevant research in related disciplines.

Other informational resources.

Scholarly Conference Papers.   Many journal articles start life as conference papers. **Conference papers** are reports of research presented by scholars at meetings with other scholars. Many convention papers are selected competitively through blind review, although the percentage of papers accepted for conventions is much higher than the percentage of articles selected for publication. Thus conference papers do not have the same prestige, or "stamp of approval," as journal articles, but they can still be a valuable source of information.

Conference papers may be hard to obtain, however. Fortunately, many of the best communication conference papers can be obtained through the Educational Resources Information Center (ERIC). Some major scholarly conferences also publish what are called **proceedings,** which are written and polished versions of the conference papers presented. When these outlets are not available, it is necessary to write directly to the author for a copy of the conference paper. Addresses for authors who are members of the Speech Communication Association are listed in the *SCA Directory* published by the SCA (5105 Backlick Road, Suite E, Annandale, VA 22003).

Periodicals. **Periodicals** include everything from daily newspapers to monthly and even bimonthly publications, such as industry magazines and government reports and documents. Periodicals tend to be oriented toward news or current events; hence the need for frequent publication. The purest news-oriented periodicals are newspapers and magazines. Periodicals published less frequently tend to be more specialized in content and readership.

HOW RESEARCH IS PRESENTED: READING SCHOLARLY JOURNAL ARTICLES

Scholarly journals present the most current research in the field, research that has passed the test of review. Journal articles are thus the bread and butter of communication researchers. For that reason, the remainder of this chapter concentrates on how to read and use scholarly journal articles effectively.

Scholarly journal articles report the results obtained from the methodology employed in a particular study. Thus there are articles about experiments performed, surveys taken, texts analyzed, and research conducted in natural settings. Experimental and survey researchers, and sometimes textual analysts tend to concentrate on quantitative, or numerical, data, while other textual analysts and ethnographers focus on qualitative, or symbolic, data.

Journal articles that analyze qualitative data are so varied that it is difficult to discuss a single model for how these articles are written. Examples of these articles, however, can be found in Friedman, Botan, Frey, and Kreps's (forthcoming) *Interpreting Communication Research.* It also should be pointed out that some articles are state-of-the-art reviews of the literature, whereas others are methodology pieces that develop and test an instrument. Some features of how articles are written are the same for all research, but one particular format is well established for presenting the results obtained from analyzing quantitative research.

A Typical Quantitative Scholarly Journal Article

A typical quantitative journal article contains a number of important subheadings (see Figure 4.7). Students often find these articles difficult to read, but understanding the accepted format will help you to know where to look in an article for the information you need and to avoid wasting valuable time.

Title. The most straightforward title presents exactly the topic that was studied by a researcher. A title might read, for example, "The Effects of Watching Television Violence on Children's Use of Threats." A title also sometimes takes the form of a question, such as "Do Workers Trust Labor Unions and Their Messages?" Sometimes, however, titles do not provide a straightforward account of what the authors were after. In such cases, the information contained in the abstract clarifies the nature of the research.

Abstract. Most journal articles start with a summary of the important points in that article. This summary, usually one paragraph long, is called an **abstract.** An abstract can be a researcher's best friend because it encapsulates the most important information contained in an article. Researchers use abstracts to determine whether articles are relevant to the research topic. If the abstract indicates relevance, the researcher then goes on to read the entire article.

An abstract contains a number of important features about the research study (see Figure 4.8). Specifically, the author identifies the general purpose of the study and explains the relevant findings. Sometimes the author will summarize the procedures that were used. As you can see, this condensed summary of the entire article can establish whether the article is relevant and should be included in a literature review.

Introduction. The introduction begins the actual body of a journal article. This section, frequently no longer than a page or two, is used to orient readers to the topic being studied and to explain why it is important to study. Sometimes this justification takes the form of identifying gaps and voids in the current body of knowledge or explaining the need (economic, social, political) for addressing that topic. The introduction thus establishes the purpose and significance of the research.

Review of the relevant literature. The literature review is one of the most difficult and crucial sections of a research article. Here a researcher identifies the work done by scholars that is relevant to the topic. Understanding what is needed next in an area of research is based on a good review of what has been done, since knowing what has been done directs researchers toward topics and questions they now consider worth studying.

Each review reflects many factors, including the author's personal style. If the research blazes a new path in the discipline, probably little specific research can be cited. In such a case, the review of the literature frames the topic being studied

Figure 4.7 Format of a typical scholarly journal article

The following format is typically used in reporting the results of a research study in a scholarly communication journal.

TITLE

ABSTRACT

INTRODUCTION

REVIEW OF THE LITERATURE

Research Question/Hypothesis

METHODOLOGY

Subjects

Procedures

Data Treatment

RESULTS

DISCUSSION

REFERENCES

within the broader goals of the discipline. By contrast, some research projects build on topics that have received considerable attention. In such a case, the review of the literature is targeted specifically to research that addresses that topic directly. Sometimes a study seeks to test whether previous research was conducted properly or whether the obtained results are accurate. This retesting of research is called **replication,** and the review of the literature concentrates on examining the methods used in previous research.

Figure 4.8 Sample abstract

ABSTRACT

This study examined the impact of gender on persuasive communication, considering the gender of both speaker and listener, and comparing the self-expectations and evaluations of the speakers before and after their communicative exchanges. Findings revealed that females expressed less confidence than males concerning their ability to communicate their arguments persuasively, even though trained communication raters indicated that both genders performed equally well. Subjects varied in their expressed self-confidence, however, depending upon whether they were addressing their arguments to a male or a female. In addition, males rated their communication "performances" more positively than did females. In attributing their perceived success to various factors, men were more likely to acknowledge their natural communication ability than were women, while women were more inclined than men to point to their effort as the cause of their success. Finally, male and female subjects differed from each other in the way they argued, with males being more inclined to present criterion-based arguments and women more likely to invent their own. Again, both genders tended to use different types of arguments, depending upon the gender of the listener. Several issues raised by the study, especially the gender differences in argument type and the apparent gender-based audience assumptions, warrant further study.

Source: P. H. Andrews, "Gender Differences in Persuasive Communication and Attribution of Success and Failure," *Human Communication Research, 13*(3), p. 372, copyright © 1987 by Sage Publications, Inc. Reprinted by permission of Sage Publications, Inc.

Research Question/Hypothesis. At the end of the literature review section, the author poses a formal research question or states a hypothesis. The author then explains how the specific research question or hypothesis grew out of what was learned from the review of the literature.

Methodology. The methodology section is where the author explains exactly how the research was conducted. This section usually contains three subheadings: "Subjects," "Procedures," and "Data Treatment."

Subjects. The methodology section typically starts by describing the **subjects,** the people who participated in the study, or the texts that were selected. The researcher advances all relevant information about the nature of the subject or text pool, such as the total number of subjects or texts, their important characteristics, and how they were selected.

Procedures. The second part of the methodology section explains the specific procedures used to conduct the research. This section is a straightforward account of what the researcher did with the subjects. The researcher explains exactly how the variables (often phrased as independent and dependent variables) were operationalized (put into observable terms), manipulated (such as exposing some subjects to a persuasive message but not others), and measured.

Data Treatment.   The final part of the methodology section explains all ways in which the data were analyzed. (This will be discussed later in this textbook).

Results.   The results section of the article explains what the researcher found. This section is typically a short, straightforward account of the findings without attempting to interpret or discuss them. The author remains objective, not allowing personal interpretations or feelings to color the reporting. You may find this section difficult to read because of the use of statistics, tables, jargon, and abbreviations. However, by the time you complete this textbook, you should be able to read and understand the gist of these data analyses.

Discussion.   In this section the author interprets the results reported in the preceding section. This is where the researcher explains the significance of the results and what they mean. The discussion section typically involves three things. First, the researcher examines the importance and utility of the results. Second, the writer identifies the problems and limitations of the study based on hindsight. Finally, the researcher uses the findings to suggest new topics worth studying, new questions worth asking, and new procedures worth trying.

References.   Because scholarly research is cumulative, readers have a right to know two things: who should get credit for each idea presented and what is the track record of each idea. It is the researcher's responsibility to identify fully, honestly, and accurately all the research referred to in preparing the article. This disclosure of indebtedness takes the form of **references,** a complete and accurate list of all sources used. All good research cites relevant references.

In addition to references, an article may have **reference notes,** which provide explanations of material in the body of the article that do not belong in the body itself. For example, such notes might include the history of a term, information about the measurement instruments used, or statistical formulas that were employed to analyze the data.

WRITING A LITERATURE REVIEW

Once researchers have located and synthesized relevant research, they use that information to revise the topic they are studying and the particular research question they are posing. This process of finding, reading, evaluating, and revising may be necessary several times. They then write a literature review that summarizes and organizes the research findings with respect to the topic being studied.

Because many of you will be asked by your professor to conduct and write a literature review similar to those you have read in the articles, we outline the steps involved.

1. Introduce the literature review by pointing out the major research topics that will be discussed, the central idea being explored, and the general importance of this topic for communication scholars or the general public.

2. Not everything written on the subject can be covered. Many students fear that they will not find enough material, but the real problem is separating the wheat from the chaff. Your job is to pick out research most relevant to the topic you are studying and the question you are asking and then to pull out of each piece the ideas that are most useful. Literature reviews are essentially evidence in arguments and should be designed to function in an argumentative context. Otherwise they are like garbage cans, and all you get out is garbage. Thus you should start out with a good idea of your research question and conduct your search and review so as to establish the place of that question in the literature. Doing so makes it easy to organize and limit the review to the most relevant literature possible.

3. You must cover research relevant to all the variables being studied. Research that explains the relationship between these variables is a top priority.

4. Ward and Hansen (1987) recommend that the following questions be answered when selecting and evaluating previous research.

   a. *Clarity:* Does the material have one unmistakable meaning?

   b. *Verifiability:* Is the information capable of being verified?

   c. *Accuracy:* Has the correctness of the information been established?

   d. *Recency:* Is the information the most recent available?

   e. *Relevance:* Is the information relevant to the subject?

   f. *Sufficiency:* Is there enough information for each main point?

   g. *Internal consistency:* Is the information consistent with itself, or are there internal contradictions?

   h. *External consistency:* Are the pieces of information consistent with one another, or does some information contradict other information?

   i. *Comparative quality:* How do pieces of information compare in quality? Is some material clearly inferior to other material?

   j. *Contextuality:* Has the information been placed within the true context?

   k. *Statistical validity:* Does the information meet tests of statistical validity? (p. 35)

5. Organizing the research you have decided to review requires a plan. There are many ways to structure this literature review. Rubin, Rubin, and Piele (1986) recommend the following patterns for organizing the literature review section.

   a. *Topical order:* Organize by main topics or issues and emphasize the relationship of the issues to the main problem.

   b. *Chronological order:* Organize by historical progression in terms of time.

c. *Problem-cause-solution order:* Organize the review so that it moves from the problem to the solution.

d. *General-to-specific order:* Examine broad-based research first and then focus on specific studies that relate to the topic.

e. *Known-to-unknown order:* Examine current literature about the problem and then identify at the end what still is not known.

f. *Comparison-and-contrast order:* Show how research studies are similar to and different from each other.

g. *Specific-to-general order:* Try to make sense out of specific research studies so that conclusions can be drawn. (pp. 45–46)

6. After reviewing the body of literature, summarize what has been done, what has not been done, and what needs to be done. Remember that a literature review functions as an argument, so this is your chance to present arguments and evidence about what research has found and what needs to be investigated in the future.

7. After the review of the literature is complete, pose a formal research question or state a hypothesis. Be sure to explain clearly how that question or hypothesis is tied to the literature you reviewed.

8. List all the sources you used in writing the literature review in alphabetical order in a bibliography. The two leading reference stylebooks are published by the American Psychological Association (APA) (see Figure 4.9) and the Modern Language Association. Ask your professor which stylebook he or she prefers, and then consult it on how to cite reference material properly.

Figure 4.9 American Psychological Association (APA) style: examples

---

A. IN THE BODY OF THE PAPER

1. **Direct Quote (A):** Sillars, Weisberg, Burggraf, and Wilson (1987) claim, "A casual look at the research on interpersonal communication would reveal that this literature has been more concerned with how people communicate than with what they say" (p. 495).

2. **Direct Quote (B):** The conclusion drawn is that "a casual look at the research on interpersonal communication would reveal that this literature has been more concerned with how people communicate than with what they say" (Sillars, Weisberg, Burggraf, & Wilson, 1987, p. 495).

3. **Acknowledging Research (A):** Fitzpatrick (1983) found that there were important communication differences between traditional, separate, and independent couples.

4. **Acknowledging Research (B):** (one or more authors) A number of researchers have been interested in the topic of conversational involvement (Cegala, Savage, Brunner, & Conrad, 1982; Cegala, 1981).

5. **Citing Secondary Research:** Mosteller (cited in Webb, Campbell, Schwartz & Sechrest, 1973) studied which sections of the *International Encyclopedia of the Social*

(continued)

Figure 4.9 American Psychological Association (APA) style: examples (continued)

Sciences were read most often by examining the wear and tear of the pages of each section. [*Note:* Provide both the original and the secondary source in the text, but provide only the secondary source in the bibliography.]

B. IN THE BIBLIOGRAPHY

1. Book by a Single Author

Stone, G. (1987). *Examining newspapers: What research reveals about American newspapers.* Newbury Park, CA: Sage.

2. Second and Subsequent Editions of a Book

Kerlinger, F. N. (1986). *Foundations of behavioral research* (3rd ed.). New York: Holt, Rinehart & Winston.

3. Book by Two or More Authors

Berger, C. R., & Bradac, J. J. (1982). *Language and social knowledge: Uncertainty in interpersonal relationships.* London: Edward Arnold.

4. Essay in an Edited Book

Fitzpatrick, M. A. (1983). Predicting couples' communication from couples' self-reports. In R. Bostrom (Ed.), *Communication yearbook 7* (pp. 49–82). Newbury Park, CA: Sage.

5. Article by a Single Author

Baxter, L. A. (1984). An investigation of compliance-gaining as politeness. *Human Communication Research, 10,* 427–456.

6. Article by Two or More Authors

Sillars, A. L., Weisberg, J., Burggraf, C. S., & Wilson, E. A. (1985). Content themes in marital communication. *Human Communication Research, 13,* 495–528.

7. Magazine or Newspaper Article

Benderly, B. L. (1981, March). The multilingual mind. *Psychology Today,* pp. 9–12.

8. Paper Presented at a Conference

Cline, R. (1982, May). *Revealing and relating: A review of self-disclosure theory and research.* Paper presented at the meeting of the International Communication Association, Boston.

Source: Based on the *Publication Manual of the American Psychological Association.* Copyright © 1983 by the American Psychological Association. Adapted by permission of the APA. Neither the original nor this adaptation can be reproduced without written permission of the APA. Consult the *Publication Manual* for more details.

CONCLUSION

Research does not take place in a vacuum. Communication researchers must therefore examine the extant literature to learn what is already known about the topic that interests them. Because time is valuable, the literature search must be as fruitful as possible, which means doing it in a logical, step-by-step manner. As a reader of research, you need to understand the structure of research libraries. The primary source of information for any researcher is the scholarly journal. Understanding the format of a typical journal article enables you to evaluate the relevance of each piece. This evaluation process leads researchers to revise the research question being asked, helps them to select the most appropriate research articles, and enables them to write an effective review of the literature. Finding, reading, evaluating, and reporting relevant literature for the purpose of clarifying a research question is a cyclical process. Once the search process is complete, researchers are ready to plan and design research, a topic we examine in Part II.

part II

PLANNING AND DESIGNING COMMUNICATION RESEARCH

chapter 5

Observing and Measuring Communication Variables

We have so far traced the early stages in the process communication researchers use to plan and conduct their investigations. You have learned how primary research topics, concepts, and variables are identified, as well as how research questions and hypotheses are constructed. Next we move on to explain what researchers do when they shift their attention from why to how—from the rationale for their study to the method they will use. The first step is translating the elements in the stream of discourse they hope to understand into terms that lend themselves to objective analysis. We will examine in this chapter how researchers develop strategies for observing and measuring the variables being studied.

OPERATIONALIZATION

Researchers never measure the abstract concepts they are interested in directly. Instead, they measure *observable, or empirical, characteristics* that they believe to be associated with a concept. To move from the conceptual to the measurement phase of research, researchers must first define an observable characteristic of a concept. For example, a researcher can't measure "communication competence" directly. An observable characteristic of communication competence must be specified, such as making eye contact with the audience during a public speech. The process of determining these observable characteristics is referred to as **operationalization.**

Only after defining a concept operationally can researchers measure it. For example, a researcher might count the number of times a speaker looks directly at audience members. The amount of eye contact then serves as the measurement for the concept of communication competence.

Operational Definitions

Operational definitions, like conceptual definitions, describe the important concepts being investigated in communication research but differ from conceptual definitions in terms of the purpose and focus of the descriptions developed. Whereas a conceptual definition describes the major components or characteristics of a concept, an operational definition describes its observable characteristics, specifying how researchers may observe the concept in actual practice. Of course, a good conceptual definition serves as the basis for a good operational definition. Miller and Boster (1989) state, "The conceptual definition contains the seeds of clear, useful ways to operationally define the construct so as to bridge the gap between the verbal and observational universes" (p. 23).

The difference between a conceptual definition and an operational definition is well illustrated by the example of a cake. A cake is defined conceptually in the dictionary as "A sweet baked food in loaf or layer form, made with or without shortening, usually with flour, sugar, eggs, flavoring, usually with baking powder or soda, and a liquid." An operational definition of a cake is the recipe that specifies the exact steps a chef must take to prepare it. It specifies the *operations* that need to be performed to bake a cake.

Evaluating operational definitions. Operational definitions of concepts must retain as much of the meaning from the conceptual definition as possible. This preservation of meaning between a conceptual and an operational definition is referred to as **conceptual fit.** The closer the conceptual fit, the more likely it is that researchers are observing the phenomenon they intend to study. The looser the conceptual fit, the more likely it is that researchers are observing a phenomenon that is different from the one they intend to study. Obviously, a poor conceptual fit seriously jeopardizes the theoretical and practical utility of the entire research project.

An operational definition, however, represents but one way of specifying some of the observable characteristics of an abstract concept. No single operational definition ever captures completely the complexity of the concepts researchers study. Researchers simply can't specify all the observable characteristics of such concepts as communication apprehension, communication competence, or communicator style. Establishing eye contact with audience members during a public speech, for example, may be one observable indicator of communication competence, but this concept could be defined operationally in many other ways.

Researchers thus often disagree about how a concept should be defined operationally. When evaluating researchers' conceptual and operational definitions and the conceptual fit between them, Barker (1989) urges you to keep in mind the following questions:

1. Is the definition or operationalization adequate? That is, does it provide a complete description of all important dimensions of the variable?
2. Is the definition or operationalization *acccurate?* Is it a valid and universally agreed-on way of viewing a variable?
3. Is the definition or operationalization *clear?* Are the terms of measurement devices described and defined familiar to the majority of report readers and future researchers? (p. 71)

Operational Procedures

Three general procedures for defining concepts operationally are self-reports, ratings by observers, and observing behavior. Choosing among these procedures depends inevitably on the purpose of the research, as some procedures are more suited to answering some research questions than others.

Self-reports.   One way to define a concept operationally in communication research is through the use of *self-report procedures.* For example, in Chapter 3 we showed how researchers could construct research questions and hypotheses about how social support is communicated within intimate relationships. The conceptual definition for social support was taken from Albrecht and Adelman (1987): "verbal and nonverbal communication between recipients and providers which reduces uncertainty about the situation, the self, the other, or the relationship, and functions to enhance a perception of control in one's life experience" (p. 19). The conceptual definition for relational intimacy is adapted from Cody and McLaughlin (1985): "the degree of emotional attachment between dyadic partners and the knowledge dyadic partners have about one another" (p. 289).

To transform these conceptual definitions into operational definitions, a researcher could use a self-report procedure. For example, social support could be defined operationally by asking partners to rate how much the verbal and nonverbal messages exchanged helped clarify the situation, self, other, or relationship and how much the messages helped the partner feel in control of his or her life on a scale from 1 to 10 (with 1 being the lowest rating and 10 being the highest rating). Similarly, to define relational intimacy operationally, partners, could be asked to indicate on a 7-point scale, with 1 being low and 7 being high, how much they are attached emotionally to the other person and how much they know about their partner.

There are both advantages and disadvantages to operationalizing concepts by using self-reports. Self-reports are extremely effective for ascertaining respondents' beliefs, attitudes, and values. These are psychological characteristics existing inside of people's heads, which makes them impossible to observe directly. Indeed, trying to infer these "black-box concepts" from actual behavior may be very misleading.

You may have just poured your heart out about your sex life to someone whom you perceive as interested because the person nods at the right times and establishes good eye contact. The listener, however, may actually feel that these experiences are boring and unremarkable. Self-report procedures are thus appropriate whenever researchers can show that they provide accurate assessments of how people think and feel.

Self-reports, however, depend on people being able and willing to provide complete and accurate information. Research on personal or controversial issues that uses self-reports may therefore be questionable. Would you answer the question "Have you stolen anything?" or "Whom do you hate?" fully and honestly? Self-reports also often demand that people reflect on their behavior, which may be difficult to remember. How many people can recall accurately how many people they have interacted with in the past week? Questions such as these also ask people to report on things they normally don't think about, so their answers may not be thought out carefully. Finally, many times, what people say they do is not what they actually do. There is often little relationship between perception and behavior, which leads to the adage "Do as I say, not as I do."

Observers' ratings.   A second way researchers define concepts operationally is through *observers' ratings*. For example, observers could be shown a videotape of a couple's interaction and then be asked to rate the messages that were exchanged on the same scales used for the self-reports of social support and intimacy.

Observers' ratings in some cases may be more accurate than self-reports. If you want to know whether a person is "helpful" or "a good friend," would it be better to ask the person or his or her friends? Observers are often more objective judges of behavior than the person being observed.

Observers' ratings, however, are also susceptible to many of the drawbacks of self-reports in terms of willingness and accuracy. In addition, observers may themselves be biased. We usually give the benefit of the doubt to people we like, for example, but not to those we dislike. Observers also don't always have enough observations on which to base accurate conclusions. Watching an example of a couple's interaction may not necessarily be indicative of how they interact day to day.

To compensate for the strengths and weaknesses of self-reports and observers' ratings, researchers often use both procedures to develop a triangulated operationalization. In group communication research, for example, researchers will ask members to rate both themselves and other group members on how much leadership was demonstrated. These self-reports and observers' ratings are then combined in some way to serve as the operational definition for the concept of leadership.

For both self-report and observer ratings, the measurement device itself, the social support and intimacy scales, for example, becomes the operational definition for the concept. Anderson (1987) explains that this type of operationalization defines the concept by the methods used to measure it. Such procedures are quite common in the physical sciences, where, for example, a ruler provides the operational definition for the variable of length. They are equally common in communication research, where, for example, the concept of communicator style is defined operationally by scores on Norton's (1978) communicator style measure.

Observing behavior.   Operational procedures don't have to rely solely on verbal reports from respondents or ratings by observers. A person's *behavior* often serves as a good operational definition for a concept. For example, to study how much different stimuli excite a person, an electrocardiograph (EKG) can be used to operationalize excitement as heart rate. The higher a person's heart rate, the greater the person's excitement.

Researchers can also define people's beliefs, attitudes, and values operationally by observing their behavior. For example, Miller and Boster (1989) offer the following ways of defining people's attitudes toward abortion operationally:

1. Solicit contributions from each person for a pro-abortion (anti-abortion) advertisement to appear in the local newspaper. Use the amount of money contributed as an index of the person's attitude toward abortion.
2. Ask each person to volunteer some time circulating pro-abortion (anti-abortion) petitions. Keep a record of the amount of time devoted to this volunteer work and use it as an index of the person's attitude toward abortion.
3. Ask each person to participate in a sit-in supporting the pro-abortion (anti-abortion) movement. Use the person's willingness or unwillingness to participate as an index of his or her attitude toward abortion. (p. 24)

Observing a person's behavior is often more accurate than self-reports or observers' ratings, as demonstrated by the saying "Actions speak louder than words." Behavioral observations, however, aren't necessarily more accurate operational definitions of concepts than self-reports or observers' ratings, for two reasons. First, behavioral observations assess only what people do, not what they believe or feel. Scholars studying persuasion know that *compliance,* performing a behavior, differs from *internalization,* valuing a behavior. A person may comply with a request to go shopping with his or her partner, for example, but that doesn't mean that the person actually wants to go shopping. Second, researchers must observe important behavior that represents the concept of interest accurately. Henny Youngman illustrates the limitations of a strictly behavioral observation when he quotes a mother who brags about her child: "He plays like Paderewski—he uses both hands."

Kerlinger (1973) calls these behavioral observations, observers' ratings, and self-reports **measured operational definitions** because they specify how a researcher ascertained the existence or quantity of a concept. Kerlinger also points out that some researchers must develop **experimental operational definitions,** which specify the behaviors researchers use to manipulate a variable.

In experimental research, for example, researchers manipulate an independent variable to observe its effects on a dependent variable. To do so, they must decide how to operationalize the manipulation. For example, the concept "immediacy" has been defined conceptually as interpersonal warmth and closeness. Andersen (1989) explains that "immediacy could be operationalized experimentally by having a confederate role-play by smiling, increasing eye contact, and touching. In either case the details of a researcher's operationalization should be specified clearly for the benefit of the reader and other researchers" (p. 11).

Quantitative and Qualitative Observations

The examples just discussed help illustrate the two primary classes of observations used to operationalize concepts: **quantitative observations,** which employ numerical indicators to ascertain the relative size of something, and **qualitative observations,** which employ symbols (words and diagrams) to indicate the presence or absence of something or categorize things into different types.

In the study of supportive communication within intimate relationships, the self-reports and observers' ratings operationalized social support and relational intimacy using quantitative observations. Social support was observed using a 10-point numerical scale, while relational intimacy was observed on a 7-point numerical scale. These were numerical, or quantitative, representations of social support and relational intimacy. To answer a research question about the relationship between these two variables, researchers would describe, compare, and analyze these quantitative data through appropriate statistical procedures.

These two variables could also have been observed qualitatively. For example, people could be asked to report in their own words their thoughts and feelings about their experiences involving social support within their intimate relationships. They could be asked, for example, to report under what conditions social support is needed most or is most likely to occur, what behaviors are associated with it, and how it makes them feel when they do and don't receive it. Similar qualitative observations can be grouped into specific content categories for the purpose of describing and comparing how social support is expressed within each category.

Quantitative and qualitative observations thus provide researchers with different yet complementary ways of operationalizing and measuring concepts. Quantitative observations provide a high level of measurement precision and statistical power, while qualitative observations provide greater depth of information about how people perceive events in the context of the actual situations in which they occur.

The choice of quantitative or qualitative observations depends ultimately on the nature of the research question, the ways in which concepts are best conceived and operationalized, and the methodology chosen for a study. Quantitative and qualitative observations follow from different research purposes and different research questions. However, both types of observations can be used together profitably to achieve triangulation, which enhances both the precision of the data gathered (with quantitative observations) and the contextual influences on those data (with qualitative observations). Using both types of observations also provides a way of assessing the accuracy of the findings from one operational procedure by comparing it with a different operational procedure. If the findings support each other, both procedures are corroborated. If the findings are different, however, this does not necessarily mean that the data are questionable. The difference could be a result of the types of data that are acquired through quantitative and qualitative observations.

MEASUREMENT THEORY

Operationalization enables researchers to observe the concepts being investigated. But observations have to be recorded and ordered in a systematic way if meaningful data are to be derived from them. Measurement is the difference between saying, "The box is heavy" and "The box weighs 80 pounds," or "He talks a lot" and "He was speaking 53 percent of the group's meeting time." **Measurement** is the process of determining the existence, characteristics, size, and/or quantity of some variable through systematic recording and organization of observations.

Measurement follows directly from conceptualization and operationalization processes. Good measurement strategies enable researchers to gather and record data about the variables being studied. Moreover, the data generated during measurement must be in an appropriate form for meaningful analysis. Effective measurement enables researchers to proceed systematically from collecting data to the data analysis phase, where conclusions are drawn.

Levels of Measurement

Earlier we described a variable as an observable concept that can take on different values. These different values are measured by using a scale, "a specific scheme for assigning numbers or symbols to designate characteristics of a variable" (Williams, 1986, p. 14). Stevens (1958) identified four levels of measurement scales that are used to describe the range and the relationships among the values a variable can take: nominal, ordinal, interval, and ratio.

These levels of measurement are arranged hierarchically—each lower level has all the characteristics of the preceding level, and each provides increasing measurement precision and information about a variable. The use of a particular level of measurement depends, of course, on the purposes of the research. The different levels of measurement precision enable researchers to use increasingly sophisticated quantitative data analysis techniques, as we shall see later in this text.

Nominal measurement scales. **Nominal measurement scales,** sometimes called **classificatory measures,** are the lowest level of measurement since they classify a variable only into qualitatively different categories. These categories may be designated by a word (such as *male* and *female, communication major* and *non-communication major,* or *yes* and *no*) or a number (such as the numbers on license plates or the numerical codes for college major). The important point is that these categories are not arranged in any particular order, such as from highest to lowest or from best to worst; they simply represent different categories. When numerical codes are used for categories, they are arbitrary and therefore nominal since they actually represent different symbolic categories. We could use the number 1, for example, to designate men and the number 2 to designate women, or vice versa. The number 2 is not greater than, or twice as much as, the number 1 in nominal-level measurement.

To measure a variable at the nominal level, it must be classifiable into at least two different categories. These categories must exhibit three qualities. First, the categories must be mutually exclusive; otherwise, comparisons between them are misleading. What if we measured students' specialization in the communication major at your school by using these categories: communication, rhetoric, speech communication, interpersonal communication, journalism, mass media, and organizational communication? If we forced students to choose among these categories, we probably would underrepresent some specializations since what is studied under one label, such as "rhetoric," may overlap what is studied under another label, such as "speech communication." By contrast, if we asked students to choose every category that was applicable, we would probably overrepresent some specializations because several categories would be chosen.

Second, the categories must be equivalent; otherwise, we will be comparing apples and oranges. For example, classifying prime-time television shows into drama, comedy, half-hour-long, and hour-long categories mixes two fundamentally different types of categories. The first two categories (drama and comedy) are equivalent and the last two categories (half-hour-long and hour-long) are equivalent, but type of show and length of show are obviously neither equivalent nor mutually exclusive.

Third, the categories must be exhaustive; otherwise, they will not represent the variable fully. If a category scheme does not represent a variable fully, the accuracy of the entire scheme is questionable. For example, if we measure the nominal demographic variable of college major on a questionnaire distributed to college students but do not list all available majors as options, we are not measuring all the possible categories of the college major variable.

Nominal measurements are very important for communication researchers. Studies of differences between people who have and have not been exposed to an experimental treatment or studies of communication differences between groups of people, such as women and men, measure the independent variable (treatment condition and gender) at the nominal level. Researchers also measure dependent variables nominally by asking people to choose the most relevant response from a checklist of exhaustive and mutually exclusive categories. An example is asking people, after they have heard a speech, to identify from a list which party they will vote for in the next election. Furthermore, when we categorize the content of written, artistic, and electronic texts or our observations about communication within natural environments, these are nominal measurements. An analysis of transcripts of adolescents' conversations that tallies comments about sports, dating, school, parents, and so on, is an example.

Once categories have been constructed, researchers may want to count up the frequency of observations for each of the categories. As shown in Chapter 13, however, these frequency counts limit the quantitative data analyses that can be performed and the conclusions that can be drawn. Although we can count the number of instances in each category, nominal measurements cannot be manipulated mathematically (added, subtracted, multiplied, or divided).

Ordinal measurement scales.   **Ordinal measurement scales** not only classify a variable into nominal categories but also rank those categories along some dimension. Each of the categories can then be compared because they are measured along some "greater than" and "less than" scale. For example, your local video store may classify movies nominally by putting them into different categories (see Figure 5.1). However, if you are asked to rank these categories along some dimension, in this case liking, this becomes an ordinal measurement.

Ordinal measurements provide researchers with more information about a variable than nominal measurements do because they transform discrete classifications into *ordered* classifications. They not only classify a variable into categories but also arrange these categories in some *ascending* numerical order along some dimension.

The ordinal level of measurement is still limited, however. Ordinal measurements only rank the variable along some dimension without telling researchers *how much* more or less of the variable has been measured. A horse race provides a good example of an ordinal measurement. It is easy to see which horse finished first,

Figure 5.1   An ordinal measurement scale

Instructions: Rank the following types of movies that are available at your local video store in order of how much you like them. Place a 1 by the type of movie you like most, a 2 by the type of movie you like second most, and so on, all the way to 7, the type of movie you like least.

_____ Adventure

_____ Comedy

_____ Drama

_____ Musical

_____ Western

_____ Science fiction

_____ X-rated

second, and third. However, the first-place finisher may have been ahead of the second-place finisher by one-tenth of a second, while the third-place finisher may have been a full second behind the second-place finisher. Likewise, your class rank indicates whether you are higher or lower than another person, but it doesn't tell how much higher or lower. Your ranking of your favorite types of movies also doesn't tell how much you prefer one over another. There is no assumption of an equal distance between the points on an ordinal scale. We know that 10 is greater than 5, but it is not twice as much. Consequently, the distance between 1 and 3 on an ordinal scale may not be the same as the distance between 2 and 4. These numbers are arranged in a meaningful order but are not considered equal in terms of distance.

Interval measurement scales. **Interval measurement scales** not only categorize a variable as in nominal measurement and rank it along some dimension as in ordinal measurement, but they also establish *standard, equal distances* between each of the adjacent points along the measurement scale. These standard units of distance enable researchers to determine exactly how much larger or smaller different interval measurements are. For example, different temperature readings can easily be compared by examining the point spread between them. The interval between the measurement points of temperature is a standard distance. Ten degrees warmer is the same size increase between 50 and 60 degrees as it is between 70 and 80 degrees.

Interval measurements also possess one additional characteristic, the use of an arbitrary zero point. This means that the zero point on an interval measure is simply another point on the scale; it does not imply that the variable doesn't exist. Zero degrees does not mean there is no temperature! Interval scales therefore have both positive and negative values. The important point, of course, is that the distances between the individual points on the scale are equal.

Interval-level measurements are relatively easy to use in describing variables of the physical world, such as temperature. They are much more difficult to apply in communication and other social scientific research. The most popular methods for measuring a communication variable at the interval level are the Likert scale, the semantic differential scale, and the Thurstone scale.

The Likert Scale. The **Likert scale,** developed by psychologist Rensis Likert (1932), identifies the extent of a person's feelings or attitudes toward another person, event, or phenomenon. A traditional Likert scale asks people the extent to which they agree or disagree with a statement (in this case a statement about our research methods textbook) by choosing a point on a 5-point scale, ranging from "strongly agree" to "strongly disagree" (see Figure 5.2). Researchers may use a 7-point scale, and they may use different answer categories, such as like/dislike or approve/disapprove, depending on the purposes of the research. Adaptations of the traditional Likert scale are referred to as **Likert-type scales.**

Likert scales are typically scored by assigning the number 1 to one end of the scale and consecutively higher numbers to the next items, up to the number 5 or 7 at the other end of the scale. Researchers share commonly the assumption that the distance between consecutive numbers is equivalent.

Figure 5.2 A Likert scale

Instructions: Indicate on the scale how strongly you agree or disagree with the statement.

Reading this book about communication research methods is more fun than I can possibly handle!

_____ Strongly agree

_____ Agree

_____ Undecided

_____ Disagree

_____ Strongly disagree

The Semantic Differential Scale. The **semantic differential scale,** developed by Osgood, Suci, and Tannenbaum (1957), measures the *meanings* people create in response to a specific stimulus. A semantic differential presents a stimulus item (a word, phrase, sentence, person, etc.) at the top of a list of scales, usually 7-point scales, representing polar-opposite terms (see Figure 5.3). Respondents choose a single point on each scale that expresses their perception of the stimulus object based on the referents given.

Figure 5.3 A semantic differential scale

Instructions: Indicate how you feel about the referent by placing a single check along each scale. For example, if you feel that the referent is extremely interesting, place a check at the extreme left side of the first scale. If you feel that the referent is extremely boring, place a check at the extreme right side of the first scale. If you feel somewhere in the middle of these two extremes, place a check in the appropriate space.

Communication Research Textbooks

Interesting	____:	____:	____:	____:	____:	____:	____: Boring
Bad	____:	____:	____:	____:	____:	____:	____: Good
Valuable	____:	____:	____:	____:	____:	____:	____: Worthless
Unnecessary	____:	____:	____:	____:	____:	____:	____: Necessary
Pleasant	____:	____:	____:	____:	____:	____:	____: Unpleasant

The selection of these bipolar adjectives is not arbitrary or random. They are chosen to represent three dimensions: activity, evaluation, and potency. Construction of a semantic differential is therefore a very difficult process requiring careful pretesting. Finally, semantic differential scales are scored like Likert scales, with numbers 1 through 7 assigned to the points on each scale, making sure that the scoring for each scale is in the appropriate direction for items phrased in a positive and negative manner. A respondent's scores on these scales can often be summed to produce an overall measurement score for that attitude object.

The Thurstone Scale. A number of scholars have argued that Likert and semantic differential scales are not adequate interval-level measurements, since researchers *assume* that the distance between the points on these scales is equal. One type of scale that attempts to ensure that the distances are equal is the **Thurstone scale,** named after L. L. Thurstone (1929, 1931).

To construct a Thurstone scale, a researcher first generates many statements, usually several hundred, related to the referent being investigated. The researcher then asks a large number of judges, usually 50 to 300, to categorize independently the statements into 11 categories, ranging from "extremely favorable" to "extremely unfavorable." The researcher selects those statements, usually about 20, that consistently have been coded into a particular category by the judges. Each statement is assigned a value based on the mean rating by all the judges. The instrument that incorporates these statements is then assumed to provide interval-level data, such that a score of 6.2 is assumed to be twice a score of 3.1.

The Thurstone scale takes a tremendous amount of time and energy to construct. Also, one can never be absolutely sure that these scaled items actually represent equal intervals; indeed, Thurstone calls them "equal-appearing intervals." Because of this difficulty in demonstrating equal intervals between adjacent points of a measurement scale, it has become customary in the human sciences to assume that Likert, semantic differential, and Thurstone scales contain equal intervals. This procedure allows researchers to subject data gathered through the use of these scales to the powerful statistical procedures reserved for interval-level data.

Ratio measurement scales. **Ratio measurement scales** not only categorize and rank a variable along a scale with equal intervals but also establish a true (absolute) zero point where the variable being measured ceases to exist. A clear and painful example of a true zero point occurs when we check our wallets to determine how much money we have available only to find out that we have spent all our cash. This is a true absolute zero point!

Because of an absolute zero point, ratio measurements cannot have negative values, since the smallest value on a ratio scale is zero. Examples of variables that have absolute zero points include amount measurements of physical variables, such as age, length, and weight (you can't weigh zero pounds), and count measures of communication, such as the number of words aired, questions asked, articles written, television shows watched, or movies produced (Tukey, 1977; Bowers & Courtright, 1984).

Measuring Unidimensional
and Multidimensional Concepts

Many concepts can be measured through the use of a single-item scale. We don't have to ask 20 questions to determine the temperature, the amount of money we have in our pocket, someone's gender, whether we like someone, or for whom we will vote. Each of these can be determined by a single question on a measurement scale.

Communication and other human science researchers can seldom, if ever, measure complex concepts adequately by having people answer one simple scale item. Instead, they use scales that consist of a series of items designed to get at the main concept. For example, recall from Chapter 3 how McCroskey and Richmond's (1987) questionnaire measured a person's willingness to communicate by a series of Likert scale items. Even our simple measure of your attitude toward communication research textbooks (Figure 5.3) had you answer four semantic differential scale items.

Scales in communication research consist of multiple indicators that are combined in some manner to yield knowledge of the underlying concept. Two types of concepts are measured by multiple indicators: unidimensional and multidimensional. The statistical procedure for determining whether a construct is unidimensional or multidimensional is called **factor analysis.** Here we should comment briefly on the complexity of measuring communication concepts.

Unidimensional concepts.   **Unidimensional concepts** are composed of a set of multiple indicators that can be added equally to derive an overall score on a measurement instrument. For example, Wheeless, Wheeless, and Baus (1984) assessed people's satisfaction with their sexual communication at different stages of relationship development. They first generated a number of statements believed to be related to satisfaction with sexual communication and asked people to indicate on a Likert scale the extent to which they agreed or disagreed with each. Factor analysis revealed that sexual communication satisfaction was a unidimensional construct composed of 22 items (see Figure 5.4). Therefore, a person's overall score for sexual communication satisfaction can be obtained simply by adding up the scores on the 22 Likert scale items (making sure to reverse the scoring for those items phrased in a negative direction). The researchers then assessed overall scores for sexual communication satisfation with people at different stages of intimate relationships.

Multidimensional concepts.   Many communication concepts are actually composed of a number of different subconcepts, called **factors.** The behavior of leaders, for example, is composed of at least two factors: how they handle *tasks* and how they handle *people.* On a leadership behavior scale, each would be assessed by a number of scale items. These factors are considered relatively separate and independent, such that answers on one factor have little or no influence on answers

Figure 5.4 Sexual communication satisfaction questionnaire

This questionnaire assesses your satisfaction with your sexual communication with your partner. Use the following scale to indicate how strongly you agree or disagree with each statement:

1 = Strongly agree
2 = Agree
3 = Neither agree nor disagree
4 = Disagree
5 = Strongly disagree

_____ 1. I tell my partner when I am especially sexually satisfied.
_____ 2. I am satisfied with my partner's ability to communicate his/her sexual desires to me.
_____ 3. I do not let my partner know things that I find pleasing during sex.
_____ 4. I am very satisfied with the quality of our sexual interactions.
_____ 5. I do not hesitate to let my partner know when I want to have sex with him/her.
_____ 6. I do not tell my partner whether or not I am sexually satisfied.
_____ 7. I am dissatisfied over the degree to which my partner and I discuss our sexual relationship.
_____ 8. I am not afraid to show my partner what kind of sexual behavior I find satisfying.
_____ 9. I would not hesitate to show my partner what is a sexual turn-on to me.
_____ 10. My partner does not show me when he/she is sexually satisfied.
_____ 11. I show my partner what pleases me during sex.
_____ 12. I am displeased with the manner in which my partner and I communicate with each other during sex.
_____ 13. My partner does not show me things he/she finds pleasing during sex.
_____ 14. I show my partner when I am sexually satisfied.
_____ 15. My partner does not let me know whether sex has been satisfying or not.
_____ 16. I do not show my partner when I am sexually satisfied.
_____ 17. I am satisifed concerning my ability to communicate about sexual matters with my partner.
_____ 18. My partner shows me by the way he/she touches me if he/she is satisfied.
_____ 19. I am dissatisfied with my partner's ability to communicate his/her sexual desire to me.
_____ 20. I have no way of knowing when my partner is sexually satisfied.
_____ 21. I am not satisfied in the majority of our sexual interactions.
_____ 22. I am pleased with the manner in which my partner and I communicate with each other after sex.

Source: Lawrence R. Wheeless, Virginia Eman Wheeless, and Raymond Baus, "Sexual Communication, Communication Satisfaction, and Solidarity in the Developmental Stages of Intimate Relationships," _Western Journal of Speech Communication_, 48(3), p. 224, copyright © 1984 by the Western Speech Communication Association. Reprinted by permission of the Western Speech Communication Association.

that apply to another factor. Whenever a concept is measured by a series of scale items that assess more than one factor, it is called a **multidimensional concept.**

For example, Norton's (1978) communicator style concept is composed of 10 independent factors or subconcepts (animated, attentive, contentious, dominant, dramatic, friendly, impression-leaving, open, precise, and relaxed), each of which is measured by four Likert-type scale items. Similarly, Giffin (1968) views trust as composed of three separate factors: expertness (the person's knowledge), character (the person's morality and intentions), and dynamism (the person's activeness and frankness). Each of these factors is measured by seven semantic differential items. In both cases, the research concept is measured in a multidimensional rather than a unidimensional manner.

MEASUREMENT TECHNIQUES

Three general measurement techniques provide communication researchers with both quantitative and qualitative data about the four levels of measurement and the unidimensional and multidimensional concepts: (1) **questionnaires,** the presentation of written questions to evoke written responses from people; (2) **interviews,** the presentation of spoken questions to evoke spoken responses from people; and (3) **observations,** the systematic inspection and interpretation of communication phenomena. Each of these general measurement techniques incorporates many **instruments,** specific, formal measurement tools researchers use to gather data about research variables.

It is important to understand that these measurement techniques are employed within the guidelines and goals of the four specific research methodologies we will discuss. Many of the same basic measurement techniques are used to gather data in these four methodologies. The guidelines for the use of these techniques differ, however, according to the purpose of the methodology. The *experimental method* uses measurement techniques to assess the causal effects of independent variables on dependent variables. The *survey method* uses measurement techniques to gather information about the attitudes and behaviors of a defined population from questions posed to samples drawn from the population. The method of *textual analysis* uses measurement techniques to classify and evaluate the characteristics of spoken, written, artistic, and electronic documents. Finally, the *ethnographic method* uses measurement techniques to observe and describe carefully the communication behaviors that occur naturally within a specific population. Here we discuss the general use of questionnaires, interviews, and observations *across* the four methodologies. We will focus on their particular uses in Chapters 8 through 11.

Questionnaires and Interviews

Questionnaires are probably the most frequently used measurement technique in communication research. They often are used in experimental studies to measure independent and dependent variables, and they are the primary measurement technique used to conduct large surveys. In textual analysis, questionnaires are often employed to elicit the messages that are analyzed as well as to provide background information for critical analyses of specific communication phenomena. Specialized questionnaires, such as communication diaries and critical-incident reports, are also used in ethnographic studies to elicit information about respondents' personal experiences in particular contexts and the meanings they create.

Interviews are also common in communication research and are employed in many of the same research situations as questionnaires. Both questionnaires and interviews gather data directly from respondents by prompting them to answer researchers' questions. They both are self-report measures because they depend on respondents providing information about their own beliefs, attitudes, and behaviors.

Directive and nondirective questionnaires and interviews. Researchers using questionnaires and interviews employ many organizational, presentational, and questioning strategies. They attempt to influence the style of responses provided, for example, by altering the directiveness of their question presentation strategy. Researchers present questions to respondents in a more or less **directive** or **nondirective** manner by constructing **closed** or **open questions**, respectively (see Figure 5.5).

Directive questionnaires and interviews use more closed questions that lead respondents to answer in specific ways by limiting the range of responses available to them. The responses may be *bipolar,* giving a choice between two opposites, such as "yes" or "no," or "good" or "bad." Closed questions may also give respondents a narrow set of potential responses, as in multiple-choice questions, checklists, or the Likert, semantic differential, and Thurstone scales. Closed questions are typically used to gather quantitative data that are analyzed statistically.

Nondirective questionnaires and interviews use more open questions that expand the range of answers available to respondents. Open questions give respondents broad latitude by inviting them to describe their perceptions as fully as they would like. For example, open questions might ask respondents to describe what they did, thought, and felt during a particular communication event. Open questions are used primarily to provide researchers with qualitative data that are described and evaluated critically.

Figure 5.5   The continuum of directive-nondirective research and closed-open questions

Directive interviews and questionnaires	Nondirective interviews and questionnaires
Closed questions	Open questions

Question strategies and formats. Questionnaires and interviews are *structured* in a variety of ways, depending on the type and arrangement of questions used. For example, demographic questions that inquire about respondents' characteristics such as name, age, gender, and education are generally asked at the beginning of questionnaires and interviews. Questions about specific topics follow. Questions about a specific topic are also generally grouped together, to make answering them easier. Furthermore, to avoid a **response bias,** a tendency to answer questions the same way automatically (such as using only one side of a scale continually), rather than thinking about each individual question, researchers often switch the side of the scale on which positive and negative responses appear to force respondents to react to each question individually.

The list of questions that guide the interview is referred to as the **interview schedule,** or protocol (see Figure 5.6). **Highly scheduled interviews** list all the questions the interviewer is supposed to ask. This interview schedule is followed carefully by the interviewer so that interviews by different interviewers and with different respondents are conducted in a similar way. **Moderately scheduled interviews** identify the specific questions interviewers are to ask but allow them the freedom to probe for additional information after responses to the primary questions are given. **Unscheduled interviews** list the primary topics the interviewer should cover but allow maximum freedom for phrasing and ordering questions as well as for probing for additional information. Which format is used depends on researchers' intent. If making generalizations about many respondents is most important, highly scheduled interviews are used. If determining fully what particular individuals think is most important, less scheduled interviews are used.

The strategic sequence of queries on questionnaires and interviews is referred to as the **question format.** An approach to questioning that is used frequently is the **tunnel format,** so called because respondents are asked a straight series of similarly organized questions. An example might be the series of Lickert scale items used to measure the unidimensional concept of sexual communication satisfaction (Figure

Figure 5.6   Highly scheduled, moderately scheduled, and unscheduled interviews

Highly scheduled interviews	Moderately scheduled interviews	Unscheduled interviews
(Rigid adherence to the specific questions scheduled)	(Adherence to primary questions scheduled, but ability to probe)	(Freedom to develop questions to fit topics and respondents)
Low freedom		High freedom

5.4). The tunnel format provides respondents with a similar series of questions to answer and researchers with a consistent series of responses to code.

Another common technique for questionnaire and interview construction is the **funnel format,** in which broad open questions are used to introduce the questionnaire or interview, followed by narrower closed questions that seek more specific information. Thus a researcher would ask, "What television shows do you watch?" before asking, "Do you watch *60 Minutes*?" This strategy avoids biasing respondents' answers by allowing them to describe first their behavior, knowledge, and attitudes regarding the overall topic before a researcher asks more specific directive questions.

The **inverted funnel format** is just the opposite of the funnel format. It begins with narrow closed questions and builds to broader open questions about a topic. This question strategy is often used in interviews to orient respondents to key issues about the research topic before opening the interview up to more in-depth questions. Some researchers suggest that the inverted funnel format should be used with very personal or taboo research topics because it introduces respondents to low-risk, closed, fixed-choice questions and then when they have become more comfortable with the topic moves on to more probing open questions. Thus it might be better to ask people first about their participation in specific religious observances than to ask them immediately to describe their religious beliefs.

Relative advantages of questionnaires and interviews. The primary *difference* between questionnaires and interviews is the method used to elicit the self-reports. Researchers using questionnaires usually do not have face-to-face interaction with respondents about the research questions and answers. Instead, their communication with them is typically via written messages. Researchers using interviews, by contrast, have direct contact with respondents.

This difference between mediated versus direct interaction between researchers and respondents provides questionnaires and interviews with relative advantages and disadvantages (see Figure 5.7). With large samples, questionnaires are often less expensive than interviews since they can reach a large audience in a short amount of time with simultaneous distribution to respondents in person or through the mail. If questionnaires are designed well, they can even be self-administered to reduce researchers' time and expenses even further. Questionnaires also increase respondents' anonymity, since they do not have to answer questions directly to researchers but instead write their answers on the questionnaire.

Another advantage is that questionnaires can be administered more consistently than interviews by different researchers, since the same form is used and the same questions are asked in exactly the same way time after time. From what we know about the idiosyncratic and processual nature of human communication, it would be unlikely that even the best-trained interviewers using a highly structured interview could ask questions as consistently as can be done with questionnaires. A

Figure 5.7   Relative advantages of interviews and questionnaires

Questionnaires	Interviews
1. Can reduce time and expense through mass production and administration	1. Can increase depth of response by probing for more information
2. Can reach a large audience in a brief amount of time	2. Can clarify questions respondents do not understand
3. Can distribute widely either in person or through the mail	3. Can encourage full participation by establishing rapport
4. Can be self-administered if well designed	4. Can observe respondents to determine demographic features
5. Can increase respondents' anonymity	5. Can detect nonverbal responses
6. Can be administered consistently by different researchers	6. Can enhance response rate through personal contact
7. Can increase data accuracy because respondents record their own data	7. Can use the telephone to reach remote respondents
8. Can use computer-coded forms to facilitate data entry as well as electronic surveys	8. Can use CATI to facilitate administration and data entry

number of researchers have found that even in highly structured interviews, there is a tendency for interviewers to introduce flexibility into their interviews by skipping questions, varying the way they ask questions, and engaging in discussions with respondents that depart from the interview format (Cannell & Kahn, 1968; Hansen, Hurwitz, Marks, & Maudlin, 1951; Hyman, 1954; Kish & Slater, 1960).

A final advantage is that questionnaires preserve people's responses exactly as presented since respondents record their own data. Furthermore, entry of responses from questionnaires on computer-coded (mark-sense) forms can be accomplished quickly and efficiently. Some researchers are even experimenting with electronic surveys where "respondents use a text processing program to self-administer a computer-based questionnaire" (Kiesler & Sproull, 1986, p. 402). Electronic surveys are obviously limited to people and organizations with access to computers, but their number is growing every day.

Interviews, by contrast, can typically provide greater depth of information than questionnaires, especially if interviewers ask respondents probing questions to clarify their answers, such as "Can you elaborate on that answer?" or "Can you give me an example of that?" Interviewers can also clarify questions respondents do not understand, encourage respondents' full participation, and gather observational data by noting their verbal and nonverbal behavior.

Interviewers encourage more full and honest answers from respondents by establishing rapport with them. The personal contact between interviewers and interviewees also helps to increase the rate of response by encouraging respondents to participate. It is far easier to ignore a questionnaire you have received in the mail than an interviewer who shows up at your front door! Some contemporary surveys use modern computer-assisted telephone interviewing (CATI) equipment. This procedure streamlines the administration and coding of interview data by having the computer dial a telephone number at random, feeds the specific questions to be asked to interviewers, and enables them to enter responses to questions as they are being given by touching a few keys on the computer keyboard. The computer analyzes the data quickly by adding respondents' answers to the existing data set.

Choosing whether to use questionnaires or interviews as appropriate self-report measurement techniques in communication research depends on three factors: the research population, the research questions, and the available resources. First, researchers consider from whom they want to gather information. If it is a small group of people who are easy to access, interviews work well. If it is a large group of people spread all over the country, questionnaires are chosen. Second, researchers consider the nature of the questions being asked. Are they better suited to mailed questionnaires where respondents can think about responses and answer them anonymously? Will researchers have to probe to gather adequate information about these questions? Finally, researchers choose a measurement technique based on practical considerations. What funds, people, and equipment are available? Is there an adequate budget to hire interviewers, pay their travel expenses, print questionnaires, or cover postage costs? Is there access to CATI or computer scanning equipment for mark-sense forms? By asking questions such as these, researchers determine the best self-report measurement technique to use.

Observations

Observations, like questionnaires and interviews, are employed widely to gather data about communication phenomena. They differ from questionnaires and interviews in that researchers themselves examine the communication phenomena, or recordings of them, directly rather than relying on respondents' self-reports.

Observations are used widely within the four research methodologies we will discuss in this text. Observational measures are used in many experimental studies to assess subjects' responses on a dependent variable, such as the number of times they nod their heads affirmatively. Observations of research populations are used in survey research to structure questionnaires or interviews and to analyze open-ended responses gathered from nondirective questionnaires and interviews. Finally, observation is the primary measurement technique used to categorize and evaluate written, artistic, and electronic documents in textual analysis and to study naturalistic behavior in ethnographic research. First we will provide a brief introduction to observations as a measurement technique; then we will describe some of the specific ways they are used.

Observational measurement techniques are divided into two primary types. Researchers use **direct observation** to watch communication systematically as it occurs. Researchers may simply observe from the "sidelines," with or without people's awareness, or they may become involved themselves, as participant-observers. The measures they use range from observational checklists to electronic, physiological measures. Researchers use **indirect observation** when they study communication artifacts, texts produced by people. Usually this calls for the systematic categorization and evaluation of the communication content of texts.

Direct observation.   Researchers often decide to investigate communication by directly observing people engaging in it. Sometimes the observations occur in a *laboratory setting* in which a researcher gathers people together, gives them a reason to interact, and then observes what they say and do. Sometimes researchers go out into the *field* to observe people as they engage in everyday activities.

Sometimes the primary target of direct observational research is a particular *person* or group of people. Burgoon and Koper (1984), for example, studied the nonverbal behavior of reticent people, observing and comparing how they talked to friends and to strangers. Because they weren't interested in a particular setting or communication activity, they set up and observed ordinary conversations between reticents and others in a laboratory context.

Sometimes the primary focus of direct observation research is a particular communication *activity*. Maynard (1985), for example, wanted to understand how children get into arguments. To study arguing as an activity, he arranged to observe first-graders working together in reading groups, presuming that disagreements would come up among them periodically. Similarly, Mehan (1983) videotaped a number of reading group sessions and then analyzed episodes of conflict. Because these researchers were not interested in a particular group of children or a particular setting, observing children in other settings doing different things would have done as well.

Indirect observation.   When using indirect observation, researchers examine *communication artifacts* rather than observing live communication events. Communication artifacts may be transcripts of discourse or products of communication. One form of communication artifacts is recordings of communication events, such as written, filmed, audiotaped, or videotaped speeches, conversations, or meetings. Other communication artifacts include the wide range of communication media that people produce, including written material (books, pamphlets, magazines, letters), electronic media (records, films, television programs), and assorted works of art (painting, sculpture).

Indirect observational measurement techniques range from objective quantitative measures, such as how often specific messages appear in a text, to the more subjective, qualitative interpretation and critical assessment of the persuasive symbols used in politicians' public speeches. All indirect observational measures, however, analyze the records or products of human communication rather than the live communication event itself.

Methods of observation.   Observations can be recorded systematically in a number of ways. One recording method is *audiotaping* conversations. Jorgensen (1984), for example, studied how tarot card readers sustain their clients' belief in the readers' special and extraordinary insight. Many of his experiences were recorded in field notes of events observed directly, but a major part of his findings were inferred by analyzing typed transcriptions of 15 audio recordings of actual tarot card readings he was able to obtain.

Many observational researchers now use *videotaping*. Pingree (1986), for example, wanted to study how children's attention to television shows was affected by how well they understand what was being portrayed. She first prepared a 30-minute version of *Sesame Street* that had several episodes, some easily understood, some in a foreign language, some with the normal sequence of events reorganized into random order, and so on. As children watched the show, a camera behind a one-way mirror videotaped their faces and eyes so that coders would later be able to note when they were paying attention to the program and whether they attended more during one episode or another.

Yet another equipment-assisted approach is *time-lapse filming*. Carey (1978), for example, tested sociologist Erving Goffman's observation that people approaching each other on the street mutually avert their gaze (practicing nonthreatening "civil inattention"). He set his camera to film at two frames per second the faces of people walking along the campus of Indiana University. The resulting film has a jerky Keystone Kops quality. But, as Weick (1985) points out, time-lapse films are

> invaluable to detect patterns of movement. . . . The viewer can get more of an event in mind to make sense of. For example, if an event lasts 180 seconds, when the event ends it is difficult to remember how it started. If, however, the event is filmed with one frame exposed every 10 seconds, then it will take 18 seconds to view the event and all portions of it will be vivid when an attempt is made to interpret it. A second advantage is that the jerky event does not look like normal behavior, so all associations made to normal behavior disappear and the viewer becomes a stranger to the segment being examined. Jerky production breaks gestalts. (p. 597)

Other technological innovations are also being used to record communication behavior. For example, Rothschild, Thorsen, Reeves, Hirsch, and Goldstein (1986) studied how people react to television commercials with an *electroencephalogram* (EEG), which records electrical activity in the brain via electrodes attached to the scalp. The researchers imbedded 18 commercials in a one-hour program and then recorded the EEGs of 26 subjects as they viewed the show to determine which kinds of commercials generated the greatest amount of EEG activity.

Computers are also being employed. Henderson (1988) developed a computer program, called EVENTLOG, by which observers can score, for example, videotapes of married couples discussing a topic about which they disagree. As the tape is shown, the observer easily codes when each person speaks and for how long by pressing a key designated for each individual and holding it down for as long as the person is speaking. The computer records the data for later analysis. Keys can also be designated for particular types of comments or nonverbal behaviors observed. Data about these kinds of behavior are then related to the process or outcome of the conflict.

Coding observations.   Observations, like questions, range from open to closed. Observers in experimental and textual analysis research often use closed-ended checklists with predetermined categories. Ethnographic researchers typically use open-ended observations to be sure to record the subtle, as well as the obvious, events being observed. Regardless of whether categories are predetermined or not, all observations eventually need to be categorized, or coded, in meaningful ways in order to make sense of the data obtained. Researchers develop **coding schemes,** classification systems that describe the nature or quantify the frequency of particular communication behaviors, either before or after the observations take place.

Developing valid and reliable coding schemes is a complex task that requires that researchers first determine the type of texts to be coded, the appropriate unit of analysis, and the relevant categories and then train coders to categorize each unit. We examine these processes in more depth in Chapter 10. For now, as an example of a coding scheme, consider Potter and Ware's (1987) examination of how antisocial acts are portrayed on prime-time television. They recorded all regularly scheduled network dramatic programs (88 hours) over a two-week period. They defined antisocial acts as "any attempt by one character to harm another" and asked their research assistants (two undergraduate students) to watch the programs and to note and code every antisocial act portrayed. Based on their own preliminary observations, Potter and Ware developed a coding form that divided antisocial acts into six categories: major felonies (murder, rape, kidnapping, and armed robbery), assaults (with and without a weapon), property crimes (robbery, burglary, larceny, and destruction of property), threats of physical violence or loss of money or reputation, insults, and lies. The resulting coding scheme is a useful research tool that can be used in future mass media research.

CONCLUSION

If communication researchers were measuring something as solid and inanimate as a plank of wood, they might have to employ only a yardstick and a level to obtain the measures necessary for carrying out their work. It's evident that they have something much more intangible to measure and therefore require much more complex measurement concepts and tools. In this chapter we delineated the standards that communication researchers try to achieve when conducting their measurements and described the three major tools they use (questionnaires, interviews, and observations) to obtain precise and meaningful measurements of communication-related phenomena.

chapter 6

Designing Valid Communication Research

Measurement is the means but not the end of communication research. Researchers may achieve precise measurement and still not make progress toward their goal of learning about communication processes. This problem is analogous to what organizations face when they assess job applicants. Their goal is selecting qualified people. They are able to measure, if they choose, every candidate's height, weight, age, years of experience, IQ, and so on, very precisely. But how well do these data tell them whom to hire? If the results of a study are to be meaningful, they must be based on unbiased data well suited to what researchers want to learn. This is a matter of **validity.** The best synonym for *validity* is *accuracy.* The measurements and conclusions in a good research study accurately reflect what that study purports to explain. Validity is the focus of this chapter.

THE NATURE OF VALIDITY

Research studies are valid in two ways. **Internal validity** concerns the *accuracy of the conclusions* drawn from a research study. Internal validity asks whether a research study is designed and conducted so that it leads to accurate findings about the communication phenomenon being investigated. If a study is valid internally, the conclusions drawn are accurate.

One of the biggest challenges researchers confront is avoiding the many factors that threaten the internal validity of their studies. Because measurement techniques are used to generate data in communication research, we first examine measurement validity and reliability and then discuss additional threats to the internal validity of a research study.

External validity concerns the *generalizability of the findings* from a research study. External validity asks whether the conclusions from a particular study can be applied to other people and other contexts. If a study is valid externally, the conclusions drawn from it are not limited to the particular people and contexts studied. The external validity of research is related to three factors: (1) how the people studied were selected, called *sampling;* (2) whether the procedures used mirror real life, called *ecological validity;* and (3) the need to *replicate* research findings.

Validity is crucial; without validity, we have no faith in the accuracy of the conclusions drawn or in the likelihood that these conclusions apply to other circumstances or people beyond one particular study. Berlo (1955) claims, "Poor research is worse than no research, just as false information is worse than no information" (p. 3).

MEASUREMENT VALIDITY AND RELIABILITY

Data collected through the use of questionnaires, interviews, and observations are worthwhile only if they are recorded in accurate and unbiased ways. Developing valid measurement techniques is thus a primary concern for all researchers.

Measurement validity indicates that researchers are indeed measuring the concepts they intend to measure. The more closely the measured data reflect the research concepts being described, the more valid that measurement technique is. Measurement validity thus refers to the ability of a measurement technique to tap the actual meaning of the concepts being investigated. If researchers wanted to measure how much you like each of your friends, which of these methods would be most valid: counting how much time you spend with each person, calculating how much money you spend on gifts for each person, determining how much you tell each person about yourself, or simply asking you to rate how much you like each person? The measure that would yield the most accurate results would have the most measurement validity, while the other three would be less valid.

For measurement to be valid, it must be **reliable,** a term that implies both consistency and stability. **Measurement reliability** involves measuring a variable in a consistent and stable manner. The more reliable a measurement is, the more dependable it is because it leads to similar outcomes when applied at different times, to different populations, and in different contexts. A camera, for example, is a reliable research tool if it works equally well every time a researcher uses it.

Measurement validity and reliability are interrelated; neither is meaningful without the other. However, a measurement can be reliable but not necessarily valid. For example, a measurement instrument that overestimates weight by 10 pounds consistently is reliable but not valid. But the opposite is not true: If a measurement is valid, it must, by definition, be reliable. An accurate instrument measuring weight must be consistent in its measurements. Therefore, reliability is a necessary but not sufficient prerequisite for developing valid measurements. For that reason, we first examine measurement reliability and then consider measurement validity.

Establishing Measurement Reliability

Measurement reliability indicates the amount of error associated with a measurement. Measurements are never perfectly reliable. Any measurement always contains a *true score component* and an *error score component*. The true score component is the person's true average score measured over the course of time. Imagine, for example, that a researcher used a questionnaire to assess your degree of communication competence every single day for an entire year. It is doubtful that your score would be the same each day. The average score, however, would be a fairly true indicator of your communication competence.

The fact is, however, that researchers don't measure people's communication competence, or any other variable, every single day for an entire year. Instead, they typically ask people to fill out a questionnaire only once and then use the score to represent the true average score. Of course, that score contains some error. The error score component is thus the amount of deviation from the true average in a person's score for a particular study.

The error score component is due partly to *random error* and partly to *measurement error*. Random error is an inevitable part of all research. Research participants misread questions, become distracted by personal problems, accidently skip a question, and so forth. Measurement error, by contrast, is more directly under the researcher's control. Although researchers cannot eliminate all measurement error, they can reduce measurement error in several ways, such as through pilot-testing questionnaire, interviews, and observations, to make sure they are effective. If measurement error is reduced, the reliability of a measurement technique will inevitably be increased.

A perfectly reliable measurement would be 100 percent reliable. Of course, no measurement technique is perfectly reliable, so reliability assessments provide a numerical indicator that tells the percentage of time a measurement is reliable, or free of error. Reliability estimates are usually phrased as an easy-to-interpret number equivalent to a percentage, ranging from 0 (no consistency) to 1 (perfect consistency). Researchers generally accept as reliable any measurement technique with a coefficient of .80 or greater.

Several techniques are used to assess the reliability of questionnaires, interviews, and observations, including (1) comparing the results taken from *multiple administrations* of the measurement procedure and (2) comparing the *internal consistency* of a measurement procedure administered once. Observational measurement techniques are also assessed by the amount of *agreement between observers*.

Multiple-administration techniques.   Reliability may be established with the **test-retest** method. A measurement procedure is administered to the same group at different times. The measurement is considered reliable if the results are consistent from one time to another.

It is possible, however, that whatever is being measured, or people's perceptions of it, might change over the course of time due to internal validity threats (discussed later in this chapter). For example, if respondents become familiar with the measurement procedures from one administration to the next, the results might change even on a reliable measurement.

To help control for this problem, the **alternative procedure** method often is used. This involves using another, equivalent procedure for the second administration. Comparing these two measurement procedures then serves as the basis for reliability. This method, however, demands that a valid and reliable alternative measurement procedure be available, which is difficult enough to obtain in the first place!

Single-administration techniques.   To avoid the problems associated with multiple administrations, reliability is often assessed for a measurement technique administered only once. With the **split-half** method, for example, a group of people answer a questionnaire. The researcher then separates their answers into two parts (half the questions are in one part and half on the other) and compares the responses between halves. If both parts measure the same thing, people will answer each part of a reliable questionnaire the same way. The separation process can be accomplished in many ways, and each way yields a slightly different reliability assessment.

Another single-administration test of reliability is the **internal consistency** method. The purpose of this method is to assess the stability of people's responses to related items. Cronbach's (1951) **alpha coefficient,** for example, pairs questions that all measure the same concept randomly to see if people are being consistent in their responses.

Interobserver reliability.   In observational research, the most common method for assessing reliability is calculating the percentage of agreement between the observations of independent coders. This is called **interobserver** or **intercoder reliability.** If the observations recorded by two or more individuals who are unaware of, or "blind" to, the purposes of the study are highly related (showing 80 percent agreement or more), their ratings are considered relatively free of individual bias and therefore reliable. The more trustworthy, or conservative, measures of interobserver reliability also control for agreement due to chance.

What do researchers do if the interobserver reliability score is lower than expected, indicating that ratings between people are inconsistent? Several options are available: (1) They can modify the observational system by improving the observation and recording conditions (schedule shorter sessions, remove distracting stimuli from the observing situation, give observers a better viewing position, etc.); (2) they can clarify more precisely the definitions of the behavioral categories being observed; (3) they can train the observers better or give them more time to get used to making the desired observations; (4) they can increase the length or number of observation sessions or people observed until consistent data are obtained (if, for example, the low reliability of the data was due to the people being observed reacting initially to the presence of the observers); or (5) they can average the observers' scores (Hartmann, 1982).

All of these methods for assessing measurement reliability are intended to show a relatively high consistency between administrations of a measurement technique, between subjects' own scores, or between observers. If we are to be confident in the conclusions researchers draw from studies, we must see indications that the measurements used were indeed reliable.

Establishing Measurement Validity

There is an important difference between measurement reliability and measurement validity. Measurement reliability is always assessed by a numerical indicator. Measurement validity, by contrast, is assessed at a conceptual level. A researcher must assert or argue that a measurement technique assesses accurately what it is supposed to assess. Brinberg and McGrath (1985) assert, "Validity is not a commodity that can be purchased with techniques" (p. 13).

To establish measurement validity, researchers often rely on measurement techniques that have been used previously in research. A researcher who intends to use a technique must make sure it has been validated at some point by its originators. Some researchers invent new and valid measurement techniques. Arguments in support of the validity of a new measurement technique revolve around content, criterion-related, and construct validity. These types of validity are not mutually exclusive; in fact, the best way researchers can make sure a new measurement technique is valid is by establishing all three.

Content validity. A measurement technique possesses **content validity** if it reflects the attributes (or content) of the concept being investigated. For example, a questionnaire designed to measure people's aggressive communication style should contain questions that are related to that style and not to something else, such as ambition or motivation.

Carmines and Zeller (1979) explain that establishing content validity involves specifying the full content domain of the concept, selecting specific attributes from this domain, and putting them into a form that is testable. Determining the full content domain of the abstract and complex concepts communication researchers study may be difficult, however. Clearly, a questionnaire that measures gender has content validity if it asks, "Are you male or female?" But what questions measure clearly how competent or credible a communicator is?

The first way a researcher can establish content validity is to make sure that the measurement instrument reflects the construct as it is defined conceptually. This technique is called **face validity.** On the "face of it," the measure seems accurate.

Although face validity is necessary, proclaiming it doesn't make it so. A stronger procedure is a **panel approach,** whereby qualified people are recruited to generate the content or determine that the technique taps the concept being measured. The validity of the measurement technique depends, of course, on the credentials of the particular panel members.

In the final analysis, there is simply no way to quantify objectively the degree to which a measurement procedure possesses content validity. As Nunnally (1978) observed, content validity rests on a researcher's appeals to reason. It should also be clear, however, that content validity is a necessary criterion for a valid measurement technique.

     Criterion-related validity.   A second form of measurement validity is **criterion-related validity.** This is established when a measurement technique is shown to relate to another technique or outcome, called the criterion, already known to be valid. If scores derived from a measurement technique are related positively to a valid criterion, it is considered valid.

There are two types of criterion-related validity: concurrent and predictive. **Concurrent validity** is established when a new measurement technique is tested against an existing valid criterion. For example, if audiologists (hearing specialists) developed a new one-minute test for hearing loss that could replace the relatively time-consuming tests now used, it would have concurrent validity if it was as accurate as the existing, well-established valid procedure.

Predictive validity refers to how well a measurement technique forecasts a future criterion. A valid employment screening instrument predicts accurately how successful potential employees turn out to be. Similarly, SAT scores are considered valid for predicting how successful college applicants will be.

Clearly, criterion-related validity can be determined only if researchers know for sure that the criterion being applied is indeed valid. Unfortunately, measures of many communication concepts have no existing valid criterion against which they can be compared. That is why they are being developed in the first place!

     Construct validity.   Most important for measuring the abstract concepts researchers study in communication is **construct validity,** validity that is inferred from theory. Construct validity is assessed for techniques that measure concepts in a theoretical framework. The theoretical framework provides conceptual as well as testable, predictive ways of validating the measurement procedure. Carmines and Zeller (1979) explain, "Fundamentally, construct validity is concerned with the extent to which a particular measure relates to other measures consistent with theoretically derived hypotheses concerning the concepts (or constructs) that are being measured" (p. 23).

For example, Berger and Calabrese's (1975) developmental theory of interpersonal communication maintains that people communicate with others they first meet in order to reduce their uncertainty about each other. Their theory makes a number of predictions about how uncertainty affects communication behavior—for example, "High levels of uncertainty cause increases in information seeking behavior" (p. 103). If a questionnaire was developed to measure uncertainty and it showed that the greater the uncertainty score, the more questions people asked, the measure would have construct validity.

Just as a theory is an intricate web of concepts and relationships, the construct validity of a measurement technique is built over the course of time. It cannot be established within a single study but is a result of accumulated findings by different researchers working on different parts of the theory.

The Relative Validity and Reliability of Measurement Techniques

Questionnaires, interviews, and observations possess comparative advantages and disadvantages with regard to validity and reliability that researchers take into account when designing research. Of course, regardless of the inherent strengths or advantages of a particular method, it must fit the concept being measured. In-depth interviews might be very useful, for example, for determining why people watch television, but a questionnaire is perfectly suitable for determining which shows they watch.

Measurement validity is greater when the data generated contain more depth of information. Thus qualitative measures generally increase validity by providing more depth of information about what is being studied than most quantitative measures. Nondirective questionnaires and interviews, for example, are likely to be more valid measures of concepts than directive techniques (including observations) because they encourage people to describe their thoughts and feelings more fully. Nondirective interviews, in turn, tend to generate more valid data than nondirective questionnaires because interviewers can ask probing follow-up questions.

Measurement reliability, by contrast, is higher with procedures that are formal and simple because these characteristics increase the likelihood of obtaining consistent measurements. Quantitative measures generally increase reliability because they are structured more formally than qualitative measures. Highly directive questionnaires and interviews, for example, follow the same format in asking questions and provide respondents with the same response categories every time they are used, which increases the likelihood that people will respond consistently. Finally, highly structured quantitative observations of communication behavior are generally more reliable than qualitative field observations because they are likely to be administered much more consistently.

Measurement validity and reliability can be increased by combining quantitative and qualitative measuring procedures in the same research study, a practice referred to as *triangulation*. By combining structured, quantitative measurements with more open-ended, qualitative measurements of the same concept, researchers enhance both the validity and the reliability of their measurements and the credibility of the conclusions they draw. The increased database also allows researchers to compare the data generated by the various measurement techniques, thereby assessing the validity and reliability of the individual measures.

THREATS TO INTERNAL VALIDITY

Besides measurement validity, many other threats to internal validity may affect the accuracy of the results obtained from any study. Many of these threats are important for all four methodologies we will discuss, but some are more relevant to a particular methodology. These threats to internal validity fall into three interrelated categories: threats due to *researchers,* threats due to *how research is conducted,* and threats due to *research subjects.*

Threats Due to Researchers

One major threat to internal validity is **researcher effect,** or the influence of a researcher on the people being studied. Two major researcher effects are the researcher personal attribute effect and the researcher unintentional expectancy effect.

Researcher personal attribute effect.   Most research involves more than simply observing people. Experimental, survey, textual analysis, and ethnographic research usually involve a researcher interacting with people. During this contact, the researcher may influence people's responses.

The **researcher personal attribute effect** applies when particular researcher characteristics influence people's behavior. Barber (1976) reports that a large number of studies demonstrate that researchers' race, gender, age, ethnic identity, prestige, anxiety, friendliness, dominance, and warmth affect subjects' responses. People answer differently when questions are posed, for example, by a male or a female, by someone warm and friendly or someone cold and aloof. Yagoda and Wolfson (1964), in fact, found that drawings made by research subjects included more mustached men when exposed to a mustached researcher!

The researcher personal attribute effect is likely to occur under two conditions. First, when the research task is ambiguous, subjects look to a researcher for cues about how to perform. Second, this effect may occur when the task is related to the personal characteristics of a researcher. For example, the race of a researcher probably affects people's responses about racial prejudice. Researchers may also be influenced by personal attributes of subjects, as when male researchers respond differently to female and male subjects.

One way researchers control for this effect is by employing a wide variety of research assistants. If it can be determined beforehand which characteristics are likely to affect subjects' responses, researchers will match assistants with the subjects they are least likely to influence.

Researcher unintentional expectancy effect. The **researcher unintentional expectancy effect** occurs when researchers influence subjects' responses by inadvertently letting them know the results they desire. Rosenthal (1966) explains that researchers do this by unintentional paralinguistic and kinesic cues that lead subjects to respond by giving researchers what they expect. Researchers may smile unconsciously when subjects do what they want or frown when they don't, for example.

To control for this problem, some researchers go to great lengths to remove themselves from the actual study. This is done by employing a research assistant to conduct the research who usually is blind to the specific purposes of the study and the desired results. Another way, to be explained shortly, is to make sure that researchers or assistants follow standard procedures so that they treat everyone the same.

Threats Due to How Research Is Conducted

A number of threats to the internal validity of a study are due to the way research is conducted. These threats include the validity and reliability of the procedures used, history, sensitization, and data analysis.

Procedure validity and reliability. **Procedure validity and reliability** requires conducting research accurately and consistently. One form of procedure validity and reliability that we have examined already is administering accurate measurement techniques in a consistent manner.

A second form of procedure validity and reliability is **treatment validity and reliability,** which applies to experimental research in which people are exposed to a manipulation of an independent variable. For example, to assess the effects of eye contact on perceptions of friendliness, some people might be exposed to a large amount and some to a small amount of eye contact. To ensure treatment validity, the eye contact provided must indeed be large in one condition and small in the other, and to ensure treatment reliability, it must be consistent from subject to subject in the two conditions.

A third form of procedure validity and reliability is controlling for **environmental influences,** which means keeping the setting in which a study is done as consistent as possible. Researchers often set up an environment in which people are observed. If more than one room is used to conduct the research, researchers certainly don't want differences between the rooms to affect the subjects, unless, of course, that is the purpose of the study. In field research, people's responses might be influenced by whether they are interviewed at their workplace or at home. So the more appropriate of the two settings should be selected and then used consistently.

The need to maintain procedure validity and reliability is crucial for interpreting the results from any study. Feldman, Hyman, and Hart (1951) found from a review of many studies that loose procedures result in different data while tight procedures result in comparable data from person to person.

History. **History** refers to all changes in the environment external to the study that may influence people's behavior. Events happening in the real world may impinge on the people being studied and influence their behavior. For example, comparisons of the effect of two ways of treating workers will produce different effects during a period of prosperity and a depression. When jobs are plentiful, ill-treated workers are likely to quit. When jobs are scarce, they may not be.

This internal validity threat is particularly important for longitudinal research that follows people over a long period of time. Any changes in the people studied may be due to changes that have occurred in the environment and not to the variables being investigated in the study.

Sensitization. **Sensitization** is the tendency for an initial measurement or procedure to influence a subsequent measurement or procedure. When a similar or identical measurement technique is used twice, the change in people's answers may not be valid because they may remember responses or have learned about the technique. People become "test-wise." When two different procedures are used, the first procedure may change people's behavior during the second procedure, giving different results than if only the second procedure had been administered.

For example, suppose that class-teaching behavior is measured. Then the teacher is trained to ask better questions. If the person improves when teaching another class, is the improvement due to the training, the practice provided by the first teaching session, or both? We discuss in Chapter 7 how sensitization threatens the internal validity of experimental research and how researchers try to control for it.

Data analysis. An important threat to the internal validity of research has to do with the way in which data are analyzed. Researchers sometimes use improper procedures to analyze data, and these will lead to invalid conclusions. We will return to examine this problem in more depth.

Threats Due to Research Subjects

Communication research depends on studying **subjects,** particular persons, groups of people, or texts people produce. Subjects often pose a threat to the internal validity of research. Subject threats include the Hawthorne effect, selection, statistical regression, mortality, maturation, and intersubject bias.

The Hawthorne effect. People aware that they are being studied often behave differently than they do when not being observed. Changes in behavior due to being observed are known as the **Hawthorne effect.**

The Hawthorne effect is derived from a famous study about the effects of illumination on worker productivity, conducted by Mayo, Roethlisberger, and Dickson (as reported by Roethlisberger & Dickson, 1939) at the Western Electric Hawthorne plant in Cicero, Illinois. As they expected, they found that when they increased illumination, productivity increased. They also found, however, that decreased lighting and even restoring the original lighting also resulted in increased productivity! The researchers realized eventually that the consistent increases in worker production were not related to the changes in the level of illumination at all. Workers produced more because they knew researchers were paying attention to them! The workers felt special because they were being observed and therefore performed in a superior manner.

To the extent that people engage in behavior different from their usual behavior because they are involved in a study, conclusions from the study have limited validity. One obvious way to control for the Hawthorne effect is not to let people know they are being observed. But this procedure raises ethical concerns (which we examine in Chapter 7).

Selection.   **Selection** of people or texts for a study may influence the validity of the conclusions drawn. For example, far different results may be obtained if supervisors or subordinates of an organization are interviewed about the communication channels available to them.

When different groups of people are studied, such as Republicans and Democrats, researchers must make sure that the subjects are valid members of these groups. When studying the effects of a treatment, however, the results should be due to that treatment and not the type of people examined, so a mixture of people is recruited for the study.

Subject selection certainly influences the internal validity of studies, and we will examine this in more depth in our discussion of the four methodologies. Subject selection also influences the external validity of research, which we examine later in this chapter.

Statistical regression.   One way in which subject selection might threaten the validity of research findings is due to **statistical regression,** the tendency for subjects selected on the basis of extreme scores to go back toward the mean on a second measurement. Suppose that researchers had measured the degree of open communication expressed by hippies during the late 1960s. They are then measured again in the 1980s after they have gotten married, and the findings show that their open communication has decreased. This change might not be due to having gotten married so much as to the fact that these people were initially studied at the height of their open communication. We would expect over time that their open communication would decrease, or regress toward the mean, regardless of life events. Of course, this change also could be due to history, since everyone might have become less open in communication during the same 20 years.

Mortality.   **Mortality** is the loss of subjects from the beginning to the end of a research study. Mortality can be caused by people moving away, losing interest, or dying. Mortality can also be a threat to the internal validity of textual analysis, such as when important documents are lost or destroyed. Mortality is obviously a critical threat to the internal validity of longitudinal research, especially when researchers try to follow the same people over a long period of time.

Maturation.   Maturation refers to all internal changes that occur *within* people studied over the course of time that might explain their behavior. These changes can be physical or psychological and can happen over a short or long period of time. A study of a yearlong method for teaching reading, for example, may seem effective because students' reading test scores increase. But their scores could also be higher because they are more mature physically and psychologically. We also need to be aware that people often answer the same question differently at the beginning and end of a two-hour experiment or survey interview simply because they grow tired, resentful, or impatient. Internal changes over time (maturation) influence responses in both instances.

Intersubject bias.   Intersubject bias results when the people being studied influence one another. Even the mere presence of other people in a study may influence some responses. Seeing a funny movie by yourself and with others is a different experience. If someone else laughs, we are likely to start laughing. Researchers know from small group studies that people often conform to the way they see others behaving, even when they know that that behavior is not right. Suppose that someone wants to study how different persuasion techniques influence people to volunteer to help a charity. After people listen to speeches using different techniques, they are asked to raise their hands if they wish to volunteer. If more people in one group raise their hands, is their response due to the speech they have heard or to seeing others in the group raise their hands?

People who have been part of a research study may also communicate with other people in the study before or even during the study itself. These conversations may influence performance in the study. Have you ever avoided taking a certain class because of what someone told you about the professor? People sometimes inform others about the purpose of the study prior to the study or tell them what the researchers are looking for, even when they are asked not to do so. Farrow, Farrow, Lohss, and Taub (1975) and Wuebben, Straits, and Schulman (1974) both found that many subjects renege on their promise not to talk with others about a study.

EXTERNAL VALIDITY

Each of the problems examined so far poses a potential threat to the internal validity of a study. In addition to knowing that the conclusions drawn from a particular study are valid, researchers want to be able to generalize these conclusions to other people and other situations. Medical researchers, for example, don't just seek to cure the subjects they studied; they also want to generalize their findings to people they didn't study directly.

External validity means that the findings about cause-and-effect relationships from experimental research, the characteristics of a group of people surveyed, analyses and critiques of texts, or understanding people's naturally occurring communication behavior from ethnographic research apply to other people, texts, and situations. External validity essentially depends on two things: the sample used in the research and the need to replicate studies.

Sampling

In communication and in most human scientific research, relatively few people are studied to find out something about large numbers of people or about trends in the general society. Obviously, every female and every male can't be studied to learn whether women and men differ in their use of the mass media. Instead, communication researchers usually study a small portion of the total population (a "sample") for the purpose of generalizing about the entire population.

Sampling terms.   Before discussing the ways samples are drawn and the implications of these procedures for generalization, we need to define the terms *population, parameter, universe, census, sample,* and *statistic.*

Population.   **Population** refers to all *people* who possess the characteristic of interest. The relevant characteristic of a population is referred to as a **parameter.**

For example, to learn whether newspaper readers are more likely to vote for independent candidates than are nonreaders, the population is all potential voters. Being a potential voter is the parameter that defines the population. Think of a parameter as a boundary around the population that defines who is in and who is out.

Universe.   A **universe** is all the *nonpeople* that share the characteristic of interest. The term *universe* applies primarily to the analysis of texts (see Chapter 10), where a researcher might, for example, sample from the universe of comments made by political speakers. Our discussion of sampling applies to both a population and a universe; we talk about sampling from a population for the sake of convenience only.

Census.   When researchers collect data from all members of a population or a universe, this is called a **census.** The federal government, for example, takes a census by attempting to count every member of the national population. If the population of interest is the membership of a small organization, it may be possible to conduct a census, but when the population of interest is larger, such as all people who attend religious services regularly, a census is not realistic.

Sample.   Because it is usually impracticable or impossible to conduct a census, researchers rely on studying the characteristics of a **sample,** a subgroup of a population or a universe. A measurement of a sample with respect to a variable is referred to as a **statistic.** Researchers often use sample statistics to infer population or universe parameters (see Chapter 12).

Random sampling. The most important characteristic of a sample is not its size but the extent to which it is **representative** of the population; that is, the extent to which it accurately approximates the population. In a representative sample, what is true about the sample should also be true of the population. If sample statistics represent the parameters of a population, researchers can generalize the results from a study of the sample to the whole population.

The best guarantee of a representative sample is the use of random sampling procedures. **Random sampling** procedures select subjects from a population so that each has an equal chance of being selected. A random sampling procedure eliminates the chance of researchers biasing the selection process because of their own opinions or desires. By eliminating such biases, random sampling is the best assurance that the characteristics of a population will be distributed in a similar fashion in a sample. The sample will then represent the population.

Of course, no single random sample is ever a perfect representation of the population from which it is drawn. A sample is representative to some degree or within a certain "margin of error." **Sampling error** expresses how much the characteristics of a sample differ from the parameters of the population. In Chapter 12 we explain how sampling error is calculated. For now, the important point is that random samples allow researchers to calculate the amount of sampling error, whereas nonrandom samples do not.

There are four types of random samples: simple random, systematic, stratified, and cluster.

Simple Random Sample. A **simple random sample** is obtained when each person in a population is assigned a consecutive number and then is selected randomly according to assigned number until the desired sample size is obtained.

To conduct a simple random sample, researchers must first have a complete list of the population or universe. If this is not possible, some other random sampling procedure must be used. The second step is using a procedure that guarantees that each person has an equal chance of being selected. Researchers typically use a random number table (see Appendix A). A random number table is a list of numbers generated by a computer in a nonpurposive way, which means that there is no relationship whatsoever between the numbers on the table.

Suppose that you wanted to draw a simple random sample of 200 students from a college of 5000. You would have to follow a number of necessary steps to conduct a simple random sample (see Figure 6.1).

It should be obvious that it is not always possible to generate a complete list of the population and guarantee that each subject has an equal chance of being represented. Slight modifications are often necessary when using a simple random sampling procedure.

For example, Hawkins, Pingree, and Adler (1987) wanted to study the effects of television's content as a subtle, global source of information about day-to-day norms and reality. They conducted a survey by first selecting telephone numbers randomly from primarily residential prefixes in Madison, Wisconsin, until a sample of 100 adults was obtained. They were attempting to use a simple random sampling

Figure 6.1 A simple random sampling procedure

The following step-by-step procedure would be used to draw a simple random sample of 200 students from a college where the total population is 5000.

1. Determine who is in the population parameter; in this case, all 5000 students who attend the college.
2. Obtain a complete list of the population, all 5000 students, from the registrar's office.
3. Assign each person in the population a number from 0001 to 5000.
4. Enter the random number table (see Appendix A) wherever you like and decide whether you wish to move up, down, right, or left in the table. The direction does not matter, as long as you move consistently in that direction. When you come to the end of a row or column, go to the beginning of the next one and proceed in the same way.
5. Use any four-number combination to pick out the 200 subjects for the study. For example, 0100 corresponds to the person on your list who has been assigned that number. You need to use a four-number combination because there are 5000 subjects in the total population. If there were 15,000 students in the total population, you would use any five-number combination.
6. If you come to the same number more than once, ignore it. Keep selecting subjects until you have 200 for your study.

procedure. But is a telephone directory a complete list of the population? Does everyone have a telephone? Does the use of primarily residential prefixes exclude some people? Could a person have more than one chance of being called if his or her home has several phones with different numbers? This gives a feel for the difficulty researchers face whenever they attempt to generate a simple random sample from a large population.

Systematic Sample.   A **systematic sample** chooses every *n*th subject from a complete list of a population after starting at a random point. The interval used to choose every *n*th subject is called the **sampling rate.** For example, if every fourth subject is chosen, the sampling rate is 1/4, or one in four. To make this procedure even more random, researchers can choose the sampling rate using a random procedure.

Systematic samples are often used with large populations, as in mass media or organizational communication research, since they are easier to do than a simple random sample. For example, Zalesny and Farace (1986) conducted a field study about how organizational members process social information by using a systematic sampling procedure to choose every tenth employee from a state government agency of approximately 1100 employees.

Although systematic samples are quite prevalent, they contain more potential error than a simple random sample. It is possible that the order of the people in a population list is biased in some manner, a problem known as **periodicity.** Every *n*th person in a population might possess a characteristic that the other people do not possess, a characteristic that could bias the sample and limit the ability to generalize to the population of interest. Selecting every twelfth student from a list of all students, for example, might yield only freshmen.

Stratified Sample.   A **stratified sample** categorizes a population along a characteristic considered important to the research, called a **stratification variable,** and then samples randomly from each category created in proportion to its representation in a population.

Suppose that a researcher has developed a valid and reliable instrument for measuring communication competence and wants to know the degree to which students of differing ability at a university are competent in communication. The researcher could first divide the students into groups based on their grade point average (high, average, low) and then administer the instrument to selected samples drawn randomly from each group.

A simple random or a systematic sample of students might produce a sample that did not account adequately for one or more segments of this population in terms of ability. By stratifying the population along this variable and selecting subjects based on their representative proportions, the different ability groups will each be represented.

Stratified samples help to ensure that variables that make a difference are factored into the study. However, the more stratification variables included in a study, the more difficult it is to obtain representatives from a population. The frequency with which subjects can be obtained from stratified populations is called the **incidence.** So if the high-ability group includes only students with a grade point average of 3.5 and above (on a 4.0 scale) and 150 students at a college maintain that average, 150 is the incidence of this particular group of potential subjects in this population.

Cluster Samples.   Each of the preceding random samples relied on obtaining a complete list of the population and then selecting individual members randomly from that list. Often, however, obtaining such a list is not possible or practical. Companies that conduct national surveys, such as the Gallup polls or the Nielsen ratings, can't get a complete list of all residents of the United States. In such cases, they must use another type of random sampling procedure.

A **cluster sample** selects units, or clusters, of subjects randomly. For example, a researcher could sample different battalions randomly from the United States Army. A type of cluster sample that is used frequently is the **multistage cluster sample,** in which successively smaller random samples of clusters are selected from a very large population. To get a random sample of the United States, for example, a researcher might start by selecting a few states randomly, then selecting a few counties, a few cities, a few streets, a few households on each street, and finally a member from each household. It's important that each of these selection processes use a random procedure.

Multistage cluster sampling is a simple idea that may become complex to carry out. Cluster sampling can introduce error into the sampling procedure if the clusters chosen are not necessarily representative of the general population. For example, if the suburb of Beverly Hills, California, is chosen randomly, the subjects might not be representative of the general population with regard to income. Sampling error is also magnified because it is present at each stage, so error in one sampling event is five times greater with five stages of cluster sampling.

Nonrandom samples. Many times, it is not possible to sample randomly from a population. Random samples, for example, can be extremely expensive. There is also the problem of finding complete population lists, which is particularly true for obtaining random samples for subjects with characteristics that are hard to find. For example, lists of couples who are happily married or people who watch late-night talk shows simply don't exist.

It is also perfectly acceptable at times for researchers not to sample randomly from a population. Exploratory or beginning research studies are concerned first with internal validity and only later with external validity. Ethnographic researchers, who often try to describe what happens in a particular context that is not easily accessible (such as a street gang or a corporate board of directors), will at first rely on any informants who can provide accurate background information.

When random samples cannot be drawn for some reason, researchers use nonrandom samples to represent the population being studied. A **nonrandom sample** does not use procedures to ensure that each subject selected from a population of interest has an equal chance of being selected. Nonrandom samples therefore do not allow researchers to compute the amount of sampling error. Even though a nonrandom sample may be representative of the population from which it is drawn, researchers have no way of calculating the amount of bias in the sample and consequently no way of knowing if a nonrandom sample differs from the population. Researchers must thus be very careful when generalizing the results of a study based on a nonrandom sample to the population of interest.

Five types of nonrandom samples are convenience, volunteer, purposive, quota, and network.

Convenience Sample. In a **convenience sample**, also called an **accidental sample**, subjects are selected nonrandomly simply because they are available. Market researchers, for example, often go to shopping malls and try to interview anyone who comes through the doors. Communication researchers often rely on college students to serve as research subjects simply because they are available. There is no guarantee that these people are similar to the general population, so these results cannot be applied with any confidence to everyone in the country or to people at large.

Volunteer Sample. In a **volunteer sample**, subjects choose to participate in the study, usually because of rewards offered. For example, to study nonverbal behaviors associated with conversational involvement during an interview, Coker and Burgoon (1987) recruited subjects by placing an advertisement in a local newspaper that offered free training in résumé preparation and interviewing skills in exchange for participation in their research study.

Research on volunteer subjects indicates, however, that they have greater intellectual ability, interest, motivation, need for approval, and sociability, as well as lower age and less authoritarianism, than nonvolunteer subjects (Rosenthal, 1965). A volunteer sample may therefore not be representative of the population.

Purposive Sample. In a **purposive sample,** subjects are selected nonrandomly because they possess a particular characteristic. For example, Stafford (1987) wanted to investigate differences in the conversational characteristics of mothers of 2-year-old twins and 2-year-old singletons. She recruited mothers of twins through a Mothers of Twins Club and mothers of singletons through a mothers' morning-out program. She then matched singletons and twins on age and gender and compared their mothers' communication differences.

A purposive sample is similar superficially to a stratification sample in that the characteristic chosen is a stratification variable. A purposive sample does not, however, select subjects randomly on the basis of this stratification variable. Instead, available subjects who possess the necessary characteristic are used, which may bias the data collected. Mothers who are club members, for example, may not behave in ways typical of all mothers.

Quota Sample. In a **quota sample,** subjects are selected nonrandomly on the basis of their known representation in the population. For example, a researcher might be interested in the different uses of television by people who do and do not own a VCR. If the researcher knows that 70 percent of the population owns a VCR and 30 percent does not, a quota sample is used to select available subjects on the basis of these proportions.

Quota sampling is also similar superficially to a stratified sample in that subjects are selected proportionally on the basis of a stratification variable. Quota sampling does not, however, select subjects randomly on the basis of this stratification variable but rather samples proportionally from available subjects who possess the characteristic.

Network Sample. In a **network sample** (Granovetter, 1976), also called the **snowball technique,** subjects are asked to refer researchers to other people who could serve as subjects. For example, Baxter and Bullis (1986) studied important turning points in romantic relationships. They asked student interviewing teams to name all the romantic pairs in their social network and then asked these people to serve as subjects in their study. These people were then asked to identify other romantic pairs in their social network. Network sampling is used commonly in ethnographic and historical research studies to locate people who will agree to provide information that is hard to acquire.

Ecological Validity

Ecological validity refers to the need to conduct research so that it reflects, or does justice to, real-life circumstances. If research findings are to be generalized to everyday people and situations, the research procedures must capture what actually occurs in real life. Otherwise, the procedures are too divorced from real life and assess only what people theoretically do in hypothetical situations, thereby limiting the generalizability of the findings.

One way to increase the ecological validity of communication research is to study message behavior as it occurs in natural settings. Anthropologist James Peacock (1986) refers to an anecdote told about the Russian general Kutuzov. Before an important battle, his advisers were detailing high-level strategies. Bored, the old general slept. On the eve of the battle, he rode around and interviewed his sentries. Kutuzov later claimed he learned more of what he needed to handle the actual situation from the sentries than from his strategists.

The general distrusted abstractions formulated at a distance from real people and real life. He sought truth from natives in their habitat, by looking and listening. He valued what we call "ecologically based" knowledge.

Studying communication behavior in natural settings increases the generalizability of research because communication processes may be thought of as streams of behavior, and like all streams, their course is shaped by the terrain through which they flow. If we ignore the banks and study only the stream or divert the stream into an artificial container and study it there, our knowledge of that stream is inevitably limited.

Mass media researchers, for example, study the impact of television on viewers. Most do so by referring to surveys or ratings reporting which programs people watch. But as Jensen (1987) points out:

> The reception situation is embedded in a socioeconomic and historical context. . . . Consequently, if we are to begin to understand the lived reality behind the ratings, we need to turn to the context of use, the physical setting where reception takes place, and ask, what is the meaning of television viewing to the audience? . . . Television viewing, for example, may work simply as an atmospheric generator, [as] an occasion for being together, or as a point of reference for fixing bedtimes and the like. It is the act of watching or not watching, together or alone, that constitutes important and recurring variables in family life, and the specific program is only of secondary importance for assessing the meaning of watching television. (pp. 24–25)

From this viewpoint, studies of reactions to television programs conducted in viewers' own homes have greater ecological validity than studies conducted in special screening rooms.

Research conducted in controlled settings can distort the findings. What actually occurs when people communicate in natural settings is often quite different from what we expect will occur. Therefore, we may not even think to study those phenomena. Hopper (1989), for example, studied how people begin telephone conversations. As data he used recordings of actual phone conversations, which provided the study with high ecological validity. He found people's behavior to be far less precise than he had expected. His observations led him to critique prevailing assumptions about communication:

> Past communication educators have conceived our task as teaching individual communicators to encode messages that are clear, precise, vivid, or well-organized. Yet in openings we observe parties succeeding by muddling through, by offering imprecise and elided speech objects across several speaking turns. This difficult-to-specify performance, in dialogue, is the dance of good persons conversing well. In the future, we must seek ways to tailor our instruction to students as community members, as well as individual achivement-units. We also must learn the value of muddling through as a supplement to the value of precise message-encoding. (p. 193).

Had Hopper written in advance and asked people to evaluate what he thought were acceptable phone conversational openings, he very likely would not have included the statements he learned people actually used. Moreover, people's responses to his hypothetical statements wouldn't necessarily have reflected how they actually respond when encountering those messages in everyday conversation.

Just because research doesn't take place within natural settings doesn't mean that it can't be ecologically valid. Researchers conducting experiments in laboratories or researchers conducting surveys using questionnaire and interviewers must pay careful attention to the ecological validity of their research. They must try to employ procedures that enhance rather than decrease the ecological validity, and hence the generalizability, of their research findings.

Replication

A third criterion for external validity of research is **replication,** conducting a second or third study on a particular topic that repeats exactly the procedures used in the first study or varies them in some systematic way. To apply research to many people and situations, researchers need to be sure that the results are based on more than one study that found the same thing. Results from any one study simply cannot be relied on, especially if any of the numerous threats to internal and external validity exist. Researchers would not want to release a new drug that supposedly cures a disease, for example, based on results from a single test. Tukey (1969) argues that no single study can establish a generalization; only when the same, or substantially the same, results are achieved from several replications of a study can the findings of the original study be confirmed and extended reliably.

Types of replication.   Lykken (1968) and Kelly, Chase, and Tucker (1979) identify four types of replication: literal, operational, instrumental, and constructive.

Literal Replication.   **Literal replication** occurs when researchers duplicate a previous research study as closely as possible. Everything done in the original study, including measurement techniques, sampling procedures, and data analysis procedures, is repeated. Literal replication demands that the authors of the original study explain the steps followed in the study fully and clearly if they are to be reproduced by other researchers working in another time and place. Of course, the subjects selected for a replication will not be the same subjects selected for the original study.

Operational Replication. **Operational replication** duplicates the sampling and experimental procedures from the previous study but typically uses different measurement techniques and analyzes the data in a different way. If different measurement techniques and data analysis procedures yield similar results as the original study, researchers are more confident about the external validity of the research findings. Say an interview study reveals that people work harder for considerate bosses. If an anonymous questionnaire reveals the same thing, researchers can feel more sure of this finding.

Instrumental Replication. **Instrumental replication** measures the dependent variable in the same way as the original study but changes the independent variable to see if a different operationalization of the experimental procedures will give the same results. Replicating a finding using different procedures means that it occurs across different conditions and thereby increases the external validity of the research. Say employee consideration is operationalized by employers giving liberal sick leave benefits in a study. If it is measured by listening to employee suggestions in another study and the same results are obtained, that finding is supported.

Constructive Replication. **Constructive replication** uses entirely different procedures, measurement instruments, sampling procedures, and data analysis techniques to study the same topic. The goal is to see if the same results can be obtained with a different study, thereby testing the replicability of the results themselves. Replication in this sense is similar to triangulation, achieving similar results through the use of different methods. Thus if the same findings are obtained in observing bosses in various settings and how workers respond to them, the generalization is substantiated.

CONCLUSION

In the final analysis, the best research is both internally and externally valid. When you read studies in communication journals and you wish to have confidence in their findings and to apply those findings to other people and other situations, you must be prepared to evaluate how internally and externally valid they are.

chapter 7

Research Ethics

Research may appear at first to be a straightforward, value-free activity, one in which a rational, correct way to operate always is evident to anyone familiar with its procedures. That's nonsense. All along the way, choices must be made that can't be decided simply on the basis of scientific logic. Communication research is conducted by human beings, about human behavior, using human beings as subjects. Whenever people deal with people, their behavior has an ethical dimension. Thomas Mann once wrote, "The great lesson of these times is to discover that the moral and the intellectual are linked." In this chapter we explore this link.

ETHICAL DECISIONS IN COMMUNICATION RESEARCH

Let's begin by understanding that ethics is not the same as legality. Laws are usually not universal principles; they are conventions particular to a given culture. It may be acceptable for politicians to defend their behavior with the famous statement "Nothing illegal was done here," but researchers have an ethical responsibility that goes far beyond not merely breaking the law. Even if it is legal, it's not necessarily ethical.

The word *ethics* is derived from the Greek word *ethos,* "character." An ethical person is a "good" person. Measurements of communicator credibility and inter-personal trust often ask for judgments about character.

Philosophers generally agree that the closest synonym for the word *ethics* is *morality,* derived from the Latin word *moralis,* meaning "customs." Therefore, **ethics** can be defined as "moral principles and recognized rules of conduct regarding a particular class of human action."

Two elements in this definition are especially important. First are "moral prin-ciples." To be ethical, communication research should be consistent with fundamen-tal moral principles that apply to all human conduct. Morals inevitably involve val-ues, standards for proper behavior. When researchers confront ethical dilemmas, they are attempting to balance competing values (Smith, 1985), such as the stan-dards of honesty and courtesy. It's sometimes hard to be both honest and courteous simultaneously, so tough choices must be made. Second is "recognized rules of con-duct regarding a particular class of human action." Communication researchers generally agree that certain forms of behavior are ethically acceptable and others unacceptable when conducting research. Ethical decisions about research are thus ones that conform as well as possible to the values and behaviors considered proper.

Ethical decisions, however, cannot be judged simply as right or wrong; they exist on a continuum ranging from clearly unethical to clearly ethical (Reese & Fre-mouw, 1984). Many are in the gray area in between, where hard choices must be made. Therefore, it is virtually impossible to develop a standard checklist that can be used to judge all the ethical decisions made in research studies. As Kimmel (1988) explains:

> The sheer diversity of ethical problems that one might encounter during the various stages of social research seems to have precluded the emergence of a clear typology or set of classifying characteristics by which to describe and contrast particular studies. (p. 26)

Here we consider ethical concerns associated with three major phases of the research process: (1) those that affect the beginning phase of research, (2) those that affect the treatment of human subjects, and (3) those that affect research findings and their use.

Ethical Decisions in Beginning Research

The beginning phase of research is affected by a number of important consider-ations, including the reasons why researchers engage in research, decisions about what to study, and threats to researchers' academic freedom.

Deciding to engage in research.   Many factors influence the decision to en-gage in research. Some are institutional, some professional, and some personal. In-stitutions—universities, government agencies, and private corporations—often in-sist that the scholars they employ conduct research. If you attend a university that awards a large number of graduate degrees, for example, chances are your professors are expected to carry on a program of research and to publish their findings in academic journals. This work is very important for the advancement of knowledge in each field of study—in many disciplines, very little research is done outside of academia—and enhances the reputation of the university. Universities are evaluated by the impact of their faculty's published research on the knowledge base in their field. Consequently, most professors feel some institutional pressure to produce and publish research. Government and corporate researchers are similarly expected to produce research that helps to achieve the goals of the institutions for which they work.

Colleagues within researchers' disciplines likewise place great importance on research. Conventions of national associations in each field, such as the Speech Communication Association or the International Communication Association, consist largely of sessions at which researchers report the results of their investigations. Journals published by these associations report the best of these studies. Articles submitted for publication are sent first to several peers (other qualified researchers in that field) to be reviewed. Only those deemed most worthwhile are selected for publication, usually fewer than 10 percent of those submitted.

Personal motivations also play a role. Most researchers enjoy the pursuit of new knowledge. Some want the rewards, such as increased prestige, promotion, and pay, that publishing acclaimed research brings.

In short, there is much pressure on researchers to conduct, complete, and publish research. To be an ethical researcher, however, occasionally slows the process. It requires taking pains to plan and conduct the work carefully and to consider effects that the research project might have on others. Being ethical occasionally forces researchers into choosing between the values of quantity and quality. That is, if they choose to do highly ethical research, they may be less productive in the short run. However, in the long run, as we hope to make apparent in the remainder of this chapter, ethical research will be more worthwhile and bring greater respect to the researcher.

Deciding what to study. Researchers in communication, as well as the rest of the human sciences, face a much harder choice in deciding what to study than it might appear at first. Communication researchers could turn their attention to a whole host of topics with a reasonable hope that their results might benefit society. But the individual researcher's choice must be taken into account. Researchers might let society's needs be their primary guide, but they shouldn't have to ignore their own interests.

Communication researchers, particularly those on the public payroll who are employed at state universities, have a general obligation to try to benefit society with their research. But if the needs of society are so important, why don't all researchers just drop whatever they are doing and concentrate on solving society's great problems, like war, crime, discrimination, or AIDS?

There are two good reasons. First, not all researchers are qualified to tackle every question. Some researchers are trained to study AIDS, and others are trained to investigate how humans construct and exchange messages. Both contribute to improving the human condition. Communication practitioners conducting public education campaigns that promote safe sex, for example, construct and disseminate important messages that help save people's lives.

Second, if all researchers turned their attention to a few major problems, they would be neglecting other important areas. This neglect might even result in the development of new problems that could have been avoided had they paid attention to them in the first place.

Academic freedom and research.   Professors at universities are supposedly guaranteed the right of "academic freedom," the ability to teach and research topics that they consider important. One reason that universities grant tenure, life-time employment, is to provide scholars with academic freedom.

Academic freedom is important for researchers at universities because without it, the decision about what to research might be influenced by political pressure. Many people and groups have political agendas to which they are strongly committed and might believe that their tax- or church-supported institution is wrong if it does not do the research they want done and find the results they already "know" to be true. This, of course, would cut off the inquiry process that forms the backbone of research, and professors might soon find themselves out of a job if they didn't give in to these political pressures.

Sometimes the threat to academic freedom is more subtle. Researchers often seek funding for their studies in the form of grants. There are two kinds of grants, public and private. *Public grants* are financial awards given by government bodies, such as the federal government, and *private grants* are financial awards given by individuals and organizations.

In either case, a researcher submits, usually in response to an announcement of potential funding, a grant proposal or outline for the research, including a complete budget. To succeed in attracting funding, however, researchers often have to orient their research in particular ways. Equally important, researchers can be tempted to offer more than they can probably deliver. A researcher who is awarded a grant is bound ethically to abide by the provisions of the granting body. If researchers cannot abide by and meet the needs of the funding agency, they must decide whether to pursue and accept funding.

Ethical Decisions Involving Human Subjects

All communication research projects inevitably intrude into the lives of the people being studied. Researchers send messages to individuals and measure how they react or observe how groups of people ordinarily exchange messages among themselves and then make their findings known to others. Such investigations can't be conducted without somehow affecting the subjects.

Up to this point, we have examined the research process from the viewpoints of two participants in the research process: the researcher (the communication scholar) and the audience (the communication consumer). Now we shift our attention to a third participant, the *subject* of communication research.

People don't say, "Hey gang, let's go out today and be in a research project." Nor do subjects usually participate in planning research projects. Researchers intend to answer questions that will ultimately help people communicate more effectively, but this benefit accrues mainly to readers of the investigation's results. The subjects of the research project, those involved in the means for achieving this noble end, have an entirely different experience and may even accrue more costs than benefits. Taking the subjects' perspective, therefore, shifts our concern from "Is this study worthwhile?" to "Are they being treated right?" Making this shift refocuses our attention on the ethics of studying human beings in communication research.

Although there are no easy answers about how subjects should be treated, guidelines have been established. Universities that receive funding from the Department of Health and Human Services are required to establish *institutional review boards* (IRBs), committees that review research proposals to ensure the protection of human beings affected in the course of research studies conducted by scholars affiliated with those universities. IRBs rely on a set of ethical guidelines established by governmental and professional associations. The American Psychological Association, for example, publishes a set of guidelines for research with human participants ("Ethical Principles," 1981; see Figure 7.1). Failure to follow these guidelines can result in censure and even expulsion from the association. In most professions, including academia, *peers* regulate each other's behavior. Ultimately, however, self-regulation prevails. The final responsibility for conducting ethical research rests with the researcher.

Ethical guidelines for the treatment of human subjects are based on four primary moral principles or rules of conduct commonly advocated by communication scholars: (1) benefit the people being studied; (2) protect their right to privacy; (3) provide them with free choice; and (4) treat people with respect.

Benefit the people being studied.   The people being studied should benefit, not suffer, from participating in a research investigation. There are numerous ways in which this precept may be violated, as well as many ways in which researchers can take it into account.

By providing information, subjects contribute to researchers' efforts. Ethical researchers in turn consider how they might reciprocate. They try to make being a research subject a pleasant or beneficial experience, or at least one participants do not regret afterward. Some studies are inherently enjoyable for participants. Elderly respondents asked to reminisce about their lives and share their knowledge with young listeners, for example, usually welcome the opportunity.

People in stigmatized or oppressed social groups may benefit, personally and as a group, from being the focus of a research study. Miller and Humphreys (1980) studied homosexuals, for example, and found many who suffered from acute depression and needed a neutral listener. They maintained contact with their subjects

Figure 7.1 American Psychological Association guidelines for ethical research

Principle 9: Research with Human Participants

The decision to undertake research rests upon a considered judgment by the individual psychologist about how best to contribute to psychological science and human welfare. Having made the decision to conduct research, the psychologist considers alternative directions in which research energies and resources might be invested. On the basis of this consideration, the psychologist carries out the investigation with respect and concern for the dignity and welfare of the people who participate and with cognizance of federal and state regulations and professional standards governing the conduct of research with human participants.

a. In planning a study, the investigator has the responsibility to make a careful evaluation of its ethical acceptability. To the extent that the weighing of scientific and human values suggests a compromise of any principle, the investigator incurs a correspondingly serious obligation to seek ethical advice and to observe stringent safeguards to protect the rights of human participants.

b. Considering whether a participant in a planned study will be a "subject at risk" or a "subject at minimal risk," according to recognized standards, is of primary ethical concern to the investigator.

c. The investigator always retains the responsibility for ensuring ethical practice in research. The investigator is also responsible for the ethical treatment of research participants by collaborators, assistants, students, and employees, all of whom, however, incur similar obligations.

d. Except in minimal-risk research, the investigator establishes a clear and fair agreement with research participants, prior to their participation, that clarifies the obligations and responsibilities of each. The investigator has the obligation to honor all promises and commitments included in that agreement. The investigator informs the participants of all aspects of the research that might reasonably be expected to influence willingness to participate and explains all other aspects of the research about which the participants inquire. Failure to make full disclosure prior to obtaining informed consent requires additional safeguards to protect the welfare and dignity of the research participants. Research with children or with participants who have impairment that would limit understanding and/or communication requires special safeguarding procedures.

e. Methodological requirements of a study may make use of concealment or deception necessary. Before conducting such a study, the investigator has a special responsibility to (i) determine whether the use of such techniques is justified by the study's prospective scientific, educational, or applied value; (ii) determine whether alternative procedures are available that do not use concealment or deception; and (iii) ensure that the participants are provided with sufficient explanation as soon as possible.

f. The investigator respects the individual's freedom to decline to participate in or withdraw from the research at any time. The obligation to protect this freedom requires careful thought and consideration when the investigator is in a position of authority or influence over the participant. Such positions of authority include, but are not limited to, situations in which research participation is required as part of employment or in which the participant is a student, client, or employee of the investigator.

g. The investigator protects the participant from physical and mental discomfort, harm, and danger that may arise from research procedures. If risks of such consequences exist, the investigator informs the participant of that fact. Research procedures likely to cause serious or lasting harm to a participant are not used unless the failure to use these procedures might expose the participant to risk of greater harm, or unless the research has potential benefit and fully informed and voluntary consent is obtained from each participant. The participant should be informed of procedures for contacting the investigator within a reasonable time period following participation, should stress potential harm, or related questions or concerns arise.

h. After the data are collected, the investigator provides the participant with information about the nature of the study and attempts to remove any misconceptions that may have arisen. Where scientific or humane values justify delaying or withholding this information, the investigator incurs a special responsibility to monitor the research and to ensure that there are no damaging consequences for the participant.

i. Where research procedures result in undesirable consequences for the individual participant, the investigator has the responsibility to detect and remove or correct these consequences, including long-term effects.

j. Information obtained about a research participant during the course of an investigation is confidential unless otherwise agreed in advance. When the possibility exists that others may obtain access to such information, this possibility, together with the plans for protecting confidentiality, is explained to the participant as part of the procedure for obtaining informed consent.

Source: Reprinted from "Ethical Principles of Psychologists," *American Psychologist, 36,* pp. 633–638, copyright © 1981 by the American Psychological Association. Reprinted by permission of the American Psychological Association.

over time, and several reported that being interviewed helped decrease their isolation and gave them an increased awareness of their identity. One even said, "You know, that research really changed my life."

Some researchers pay their subjects a small fee for their participation. Focus group members, who meet as a group under the guidance of a facilitator (see Chapter 9), for example, are usually rewarded financially for their time. Other researchers give their subjects a copy of the research report and thus reciprocate by sharing that knowledge with them. Organization heads often encourage their employees to participate in particular research projects because they believe that the results will prove useful to their organization.

The more uniquely and comprehensively the findings relate to particular research subjects, the more attention must be given to benefits. For example, Spradley (1980) recalls:

> James Sewid, a Kwakiutl Indian in British Columbia, was an excellent informant, and together we recorded his life history about growing up during the early part of this century. When it became apparent that the edited transcripts might become a published book, I decided to safeguard Mr. Sewid's rights by making him a full partner who signed the contracts with Yale University Press. He shared equally in all royalties and had the right to decide with me, on crucial matters of content. I also wanted to safeguard his sensitivities, so before we submitted the final manuscript I read the completed

version to both him and his wife. They made deletions and changes that were in their best interests, changes that reflected their sensitivities, not mine. (pp. 21–22)

The flip side of benefiting subjects is not causing them harm. Suppose that a researcher wants to study the effects of a negative condition, such as high stress or pain, on how people communicate or whether certain messages, such as those contained in violent or pornographic films, cause harm. While studying such conditions, the researcher might exacerbate them.

This danger may be avoided in several ways. One is studying people already in that condition. For example, instead of creating experimental conditions that frighten their subjects, researchers studying the effects of stress can study people who are already experiencing stress, such as patients facing dentistry or surgery or students about to take examinations.

A second approach is studying minimal levels of negative states. Say researchers are studying stage fright. Instead of comparing the behavior of people who feel normal and high communication apprehension when giving a speech, the researchers may be able to test their theory equally well by comparing speakers with low and normal apprehension and thereby avoid subjecting highly apprehensive people to an upsetting experience. Or they might require that the subjects be in the negative state for a minimal amount of time, say, by making the highly apprehensive people speak only as briefly as needed to make the required measurements.

Researchers must be attentive to causing discomfort to their subjects inadvertently. Activities that don't disturb most people may be upsetting to a few. Subjects whose parents are deceased or divorced, for example, may feel uncomfortable or even angry when asked to provide their mother's age, occupation, or address. Pretesting experimental conditions and consulting with people familiar with the research population help researchers to identify and eliminate or at least reduce instances of avoidable discomfort.

When communication researchers study how well particular treatments alleviate problems and use control groups that do not receive the treatment (see Chapter 8), they face the ethical dilemma of not benefiting their subjects as well as they might. Say researchers devise a new way to alleviate fear of public speaking. Is it fair to teach it only to an experimental group and give no help to the control group? One approach some researchers use in such circumstances is to solicit volunteers for the treatment and then select some randomly for the treatment groups and some for a "waiting list" control group. They then offer the experimental treatment to the control group at a later date, or they offer the control group some other known treatment rather than no treatment at all.

When publishing the results of their study, researchers must also consider whether they are benefiting or harming their subjects. For example, a study of drug use, cheating, or sexual behavior on a college campus that doesn't take into account the effect on trustees, parents, or alumni donors may do much harm. To minimize harm, ethical researchers might either avoid naming the institution in the article or make very clear how the behavior they report compared with data from similar institutions.

Protect the right to privacy. Researchers measure subjects' behavior and elicit information from them. This information should not be used to violate the subjects' privacy. Researchers usually protect privacy by ensuring their subjects of anonymity or confidentiality. **Anonymity** exists when researchers cannot connect responses to the individuals who provided them. **Confidentiality** exists when researchers know who said what but promise not to reveal that information publicly. Anonymity is usually ensured by identifying research participants with a code number rather than their names. Confidentiality is usually assured by publishing *aggregate,* or grouped, data rather than individual data; if the latter are necessary, names are omitted or disguised.

Whenever possible, anonymity is preferable, since research data can leak out inadvertently. Babbie (1986) reports an example. He studied the attitudes and behavior of churchwomen by asking ministers in a sample of churches to distribute questionnaires, collect them, and return them to his office. One minister read through the questionnaires before returning them. Then he "delivered a hell-fire and brimstone sermon to his congregation, saying that many of them were atheists and were going to hell" (p. 452). Even though the minister could not identify particular respondents, many people felt that their privacy had been violated.

When conducting interviews, subjects and researchers are face to face, so anonymity is impossible. Researchers usually protect privacy in such cases by being cautious themselves, by recruiting responsible and mature interviewers to assist them, and by training and supervising their interviewers carefully.

The appropriateness of protecting respondents' privacy is sometimes called into question. Some researchers have found themselves in the dilemma of learning information that might be incriminating to their subjects. Hartman and Hedblom (1979) give the example of a researcher observing a badly battered child in a home where she was conducting the interview. As they ask:

> In seeking the cooperation of the respondent and promising anonymity, had the interviewer lost the right or the responsibility to report legal violations to the authorities? . . . The interviewer's presence in the home was contingent on a single role; did the interviewer have the right or the mandate to play another? (p. 345)

These are difficult ethical questions. In this particular case, fortunately, the interviewer called the mother and guided her subtly toward making contact with a community agency that would help her rather than prosecute her.

Provide free choice. Ethical researchers do not coerce subjects into contributing to their investigations. Whenever possible, subjects first provide **informed consent.** That is, subjects agree to participate only after they have been fully informed about the study. When seeking subjects' consent, we believe that researchers ought to provide them with some important information (see Figure 7.2).

The principle of informed consent presents a dilemma to communication researchers who wish to study unpleasant phenomena, such as conflict or social embarrassment, or socially desirable phenomena, such as helpfulness or cooperation.

Figure 7.2   Information necessary when requesting informed consent

Researchers ought to provide subjects with the following information when requesting their consent to participate in a research study.

1. The purpose of the research
2. The procedures to be followed (including identifying those that are experimental)
3. The identities of the individuals conducting the research and their educational and other credentials
4. A description of the immediate and long-term discomforts, hazards, and risks involved and their possible consequences
5. An offer to answer any inquiries concerning the study at any time
6. A means of contacting the principal investigator (address and phone)
7. An instruction that the subjects are free to withdraw their consent and to discontinue participation in the project or activity at any time without prejudice
8. Assurance that any information derived from the research project that personally identifies the subject will not be released voluntarily or disclosed without the subject's separate consent, except as required by law
9. Assurance that if the study design or use of information is changed, subjects will be informed and their consent reobtained.

If participants are warned fully about what is being studied and why, as informed consent insists, that knowledge may distort the data they provide. They might deny or hide socially unacceptable behavior or exaggerate in reporting behavior they believe they should be engaging in. To avoid this problem, researchers often omit information, are vague, or are even deceptive regarding what will occur or be measured in an upcoming study. Several approaches have been employed to approximate informed consent when foreknowledge must be limited.

Berscheid, Baron, Dermer, and Lebman (1973) suggest that a complete description of the experiment be given to a sample of the population from which the participants in the study will be chosen. These people are then asked whether they would volunteer to participate in the study. If most people say that they would, researchers may conclude that the study would be acceptable to most participants.

A related procedure is what Sable (1978) calls "prior general consent plus proxy consent." A researcher first obtains the general consent of a subject to participate in a study that may involve extreme procedures. The person then empowers a friend to serve as a proxy; that is, to examine the details of the specific procedures in advance and to make a judgment as to whether the subject would have consented to it given the choice. If the proxy says yes, the researcher may proceed.

Lewin (1979) suggests running a pilot study with just a few subjects, then discussing the purpose of the study with them. If they don't object and believe that their participation was acceptable, researchers are on firmer ground for inducing others to participate. If they regret their participation, researchers should modify or drop the planned study.

Kelman (1967) suggests role playing as an alternative to the use of deception.

A researcher invites participants to be partners in the investigation and encourages them not to behave in ways they think the researcher wants but conscientiously to assume the role and carry out the tasks that the researcher assigns.

A particular problem related to informed consent arises when faculty members or graduate students in a communication department are conducting research that involves students as subjects. Should students be required to participate in research projects? Some people say yes: Current students benefit from knowledge obtained in studies involving the students who preceded them, so they should make a parallel contribution to the students who will come after them. Others believe that coercing students yields only contaminated data and damages the teacher-student relationship. Requiring student participation in research is an unresolved issue. What do you think?

Whenever students are required to participate in studies, Lewin (1979) suggests several guidelines:

1. Students should first be convinced about the importance of their participation, so they will not withhold it for minor reasons.
2. Researchers should make participation as educational as possible by devoting adequate time to explaining its purpose and results.
3. An alternative means of satisfying the participation requirement, such as writing a report, should be available.
4. A mechanism, such as a departmental research ethics committee, should be available for reviewing projects before they are used as course requirements and for students who wish to complain about a particular study.

Another problem arises when conducting *field* studies. One cannot observe and record people's behavior unobtrusively if they are informed in advance, since knowing they are being studied may distort their behavior (the Hawthorne effect). Therefore, many researchers involve people in their research involuntarily. Piliavin, Rodin, and Piliavin (1969), for example, studied helping behavior by having a confederate stagger and fall to the floor in a subway car. In some cases the confederate appeared to be sick; in other cases he appeared to be intoxicated. They compared how many people helped, and how quickly, in each case. These bystanders did not know they were involved in a research study. Bochner (1979) calls this "street theater strategy"; typically, an incident is staged, and the reactions of people affected by it are recorded.

Cook and Campbell (1979), otherwise advocates of unobtrusive research, point out that "from ethical and perhaps legal perspectives, much technically feasible unobtrusive experimentation is not desirable since it violates the ethical requirement of 'informed consent'" (p. 369). They maintain that research is justified ethically only if what subjects are asked to do is innocuous, takes very little time or effort, and is within the range of the subjects' normal experience.

Another way researchers deal with the mandate to inform their subjects is providing a **debriefing** session *after* a study is completed. At this point, they clear up any deception used in the study and explain the full purpose of the study, as well as learn for themselves whether their hidden intentions were effective or were discovered by the subjects. Aronson and Carlsmith (1968) recommend the following procedures when conducting poststudy debriefings:

1. Ask the participants whether they have any questions, and answer them honestly and completely.
2. Ask participants if they did not understand parts of the study or whether they were confusing or disturbing.
3. Ask what they thought was being studied and how they felt about the study.
4. Provide any additional information so that participants are completely aware of all aspects of the study and why deception was necessary.

Being completely open when informing subjects about the results of their investigations during a debriefing is not always beneficial, however. In some studies, participants perform in ways that aren't commendable. Subjects in Milgram's (1963) famous study of obedience to authority, for example, found that they could be pressured to obey an authority even when such obedience (apparently) involved inflicting severe pain on another human being. Did it help or hinder the subjects to learn in the debriefing session that the doctor ordering the painful electric shocks was an actor who intimidated them into administering the electric shocks with his white coat, name tag, and authoritative voice?

Baumrind (1979) calls such feedback "inflicted insight" and maintains that it is not necessarily more ethical to reveal negative information about the subjects in a debriefing than to refrain from doing so. Dawes and Smith (1986) compare deception from debriefing in research to adultery and confession in marriage. In both cases, they suggest, "the debriefing may do more harm than the act itself. Besides, it doesn't undo the act" (p. 550). They maintain that if researchers think their deception is wrong in the first place, they shouldn't do it, and if they don't think it's wrong, they should shut up about it. So they recommend no debriefing at all and deception only in situations where debriefing wouldn't be necessary.

Treat people with respect. Most research is undertaken in an effort to learn something about how all people (or large groups of people) communicate. Thus an easy trap for researchers to fall into is forgetting to view and treat research subjects as individuals worthy of respect. Garfinkel (1967) reports that when one of his students conducted an ethnomethodological experiment on his family with no advance warning or explanation, his sister said, "Please, no more of these experiments. We're not rats, you know" (p. 49). Some authorities disapprove of the term *running subjects,* commonly used by researchers when conducting experiments, because of its dehumanizing implication that human subjects are like rats in mazes.

Sexism in research is one manifestation of a dehumanized view of people, according to Eichler (1988). She identifies four major symptoms of sexist research:

1. *Androcentricity,* viewing the world from a male perspective, such as assuming that power over others is something everyone wants.
2. *Overgeneralization,* when a study deals only with one sex but presents itself as applicable to both sexes, such as using the term ''parenting'' but studying only mothers.
3. *Gender insensitivity,* ignoring sex as a variable, such as not reporting the sex of research subjects or studying the speeches of a politician without considering their different effects on men and women.
4. *Double standards,* treating identical behaviors, traits, or situations in different ways, such as viewing interruptions during conversations by women as indicating poor listening ability and interruptions by men as indicating social power.

Comparable manifestations of bias, in terms of age or race, also violate the principle of respecting people. Researchers must be careful not to assume that their own world view encompasses all the ways that a research study or its findings may be perceived. Thus ethical researchers often invite their research subjects or at least representatives of the population being studied to provide input on the design of the studies and the interpretation of the results.

Ethical researchers also express their respect for people by using subjects' time and energy as efficiently and as effectively as possible. Efficiency means doing things right; effectiveness refers to doing the right things. Efficient researchers pilot-test their studies in order to be certain that all their procedures are clear and necessary. Investigators doing survey research, for example, will try out their questionnaire or interview protocol with a small sample of respondents to be sure that the meaning of each question is clear and that questions eliciting redundant information are eliminated. Effective researchers think long and hard in advance about the question being investigated; they consult with colleagues and review previous theory and research carefully before launching their study. In short, to be ethical, research must be competent.

Besides subjects, other individuals to whom researchers are accountable and whom they must respect include colleagues in their profession and members of society at large. Researchers who deceive their subjects unnecessarily, for example, encourage the stereotype that researchers are not to be trusted, that research is never about what researchers say it is, and the whole research community is tarnished as a result.

In the final analysis, a good commonsense guideline for treating research subjects with respect is the golden rule: Researchers should treat subjects as they would like to be treated—or even better.

Ethical Decisions Involving Research Findings

The findings from research are used to make important decisions. Here we consider ethical issues regarding how data are analyzed and reported, the public nature of scholarly research, and the general use of research findings.

Analyzing data and reporting findings.   Scholarship is cumulative and self-correcting, building on itself in a step-by-step process. The findings from scholarship, however, depend on the data collected and appropriate analyses of them.

Consumers of research rarely see the actual data themselves; instead, we take the findings on faith and read about the conclusions drawn from the analysis of the data. Only researchers see the actual data they collect. Therefore, they have an ethical responsibility to make sure that their data are collected in a valid and reliable manner and that they are analyzed using appropriate procedures. We know, however, that researchers often make mistakes when collecting data. For example, mistakes may occur in counting subjects' scores and recording their responses. The majority of the time these mistakes are in the direction of their research hypotheses (Kennedy, 1952; Laslo & Rosenthal, 1971; O'Leary, Kent, & Kanowitz, 1975; Rosenthal, 1966; Silverman, 1968). Ethical researchers therefore look closely at their data to catch, for example, skewed responses (such as someone answering all the questions "True" to get through a form quickly); incorrect coding, keying, or computer reading of data; and exceptions to the qualitative generalizations they would like to make about the context they are studying.

Worse yet, instances of outright falsification of data occasionally occur. False data may be given when research assistants are hired who have little commitment to professional ethics. For example, interviewers falsify data if they do not ask a question but record responses anyway or simply do not even conduct the interview but say they have (Andreski, 1972; Guest, 1947; Hyman, 1954; Roth, 1966; Sheatsley, 1947; Wyatt & Campbell, 1950). In observational research, interrater reliability coefficients have been increased by observers communicating with each other and then changing their coding to reflect greater agreement (O'Leary & Kent, 1973). Azrin, Holtz, Ulrich, and Goldiamond (1961) even found researchers who reported conducting an experiment that by design was practically impossible!

When scholars critique research reports, they occasionally find serious mistakes made in analyzing data. For example, some researchers use inappropriate statistical procedures that don't fit the nature of the data (Chapanis, 1963; Wolins, 1962), conduct too many post hoc, or follow-up, analyses that weren't planned (Lipset, Trow, & Coleman, 1970), perform a large number of statistical tests that will inevitably make some findings significant and then report only the significant ones (Barber, 1976; McNemar, 1960), report significant findings without indicating that the power of the findings is relatively low (Kish, 1970), or simply fail to report data that do not support the hypotheses (Lipset, Trow, & Coleman, 1970; Selvin, 1970).

Some data analysis deficiencies may actually be encouraged by the nature of academic publication procedures. Some journals, for example, tend only to accept articles for publication that report significant findings. Rosenthal (1966) argues that research needs to be reviewed on the basis of the importance of the questions it asks, the appropriateness of its design, and how effectively it was conducted, not by the results obtained.

Because it is difficult to evaluate the actual research data, researchers need to be as clear as possible when reporting what they were looking for, how they got the data they did, and how the data were analyzed. After all, the conclusions drawn from data are only as worthwhile as the data themselves and the analyses performed on them.

The public nature of scholarship. Fundamentally, scholarly research is public research. Researchers should not withhold the results of their research unless they honestly believe that releasing the results could be damaging or misleading. Professional ethics require that scholars be free to examine each other's research. But this principle does not always apply to privately funded research. Private research may be proprietary—firms may withhold findings, particularly from competitors. Laws exist to protect original discoveries, usually in the form of a patent or copyright.

One way in which researchers can subject their work to public scrutiny is to save their data and make them available to fellow researchers who have an honest need for them. Wolins (1962), wanting to study how well scholars abide by this standard, asked to see the original data from articles published in psychology journals. Fully 70 percent of the authors either did not respond or claimed that their data were lost. In 1973, Craig and Reese found that half of the authors they contacted did not supply their original data or a summary of them.

Researchers certainly have the right to protect themselves from having the fruits of their labors stolen under the guise of a request to examine data. However, if a researcher's results are ever challenged by a competent authority, such as a colleague, he or she should be able to substantiate the findings. So data generally should not be destroyed. Research is a collaborative process, requiring that data, and the findings obtained from them, be available as public information.

The use of research findings. Research findings are often used by people taking actions that affect society as a whole, such as advertisers, government officials, and business managers. Researchers therefore have the potential to affect the lives of many people. Kimmel (1988) explains, "Many individuals within the scientific community would argue that research ethics become increasingly important as the results of investigations acquire policy, professional, and personal implications outside the social science professions" (p. 12). In fact, Baumrin (1970) and Weber (1949) have argued that it is unethical *not* to use research findings to improve society.

Researchers need to consider the effects of their research on the people who use them or are affected by them. Lewin (1947) argued that researchers can be both scientists and practitioners simultaneously; the roles are not mutually exclusive. Although some researchers prefer to view themselves as testing pure theories, not practical applications, they need to realize that there is an important relationship between theory and practice.

As a final thought on the public use of research findings, we offer you a case and ask you to be the judge. During the Second World War, Nazi scientists conducted research on how people are affected by extremely cold weather by subjecting inmates at the Dachau concentration camp to freezing weather and letting them die.

Obviously, these experiments were completely unethical on all four of the bases we covered earlier. The fact is, however, that about 1000 people in the United States die each year from freezing weather (Moylan, 1988). Some doctors and researchers claim that they can save lives by using the knowledge obtained from these experiments.

The possible use of the knowledge obtained from these experiments is very controversial. Consider two points of view. Dennis B. Klein, director of the Anti-Defamation League International Center for Holocaust Studies in New York City, claims, "No matter how valuable this information may be, it should never be used because that could legitimize the Nazi experiments in some people's minds" (Moylan, 1988, p. 6). Professor Robert Rozos, a physiologist and a nationally known hypothermia expert at the University of Minnesota at Duluth, claims, "If there is some information we could glean in the experiments and help people live, should we use that information? Or should we let the Dachau people die in vain? I think we should use it" (Moylan, 1988, p. 6).

What do you think?

CONCLUSION

Ethical research involves important and complicated moral decisions about appropriate modes of conduct throughout the entire research process, including why researchers engage in research, how researchers treat subjects, what researchers do with data, and how they report the findings. Ethical research particularly requires taking into account the perspective of research subjects, looking after their interests, respecting their privacy, giving them as much information and free choice as possible, and treating them as worthwhile people, not just numbers. Finally, ethical researchers make great efforts to collect, analyze, and report their findings carefully and to consider the impact of their research on their colleagues and on society at large. Ethical research, in the final analysis, is thoughtful, competent research.

part III

METHODOLOGIES FOR CONDUCTING COMMUNICATION RESEARCH

chapter 8

Experimental Research

Albert Einstein once wrote, "Development of Western science is based on two great achievements: the invention of the formal logic system and the discovery of the possibility to find out causal relationships by systematic experiment" (Mackay, 1977, p. 51). Since the scientific method was pioneered during the Renaissance, human beings have grown enormously in their understanding and mastery of natural and social forces—and much of this growth can be attributed to creative and careful experimentation. Indeed, much knowledge in the field of communication was derived in this way.

Underlying experimentation work is the faith that behavior is not random. The messages we send are caused by what occurred beforehand and in turn cause how listeners respond—an ongoing cause-and-effect sequence. If we understand how one thing leads to another, we can predict communication processes and thereby control the social forces they influence. An **experiment** is a test of cause-and-effect sequences that researchers suspect exist.

Like a detective hot on the trail of a criminal guilty of a crime, the experimental researcher in communication believes that he or she knows what is cause and what is effect in a social situation. Let's call the suspect the independent variable and the victim or criminal act the dependent variable. The experiment is a controlled reenactment of the crime to assess the accuracy of the detective's hunches.

Does watching violent cartoon programs, for example, lead children to develop aggressive tendencies? Are some communication strategies more effective than others for persuading audience members to change their minds? What behaviors help speakers to be perceived as credible? Each question is concerned with establishing a **causal relationship** by determining whether changes in an independent variable produce changes in a dependent variable. When researchers want to establish causal relationships between variables, they use the *experimental method*—the subject of this chapter.

THE NATURE OF CAUSATION

Three requirements are necessary for establishing a causal relationship between an independent and a dependent variable (Lazarsfeld, 1959). All three requirements are necessary for inferring causality; none is sufficient in and of itself. First, the independent variable must precede the dependent variable. Unless something comes first in time, it cannot cause something else to occur. Second, the independent and dependent variable must be shown to covary, or go together. Unless two things are related in a *meaningful* way, how can one cause the other to occur? Running through a red light, for example, not only precedes causing an accident but is also related to the accident in a meaningful way. Third, the changes observed in the dependent variable must be the result of changes in the independent variable and not some other, unknown variable. This last criterion requires researchers to make sure that the causal relationship is a valid one, rather than the result of the various internal validity threats discussed in Chapter 7.

The first two criteria are fairly easy to meet in experimental research. Researchers can expose children to violent cartoons, for example, and observe whether there are meaningful changes in their aggressive behavior. It is much harder, however, to rule out alternative explanations, called **alternate causality arguments,** that might account for the changes in the dependent variable, especially for the complex phenomena studied in the human sciences. Experimental research was pioneered in the natural sciences, where consistent causal relationships are fairly easy to establish. In the human sciences, however, causal relationships are more difficult to measure. Many hereditary and environmental factors may cause children to develop aggressive tendencies, only one of which is watching violent cartoons. Therefore, we must talk about causation in the human sciences tentatively. In the human sciences, experimental research is used to look for the partial effects, or probable influences, of independent variables on dependent variables.

EXERCISING CONTROL IN EXPERIMENTAL RESEARCH

To measure the effect of an independent variable on a dependent variable, experimental researchers must exercise a good deal of control. **Control** means that a researcher "tries systematically to rule out variables that are possible 'causes' of the

effects he is studying other than the variable that he has hypothesized to be 'causes''"
(Kerlinger, 1973, p. 4).

Control is not either present or absent. It exists on a continuum, ranging from
tightly controlled experiments to experiments that demonstrate little control. What
distinguishes one end of the continuum from the other is the extent to which researchers are able to do three things: (1) manipulate an independent variable, (2)
establish equivalent experimental groups, and (3) control for the influence of extraneous variables.

Manipulating an Independent Variable

To be sure that changes in an independent variable cause observed changes in a
dependent variable, subjects' exposure to the independent variable must be controlled. Being able to regulate the extent to which people are exposed to an independent variable provides a high degree of control. Conversely, not being able to regulate exposure to an independent variable provides a low degree of control.

In highly controlled experiments, researchers *manipulate* an independent variable by controlling when, how, or how much of it subjects receive. When researchers
manipulate an independent variable, it is called an *active variable.*

A classic experimental manipulation of an independent variable is to divide
subjects into two different **experimental conditions** or **groups,** one group that receives a manipulation (the **treatment group**) and another group that does not (the
control group). For example, W. Douglas (1985) wanted to see the effects of anticipated interaction on information seeking. All subjects watched a videotaped interaction between a female (the target) and a male, but those in the treatment group were
told to expect interaction with the target after viewing the videotape, whereas those
in the control group received no such instructions. After watching the videotape,
subjects were asked to indicate all they had seen or heard that was informative. The
results showed that subjects' recall of the interactional sequences in the treatment
group was more complete than that of the passive observers, which suggests that
anticipated interaction leads to more vigilant information seeking.

Another way to manipulate an independent variable is by exposing subjects to
different levels or types. Hoffner, Cantor, and Thorson (1988), for example, studied
how children understand a televised narrative by exposing children of three age levels to a story in one of three videotape formats: audiovisual, video only, or audio
only. By comparing children's comprehension and recall in the nine experimental
conditions, the researchers were able to conclude that "understanding and integrating temporal aspects of a narrative are more difficult for young children when the
story is presented visually than when it is presented verbally, whereas older children
comprehend narratives in both formats equally well" (p. 227).

Many researchers also manipulate an independent variable by establishing different treatment groups as well as a control group that does not receive the treatment. For example, Berger and Kellermann (1989) explored the tactics by which
individuals withhold information from inquisitive others. One treatment group was

told to reveal as little as possible about themselves (low revealers), while another treatment group was told to reveal as much as they could about themselves (high revealers). Subjects in the control group were told just to have a typical conversation. Each group of subjects was then paired with a person told to find out as much as possible about his or her partner (high seekers) in a five-minute conversation. The interactions were videotaped, and observers rated each participant on a number of scales. Comparisons of the experimental groups revealed that evasiveness was accomplished primarily by proffering uninformative content and by refocusing the conversation on one's partner. The behavior of high revealers was also judged to be less appropriate than normal revealers but not as inappropriate as that of low revealers. Berger and Kellermann conclude, "It appears that being evasive is a greater social sin than being overly disclosive" (p. 341).

It is not always possible, or even desirable, to manipulate an independent variable. Suppose that researchers wanted to find out whether a pay raise leads to increased job performance. In a highly controlled experiment, they could bring subjects into a laboratory setting, create jobs for them, and manipulate a reward by giving it to some subjects and not to others. Then they could observe whether the people who received the reward performed better than those who did not receive it. However, this procedure probably decreases the real-life nature of the experiment, its ecological validity, since the subjects would not have the same kind of emotional investment in an environment that is created artificially as they would in their actual work environment. This environmental artificiality might result in finding no relationship, or a relatively small one, between pay raises and employee job performance, even if a large relationship was in fact present.

Researchers therefore usually exercise less control in natural settings. In the real world, however, some employees get pay raises while others don't; the former may be considered a treatment group and the latter a control group, and their job performance could be compared. An independent variable that is not manipulated directly by a researcher (either because it occurs naturally, such as a tornado, or is controlled by another person, such as an employer) is called an *observed variable*. Just observing, of course, affords less control over the experiment than manipulating an independent variable does.

Creating Equivalent Experimental Groups

When experimental researchers manipulate an independent variable, they typically use at least two groups, one that receives the manipulation and one that doesn't, or two groups that differ in the type or amount of manipulation they receive. The term **comparison group** is used in the broad sense to imply any group against which another is compared to look for differences, whereas the term **control group** refers to a no-treatment comparison group.

Researchers need to be as certain as possible that the experimental groups started off equivalent; otherwise, changes in a dependent variable might be a result of the initial differences between the groups, called subject selection, rather than the manipulation of the independent variable. Suppose that a researcher wants to know whether a particular advertisement makes subjects more likely to vote for a candidate. Some subjects are exposed to the ad, while others are not, and their intended voting behavior is assessed. It is possible, however, that the majority of subjects who are exposed to the ad are supporters of the candidate while those in the control group are primarily opponents of that candidate. In this case, differences in the subjects selected, not the advertisement, account for the voting behavior.

Experiments that demonstrate high control are able to rule out initial differences between the experimental groups, whereas those low in control cannot rule out this internal validity threat. Researchers thus strive to establish equivalent experimental groups, which is accomplished by using random assignment. When this procedure is not possible, researchers attempt to establish quasi-equivalent experimental groups, which is accomplished by using pretests. When researchers don't check on initial differences, they create *nonequivalent* experimental groups. In such cases, there is no assurance that changes in a dependent variable are the result of changes in an independent variable, because the threat of subject selection cannot be ruled out. Of course, nonequivalent experimental groups provide slightly more control than using no comparison group.

Random assignment. In Chapter 6 we stressed the importance of *randomly selecting* subjects for establishing external validity so that the results from a sample can be generalized back to the population from which it came. A procedure called *random assignment* is used to control for the internal validity of an experiment. With **random assignment,** also known as **randomization,** each person has an equal chance of being assigned to any particular experimental group.

Random assignment is done like random sampling, except the random numbers table now is used to put subjects into the various experimental conditions. Random sampling is thus concerned with how subjects are selected in the first place, whereas random assignment is concerned with how subjects are placed into the experimental conditions. None of the experiments reviewed so far in this chapter, for example, selected subjects randomly, but subjects were assigned randomly to the experimental conditions. Research that uses both random sampling and random assignment is high in external and internal validity.

Random assignment gives the greatest possible assurance that experimental groups are equivalent because initial differences between people that threaten internal validity are distributed evenly across the experimental conditions. As Wright (1979) notes:

> The advantage of randomization is thus that important variables and processes which can potentially produce the observed differences between experimental and control groups operate as *random error.* In the vocabulary of statistics, random error has the characteristic that its expected or long run average is zero—that is, some errors will be positive, some will be negative, but in the long run they average out to zero or cancel out. (p. 38)

Random assignment therefore assures that any changes in a dependent variable are not due to differences between the subjects selected for the experiment.

Random assignment, however, does not guarantee perfectly equivalent experimental groups in any single instance. Suppose that researchers wanted to conduct an experiment to find out which of two basketball coaching philosophies (the independent variable) leads to higher scores (the dependent variable). They could divide 10 people randomly into two basketball teams and have a pretty good chance of creating teams that were balanced equally. Unfortunately, if one of the players is named Michael Jordan or Magic Johnson and the other nine players are schoolyard players, random assignment will not result in equally matched teams. In most cases, however, random assignment gives the best possible odds of creating equivalent experimental groups.

Pretests. When researchers aren't able to assign subjects randomly to experimental conditions or want additional assurance that random assignment was successful in creating equivalent groups, they can assess whether some initial differences exist between subjects by using *pretests*. A **pretest** measures subjects in the experimental groups on relevant variables that need to be accounted for *before* exposing the treatment groups to the manipulation of the independent variable. For example, Smith (1989) conducted an experiment to determine how design and color affect newspaper credibility. To rule out subject selection as a competing explanation, subjects were pretested and those who were not frequent readers of the newspapers being used in the experiment were excluded from the study.

Pretests are most often used to measure subjects on a dependent variable before the experimental manipulation occurs. If subjects' scores in the experimental groups are generally equivalent, researchers are more assured that any differences between the groups after the treatment are probably due to the treatment and not subject selection.

Pretesting is not as effective as random assignment for assuring equivalent groups because there may be important differences between subjects in the experimental groups that can't all be accounted for by pretests. In addition, pretests of a dependent variable may interact with an experimental treatment and cause a change that the treatment alone would not have produced. Pretests may also sensitize subjects in the two groups differently, which can lead to misleading results. For these reasons, only using pretests creates what we call "quasi-equivalent experimental groups."

Controlling for Extraneous Variables

Manipulating the independent variable and controlling for subject selection through random assignment and/or pretests are the most powerful tools researchers have for controlling for the influence of extraneous variables. These procedures do not, however, control for all of the potential threats to internal validity discussed in Chapter 7. Here we review the three general threats to internal validity that experimental researchers must control for: threats due to researchers, how the research is conducted, and subjects.

Threats due to researchers.   Researchers' behavior can be a threat to the internal validity of experiments because it introduces the possibility that changes in a dependent variable are a result of responses to the researcher rather than to the manipulation of an independent variable. Members of experimental groups may respond differentially to a manipulation of an independent variable because of the personal characteristics of the experimenter (the researcher personal attribute effect) or because a researcher unintentionally gives cues as to the "correct" response (the researcher unintentional expectancy effect).

To control for the researcher personal attribute effect, subjects can be matched with researchers, or a wide variety of researchers can be employed to try to limit the effect to a few subjects. The most common procedure for controlling for the researcher unintentional expectancy effect is to employ an assistant to conduct the research who does not know the purpose of the research or the hypothesized results. In addition, when researchers want to manipulate a person's behavior, such as lying or self-disclosure, to see its effects on another person's behavior, they typically employ **confederates,** people who are part of an experimental manipulation. To control for the unintentional expectancy effect, confederates usually aren't told the goals of the research. In both cases, researchers are separated from the actual research conducted so as not to influence subjects' behavior.

Threats due to how research is conducted.   The way research is conducted can also pose a major threat to the internal validity of an experiment. A lack of procedural reliability, for example, makes it unclear whether differences between groups are due to the independent variable or the different treatments. Treatment reliability requires that researchers conduct the experiment in as similar a manner as possible with all subjects. This includes what is said during an experiment and exposing subjects to the experimental treatment in exactly the same way. For example, Tamborini, Stiff, and Zillman (1987) studied people's preference for graphic horror by manipulating whether subjects saw a film containing male or female victimization. To make sure that the subjects in their experiment got *precisely* the same treatment, they had them listen to tape-recorded instructions.

To make sure that procedures are valid and reliable, researchers will pretest their methods. Some researchers conduct a **pilot study** wherein procedures that will be used in the experiment are given to a small subsample, and any perceived problems are remedied. Other researchers use independent-variable manipulations or measurement techniques that have been found to be valid and reliable from other studies. Runco and Pezdek (1984), for example, tested the effects of television and radio on children's creativity by using videotapes from a previous study by Greenfield, Gerber, Beagles-Roos, Farrar, and Gat (1981) as well as a standardized measure of creative potential developed and tested by Torrance (1974).

When employing confederates, researchers must train them to manipulate their behavior in a consistent manner. For example, Schultz (1982) wanted to manipulate a leader's argumentativeness to see its effects on group decision making and leadership perception. She first had groups discuss a problem and then had members rate all other members on 19 variables associated with leadership emergence. The top-scoring individual from each group was chosen as a confederate and received special training in how to argue for unpopular or minority views. The confederates then participated in the actual experiment by being assigned to a group and asked to advocate an extreme position and to argue forcibly and with persistence but not to reveal that they were playing a role.

In addition to pretesting procedures, researchers will conduct **manipulation checks** using questionnaires, interviews, and observations to make sure that the manipulation of the independent variable was successful. Schultz (1982), for example, used self-report scales to assess whether the confederates had indeed been argumentative. The rating showed that trained confederate leaders were significantly more argumentative than untrained leaders. Conscientious pretesting and manipulation checks thus give researchers more confidence in the accuracy and reliability of their experimental manipulations.

The way in which variables are measured also enhances or threatens the internal validity of an experiment. Experimental researchers, like all researchers, rely on questionnaires, interviews, and observations to measure variables. For example, Tamborini, Stiff, and Zillman (1987) used questionnaires to assess subjects' preferences for graphic horror in films, whereas Lewis (1989) interviewed subjects in their own homes to find out how they responded to different formats and locations for newspaper ads. deTurck and Miller (1985) observed deceivers' and truth tellers' arousal every second on a skin resistance amplifier. Whatever measurement technique is employed, it must be reliable if researchers are to establish a high degree of control necessary for ascertaining causal relationships between independent and dependent variables.

Another threat due to how research is conducted is history, changes in the environment external to the experiment that may influence subjects' responses. To control for this threat, researchers run experimental groups at the same time. They also inquire in debriefing sessions about any environmental factors that impinged on subjects' behavior during the experiment.

Threats due to subjects.   Threats due to subjects, such as selection, statistical regression (the tendency for subjects selected on the basis of extreme scores to regress toward the mean on a second measurement), and maturation (internal changes in subjects over time), are largely controlled for through random assignment. Pretests also reveal whether an extreme group has been selected. Researchers also control for maturation by measuring subjects in the experimental groups on the dependent variable at the same time.

Experimental researchers also attempt to control for such subject threats as the Hawthorne effect (the tendency for subjects to change their behavior because they know they are being observed), mortality (differential loss of subjects from experimental conditions), and intersubject bias (subjects influencing one another). Researchers control for the Hawthorne effect by not letting subjects know they are being observed, perhaps by using a one-way mirror or misleading subjects about the true purpose of the experiment or about which part of a multistage experiment is the actual manipulation. Researchers also employ many subjects to minimize the threat due to subject mortality. Finally, researchers take great care to prevent subjects from discussing an experiment. For example, to study differences in communication processes and outcomes between face-to-face and computerized conferences, Hiltz, Johnson, and Turoff (1986) assigned students from the same class to different groups, which helped minimize communication between them. Researchers also stress during debriefings the importance of not discussing an experiment with future subjects.

LABORATORY AND FIELD EXPERIMENTS

Experiments differ according to the setting in which they are conducted. A **laboratory experiment** takes place in a setting created by researchers, while a **field experiment** takes place in subjects' natural setting.

Experimental research is typically conducted in a laboratory setting because it allows researchers to manipulate independent variables easily, assign subjects randomly to experimental conditions, control for the influence of extraneous variables, and measure subjects' behavior, especially communication behavior. For example, Hiltz and colleagues (1986) conducted their research on computerized and face-to-face conferences in a laboratory. Subjects in the computerized conference (CC) condition received training for one week on how to use the computer terminal prior to participating in the experiment. During the experiment, subjects in the CC condition worked alone in a room with the door closed, and all instructions were delivered via computer. Subjects in the face-to-face condition met in "a room with a round table, a microphone connected to recorders at each place, and one-way mirrors on two sides for observation" (p. 233). These procedures enabled the researchers to record all of the communication that took place between group members. Thus laboratories help researchers conduct highly controlled experiments.

Although people typically picture a laboratory as a place with scientists in white coats, test tubes, and Bunsen burners, a laboratory is actually any research environment that is set up by researchers, including ones created in subjects' natural setting. For example, when Hoffner and coworkers (1988) studied children's understanding of a televised narrative, they wanted the experiment to take place in a natural but controlled setting, so they used "a quiet room within the child's school building" (p. 233). This laboratory setting maximized both the internal and the external validity of the experiment.

Laboratories allow researchers to exercise high control, but often they can minimize external validity because subjects may respond differently in laboratories than in natural settings. Many experimental researchers, particularly organizational communication, public communication, and journalism researchers, maximize external validity by conducting field experiments in subjects' natural settings. For example, Miller and Monge (1985) wanted to study the effects of information on employee anxiety about organizational change. The experiment was conducted in a company that was planning a move to a new building within six weeks. The independent variable of information was manipulated by sending some employees positive information about the move and others negative information, while a control group received no information about the move. Employees' level of anxiety about the organizational move then was assessed. One finding from this field experiment was that any information, whether positive or negative, was better at reducing anxiety than no information.

Field experiments are often conducted to take advantage of particular situations or events. Pfau and Burgoon (1988), for example, wanted to know how to design political campaign messages so as to inoculate supporters of candidates against subsequent attack messages by opposing candidates. They first selected 733 adult residents in the Sioux Falls, South Dakota, metropolitan area during a U.S. Senate campaign and assigned subjects randomly to treatment or control conditions. They then sent subjects political campaign messages that were manipulated in three ways: political party orientation (strong, weak, none, or crossover), inoculation condition (none, refutational same, or refutational novel), and attack messages (issue or character attacks). The findings showed that inoculation messages do confer resistance to attitude change following exposure to a persuasive attack, but the effect is most apparent among strong political party identifiers.

The quality of experimental research is thus determined not by where it takes place but by the amount of control researchers exercise. Whether in a laboratory or in the field, experimental researchers exercise high control when they are able to manipulate independent variables, assign subjects randomly to experimental conditions to create equivalent groups, and control for the effects of extraneous variables. Typically, however, laboratory experiments maximize internal validity, and field experiments maximize external validity.

EXPERIMENTAL RESEARCH DESIGNS

Campbell and Stanley (1963) identify three general types of experimental designs: (1) **full,** or **true, experiments,** (2) **quasi-experiments,** and (3) **preexperiments.** These experimental designs differ according to whether an independent variable is manipulated or observed, whether random assignment is used, and what types of equivalent experimental groups are created. These three types of experiments can be charted on a continuum of control, ranging from highly controlled experiments (full experiments) to ones that demonstrate little or no control (preexperiments; see Figure 8.1).

Full experiments are the most controlled because the independent variable is manipulated and subjects are assigned randomly to conditions, thus creating equivalent experimental groups. If these three controls are not present, the study is not a full experiment.

Figure 8.1 A comparison of full experiments, quasi-experiments, and preexperiments

Type of Experiment	Manipulation of Independent Variable	Random Assignment	Experimental Groups	Control of Extraneous Variables
Full experiment	Manipulate	Yes	Equivalent	High
Quasi-experiment	Manipulate or observe	No	Quasi-equivalent or multiple intragroup comparisons	Moderate
Preexperiment	Manipulate or observe	No	Nonequivalent or no comparison group	Low

Quasi-experiments either manipulate or observe the independent variable and may or may not have a comparison group. When there is a comparison group, subjects are not assigned randomly to conditions; hence the experimental groups are not equivalent. Researchers do, however, attempt to establish quasi-equivalent experimental groups by using pretests. In cases where there is only one experimental condition, multiple observations are used as baseline measures to assess changes before and after the experimental treatment.

Preexperiments manipulate or observe the independent variable and may or may not have two experimental groups. When there is a comparison group, subjects are not assigned randomly to conditions, nor are individual differences between experimental groups assessed, which means that the groups are nonequivalent. Preexperiments thus demonstrate the least amount of control of the three types of experiments.

Full Experimental Designs

Three full experimental designs are the pretest-posttest control group design, the posttest-only control group design, and the Solomon four-group design (see Figure 8.2). Each of these full experimental designs manipulates an independent variable, assigns subjects randomly to experimental conditions, and thus creates equivalent experimental groups.

Pretest-posttest control group design. A traditional full experiment is the pretest-posttest with control group design (see Figure 8.2a). Subjects are first assigned randomly to a treatment group or a control group. All subjects are then given a pretest that measures the dependent variable prior to the experimental manipulation. Remember that random assignment does not always *guarantee* equivalent groups for any single experiment. Comparing the pretests of the two groups adds assurance that they start off equivalent. The treatment group then receives the experimental manipulation while the control group does not. Finally, all subjects are given a **posttest** that measures the dependent variable after the manipulation of the independent variable. Posttest scores for the experimental groups are compared to learn what effect, if any, the independent variable had on the dependent variable.

This pretest-posttest control group design gives a researcher a great deal of control by minimizing the various internal validity threats. Random assignment and the pretest ensure, as much as possible, that the groups started equivalent and thus that any posttest differences between the experimental groups are not due to subject selection. A researcher can also be relatively confident that changes in the independent variable are due to the experimental treatment if the posttest score for the treatment group (O_2) is greater than the posttest score for the control group (O_4) and if O_1, O_3, and O_4 are equal.

Posttest-only control group design. One possible shortcoming of the pretest-posttest control group design is that the pretest may sensitize subjects to the depen-

Figure 8.2 Full experimental designs

(a) Pretest-Posttest Control Group Design

$$R \; \diagdown \; \begin{matrix} O_1 & X_1 & O_2 \\ O_3 & X_0 & O_4 \end{matrix}$$

(b) Posttest-Only Control Group Design

$$R \; \diagdown \; \begin{matrix} X_1 & O_1 \\ X_0 & O_2 \end{matrix}$$

(c) Solomon Four-Group Design

$$R \; \diagup \; \begin{matrix} O_1 & X_1 & O_2 \\ O_3 & X_0 & O_4 \\ & X_1 & O_5 \\ & & O_6 \end{matrix}$$

Note: The following notation system is used to explain all experimental designs:

R   = random assignment of subjects to an experimental group (creates equivalent experimental groups)

O   = observation (measurement) of subjects on a dependent variable

X   = experimental manipulation of an independent variable (X_1 = a treatment; X_0 = no treatment). (For the purposes of discussion, a treatment group will be contrasted against a control group in all designs; however, these designs also could include different treatment types or levels, such as X_1 and X_2.)

Y   = experimental manipulation of a second independent variable

----   = quasi-equivalent experimental groups

. . . .   = nonequivalent experimental groups

dent variable and affect posttest scores. When sensitization occurs, changes from O_1 to O_2 are not a result of the treatment but of having taken the pretest. Consider, for example, how much better you'd be likely to do on a "second chance" final examination!

When researchers believe that a pretest may sensitize subjects to a posttest, they use a posttest-only control group design (see Figure 8.2b). This design is the same as the previous design, except that pretests are not used. Because subjects are assigned randomly to conditions, the experimental groups are assumed to be equivalent with or without pretests. As Campbell and Stanley (1963) argue:

> While the pretest is a concept deeply embedded in the thinking of research workers, . . . it is not actually essential to true experimental designs. For psychological reasons it is difficult to give up "knowing for sure" that the experimental and control groups

were "equal" before the differential experimental treatments. Nonetheless, the most adequate all-purpose assurance of lack of initial bias between groups is randomization. (p. 25)

Huck, Cormier, and Bounds (1974) conclude that "there is general agreement that, unless there is some question as to the genuine randomness of the assignment, the posttest-only design is as good as, if not better than, the pretest-posttest design" (p. 253).

Solomon four-group design.   The Solomon four-group design combines the pretest-posttest control group and the posttest-only control group designs (see Figure 8.2c). This design both controls for the influence of the pretest on the posttest (by comparing O_2 against O_5 as well as O_4 against O_6) and shows whether the combination of the pretest with the experimental treatment produces an effect different from the experimental treatment alone (by comparing O_2 and O_5). Any effect that is due to a combination of two or more things (such as a pretest and an experimental treatment or two different treatments) is called an **interaction effect,** discussed later in this chapter.

Although the Solomon four-group design is a powerful one for determining the effects of an independent variable on a dependent variable, it also requires twice as many subjects as the other two full experimental designs. Thus it has not been used as frequently as the other two designs in communication research.

Quasi-experimental Designs

It is frequently not feasible or desirable to conduct full experiments, particularly in natural settings. Effects demonstrated in the laboratory must also be studied in the real world. Just because a particular group discussion technique (such as consensus) leads to a better decision in a controlled laboratory experiment doesn't mean it will work equally well within organizations. The demands of the real world are often quite different from the conditions established in the laboratory.

Researchers conducting field experiments are usually visitors in the natural setting and must work within restrictions imposed by that setting. These restrictions might mean, for example, that it is impossible to manipulate an independent variable by having different experimental conditions. People in the groups may discuss their different treatments and infer reasons for being treated differently that influence their reactions and confound the results. Withholding a treatment from a control group may also be unethical if the treatment is likely to work. Most important, researchers conducting field experiments are usually unable to assign people randomly to experimental conditions. Thus many factors may prevent the use of full experimental designs in the field.

Nevertheless, field experimenters often study causal relationships between variables with some degree of control by using quasi-experimental designs. Quasi-experimental designs are a compromise between highly controlled experiments and ones with little or no control. Quasi-experimental designs maximize the real-world transferability of research findings, while sacrificing some degree of internal validity. Huck and colleagues (1974) explain:

> Quasi-experimental and true experimental designs differ in the degree to which threats to internal and external validity are controlled. Generally, true experimental designs can have greater control over internal threats than over external threats, while quasi-experimental designs have greater control over external threats to validity. (pp. 301-302)

Although quasi-experimental designs are numerous, with many variations on each, we examine three designs: the nonequivalent control group design, the time series design, and the multiple time series design (see Figure 8.3).

Nonequivalent control group design.   Suppose that an oganization is getting ready to send some, but not all, of its managers to a communication training program to increase their supervisor-subordinate communication skills. In this situation, all the ingredients for a quasi-experimental design exist. A treatment group, those who will receive the training, and a control group, those who will not, can be observed. However, they are not equivalent because the managers aren't assigned randomly to each group.

The nonequivalent control group design (see Figure 8.3a) could be used in this case to examine the effects of the independent variable (the communication training program) on the dependent variable (the increase in supervisor-subordinate communication skills). This design has a treatment group and a control group, as well as pretest and posttest observations, which makes it similar superficially to the pretest-posttest control group full experimental design. This design differs, however, be-

---

Figure 8.3   Quasi-experimental designs

(a) Nonequivalent Control Group Design

$$O_1 \quad X_1 \quad O_2$$
$$\text{-----------------------------}$$
$$O_3 \quad X_0 \quad O_4$$

(b) Time Series Design

$$O_1 \quad O_2 \quad O_3 \quad X_1 \quad O_4 \quad O_5 \quad O_6$$

(c) Multiple Time Series Design

$$O_1 \quad O_2 \quad O_3 \quad X_1 \quad O_4 \quad O_5 \quad O_6$$
$$\text{---}$$
$$O_1 \quad O_2 \quad O_3 \quad X_0 \quad O_4 \quad O_5 \quad O_6$$

---

cause people are not assigned randomly to the experimental conditions, in this case because preselected managers will be sent to the communication training program.

Since random assignment is not used, the experimental groups are not equivalent. Cook and Campbell (1979) explain that this means that "the task confronting persons who try to interpret the results from quasi-experiments is basically one of separating the effects of a treatment from those due to the initial incompatibility between the average units in each treatment group" (p. 6). However, what differentiates a quasi-experimental design from a preexperimental design is the attempt to establish some equivalence between the experimental groups.

The pretest in a nonequivalent control group design accounts partly for initial differences by measuring whether the treatment and the control groups start off significantly different on the dependent variable, although the pretest may sensitize subjects to the posttest. The pretest does not, however, ensure that the experimental groups are equivalent, as random assignment does. For this reason, the comparison group is a *quasi-equivalent comparison group,* and we prefer to call this the **quasi-equivalent control group design.**

Time series design.   Field researchers cannot always provide an experimental group against which to compare a treatment group. Sometimes they are interested in the effects of an independent variable on a dependent variable for an entire population or a specific sample. For example, an organization might want all its managers to attend a communication training program, making it impossible to compare people who attended with people who did not. In such a case, the time series quasi-experimental design can be used (see Figure 8.3b).

Campbell and Stanley (1963) explain, "The essence of the time-series design is the presence of a periodic measurement process on some group or individual and the introduction of an experimental change into this time series of measurements" (p. 37). Although this design does not have a control group against which to compare the treatment group, an attempt is made to determine whether changes in a dependent variable are due to the influence of an independent variable. To do this, the time series design uses multiple pretests to establish intragroup baseline comparisons. If differences between the pretests are not significant but differences between the last pretest and the first posttest are, researchers are more confident that any changes are the result of the treatment. In addition, multiple posttests help to measure the long-term effects of a treatment. Using multiple pretest or posttest measurements (or multiple treatments) with the same set of subjects within any experimental design is known as a **repeated-measures design.**

Using multiple pretests, however, may sensitize subjects to the posttests. The lack of an equivalent comparison group also limits the confidence researchers can place in the results. They do not know for sure whether a group not exposed to the treatment would demonstrate the same kind of changes as the treatment group.

Multiple time series design.   The multiple time series design combines the nonequivalent control group design with the time series design (see Figure 8.3c).

This is done by assigning subjects nonrandomly to either a treatment group or a control group and measuring both groups using a series of pretests and posttests.

This quasi-experimental design contains some important features that increase researchers' confidence regarding a causal relationship between two variables. If the pretests for the groups are not significantly different, quasi-equivalent comparison groups are established. In addition, if scores for the last pretest and the first posttest are significantly different for the treatment group but not for the control group, researchers are more confident about the effects of the treatment than with a time series design alone. Finally, the long-term effects of the treatment can be seen by comparing the posttests for both the treatment and the control groups. Unfortunately, the pretests might still sensitize subjects to the posttests.

The multiple time series design maximizes the internal validity of a study when random assignment cannot be used. This design, like the other quasi-experimental designs, thus represents a compromise, providing a moderate degree of control when full experimental designs are not possible or desirable.

Preexperimental Designs

Preexperimental designs are superficially similar to quasi-experimental designs in that a treatment may or may not be manipulated, different experimental conditions may or may not be created, and random assignment is not used when there are multiple experimental groups. Preexperimental designs differ from quasi-experimental designs, however, in that no attempt is made to establish equivalence between the treatment group and any comparison group. In addition, when there only is one treatment group, preexperimental designs do not use multiple pretests to establish an intragroup baseline comparison.

Preexperiments thus demonstrate the least amount of control when compared to full and quasi-experimental designs. Indeed, Huck and colleagues (1974) call these "pseudoexperimental designs" because they do not allow researchers to rule out competing explanations for changes in the dependent variable. They argue that "it is impossible to make completely valid inferences from the results of studies that use pseudoexperimental designs" (p. 227).

Nevertheless, preexperimental designs are quite common in communication research. These designs include the one-shot case study, the one-group pretest-posttest design, and the static group comparison design (see Figure 8.4).

One-shot case study design. The one-shot case study measures a treatment group after exposure to an independent variable (see Figure 8.4a). Suppose that a television advertising salesperson is trying to convince a client to continue advertising on that channel because the company's product sales increased during the past year. A first glance, this might appear to be a valid causal argument: Increased advertising leads to increased sales.

There are, however, many problems with this claim. Suppose that all products advertised on all channels experienced increased sales in the past year because of an

Figure 8.4 Preexperimental designs

(a) One-Shot Case Study Design

X_1 O_1

(b) One-Group Pretest-Posttest Design

O_1 X_1 O_2

(c) Static Group Comparison Design

X_1 O_1
....
X_0 O_2

upturn in the economy. Perhaps products sold on other television channels had bigger sales increases. It is not possible to know what caused the rise in sales since no comparison group was used—a preexperimental design. It even is possible that the product would have experienced a greater increase in sales if it had not been advertised at all!

Though this design is extremely problematic, there are instances where the one-shot case study is the only design possible. What if a researcher wanted to know whether an unexpected disaster, such as the explosion of the *Challenger* space shuttle, changed the public's stance on an issue? If that stance had been tested prior to the disaster, a quasi-experimental design could be used. But since such a disaster was not anticipated, there is no pretest score. In such instances, the one-shot case study is the only feasible design. In addition, case studies often serve as preliminary research, the results of which are then used to design quasi- and full experiments to assess the observed effects in a more controlled fashion.

One-group pretest-posttest design.   The one-group pretest-posttest design (see Figure 8.4b) is superior to the one-shot case study because it adds an important feature, a pretest. This pretest allows researchers to compare the time$_1$ with the time$_2$ measurements. For example, if a researcher had measured the public's support for the space program prior to the *Challenger* disaster and immediately after it, more would be known about the effects of that disaster on the public's support for the space program.

There are, however, many rival explanations that may not be controlled for by this design. If the pretest and the posttest are far apart in time, extraneous variables, such as other events—say, an announced rise in the federal budget deficit or a successful space launch by the Soviet Union—could explain changes in the dependent variable. Sensitization may also be a problem, and there is no comparison group in this design.

At times, this preexperimental design is the only one available. This design also can lead to the quasi-experimental time series design if additional pretests and posttests are possible. However, because of the threats to internal validity, researchers cannot be confident about the effects of an independent variable on a dependent variable when using the one-group pretest-posttest design.

Static group comparison design. The static group comparison design (see Figure 8.4c) affords researchers the most amount of control of these preexperimental designs. This design is similar to the one-shot case study design except that it adds an important feature, a control group that does not receive the treatment.

There are, however, many threats to the internal validity of this preexperimental design. Without random assignment of subjects to the experimental groups, they are not equivalent. In addition, no attempt is made to create quasi-equivalent experimental groups through the use of a pretest. Therefore, a nonequivalent control group is being compared with a treatment group. As a result, researchers can never be sure that changes in a dependent variable are the result of a treatment and not due to initial differences between the groups.

Again, at times the static group comparison design is the only one feasible, as when researchers study how an observed treatment affected two different intact groups (hence the term *static*). For example, a researcher might use this design to study the effects of a hastily called televised presidential address on the public's support for the president. The researcher probably could find people who had and had not watched the televised address and could compare these groups. If the researcher found that the people who watched the address were more likely to vote for the president in a coming election than those who didn't watch the address, could it be assumed that the single address caused the difference? Of course not. It could be that the two groups differed initially on their support for the president. Perhaps there were other circumstances that members of the treatment group knew about (such as a nuclear arms treaty with the Russians), but the control group did not, which increased their support.

Notice that this design, however, could be converted into a nonequivalent control group quasi-experimental design by adding pretests for each group. It could also be converted into a posttest-only control group full experimental design if subjects can be assigned randomly to the conditions.

In summary, researchers conduct full experiments whenever possible. When full experimental designs are not possible or place severe limits on the external validity of the research, researchers conduct quasi-experiments. Researchers conduct preexperiments whenever that is the only design available.

FACTORIAL DESIGNS

Up to now, we have referred to the independent variable as if there is only one, and subjects either do or don't experience it or are exposed to different types or amounts of it. Because communication is such a complex process, researchers are usually interested in examining the effects of more than one independent variable on a dependent variable. For example, Schenck-Hamlin (1978) manipulated both dialect (southern and midwestern) and message relevance (one relevant and one irrelevant to the southern stereotype) to observe the effects of dialectical similarity, stereotyping, and message agreement on the speaker evaluation variables of source competence, character appeal, interpersonal attraction, and message coherence. Meadowcroft and Reeves (1989) manipulated three variables to study the influence of story schema development (schemata are organized memory structures that lead to predictions about upcoming material, and story schema is memory about how stories are structured) on children's attention to television: story schema development (low or high), story content (central or incidental), and story structure (story versus nonstory).

In theory, researchers can investigate the simultaneous effects of as many independent variables as they deem important. When there is more than one independent variable in a study, the independent variables are called **factors,** and the study is called a **factorial study.** Depending on how they are designed, experimental factorial studies can be full experiments, quasi-experiments, or preexperiments.

Earlier we used the example of an organization that sends some managers to a communication training program in order to improve their supervisor-subordinate communication skills. Suppose that there were two possible communication training programs to which managers could be sent, one on interpersonal communication skills and one on group communication skills. To test which training program was more effective, a full field experiment could be conducted by assigning subjects randomly to one training program or the other and comparing their improvement. But what if the company suspected that managers who received training in *both* interpersonal and group communication would show the most amount of improvement? A single independent variable experimental design simply can't test this prediction at all, so a factorial experiment is needed.

For example, a full experimental posttest-only control group factorial design for such a study (see Figure 8.5) begins by assigning subjects randomly to four different conditions. Subjects in the first condition receive both treatments, the interpersonal (labeled X) and the group communication (labeled Y) programs. Subjects in the second condition receive the interpersonal program but not the small group program, while subjects in third condition receive the small group program but not the interpersonal program. Subjects in the fourth condition serve as a control group by not being exposed to either program. Finally, all subjects' supervisor-subordinate communication skills are measured.

This experimental design reveals two things. First, it assesses the effects of each independent variable alone, by comparing O_2 against O_4 to see whether the interpersonal program was effective and O_3 against O_4 to see whether the small group program was effective. The effects due to each of the independent variables in a factorial study are called **main effects.**

A second important effect can also be examined, whether the combination of the interpersonal and the small group communication programs is more effective than the interpersonal program alone (by comparing O_1 against O_2), the small group

Figure 8.5 Posttest-only control group full experimental factorial design

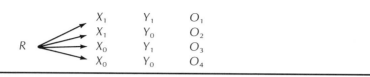

$$
R \quad
\begin{array}{ccc}
X_1 & Y_1 & O_1 \\
X_1 & Y_0 & O_2 \\
X_0 & Y_1 & O_3 \\
X_0 & Y_0 & O_4
\end{array}
$$

program alone (by comparing O_1 and O_3), or no treatment whatsoever (by comparing O_1 against O_4). Effects due to the unique combination of independent variables are called **interaction effects.** Interaction effects are important in communication research because they do justice to the complex nature of causation in the human sciences as well as the complex nature of communication itself. Consequently, much experimental research in communication uses factorial designs.

Factorial Design Statements

Factorial studies may seem complex, but understanding them is not hard. For shorthand purposes, studies with more than one independent variable are summarized with a design statement. A **design statement** is a series of numbers, one for each independent variable in the study, separated by a multiplication sign ($\times$). The numbers represent the total number of levels for each independent variable.

Suppose that a researcher has reason to believe that the independent variables of gender and year in college influence people's judgment about the persuasiveness of a particular advertisement. The design statement for this study would be 2 × 4 (the order is arbitrary) because there are two independent variables, the first one (gender) having two levels or conditions (male and female) and the second (year in college) having four levels (freshman, sophomore, junior, and senior).

Suppose that a researcher has reason to believe that in addition to the independent variables of gender and year in college, the type of ad to which subjects are exposed affects judgments about the ad's persuasiveness. To test this idea, the researcher divides subjects into the eight different conditions based on gender and year in college. Half of the subjects in each of these eight conditions are then exposed to a message based on a logical appeal, while the other subjects in each condition are exposed to a message based on an emotional appeal. The addition of this independent variable of advertisement (which has two levels, logical and emotional) makes this a 2 × 4 × 2 design (gender with two levels, year in college with four levels, and type of ad with two levels, respectively).

Design Diagrams

A **design diagram** is a visual depiction of a factorial design statement. In a simple, two-factor design, a design diagram is a box with one independent variable represented on an *x,* or horizontal, axis and one on a *y,* or vertical axis. Figure 8.6 is the

Figure 8.6 A 2 × 4 factorial design

	Male	Female
Freshman	I	II
Sophomore	III	IV
Junior	V	VI
Senior	VII	VIII

design diagram for the 2 × 4 design statement about the effects of gender and year in college on judgments about the persuasiveness of a particular advertisement. Notice that the design diagram plots only the independent variables (gender and year in college) and not the dependent variable.

A design diagram shows researchers all the possible combinations of the independent variables. Each possible combination is called a **cell,** and the study must include subjects for each cell, eight in this particular case. You always can tell how many cells a study has simply by multiplying the numbers in the design statement. In the case of Figure 8.6, there are 8 cells (2 × 4).

To have a cell for every possible combination of the independent variables in a three-factor study, two of the variables are reported on one dimension of a matrix. Figure 8.7 shows the design diagram for the 2 × 4 × 2 design statement about the effects of gender, year in college, and type of ad on judgments about the persuasiveness of advertisements. In order to conduct this study, there must be subjects for each of the 16 cells (2 × 4 × 2).

Repeated-Measures Factorial Designs

As more independent variables are added and more cells created in a factorial study, more subjects are needed to fill the cells. A generally accepted rule is that at least five subjects are needed for each cell in a factorial design (Kidder, 1981). A 2 × 4

Figure 8.7 A 2 × 4 × 2 factorial design

	Logical Ad		Emotional Ad	
	Male	Female	Male	Female
Freshman	I	II	III	IV
Sophomore	V	VI	VII	VIII
Junior	IX	X	XI	XII
Senior	XIII	XIV	XV	XVI

× 5 factorial design has 40 cells and thus demands 200 subjects. At some point, the need to recruit subjects becomes a burdensome responsibility for researchers using complex factorial designs.

The large number of interaction effects in a complex factorial design also makes data analysis difficult to handle. With three independent variables, there are three two-way interactions effects (*xy, xz,* and *yz*) and a three-way interaction effect (*xyz*). Calculate how many different interaction effects exist with four or five independent variables! As a result, researchers typically choose only independent variables that are most crucial and can be examined reasonably within a single study.

One solution to the problem of acquiring additional subjects is exposing the same subjects to different treatments. This is called a **repeated-measures factorial design.** Let's say that researchers want to see whether men or women are more effective in presenting four different types of speeches (impromptu, informative, persuasive, and entertainment). One possibility is to use different subjects for each cell, which is known as a **between-subjects design.** Another possibility, requiring fewer subjects, is to have the same men and women give all four of the speeches. Of course, not all independent variables can be used in this way. Subjects can't experience being both male and female without some radical operations!

Repeated-measures factorial designs allow researchers to use subjects as their own comparison, since they chart the same subjects across different treatments. For this reason, repeated-measures factorial designs are known as **within-subjects designs.** The order of treatments can make a difference, however, because earlier treatments might sensitize subjects to later treatments. For this reason, researchers usually randomize the order of the treatments in a repeated-measures factorial design. They must also be sure that the effects of each treatment have passed before exposing subjects to subsequent treatments. This design thus reduces the number of subjects needed for complex experiments, but care still is needed to make sure that a dependent variable is influenced only by the independent variables being studied.

CONCLUSION

Experimental research is conducted in order to establish causal relationships between variables. Establishing causal relationships demands that researchers exercise high control so that alternate causality arguments can be ruled out. Regardless of whether the experiment is conducted in a laboratory or a field setting, control is the central characteristic of an experiment. The degree of control revolves around three things: manipulating the independent variable, creating equivalent experimental groups, and controlling for the influence of extraneous variables. The extent to which these three things can be accomplished determines whether researchers use full, quasi- or preexperimental designs. Finally, because communication is a complex phenomenon, researchers often design factorial experiments to investigate the causal effects of more than one independent variable on a dependent variable.

chapter 9

Survey Research

A researcher once sought to determine what was actually learned from experiments in human behavior. A group of people with little formal education and much life experience were told the hypotheses tested in a number of experiments and asked to predict the results. They were remarkably accurate! They had learned quite a bit about human behavior from the "school of hard knocks." This finding doesn't imply that social scientific experiments needn't be done. Their results contradict common sense often enough to make empirical tests of hunches and folk wisdom necessary. But it does imply that we can learn a lot simply by *asking* people what we want to know. This is one premise of survey research. When the **survey method** is used, respondents representing a specific population are asked questions concerning their beliefs, attitudes, and behaviors. Their answers are analyzed to describe characteristics of both the respondents and the populations they were chosen to represent.

USE OF SURVEYS IN COMMUNICATION RESEARCH

The survey method may be the methodology used most often in communication research. One reason is that survey research is particularly useful for gathering descriptive information about populations too large for every member to be studied.

For example, it would be impractical to observe the study habits of the entire fresh-man class at a large state university, but it would be relatively simple to ask represent-ative members of the freshman class about their study habits. Similarly, it would be very difficult, as well as unethical, to observe the voting behavior of all Americans in a national election, but political pollsters commonly interview representative voters before and immediately after they vote. Surveys thus provide researchers with a convenient method for gathering descriptive information from representatives of a population.

A second reason for the popularity of the survey method in communication research is that it involves a relatively straightforward research strategy: Ask people questions and analyze their answers. Communication scholars and practitioners alike frequently use the survey method to study people's beliefs, attitudes, and be-haviors.

Use of Surveys in Scholarly Communication Research

Groves (1987), a senior study director at the Survey Research Center at the University of Michigan, begins his overview of survey research by pointing out:

> Survey research is not itself an academic discipline, with a common language, a com-mon set of principles for evaluating new ideas, and a well-organized professional refer-ence group. Lacking such an organization, the field of survey research has evolved through the somewhat independent and uncoordinated contributions of researchers trained as statisticians, psychologists, political scientists, and sociologists. (p. S156)

Many of these contributions have also come from communication scholars who have used the survey method to describe people and their communication be-havior. Figure 9.1 provides some recent examples of how the survey method has been used to study topics relevant to speech communication, mass communication, and journalism research. As is apparent, survey research has been used to examine the nature of communication within organizations, the relationship between con-sumers and their use of the mass media, and the characteristics of mass media pro-ducers, especially newspaper personnel.

These examples illustrate how the survey method can be used to answer the two primary questions that guide scholarly communication research (see Chapter 3): What is the nature of communication, and how is communication related to other things? Survey researchers often describe communication characteristics of respondents for the purpose of building theories or generalizations about the popu-lation they represent. At other times survey researchers test theoretical predictions about the relationship between communication and other behavior in a population of interest.

When testing predictions, however, survey researchers typically don't exercise the same amount of control as experimental researchers. Survey researchers usually don't use experimental designs to manipulate independent variables to determine their influence on dependent variables. Instead, they tend to use **correlational de-**

Figure 9.1 Some recent examples of communication survey research

Speech Communication

1. Frey and Botan (1988) described whether and how the introductory undergraduate communication research methods course was being taught based on 184 responses from a questionnaire mailed to all 421 departments of communication at all universities in the United States.

2. Glasser, Zamanou, and Hacker (1987) used questionnaires and interviews to survey 195 government employees representing every level and division in their department (line workers, supervisors, clerical, professional-technical, and top management) about their satisfaction with factors influencing their organizational climate, such as teamwork, communication and information flow, and meetings.

3. Pettey (1988) conducted a telephone survey of 737 adults during the 1984 presidential campaign to see how the politicalization of respondents' family, friends, and coworkers related to their motivations for obtaining political knowledge, such as political interest and attention to public affairs media.

4. Trombetta and Rogers (1988) surveyed 521 nurses in four general-care hospitals to see how information adequacy (actual versus desired information available), communication openness (perceived willingness on the part of organization members to send and receive messages), and participation in decision making (actual versus desired) were related to employees' organizational commitment and job satisfaction.

Mass Communication

1. Christenson and Peterson (1988) used a survey questionnaire to examine the differences between 239 male and female college students regarding their preference for 26 different types of music.

2. Finn and Gorr (1988) examined the relationships between motivations for watching television, six individual characteristics (including shyness, loneliness, and self-esteem), and social support by interviewing 290 undergraduates through the use of specially programmed computer terminals.

3. Rubin, Perse, and Taylor (1988) surveyed 392 adults to examine the relationships between television exposure (how much they watched it, type of programs watched, and attitude toward viewing) and positive social attitudes, such as trust in others and life satisfaction.

Journalism

1. Bergen and Weaver (1988) conducted a systematic random sample of 470 daily newspaper journalists from 1001 U.S. journalists to see whether the size of the newspaper as measured by circulation was related to employee job satisfaction.

2. Buddenbaum (1988) described the characteristics of the typical religion journalist from 141 responses received from a questionnaire mailed to all 250 religious newspapers listed in *Editor and Publisher Yearbook.*

3. K. A. Smith (1988) interviewed community residents in person and verified by telephone to see how perceptions of neighborhood and community issues were related to coverage of those issues in the local newspapers.

4. Tichenor, Donohue, and Olien (1987) conducted telephone interviews with 100 people from each of 10 communities (including a small rural community, an outlying regional center in the process of growth, a metropolitan core city area, and a group of metropolitan suburbs) to learn the relationship between reading local newspapers and shopping behavior.

signs, wherein the strategy is to assess all the variables of interest at one point in time in order to describe the relationships among them. Though causation can sometimes be argued from these designs, survey researchers are typically more interested in establishing noncausal relationships between variables. For example, if survey respondents indicate that they are attracted to people with whom they engage in mutual self-disclosure, a researcher would not assume that mutual self-disclosure causes attraction. Since the variables were assessed at the same point in time, the survey researcher posits a mutually causal, rather than a linearly causal, relationship between mutual self-disclosure and interpersonal attraction. The survey researcher recognizes that these two variables probably influence each other. The more mutual self-disclosure, the more attraction, and vice versa. In Chapter 14 we examine the data analysis procedures used to assess relationships between variables.

Three Applied Uses of Survey Research

The survey method is also used extensively in applied research to measure public opinion, referred to as **public opinion research.** Three major applications of public opinion research are of particular interest to communication researchers: **political polls,** in which surveys are conducted to describe public opinion on political issues and potential voting patterns; **evaluation research,** in which surveys are used to assess the performance of specific programs, products, or organizations; and **market research,** in which consumer attitudes and product preferences are described.

Political polls. Political polls are one of the most common and best-publicized applications of the survey research method. The results of political polls are presented to us routinely by television news programs, newspapers, and newsmagazines. Researchers conducting political polls typically survey large samples of potential voters to measure popular support for different candidates or political issues, particularly with regard to voting in upcoming elections. Since these polls are often designed to predict the results of elections, they provide extremely useful information for political candidates and political parties. The accuracy of a political poll, however, depends on a number of factors, such as the sample of respondents surveyed and the kinds of questions asked.

Decades ago, political polls were held in disrepute after highly publicized election predictions were shown to be inaccurate. For example, in 1936 the *Literary Digest* (a popular national newsmagazine), after sending out more than 10 million questionnaires through a mail survey and receiving over 2.3 million ballots, predicted a stunning 57 to 43 percent upset of incumbent president Franklin Roosevelt by the Republican challenger Alf Landon. However, Roosevelt posted one of the largest victories in presidential elections, winning 61 percent of the popular vote and 523 electoral votes to Landon's 8. Squire (1988) points out that the pollsters were so inaccurate for two reasons. First, they contacted people listed in telephone directories and on automobile registration lists, without realizing that at that time, telephones and automobiles were owned by an overwhelming number of registered Republicans (Babbie, 1973). Second, less than 25 percent of the sample selected returned ballots, producing a flawed estimate of the population vote. Sample selection and response rate thus are two important concerns for survey researchers.

Recent political polls, however, have been remarkably accurate at predicting the results of elections because of the increasingly sophisticated design and administration of these surveys and the representative sampling techniques being used. Modern political polls tend to use very large samples that have been selected randomly. In addition, modern pollsters have found that exit polls of voters, asking them how they voted just after they have cast their ballot, produce accurate predictions. There is, however, some concern about whether exit polls influence potential voters. Sudman (1986), for example, found in a review of studies that

> there is a possibility of a small decrease ranging from 1 to 5 percent in total vote in congressional districts where polls close significantly later than 8 P.M. EST in those elections where the exit polls suggest a clear winner when previously the race has been considered close. (p. 338)

Still, modern political polling techniques are extremely accurate. Indeed, Babbie (1973) noted that by 1968, the Gallup and Harris polls predicted that Richard Nixon would receive between 41 and 43 percent of the popular vote for president, and he received 42.9 percent!

Evaluation research.   The survey method is often used to evaluate the effectiveness of specific programs or products by inquiring about the relevant experiences and feelings of clients or customers. A **summative evaluation** is conducted after a program or product is completed to learn its overall effectiveness, usually to determine whether to continue or discontinue it. A **formative evaluation** is conducted while a program or product is in process to identify ways to refine it.

One specific type of evaluation research is **need analysis,** which uses surveys to identify specific problems experienced by a target group, usually by comparing what exists with what would be preferred, as well as potential solutions to those problems. The data collected in need analysis surveys are used to develop and implement intervention programs to help relieve the identified problems; these programs are then evaluated by surveying the people who were exposed to them.

Another type of evaluation research is **organizational feedback surveys and audits,** in which members of organizations and representatives of relevant organizational publics, or "stakeholders," are questioned about current or potential opportunities and constraints facing the organization. The International Communication Association's communication audit (see Chapter 3), for example, has been used as a survey instrument to evaluate the strengths and weaknesses of communication within organizations concerning information adequacy, use of communication channels, information flow, quality of information, communication relationships, and communication climate. Information gathered from these surveys provide communication consultants with important information that is used to develop intervention and change strategies to help organizations meet their challenges.

One important type of evaluation research is **network analysis,** which uses the survey method to examine the pattern of interactions between members of a *social network.* A network is a grouping of individuals within a social system (groups, organizations, and societies) who engage in interaction (Kreps, 1986). Researchers use network analysis to construct a "blueprint" of the kinds of communication networks that comprise social systems.

The network analyst identifies the patterns of interaction within a given social system by gathering information about whom system members communicate with, either by surveying members of the system or by observing their interaction. Typically, members of an organization are asked to identify whom they communicate with and how often they communicate with other members of the organization. This information is used to map the actual patterns of interaction within the social system, often with the help of a computer network analytic program.

Rogers and Agarwala-Rogers (1976) identify three types of communication networks that can be studied through network analysis: (1) *total system networks,* which describe the patterns of communication throughout an entire social system; (2) *clique networks,* which describe groups of individuals within a social system who communicate more exclusively with each other than with other members of the social system; and (3) *personal networks,* which describe whom an individual interacts with commonly within a social system.

By identifying total system networks, clique networks, and personal networks, researchers and practitioners can describe and evaluate communication patterns and information processing within social systems. Data about the total system network helps a communication consultant examine the general flow of messages within an organization, by identifying, for example, the grapevine by which rumors are spread or potential blocks to communication between interdependent members or departments of the organization. Examining clique networks helps identify which groups of individuals share information regularly and which don't. Finally, analyzing personal networks provides information about what roles individuals play within an organization. Kreps (1986), for example, identified the following roles that members might play within communication networks: (1) *isolates,* members of a social system who have minimal contact with other members; (2) *opinion leaders,* members who guide other members' behaviors and influence their decisions, although they are not necessarily formal leaders within a social system; (3) *gatekeepers,* members who control information flow within a social system; (4) *cosmopolites,* members who make connections between social systems; (5) *bridges,* members who connect a clique to which they belong to another clique; and (6) *liaisons,* members who connect cliques but do not belong to either clique. Information about these networks and roles are then used to formulate intervention and change strategies if necessary.

Market research. The survey method is commonly used in market research to identify consumer reactions, interests, and preferences for purchasing and using specific goods and services. Market research serves several purposes. It is used to determine current levels of consumption of products and services, as well as to predict future consumption trends. It is also used to evaluate consumer satisfaction with the performance of existing products and to predict consumer preferences for new products. In addition, market research is used to identify persuasive strategies for product packaging, pricing, and advertising.

Market research also performs an important role for mass media producers. **Readership surveys,** for example, are conducted regularly to determine how often magazine subscribers read the magazine, which articles they like and don't like, and what topics they would like to see covered in the publication. These surveys provide magazine editors with important feedback on how their audience views the publication, information that is used to establish publication policies.

Audience ratings are another important application of survey research that pervades all aspects of the mass media. These ratings identify the size and composition of the audience that different programs and stations reach. Audience ratings determine the market shares held by particular programs and stations and serve as the major indicator of the relative success of stations, programs, and their staffs. Audience ratings influence how media executives schedule programs, determine which shows companies will advertise on, and are used to establish the prices for commercial time.

A variety of measurement techniques have been used by rating services, such as Nielsen (for television) and Arbitron (for radio). For example, audience members have been asked to keep daily diaries and logs of which shows they watch or listen to. Questionnaires have been distributed and telephone interviews have been conducted to determine audience viewing and listening behavior. More recent ratings measurement techniques use sophisticated electronic equipment. Electronic meters, for example, have been attached to television and radio sets to monitor automatically the programs that are turned on at any given moment. The "people meter" is a device that allows audience members to push buttons on a small keypad and registers their responses automatically (Beville, 1988). Some of these people meters actually contain heat-sensitive devices that determine the number of people in the room (Beniger, 1987). There even is talk of using cameras to watch audience members watching the television set! Each of these techniques provides important ratings information for mass media producers.

SURVEY RESEARCH DESIGN

Designing effective surveys can be deceivingly complex. For example, the appropriateness of the sample of people who are asked to respond to survey questions strongly influences the kinds of responses elicited as well as the generalizability of the data generated. The strategy used to reach survey respondents (telephone, mail, personal contact) influences both response rate and responses. And, of course, the ways in which survey questions are worded and the order in which they are asked also influence respondents' answers. Therefore, survey researchers must establish clear goals and administer these techniques carefully if they are to generate valid data.

Designing survey research involves identifying the specific population to be described and developing strategies for sampling that population effectively. Researchers also need to determine whether the survey will be conducted over a short or a long period of time.

Selecting Survey Respondents

Sampling is essential when surveying large populations. It is often unreasonable, as well as unnecessary, to study every member of a large group. Researchers generally select, through standardized sampling techniques, representative members of a population to survey. The data these respondents provide are presumed to reflect the characteristics of the defined population.

Sampling frame.   To select a sample, communication researchers first identify the population they want to describe. Researchers next identify (or develop their own) "sampling frame" from which to select specific respondents. Ideally, a **sampling frame** is a list of all members of a population, although in actual practice the sampling frame is as exhaustive a list of population members as researchers can obtain.

Survey researchers often use telephone directories as sampling frames because these are assumed to be a full list of people living within a geographic area. Though most people in the United States have telephones, not everyone does, and even those who do have phones do not always have their numbers listed in the phone directories. Individuals listed several times in the telephone directory for multiple numbers, multiple residences, or business purposes also have a greater likelihood of being selected. Most telephone directories are also slightly out of date since they don't include people who have moved recently into and out of an area.

Random-digit dialing solves some of these problems by having a computer generate randomly all possible combinations of telephone numbers in a given exchange. All telephone numbers within the bank of numbers then have an equal chance of being selected. This method does not, however, overcome the problem of providing an equal chance of selecting people who do not have telephones or who share telephones with others.

Generalizing the findings from a sample to a population requires the use of a full and accurate sampling frame. Using incomplete lists of people living in a specific region produces a **biased sampling frame.** The result is that the sample drawn may not necessarily be representative of the population because the people left off the sampling frame do not have an opportunity to participate in the survey.

Sampling method.   Once the sampling frame is identified (or created), survey researchers must choose a method for selecting respondents from it. A random sample provides the best guarantee of an externally valid sample for describing a population (see Chapter 6). For this reason, most modern survey researchers, especially political pollsters who want to predict public attitudes and potential voting behaviors precisely, use a random sampling method (simple random, systematic, stratified, or cluster).

When surveying large populations, as is common in national, regional, state, or city surveys, it is often difficult, if not impossible, to obtain a complete list of all members of the population. For this reason, many large-scale surveys use a multistage cluster sampling procedure to select respondents. A researcher conducting a national survey selects states, counties within the state, cities within the counties, streets within the cities, houses on the streets, and finally household members, all in a random manner.

Survey researchers also often use stratified samples to select individuals with particular characteristics, such as males or college graduates, in numbers proportional to their occurrence in the actual population. This stratification procedure enhances the representativeness of a sample by increasing the homogeneity, or similarity, of respondents. For example, using the survey method to compare the television-viewing habits of college students at different undergraduate class levels (freshman, sophomore, junior, and senior), a researcher could stratify and select the sample proportionally by these class levels. This procedure maximizes the similarity between the sample and the actual population, thereby increasing the external validity of the conclusions drawn from the data.

Market researchers are least likely to use random samples, often using purposive samples to identify preferences about a specific product from available consumers with particular characteristics. You have probably encountered an interviewer working for a market research firm in a grocery store or shopping mall. This person typically approaches consumers and asks whether they will answer a few questions about specific products. These interviews are not random. The interviewers are trained to approach particular individuals based on key market segmentation characteristics that can be observed, such as age, gender, income level, or parent status. These purposive samples, though not as representative of a population as random samples, do provide market researchers with "quick and dirty" information for making product decisions.

Volunteer sampling techniques are also being used by applied survey researchers. For example, 900-number polls, wherein respondents are asked to call one of several numbers to register their vote, have become quite popular. The first 900-number poll was used to judge the winner of the Carter-Reagan debates on television (Frankel & Frankel, 1987), and today these polls are used extensively on television. The validity of these polls, however, is questionable. Researchers know that volunteers are different from nonvolunteers and thus may not represent the population of interest. Schiavone (1984), for example, reported that the ABC program *Nightline* found from using a 900-number poll that 67 percent of more than 186,000 callers wanted the United Nations out of the United States. A random scientific poll, however, found that 72 percent wanted the UN to remain in the country. Perhaps the real winner of these "pseudosurveys" is the telephone company, which collects at least 50 cents per call!

Sampling unit of analysis. Survey researchers usually obtain responses from individuals, but individuals are not always the unit of analysis in the survey. Individuals are often asked questions about a larger unit of analysis, such as their family or work unit. The danger in having respondents represent a larger unit of analysis is the chance that these individuals will not portray the larger group accurately.

For example, in some studies of family sexual communication patterns, college students are asked to describe conversations that occurred in their families. Do you think what these students report will be the same information their parents would provide?

Ecological fallacy errors exist when the data collected from respondents representing one unit of analysis (such as college students) do not describe accurately the larger unit of analysis (such as their families). Survey researchers must be careful to gather adequate information about the unit of analysis in which they are interested if they are to avoid ecological fallacy errors.

Cross-sectional versus Longitudinal Survey Designs

Some surveys gather information about respondents at one point in time, like a snapshot of a research population. Others are more like a motion picture; they provide data about respondents at several points in time. Surveys that study respondents at one point in time are called **cross-sectional designs**; those that study respondents at several points in time are called **longitudinal designs**.

Cross-sectional survey designs. Cross-sectional surveys describe the current characteristics of a sample that represents a population at one point in time. Cross-sectional surveys are used most frequently, perhaps because they are easier to conduct than longitudinal surveys. Moreover, they are extremely effective for describing the status quo. For example, political polls are almost always cross-sectional, determining respondents' current position on a political issue. A typical cross-sectional political poll might ask respondents the question "If the election were held today, whom would you vote for?"

When evaluating the results from a cross-sectional survey, it is important to take into account the particular point in time when the survey was conducted. The results of a cross-sectional survey are time-bound in that they may be quite different if conducted at a different point in time, even if the same sample is surveyed. Results of cross-sectional surveys can be very misleading if the data are gathered at an unrepresentative point in time. There are many reasons why people may not respond to a single survey in representative ways. These include personal as well as environmental circumstances. Support for a politician, for example, usually changes radically after improprieties have been discovered. Therefore, the data gathered from a cross-sectional survey may be more indicative of that specific point in time than it is about the enduring characteristics of a research population.

Cross-sectional surveys also depend on the assumption that the processes involving variables have reached relative stability, which may not be the case. Conducting a cross-sectional survey is like taking a single picture with a camera. A picture taken while kids are coming through the schoolroom door, for example, does not tell much about order or seating arrangements in the classroom.

Longitudinal survey designs. Longitudinal survey designs help to overcome many of the limitations of cross-sectional surveys. By gathering data from respondents at several points in time, survey researchers can assess the impact of unusual or unique environmental events on a population, as well as a population's enduring beliefs, attitudes, and behaviors. Therefore, longitudinal survey designs are much more effective than cross-sectional designs at capturing the processual nature of human communication.

Three primary techniques—trend, cohort, and panel studies—are used to conduct longitudinal survey research. In a **trend study,** a measurement is made at two or more points in time to identify changes or trends in people's beliefs about the measured variable. In a **cohort study,** responses from specific subgroups of the population, such as all group members born during the 1960s, are identified and compared over time. In a **panel study,** responses are obtained from the same people over time to learn how their behavioral or attitudinal patterns change. Since panel members cannot be replaced, panel studies are threatened by subject mortality, referred to as **panel attrition.** For example, a panel study of the communication development of identical twins designed to observe them every 2 years over a 10-year period may have several pairs of twins drop out of the study, thereby decreasing the size of the research sample. Survey researchers using longitudinal panel designs must therefore begin with relatively large samples to withstand panel attrition and must also persuade respondents to cooperate with a study over several administrations of the survey instrument.

SURVEY MEASUREMENT TECHNIQUES

Questionnaires and structured interviews are the primary measurement techniques employed in the survey method, although observational techniques are often used as secondary measures. For example, direct observation of the demographic and communication characteristics of potential members of survey populations are used to design questionnaires and interviews that contain appropriate language and culturally sensitive questions. For example, Botan and Frey (1983) studied communication in labor unions but had to substitute some terms contained in Giffin's (1968) trust instrument because they observed that workers were having difficulty answering some of the questions. Observational measurement techniques are also used by survey researchers to classify the content of open-ended responses generated by non-directive questionnaires and interviews into distinct categories that can be compared qualitatively (by theme) and quantitatively (by frequency of occurrence). In these cases, observations are being used to help develop effective questionnaires and interviews and to process the data.

Use of Self-report Measurement Techniques

The survey method depends on the use of self-report questionnaires and interviews. In Chapter 5 we examined the strengths and weaknesses associated with self-report measures. Because survey researchers rely almost exclusively on these measurement techniques, extreme care in using them is warranted.

To gather valid data, researchers must create questions that are appropriate for the specific respondents they intend to survey. Appropriate survey measurement techniques take into account respondents' educational levels and cultural backgrounds by posing questions that use language and ideas with which they are familiar, thus maximizing the chances that the survey questions will be understood and answered.

Survey interviewers can also help to increase the validity of the data they gather as they interact with respondents. They can clarify questions respondents do not understand fully, and they can probe with follow-up questions when respondents answer a question incompletely or inappropriately.

Survey researchers can encourage respondents to provide full and accurate information by the way they represent the study and generally communicate with respondents. They need to explain the purpose and significance of the study. They also need to assure respondents that their names and all the answers they provide will be kept confidential and reported as aggregate data (grouped with responses of many other respondents) to relieve people's anxieties about divulging sensitive information. In addition, researchers establish rapport with respondents by treating people in a professional, friendly, and respectful manner.

Designing Questions for Survey Questionnaires and Interviews

The value of questionnaires and interviews used in survey research rests on developing effective questions. Researchers must consider three things: (1) the types of questions to be asked, (2) the way questions are constructed, and (3) the question format that will be used.

Types of questions.   The choice of what questions to ask obviously determines the kinds of responses given. Figure 9.2 offers two category schemes for the types of questions asked on questionnaires or in interviews. Patton (1980) describes six "generic" types of questions, each of which can be phrased in terms of the past, present, and future—by asking, for example, what respondents did when a certain

Figure 9.2   Two category schemes for the types of survey questions asked

---

A hypothetical study of respondents' reactions to former President Reagan's speeches is used to formulate illustrative questions.

Patton (1980)

1. *Experience* and *behavior* questions that elicit what respondents do or have done ("Did you watch President Reagan's speech about treaty X on television?")

2. *Opinion* and *value* questions that elicit how respondents think about their behaviors and experiences ("What do you believe was President Reagan's most important argument in that speech?")

3. *Feeling* questions that elicit how respondents react emotionally to their behaviors and experiences ("Did you feel more or less positively about treaty X after you heard the speech?")

4. *Knowledge* questions that elicit what respondents know about their world ("What do you know about the terms of treaty X?")

5. *Sensory* questions that elicit respondents' descriptions of what they see, hear, touch, taste, and smell in the world ("Can you describe what you remember about President Reagan when he delivered that speech?")

6. *Background* and *demographic* questions that elicit respondents' descriptions of themselves ("Do you tend to vote for Republican or Democratic candidates?")

Schatzman and Strauss (1973)

1. *Reportorial* questions that elicit respondents' knowledge of factors in a social situation, usually preceded by interrogatives, such as *who, what, when, where,* and *how* ("Who else in your family watched that speech?")

2. *Devil's advocate* questions that elicit what respondents view as controversial ("What issues did President Reagan avoid addressing in that speech?")

3. *Hypothetical* questions that encourage respondents to speculate about alternative occurrences ("How would you have felt about treaty X if Secretary of State George Shultz had made the same speech?")

4. *Posing the ideal* questions that elicit respondents' values ("What else should he have done to promote Senate approval of treaty X?")

5. *Propositional* questions that elicit or verify respondents' interpretations ("Are you saying that you formed your opinion of the treaty more from newspaper accounts than from President Reagan's speech?")

---

event occurred in the past, what they do now, and what they expect to do in the future. Schatzman and Strauss (1973) offer a different typology, identifying five categories.

The types of questions posed depends on the researcher's intent. Moreover, several elements of question articulation affect how accurately and readily respondents answer. Recent and important events are recalled more easily. To illustrate, Mooney (1962) found that people reported far fewer incidences of illness for the fourth week prior to an interview than the most recent week. The difference was much lower, however, for important illnesses, those serious enough to restrict activity or require medical attention.

People also tend to report inaccurately incidents that are unpleasant or ego-threatening. Wenar (1963), for example, reported that mothers being interviewed about their children's upbringing usually exaggerate their children's precociousness and underreport their misbehaviors. Clark and Wallin (1964) interviewed husbands and wives separately about their relationship and found general disagreement about the frequency of sexual intercourse reported by couples who were less satisfied with their sexual relations.

Question construction.   Questions used in questionnaires and interviews must be appropriate, meaningful, and nonbiasing. The importance of asking appropriate questions, for example, is well illustrated in this folk story:

> Jane and a big dog are standing at a bus stop. Bill approaches them and asks her if her dog bites. Jane assures him that her dog is very friendly and doesn't bite, whereupon Bill pets the dog. The dog bites Bill's arm and thoroughly mauls him. He screams at Jane, "I thought you said your dog doesn't bite." Jane responds quite innocently, "Oh, that's not my dog."

To avoid asking ineffective questions, we offer five general guidelines for constructing questions:

1. Good survey questions are straightforward, to the point, and stated clearly. Respondents must understand questions clearly if they are to provide survey researchers with valid and reliable information. Questions should be kept simple, using language that is understood easily by the intended respondents.

2. Good survey questions should ask about one and only one issue. **Double-barreled questions** that ask about several issues at once must be avoided. For example, consider the following statement: "I am in favor of better education and a strong military." If researchers ask people how much they agree or disagree with this statement (perhaps by responding on a 5-point agree-disagree Likert scale), the answer is confusing and difficult to interpret, since the question asks about two issues that are probably unrelated.

3. Good survey questions are worded so that they do not lead people to respond in certain ways. For example, a question that begins "Don't you think that . . ." leads the respondent to answer the question in a specific manner. Loftus (1979) reports many studies indicating that eyewitness accounts in interviews change depending on how questions about an event are worded. Even apparently insignificant words make a difference. For example, Loftus showed people a film depicting a multiple-car accident. Afterward she asked them questions about what occurred. The questions posed to half the people began "Did you see a . . ." as in "Did you see a broken headlight?" The other half were asked, "Did you see the . . ." as in "Did you see *the* broken headlight?" The results showed that witnesses asked *the* questions were more likely to report having seen that object than witnesses asked *a* questions, regardless of whether or not the object had actually appeared in the film.

4. Good survey questions avoid using emotionally charged terms that can bias people's responses. For example, researchers inquiring about people's attitudes toward abortion are unlikely to gather accurate information by asking them to agree or disagree with the following statement: "Fetuses should be murdered." How many people would acknowledge that they agree with such a statement?

5. Sometimes it is helpful to use indirect questions, especially when people fear that their responses might seem undesirable to an interviewer. A common form of indirect question uses the third person. For example, when Lansing and Blood (1964) investigated attitudes toward foreign travel, they found respondents repressing some of their real concerns for fear of appearing provincial or incompetent to cope with new and strange situations. So they asked, instead, why the respondents thought "some people" did not want to visit foreign countries.

Question strategies and format. Survey researchers use directive or nondirective questions (or both). Directive questioning employs closed questions that limit the kinds of answers respondents can provide, such as yes-no bipolar responses or Likert-type agree-disagree scales. Nondirective questioning uses open questions that allow respondents to frame their own answers, such as "How do you feel about . . . ?" or "What are your experiences with . . . ?"

The organizational format of questions is an important issue in developing effective questionnaires and interviews. In Chapter 5 we described three general formats that are often used: the tunnel, funnel, and inverted funnel formats. Recall that the tunnel format asks a series of questions that are organized similarly, the funnel format begins with broad open questions followed by narrower closed questions, and the inverted funnel format begins with narrow questions followed by open questions.

Survey researchers choose the questioning strategy and format that best suit their research purpose and the sample being studied. Three guidelines are generally applied: (1) demographic questions should come first, (2) questions about the same topic should be linked together, and (3) the format of scales used should be varied (that is, reverse the polarities throughout a questionnnaire) to minimize the tendency for respondents to get into a "response set."

Use of Questionnaires in Survey Research

Questionnaires are commonly used in survey research to gather information from large samples. Since questionnaires can be mass-produced easily and inexpensively and distributed widely in person or through the mail (or even through an online computer network), they are useful for reaching large samples. Moreover, the fact that many respondents can be given identical questionnaires makes them a reliable measurement technique for survey research.

Questionnaire administration.   There are two general strategies for administering questionnaires: **researcher-administered questionnaires,** which are administered in person by researchers, and **self-administered questionnaires,** which individuals complete by themselves at their own discretion.

When researchers administer questionnaires, they are available to provide respondents with instructions and to answer questions, which helps minimize errors
in filling them out. Since researchers do not have direct contact with respondents
when using self-administered questionnaires, they must provide clearly written instructions for filling out the instrument correctly. Self-administered questionnaires
must therefore be worded simply, straightforward, and easy to fill out.

Questionnaires can also be administered individually or to a group of people
at one time and in one place, just as teachers administer exams to their classes. By
the way, written exams may be viewed as examples of questionnaires used in evaluation research. Students' performance on them is one gauge of a course's effectiveness. Group administration of questionnaires is obviously more efficient than individual administration because a large number of respondents can be surveyed in a
short amount of time. Group administration can affect the data, however, since
verbal and nonverbal comments made by some respondents in the presence of others
can influence responses. Questionnaires administered individually thus provide
people with more privacy and anonymity than researcher-administered questionnaires.

Using the postal service to distribute self-administered questionnaires is a relatively efficient and inexpensive way to reach representatives of large, geographically
dispersed populations. Researchers do not have to travel to these people, nor must
they transport them. Mailed questionnaires also afford respondents more privacy
and anonymity than researcher-administered questionnaires.

The use of mailed questionnaires, however, can jeopardize the **response rate,**
the percentage of individuals who complete and return the questionnaires out of the
total number of people to whom they are sent. The acceptable level depends on the
purpose of the survey, but most researchers try to get more than 60 percent of people
to respond. Mailed questionnaires generally result in a lower response rate than in-
person questionnaires, however, because respondents do not feel as obligated to
complete them.

Survey researchers use several strategies to increase the response rate to acceptable levels. Prenotification of the survey prior to its arrival has been found to increase response rate by as much as 47.4 percent (Fox, Crask, & Kim, 1988). To make
responding easy, researchers will send respondents questionnaires that are quick and
easy to fill out. They will describe the purpose, sponsorship, and importance of the
research in a cover letter and promise to send respondents a summary of the results
from the study. Sponsorship of a survey by a university, in particular, has been
found to increase returns (Houston & Nevin, 1977; Jones & Lang, 1980; Jones &
Linda, 1978; Peterson, 1975). Some researchers even provide respondents with rewards such as cash, discounts, or presents to complete the questionnaire. Most mail
surveys also provide respondents with an addressed, postage-paid, return envelope

to encourage respondent compliance. Armstrong and Lusk's (1987) review of the literature found that first-class postage yielded an additional 9 percent return over business reply rates. These researchers also found that using commemorative instead of standard stamps increased responses. Even the color of questionnaires has been found to affect response rates, with green questionnaires producing a higher response rate than white ones (Fox, Crask, & Kim, 1988).

Researchers also often attempt to increase compliance with a survey by sending people who haven't responded a few weeks after receiving the original mailed survey a *follow-up mailing* that reminds them to complete and return the questionnaire. The follow-up mailing includes another questionnaire as well as a reply envelope in which to return the completed questionnaire. Another follow-up strategy is to call reluctant respondents on the telephone to remind them to return the questionnaire, hoping that the more personal contact will increase the likelihood of compliance.

It should be pointed out, however, that increasing response rate doesn't necessarily result in a more representative sample. Berry and Kanouse (1987), for example, argue that "in fact, some methods of boosting response rate may do so at the expense of introducing further bias. Because incentive payments may appeal more to some types of respondents than others, they certainly have this potential" (p. 112).

Use of Interviews in Survey Research

Interviews, like questionnaires, are a major tool of survey research. Interviews enable survey researchers to question respondents personally about research topics. The personal nature of the interview provides researchers with both benefits and potential detriments in conducting surveys. Because interviews are an interactive measurement technique, the **interviewer,** the person conducting the interview, and the **interviewee,** the person being interviewed, engage in interpersonal communication and begin to establish a relationship. If the interviewer can establish *rapport* with interviewees, by putting them at ease through personal identification and comfortable interaction, interviewees will be encouraged to provide full and accurate information in response to all the questions.

However, the personal nature of interviews can intimidate interviewees and bias their responses. The validity of interview data is highly dependent on how respondents view the interviewer and how effectively the interviewer manages the interaction.

Hyman (1954), for example, reported on a study of 1000 black respondents, conducted by the National Opinion Research Center in Memphis in 1942. Researchers compared the information elicited by white and black interviewers when interviewing black respondents. Hyman says:

> On almost all the opinion and attitude questionnaires, the white interviewers obtained significantly higher proportions of what might be called by some people "proper" or "acceptable" answers. Negroes were more reluctant to express to the white interviewers

their resentments over discrimination by employers or labor unions, in the army, and in public places. (p. 159)

Researchers therefore frequently make sure that interviewers are in crucial ways similar to the interviewees. Douglas (1987), for example, studied how people on dates assess how attractive they are to the other person. Fifty college students were interviewed and asked, "I would like you to describe, as completely as you can, all the things you do to find out how much somebody of the opposite sex likes you." To ensure frank responses, Douglas reported, "The interviewers met only with subjects of the same sex as themselves. This precaution was taken to maximize subjects' willingness to disclose" (p. 6).

Researchers are also aided in developing rapport if their own past experiences are similar to those of their interview respondents. For example, Lee (1988), who interviewed Holocaust survivors, was once herself a concentration camp inmate. As she put it, "Being a survivor myself facilitated my empathy and the sensitivity to know when not to probe or be too intrusive" (p. 75).

Another limitation of the interview is interviewers' ability to record answers accurately while engaging in interaction with respondents. Respondents record their own answers to questionnaires, but in interviews the interviewer must record the data provided by interviewees without omitting anything important. Audiotaping or videotaping interviews records responses effectively, but, like the personal nature of the interview itself, the presence of these devices can make respondents act artificially because they become self-conscious about being recorded (a variation on the Hawthorne effect).

Training interviewers.   Smith (1987) points out that back in the 1930s, survey interviews lasted only about 10 minutes. Surveys today have increased considerably in terms of the time it takes to complete them and the complexity of the questions asked. The potential problems demand that survey interviews should be conducted only by competent and responsible interviewers, since the quality of the data gathered in the interview is largely dependent on the skills of interviewers. Lofland (1971) notes:

> Successful interviewing is not unlike carrying on unthreatening self-controlled, supportive, polite, and cordial interaction in everyday life. If one can do that, one already has the main interpersonal skills necessary to interviewing. It is my personal impression, however, that interactants who practice these skills (even if they possess them) are not overly numerous in our society. (p. 90)

Unskilled interviewers can destroy the validity of a well-designed survey by misrepresenting the goals and questions of the survey, biasing respondents' answers, or recording respondents' answers incorrectly. Furthermore, ineffective interviewers not only compromise the effectiveness of the specific research project but can also impugn the reputation of the research organizations sponsoring the survey.

Many researchers therefore train interviewers beforehand, helping them to become comfortable with the interview procedure by practicing it in a supervised setting before they use it in the actual study. Somers, Mannheimer, Kelman, and Mellinger (1982), for example, studied changes in college students' values and lifestyles between their freshman and senior years. The interviewers they hired were required to participate in "all-day group discussions in which a large proportion of the time was spent on 'mock' interviewing and review and criticism of practice interviews with friends and randomly selected strangers outside the training session" (p. 150).

Brown (1985) employed three assistants to help her conduct interviews of employees in nursing homes. To be sure that she and the assistants conducted equivalent interviews, she trained them beforehand. Then she assessed the effectiveness of her training program. She asked five graduate students to rate samples of the assistants' interviews taped during training on "content, style, and strategy" (p. 29). Her training program was effective—the judges all found the taped interviews to be very similar. In fact, four of the five judges thought all the interviews were conducted by the same person!

Though all interviews demand skilled interviewers, different types of interviewing demand different interviewing skills. For example, nondirective interviews demand far more interviewer knowledge and skills than directive interviews. Directive interviews demand only that interviewers read questions to respondents clearly and accurately and then record their answers. Nondirective interviews demand much more sensitivity, flexibility, and communication skills on the part of interviewers. In nondirective interviews, interviewers must phrase questions appropriately for the specific individual being interviewed, know when to direct respondents, when to let interviewees speak, and when and how to probe for more information. These are all skills that interviewers should be trained to perform.

Initially, all interviewers should be educated about the goals and methods of the survey so that they can answer respondents' questions accurately. Interviewers should become very familiar and comfortable with the interview instrument to be used in the survey. They should be given opportunities to practice administering the interview in a supervised setting before they actually conduct the interview with respondents. Training programs also help interviewers develop strategies for establishing rapport with interviewees. Billiet and Loosveldt (1988) report that training programs optimally should teach interviewers "to convey to the respondents what is expected of them by means of instructions, to probe, and to give adequate positive and negative feedback" (p. 205). Effective training programs for interviewers helps identify and rectify potential research administration problems before these problems compromise the validity and reliability of the study. Well-trained interviewers encourage respondents to provide full and honest information, thus increasing the validity of their data.

Interviewer training programs thus minimize damage that could be caused by unskilled interviewers and increase the likelihood that the interviews will accomplish the goals of the survey. Nevertheless, some variation among interviewers' personal traits and communication ability is inevitable. Researchers sometimes turn this potential problem into an advantage by having interviewers work in teams. Murphy

(1980) says, "Team interviewing can bring different perspectives to the questioning, provide a double check on what was said, and lead to productive postinterview discussions about what it all meant and whether the subject was reliable" (pp. 80–81).

Individual versus group interviews.   For the most part, survey researchers interview respondents individually, unless, of course, the research purpose demands that respondents be interviewed as a couple—in studies of marital relationships, for example. In addition, market and evaluation researchers often use a *focus group interview* to complement survey data regarding what people buy with insights into why they make those choices. In a **focus group interview,** a facilitator leads a small group of people (usually five to seven members) in a relatively open discussion about a specific product or program. The facilitator introduces topics, encourages participation, and probes for information in a flexible, interactive way to elicit consumers' genuine views. Focus groups also encourage people to "piggyback" on others' ideas, which sometimes makes it easier for reluctant communicators to participate.

Face-to-face versus telephone interview administration.   Interviews can be administered in person ("face to face") as well as over the telephone. There are many similarities between face-to-face and telephone interviews, but each has advantages and disadvantages.

In face-to-face interviews, interviewers can identify when interviewees do not understand questions, when they seem unsure about their answers, or even when they are providing misleading answers. Such immediately available feedback is instrumental in helping interviewers decide when to probe or to restate questions. In face-to-face interviews, interviewers can also make note of respondents' demographic characteristics revealed by their appearance and need not ask about them directly.

Using the telephone to conduct interviews is convenient, but the amount of nonverbal information available to the interviewer is limited to paralinguistic cues, which may make it difficult to identify whether the answers are honest. In addition, the telephone obviously limits an interviewer's ability to identify respondents' demographic characteristics.

The face-to-face interview strategy poses several limitations for survey researchers. It takes more time to gather data via face-to-face interviews. If interviewers have to travel long distances to reach interviewees, the time and expense of conducting interviews increases even more. Face-to-face interviews also decrease the privacy and anonymity of interviewees, making it difficult to gather data about personal, risky, or embarrassing topics.

Telephone-administered interviews can overcome some of the time, expense, and reactivity problems of face-to-face interviews. Groves and Kahn (1979) and Hochstim (1967) both found that a telephone survey costs as little as half as much as a face-to-face survey. The telephone can also be used to reach interviewees over long distances and can increase respondents' privacy and anonymity, especially if they know they were selected through a random-digit dialing procedure. Computer-assisted telephone interviews further increase interviewing efficiency by selecting and calling respondents automatically, cuing interviewers to questions, and providing a simple mechanism for recording, coding, and processing the responses.

Beginning the interview. How interviews are begun often determines whether, and then how fully, respondents cooperate. Cannell and Kahn (1968) suggest that interviewers begin by identifying themselves, the research agency they represent, the general research topic, how the person was selected to be interviewed, and the amount of time the interview will take. Figure 9.3 is an example of an introduction an interviewer might use when beginning a telephone survey of public reactions to televised presidential debates.

In-depth interviews call for a great deal of time and disclosure from respondents. J. D. Douglas (1985) recommends that in such cases, researchers need to make a greater effort to convince respondents of the importance of the research project and their contribution to it. He believes that interview researchers should be "supplicants" and "sell" themselves. Douglas says, in effect, to potential respondents:

> The world is a serious place where only people who are directly involved in it can know completely what it's like. *You* are that expert and I meekly beseech your help in gaining a more complete—never complete—understanding of it. (p. 60)

Planning the interview questions. Interviewers usually prepare the major questions they will ask long before they meet the respondents. Miall (1986), for example, studied the social experiences of women who were infertile. She reports that questions used in her interview "were based on previous research on infertility, over one-and-a-half years of participant observation in an infertility self-help group, discussions with infertile individuals in the community, and popular anecdotal literature on infertility" (p. 271).

A preliminary set of questions is devised and often pretested in some trial interviews. This step is especially important when respondents' verbal abilities differ from the investigator's. Hart and Damon (1986), for example, studied how "self-

Figure 9.3   A telephone survey introduction

"Hello. My name is Gary Kreps. I'm from the Northern Illinois University Communication Research Center. We're doing a survey about public reactions to the recently televised presidential debates. The study is being conducted across the country, and the results will be used to increase our understanding of the influence of the media on political campaigns. Your phone number was chosen at random by a computer from all possible numbers within this area code. The interview will take only about fifteen minutes to complete. All information you provide will be kept strictly confidential."

understanding" develops among children by interviewing children of several different ages. They first prepared a large number of possible questions that were "pilot-tested extensively, and only the questions that were comprehensible at all age ranges and that were consistently successful in eliciting responses relevant to self-understanding were retained for the study" (p. 393).

The major questions to be posed are articulated in an **interview schedule** or **guide,** particularly if many interviewers or respondents are to be involved and the information from them all is to be compiled and compared. Merrill (1987), for example, interviewed representatives from 58 countries about their governments' control of the press. He first divided governmental control of the press into six primary areas (for example, one was "licensing of journalists"). Then he developed a basic question to begin his inquiry into each of the areas: "How do you (or your government) feel about the licensing of journalists? Are you favorably disposed to it, or are you against it?" Since Merrill was concerned about the governments' "inclination" to control the press, not an objective description of specific practices in each country, the questions he actually posed about the six areas varied a bit, asking at times, "What do you think about . . . ?" "What is your opinion of . . . ?" or "Is your government inclined to support . . . ? But he followed the essential interview guide in each interview.

The kinds of interview schedules used range from highly scheduled to unscheduled. Recall from Chapter 5 that in highly scheduled interviews, interviewers ask only the questions (usually directive, closed questions) written on the interview guide and follow the specific wording of each question, making this approach closely akin to the formal structure and consistency of questionnaires. In moderately scheduled interviews, interviewers ask the specific primary questions provided on the interview guide but can also ask probing secondary questions, usually to gather specific details or to obtain more complete answers. In unstructured interviews, interviewers are provided with a list of topics but have the freedom to decide what questions (usually nondirective, open questions) to ask and how to phrase these questions.

Cannell and Kahn (1968) provide an overview of interview planning. They recommend conducting the entire interview:

> To make the total experience as meaningful as possible, to give it a beginning, a middle, and an end. More specifically, the early questions should serve to engage the respondent's interest without threatening or taxing him before he is really committed to the transaction, and to exemplify and teach him the kind of task the interview represents. The most demanding of questions might well be placed later in the interview, when respondent commitment can be presumed to have peaked—and fatigue has not yet set in. Sometimes the riskiest of questions may be put very late in the interview, so that if they trigger a refusal to continue, relatively little information is lost. This procedure seems prudent, but it risks also the possibility of an unpleasant leavetaking. (p. 571)

Responding to answers.   Interviews are influenced as much by how researchers respond to answers they receive as by how initial questions are posed. Whyte (1984) provides this advice:

> Like the therapist, the research interviewer listens more than he talks, and listens with a sympathetic and lively interest. We find it helpful occasionally to rephrase and reflect back to informants what they seem to be expressing and to summarize the remarks as a check on understanding.

> The interviewer avoids giving advice and passing moral judgments. We accept statements that violate our own ethical, political, or other standards without showing disapproval in any way. (p. 98)

Such neutrality is not easy to maintain. Interviewers' attitudes may leak without their awareness. Zaleski (1987) makes this point in her book of accounts of near-death experiences. She found very few negative reports in her review of the literature and suspects that this omission may be due somewhat to interviewers' behavior. She points out that even

> the most noncommittal line of questioning still falls short of providing sterile laboratory conditions; the mere presence of the interviewer contaminates the data. . . . The interviewer can unwittingly steer the conversation by subliminal signals more subtle than direct speech or overt body language. Our social experience is a web of such mutual influencing, much of it below the threshold of conscious communication. (p. 149)

To obtain accurate and complete information, interviewers also probe for more information when responses at first are too brief or too general. For example, Wenner (1983) and colleagues interviewed people regarding why they watch, or why they avoid watching, presidential campaign coverage on network news programs. Interviewers were instructed "to probe beyond the 'easy answer,' a type of superficial response which is often categorized as 'surveillance' (i.e., 'to find out what is going on in the world,' or 'to keep up with things')" (p. 383). By using probes, Wenner was able to identify 17 distinct categories of responses to his research question.

Probes are sometimes planned in advance, and sometimes they are improvised by interviewers on the spot. J. D. Douglas (1985) advocates a strategy of "research opportunism." He suggests being prepared to make:

> creative adaptations of the plans at all levels and all times, depending on the situations that emerge and especially on the particular quirks of the always perverse and intriguing human animal you are confronted with . . . always ready to pounce on any phenomenon that shines with the promise of a new truth—discovery. (p. 69)

THE NATURE OF SURVEY DATA

The survey method can provide researchers with both quantitative (numerical) and qualitative (verbal) data. Directive questionnaires and interviews use closed questions that limit the answers respondents can give and so usually provide researchers with quantitative data. Conversely, nondirective questionnaires and interviews use open questions that place few restrictions on the kinds of responses subjects can give and so provide researchers with primarily qualitative data.

Directive, closed survey questions are easier and less time-consuming for respondents to answer than nondirective, open questions, since they provide respondents with limited options and fixed choices. Data generated by closed questions are also easier and less time-consuming for researchers to code and analyze than unstructured responses to open questions. The process of assigning meaning, whether numerical or verbal, to survey answers is called **coding.** Directive, closed questions provide quantitative data that can be analyzed through the use of statistical procedures. Survey researchers can then make quantitative statements about the nature of the people sampled as well as infer from a sample to a population. These more directive, closed survey questions are therefore more likely to be used with large samples of respondents because of their ease of administration, response, coding, and analysis.

Nondirective, open survey questions are time-consuming for researchers to administer and for respondents to answer. They are also difficult to code and analyze since respondents' answers can vary widely. These open questions, however, may evoke more information about the particular perspectives of individual respondents than closed questions since they do not lead them to answer in any preconceived way, and they allow wide latitudes regarding the depth of information respondents can give. Qualitative survey data are generally content-analyzed (see Chapter 10) to identify the type and frequency of recurring thematic patterns. Open survey questions are therefore used with small samples about whom the researcher wants to know a great deal.

Quantitative survey measurement techniques thus provide researchers with more **horizontal data,** data with great breadth, covering a broad range of respondents. Qualitative survey measurement techniques, by contrast, provide researchers with more **vertical data,** data of great depth, describing the perspectives of particular respondents fully. It should be apparent that by combining directive and nondirective question strategies on questionnaires and interviews, researchers can generate both horizontal quantitative and vertical qualitative data. By triangulating these measurement techniques, survey researchers can increase both the breadth and the depth of their descriptions of research populations.

CONCLUSION

From surveys we can learn how large groups of people think and act. To trust generalizations made on the basis of surveys, however, the sample must be representative, the response rate sufficient, the questions unbiased, the data collection procedures uniform, and the data coding and analysis accurate.

chapter 10

Textual Analysis

In earlier chapters we discussed research methods—experiments and surveys—that generate new messages. People must respond to situations or answer questions and thereby provide information not previously available. Other researchers prefer to study messages that already exist in recorded or visual form. **Textual analysis** is the method communication researchers use to describe and interpret the characteristics of a recorded or visual message. Communication texts can be written transcripts of speeches and conversations, written documents (like letters, personnel records, newspapers, and magazines), electronic documents (like audiotapes, films, videotapes, and computer files), or visual texts (like paintings, photographs, and architecture). There are a great many texts; in fact, there are as many kinds of texts as there are communication media. This chapter examines the general nature of textual analysis and then explores in more detail some specific methods textual analysts use.

PURPOSE OF TEXTUAL ANALYSIS

Textual analysis, like experimental and survey methods, can be used to answer the two major questions posed in communication research: What is the nature of communication, and how is communication related to other variables? In answering the first question, researchers describe the content, structure, and functions of the messages contained in texts. For example, researchers might categorize the types of message strategies politicians use in public campaign speeches into fear and reward appeals.

To describe the communication embedded in a text may involve answering the questions "What does the text mean, and how does it achieve that meaning?" The answers to these questions depend, however, on where researchers locate the meaning of a text. Lindkvist (1981) points out that "the meaning of a text can be identified with the producer, the consumer or the interpreter of a text or with the text itself" (p. 23). Hirsch (1967), for example, argues that the purpose of textual analysis is to ascertain the meaning intended by the producer of a text. Other researchers study how consumers perceive and interpret texts. The meaning of a text can also rest in how it is viewed by qualified interpreters. For example, the Supreme Court justices are the final authorities for interpreting the meaning of the Constitution of the United States.

Besides describing the communication embedded in a text from a chosen perspective, researchers also ask how that communication is related to other variables. Some researchers study how *input* variables, variables that precede communication, are related to the messages contained in a text. One example is investigating how politicians' personalities affect their use of fear and reward appeals. Researchers also study relationships between the type of communication embedded in a text and various *outcomes,* such as how the use of fear and reward appeals relates to listeners' perceptions of politicians' credibility.

Researchers using textual analysis also often go beyond these two questions to *evaluate* texts by using a set of standards, or criteria. For example, researchers might evaluate the effectiveness of a politician's public campaign speech, focusing perhaps on how well he or she used fear and reward appeals to influence voting behavior and, in the case of a losing campaign, what types of appeals should have been used. Indeed, political candidates' campaign messages are subjected to in-depth critiques by the media. Of course, to critique messages embedded in texts, researchers and critics must establish a set of standards against which the communication can be compared.

IMPORTANT CONSIDERATIONS IN TEXTUAL ANALYSIS

Researchers conducting textual analysis must make a number of important decisions. These decisions include the types of texts to be studied, how appropriate texts will be acquired, and which particular approach will be used to analyze texts.

Types of Texts

Texts can be divided into two major categories: transcripts and outputs of communication. **Transcripts of communication** are verbatim recordings of actual communication, such as written transcripts of courtroom behavior made by a court stenographer or audio and audiovisual recordings of group meetings. **Outputs of communication** are messages produced by communicators themselves, including written artifacts (such as letters, graffiti, or books), works of art (such as paintings, statues, or films), and other symbolic outputs (such as footprints or refuse).

Both transcripts and outputs texts may range from *scripted* (planned ahead) to *unscripted* (spontaneous) and from *public* to *private.* Whereas some scholars argue that all communication is intentional, the amount of preparation varies, as does the purposes and the audience for which the communication is produced. A transcript of a political speech, for example, is probably a well-planned or scripted form of communication that was designed for public consumption and analysis. By contrast, a videotaped recording of a family reunion is representative of a more unscripted, spontaneous form of interaction, intended primarily for relatively private viewing only by the members of that particular family.

Studying transcripts and outputs of communication relies on *indirect,* rather than direct, *observation.* Recall that researchers use direct observation to examine live communication behaviors and indirect observation to examine recordings of communication behavior. The use of indirect observation in textual analysis makes this a relatively **nonreactive** research methodology. That is, textual analysis is a fairly "clean" way of gathering data (free from contamination by the research procedure) because generally it does not depend on using self-reports or direct observational measures. Many texts are also the result of natural communication behavior, as opposed to being generated at a researcher's request. In fact, one of the four major approaches to textual analysis, unobtrusive measures, was developed especially because it is a nonreactive way to gather data.

Acquiring Texts

A challenge for researchers is identifying, acquiring, and analyzing the texts most appropriate for the purposes of their research. Outputs of communication are available more readily for analysis than transcripts. Even dated outputs such as old television shows or newspapers can be acquired from libraries and media archives. Transcripts of communication, however, may be more difficult to acquire. Most communication events are not recorded or available in the form of transcripts. Public speeches by major political figures are sometimes recorded, but most interpersonal, group, and organizational communication is not preserved. Researchers often introduce recording devices to preserve communication, but these can make people nervous and distort their normal behavior (the Hawthorne effect).

Acquiring a database is therefore a primary consideration in textual analysis, particularly when texts are not readily available. Consider, for example, four procedures Grimshaw (1974) identifies for acquiring texts of dyadic conversation. First, some researchers listen in on conversations that occur in natural, everyday settings. Second, "natural" conversation is produced under conditions controlled by researchers by bringing people into a laboratory and giving them a reason to converse. Third, researchers request samples of specific conversation from people directly.

For example, couples might be asked to talk about a topic on which they often disagree. Fourth, researchers use spoken, interpersonal discourse or dialogue taken from literary or historical sources, such as novels or films. McLaughlin (1984) also adds a fifth procedure: Some researchers construct examples of conversation themselves, much as playwrights do.

A second issue in acquiring texts concerns how well they represent the universe from which they are selected. Sometimes researchers can conduct a census of all relevant texts if the database is limited. For example, Frey and Snider (1986) were interested in comparing public policy statements about space exploration made by Presidents Kennedy and Reagan. Using such reference material as the *New York Times Index,* they were able to locate all the relevant texts.

Most times, however, it is not possible to conduct a census of all relevant texts, so researchers rely on sampling for identifying representative texts. For example, if researchers want to examine the newspaper coverage devoted to a particular political event, they can identify a sampling frame of appropriate newspapers and select a random sample of papers. The actual date of the political event to be studied indicates the appropriate time frame for selecting newspapers, but if the event occurred over a long period of time, random sampling procedures can also be used to select representative issues of the newspapers.

A third issue in acquiring texts concerns the need for complete and accurate texts. Researchers analyzing historical texts, for example, find that texts are often incomplete or, worse, have been destroyed. Also, audiotaped or videotaped interactions are not always of sufficient quality to permit understanding of everything recorded. Moreover, audiotapes and videotapes are typically transcribed into written form, and information can be lost in the process, especially important nonverbal communication.

Approaches to Textual Analysis

How a text is analyzed depends on the purposes of the research and the particular method used. We will describe four major approaches to textual analysis: rhetorical criticism, content analysis, conversation analysis, and unobtrusive measures. These four approaches differ in terms of purpose, ranging from descriptive to critical, and observational strategy, ranging from qualitative to quantitative, but they all share a common focus on examining the communication embedded in texts.

RHETORICAL CRITICISM

To the average person on the street, the words *rhetoric* and *criticism* conjure up some interesting images. Some people view rhetoric as grammar and syntax, as in, "Oh, I took my freshman English rhetoric course." Rhetoric also often carries negative connotations. For example, rhetoric is sometimes applied to grand, eloquent, bombastic, or verbose discourse—as Shakespeare said, "Full of sound and fury, signifying nothing.'' Rhetoric is also viewed as the process of "prettying up" an idea, the clothing that surrounds the substance. Finally, we often hear, "That's mere rhetoric,'' which usually means talk without action.

The word *criticism* also carries certain connotations. Andrews (1983) argues that criticism is typically associated with tearing down or denigrating comments— we ask people to "stop being so critical." Criticism is usually thought of as advice, which when perceived as helpful is called "constructive criticism."

For scholars, the word *rhetoric* is traditionally associated with Aristotle's definition: "the available means of persuasion." And *criticism* is thought to be "the systematic process of illuminating and evaluating products of human activity" (Andrews, 1983, p. 4). **Rhetorical criticism,** therefore, involves the "description, analysis, interpretation, and evaluation of persuasive uses" of human communication (Campbell, 1972, p. 12).

Rhetorical criticism serves five important functions, according to Andrews (1983). First, rhetorical critics often search for the intended effects of persuasive discourse. Wichelns (1925), for example, observed that rhetorical criticism "regards a speech as a communication to a specific audience and holds its business to be the analysis and appreciation of the orator's method of imparting his ideas to the hearers" (p. 32). Second, some rhetorical critics seek to understand historical events in a social and cultural context, explaining how the persuasive use of communication relates to the events occurring at that time and place. Third, rhetorical criticism may shed light on current persuasive practices, providing a form of social criticism, by analyzing, for example, how television commercials influence political campaigns. Fourth, rhetorical criticism contributes to understanding how theories apply to the practice of persuasive discourse. An example might be applying a theory of emotional arousal to analyze the speeches of a demagogue. Finally, rhetorical criticism serves a pedagogical function by teaching people something about how persuasion works and what generalizations are possible. Rhetorical critics are needed, for example, to alert us to techniques advertisers use to promote product sales.

Rhetorical criticism holds an honored place in the history of communication inquiry, and textual analysis in particular, since the earliest studies of human communication were rhetorical studies of public discourse. **Classical rhetoric** emphasized the central role of public communication in developing and maintaining government and society, which established the importance of the oral tradition in communication inquiry.

Contemporary rhetorical criticism has expanded from its early Greek and Roman roots to incorporate a wide range of philosophical, theoretical, and methodological perspectives and is used to examine a broad spectrum of persuasive messages. For example, contemporary rhetorical critics study mediated as well as oral communication and nonverbal as well as verbal communication. They examine the role of rhetoric in organizational life (such as how it is used to express organizational power or to develop organizational culture), conduct longitudinal studies on the role of rhetoric in social movements and politics, and evaluate the ethicality of rhetorical strategies.

Here we examine five types of rhetorical criticism: neo-Aristotelian criticism, genre criticism, historical criticism, dramatistic criticism, and fantasy theme analysis. Each provides a distinct approach to examining persuasive messages, although rhetoricians often combine two or more approaches to critique a particular text. Most important, each approach serves a common purpose: to examine the role of communication in social influence by examining texts and presenting an argument about how the messages in those texts achieved or failed to achieve their purposes (Brockriede, 1974).

Neo-Aristotelian Criticism

Neo-Aristotelian criticism is based on the classical rhetorical tradition established by the ancient Greek and Roman rhetoricians, who were influenced strongly by the writings of Aristotle. The purpose of neo-Aristotelian criticism is to evaluate the means of persuasion used by a speaker according to the specific set of criteria given in Aristotle's *Rhetoric*. Hill (1972) explains that the goal of neo-Aristotelian criticism is "to discover whether the speaker makes the best choices from the inventory [in Aristotle's *Rhetoric*] to get a favorable decision from a specified group of auditors in a specific situation" (p. 106).

Aristotle's inventory for describing and evaluating rhetoric focuses on five major *canons* of classical rhetoric. The five canons are (1) *invention,* the development of persuasive arguments through *ethos,* the credibility of the speaker, *pathos,* appealing to the emotions of the audience, and *logos,* presenting logical evidence; (2) *disposition,* the organization of persuasive messages; (3) *elocution,* a speaker's style or use of language to express ideas; (4) *delivery,* the nonverbal manner in which a speaker presents the message; and (5) *memory,* the strategy a speaker employs to recall information for a presentation.

Despite some critics' doubts as to whether this particular set of criteria can be applied to all forms of rhetoric, neo-Aristotelian criticism has remained popular. Indeed, Black (1965) maintains that neo-Aristotelian criticism has been "the dominant mode of rhetorical criticism of the present century in the United States" (p. 27).

Genre Criticism

Genre criticism is the analysis of certain types, or genres, of text that are similar in function and form. Genre criticism differs from neo-Aristotelian criticism by applying standards that are intrinsic to the type of rhetorical act being studied, instead of applying a single set of standards to all rhetorical acts. Criticism is viewed as being constrained by the particular genre of texts being analyzed.

Aristotle originally argued that there were three genres of rhetoric: forensic, epideictic, and deliberative. *Forensic* speeches deal with the past and concern issues involving legality and justice. *Epideictic* speeches deal with the present and are ceremonial. *Deliberative* speeches deal with the future and involve political oratory.

In the years since this early classification, scholars have studied a number of other rhetorical genres. For example, *apologias* are speeches that present a public defense of character, such as Richard Nixon's apology given during the Watergate scandal (Katula, 1975). In *campaign speeches,* rhetors urge the audience to adopt their preferred view of an issue or candidate, an example being Abraham Lincoln's Cooper Union Address (Leff & Mohrmann, 1974). *Eulogies* are speeches in honor of a deceased person, such as those given for Adlai Stevenson (Brownlow & Davis, 1974). *Inaugural* speeches are delivered when political figures are inducted into office, such as Richard Nixon's 1973 presidential inaugural address (Hillbruner, 1974). *Jeremiads* are speeches that castigate a specific group, blaming the group for current problems and urging the group to remedy its ways. Johannesen (1986), for example, showed how Ronald Reagan's speeches blamed economic woes on the tendency of the general public to be swayed by bad leadership and their easy lifestyles, urging them to return to the Puritan values of hard work and competition.

Historical Criticism

The purpose of **historical criticism** is to describe and evaluate important past events by compiling and analyzing relevant documents (Gronbach, 1975). Understanding an important communication event from the past provides a point of comparison for understanding current communication events. In historical criticism, researchers go beyond merely describing and re-creating past events from documents to evaluate the reasons why the past events occurred as they did.

The four major types of historical studies are oral histories, case studies, bibliographical studies, and movement studies. Each approach to historical criticism studies the role of communication in historical events and the accomplishments of historical individuals (Bowers & Ochs, 1971; Riches & Sillars, 1980; Stewart, Smith, & Denton, 1984).

Oral histories.   **Oral histories** examine spoken, as opposed to written, accounts of past experiences. Oral histories are conducted by compiling and analyzing recordings of speakers or by gathering data from interviews with people who participated in historical events. The strength of oral histories is that researchers study *primary sources* of information, firsthand, eyewitness accounts of historical events, instead of *secondary sources,* descriptions and interpretations of events by people who did not experience them personally. Oral historians will interview people who lived during the depression era of the 1930s, for example, rather than rely on information from newspaper accounts of that period.

Case studies.   **Case studies** examine a single, salient social situation to interpret the role played by communication. The researcher first describes the key events that precipitated the situation (the case) and then analyzes the case in light of current communication theory and research. The goal is to identify appropriate strategies that were used or that could have been used to solve problems experienced in that particular situation.

The case study is commonly used as a pedagogical tool in many educational programs to help students examine problems that others have encountered and to develop strategies for analyzing and solving cases that are theoretically sound. A case study might examine, for example, how labor-management negotiations broke down, precipitating a costly strike in the steel industry. Analyzing one such event in depth might yield valuable insights into the process of labor-management negotiation, leading to some generalizations that can be applied to many other situations.

Biographical studies.   **Biographical studies** examine the public and private communication of prominent, influential, or otherwise remarkable individuals. Biographical studies analyze how the messages used by these individuals helped them to accomplish what they did. Biographical studies have focused, for example, on (1) political figures, such as Winston Churchill (Weidhorn, 1972, 1975), Adolph Hitler (Bosmajian, 1974), and Ronald Reagan (Johannesen, 1985); (2) leaders of social movements, such as Anita Bryant (Fischli, 1979), César Chávez (Hammerback & Jensen, 1980), and Malcolm X (Benson, 1974); and (3) scientists and scholars, such as Charles Darwin (Campbell, 1974, 1975) and Cicero (Enos, 1975).

Social movement studies.   **Social movement studies** examine the historical development of common causes and the rhetorical strategies used to rally people to them. Social movements include the rise (and eventual fall) of religious denominations and cults, political parties and campaigns, and civil rights activism. Scholars have studied such social movements as the American Revolution (Wiethoff, 1975), black nationalism and liberation (Hope, 1975), Christian Science (Chapel, 1975), communism (Burgchardt, 1980), the Equal Rights Amendment (Foss, 1979), Irish nationalism (Shields, 1974), Jewish statehood (Polisky & Wolpaw, 1972), Nazism (Bytwerk, 1975, 1978), the right-to-life movement (Solomon, 1980), the Roman Catholic church (Jablonski, 1980), and feminism (Campbell, 1973). Critics studying social movements analyze a variety of texts, including movement leaders' speeches, correspondence, and writings, as well as the public relations media campaigns used to promote them.

Dramatistic Criticism

Dramatistic criticism is based on the work of Kenneth Burke (1945, 1950, 1966), who argued that all symbolic acts can be viewed as "dramas." The concepts used to talk about plays acted on a stage are therefore used to analyze social events. For Burke, a drama consists of five essential elements: act, purpose, agent, agency, and scene. This *pentad* can be used to isolate essential elements of and differences between symbolic acts.

An *act* is a particular behavior performed by a communicator. The *purpose* is the reason for a symbolic act. Communication is not a random event, for a communicator makes rhetorical choices when engaging in a symbolic act, choices dictated by the purpose. The *agent* is the person who performs a symbolic act. The *agency* is the medium or code through which communication takes place, such as verbal and nonverbal channels. The *scene* is the backdrop or the setting for a symbolic act. A practice delivery of an inaugural speech in an isolated room is far different, for example, from the actual delivery of that speech in front of the nation, primarily because it takes place in a different scene.

Burke contends that within a given piece of discourse, two of the five elements of the pentad are expected to emerge as more important than the others, which is called a *ratio*. A rhetorical act that emphasizes agent and scene, for example, may be contrasted with a rhetorical act that emphasizes agency and purpose. Dramatism thus calls for assessing how rhetorical acts highlight a particular ratio of the pentad.

Highlighting a particular ratio of the pentad makes it possible to understand and critique the purpose and nature of rhetorical acts. For example, Fisher (1974) used the pentad to explain people's motives for murder and suicide, and Brummett (1979) examined ideology contained in gay rights rhetoric. The pentad has also been used to critique presidential rhetoric in general (Ivie, 1974), as well as the specific rhetoric of Presidents Kennedy (Berthold, 1976) and Nixon (Brummett, 1975).

In the dramatistic model, rhetoric refers to the conscious and unconscious strategies that actors employ to evoke cooperative performances with other actors on life's stage. The more actors *identify* with one another, the more effective rhetors are in evoking cooperation. Rhetorical critics using dramatistic criticism seek to "discover and illuminate the strategies operating through language that promote the desired end of identification" (Andrews, 1983, p. 59). Identification leads to coordinated, harmonic understanding, an ideal relational state called *consubstantiality*.

Fantasy Theme Analysis

Fantasy theme analysis, based on the work of Ernest Bormann (1972, 1973, 1982), is another form of dramatistic criticism. Rhetoric is examined for embedded narrative dramatizations that influence people by shaping how they interpret social reality.

Four symbolic categories are analyzed in fantasy theme analysis: fantasy themes, fantasy types, rhetorical visions, and rhetorical communities. *Fantasy themes* are mythic stories present in communication involving characters with whom people identify. The activities of the dramatic characters (such as "good guys" and "bad guys") symbolize general moral principles or philosophies. Leaders of a country going to war, for example, will portray the enemy as villains carrying out evil deeds or philosophies. Fantasy themes form patterns that recur throughout a text, referred to as *fantasy types*. These recurring types become powerful rhetorical symbols that unite an audience in its perception of social reality. Speaking about a "war on poverty" or "the evil empire" rallies people to support a cause. These fantasy types create *rhetorical visions,* interpretive schemes about reality shared by groups of people, who are called *rhetorical communities*. Rhetors who evoke shared rhetorical visions among an audience can transform that audience into a rhetorical community that identifies strongly with specific fantasy themes and types.

Rhetorical critics thus use fantasy theme analysis to understand how rhetoric creates a shared reality for a group of people. Communication is seen as influencing an audience through the use of dramatic fantasy themes and the extent to which fantasy types contribute to the rhetorical visions that members of rhetorical communities share (Cragan & Shields, 1981). Bormann (1972), for example, showed how fantasy themes "chain out" in a group when people jump on the bandwagon and how this process creates a common rhetorical vision. Executives who talk about "running an idea up a flagpole to see if anyone salutes" can set off a series of references to military or patriotic images, which in turn create an *esprit de corps* among the group.

CONTENT ANALYSIS

Content analysis is "a research technique for making inferences by systematically and objectively identifying specified characteristics within a text" (Stone, Dunphy, Smith, & Ogilvie, 1966, p. 5). For communication researchers, content analysis involves identifying and examining messages contained in a text.

Content analysis was developed primarily as a method for studying mass-mediated and public messages. Indeed, the roots of content analysis stretch back to the eighteenth century, when scholars in Sweden counted the number of religious symbols contained in a collection of 90 hymns to see whether they were preaching against the church (Dovring, 1954–1955). At the end of the nineteenth century, scholars started conducting quantitative content analyses of newspapers. Sneed (cited in Krippendorf, 1980), for example, counted the number of various types of articles in New York newspapers and showed that the content was changing from a focus on religious, scientific, and literary matters to an orientation toward gossip, sports, and scandals. Quantitative content analysis was soon applied to radio and public speeches. McDiarmid (1937), for example, content-analyzed presidential inaugural addresses in terms of the number of symbols used to promote national identity.

Content analysis also proved to be a valuable tool for applied researchers and communication practitioners. For example, scholars determined authorship by comparing the content and structure of new documents with known examples of authors' work. During the Second World War, researchers content-analyzed music played on German radio stations and the messages exchanged between Japan and various island bases to detect troop movements (Wimmer & Dominick, 1987). After the Second World War, newspaper editors content-analyzed reporters' stories using readability formulas, such as Flesch's (1949), to assess whether words and sentences could be understood by a person with an eighth-grade education. Editors still use these formulas today as "fog indexes" to determine whether an article is readable.

Content analysis is currently one of the dominant methodologies employed in public communication, journalism, and mass media research. Comstock (1975), for example, found more than 225 content analyses of television programming, and a survey by Jackson-Beeck and Kraus (1980) showed that content analysis was used in one-third of journal articles published on political communication in 1978 and 1979.

Value of Content Analysis

The primary goal of content analysis is to describe the characteristics of messages embedded in public and mediated texts. However, researchers also relate the content of messages to important input variables, such as how the context influences the type of messages constructed, as well as to important outcomes, such as how message content leads to attitude change.

Krippendorf (1980) identifies four advantages of content analysis that potentially make it a more powerful technique than questionnaires or interviews for describing the nature of communication and for inferring the relationship between input variables, communication, and outcomes. First, content analysis is an unobtrusive technique because it studies texts that already exist rather than having researchers get people to produce texts. Second, content analysis accepts unstructured material, which observers categorize. Structured questionnaires and interviews, by contrast, ask predetermined questions that limit respondents' answers. Third, questionnaires and interviews often obtain data in settings far from the context in which the communication occurs, but content analysis studies the data as they apear in a context. Krippendorf argues that "content analysis is a research technique for making replicable and valid inferences from data to their context" (p. 21). Consequently, researchers not only examine the content of texts but can also infer such things as the underlying motivations of the texts' producers and the effects of the texts on consumers (Hsia, 1988). Finally, content analysis is able to handle massive amounts of data, especially with the increased use of computers to store information. Gerbner, Gross, Signorielli, Morgan, and Jackson-Beeck (1979), for example, content-analyzed 15,000 characters from 1000 hours of television fiction to describe how power and violence are depicted on prime-time television shows.

Content-analytic Procedures

Content analysis is a systematic, step-by-step procedure used to answer research questions. The procedure involves selecting texts, determining the units to be coded, developing content categories, training observers to code units, and analyzing the data.

Selecting texts.   In the beginning of this chapter we observed that all textual analysts must acquire appropriate texts. Some content analysts may well be able to conduct a census of all relevant texts. For example, a researcher may want to know the sexual stereotypes portrayed in a particular television show, such as *Roseanne,* or in the top 10 rock songs on the *Billboard* charts from a particular year. In cases where there is a limited database, researchers conduct a census of all texts.

Most often, however, content analysts face the same problem as all researchers, the need to acquire a representative and sufficient sample. Kaid and Wadsworth (1989) explain that researchers using content analysis "must devise a method of obtaining a sample which is (1) representative of the universe from which it comes and (2) of sufficient size to adequately represent that universe" (p. 201).

Content analysts, therefore, first specify the universe of texts to which they wish to generalize and then use some procedure for selecting a sample from this universe. Of course, to generalize from a sample to a population or universe, researchers must use a random sampling procedure (see Chapter 6). Thus whenever possible, content analysts use simple random, systematic, stratified, or cluster sampling techniques to acquire representative samples. When these procedures are not feasible, researchers rely on nonrandom samples, such as convenience or purposive samples.

Determining the unit of analysis.   Content analysis involves coding messages embedded in a sample or census of texts according to categories. To accomplish this, researchers must identify the proper message unit that will be coded, a process referred to as *unitizing.* While the research question itself ultimately leads researchers to determine the appropriate unit to be studied, a number of different units are possible.

Krippendorf (1980), for example, identifies five units that researchers study: physical, syntactical, referential, propositional, and thematic units. *Physical units* are the texts that are to be used in the study, such as newspapers, books, or television shows. A bibliographic study of the number of books written about communication during different time periods (1960s, 1970s, etc.) or a study of television shows involving minority characters, for example, call for content analysis at the physical unit level. *Syntactical units* consist of individual symbols (words), as when counting the number of times the term *communism* appears in newspaper editorials. *Referential units* link symbols to particular referents, as when counting the number of positive words written in newspaper editorial comments about President Bush. Content analysis thus can be used to ascertain the evaluative meaning observers associate with words and sentences. *Propositional units* carry explicit proposals. For example, Gerbner (1964) studied how ideological biases were apparent in proposals advocated in newspaper articles. Finally, *thematic units* are topics contained within messages, as when identifying sexist or racist themes in the content of television shows.

Developing content categories.   Once researchers have identified the appropriate unit of analysis, they use nominal measurement procedures to develop categories into which units can be classified. These categories must be mutually exclusive, equivalent, and exhaustive (see Chapter 5).

Berelson (1952) identifies two general types of categories used to classify units in content analysis: substance (the content of the message) and form (the way it is said). For example, Alderton and Frey (1983) classified the substance of small group argumentation into majority and minority arguments. They could also have classified each argument according to whether it took the form of a statement or a question.

The value of a content-analytic study rests on developing valid categories into which units can be classified. Developing these categories is a creative process, but diligent researchers try to follow all the valid measurement procedures discussed in Chapter 6.

Coding units. Once the appropriate units have been determined and the categories have been developed, researchers train observers, called **coders,** to identify the appropriate category for each unit. Researchers usually use two coders, and preferably more, who classify each unit into its appropriate category independently. Researchers then use a procedure to assess the reliability of these codings. For example, the percentage of agreement between coders can be computed on a unit-by-unit basis. Other formulas, such as Scott's (1955) *pi,* also take into account chance agreements as well as the complexity of the category system itself. Each procedure yields a coefficient of interobserver reliability. A coefficient of .80 or above usually is considered reliable, whereas one below .80 is suspect (Kassarjian, 1977). Finally, coders are asked to work together and reach agreement on coded units about which they disagreed.

Analyzing the data. Coding units into nominal categories yields qualitative data; counting the number of units in each category yields quantitative data. Knowing the types of categories informs researchers about what is being communicated; knowing the number of units in each category informs them about how often these types of messages are being communicated.

Both types of data are useful for describing, understanding, and critiquing the content of the communication being studied. For example, knowing the types and amount of psychoanalytic themes in traditional folk and fairy tales can lead to rich descriptions and interpretive insights about what morals the culture values. Furthermore, researchers can use this information to understand how input and output variables relate to message behavior. It may be possible, for example, to show how different cultures (an input variable) emphasize different values through the tales told. It may also be possible to show how such tales influence children's thoughts and behaviors (an output variable). Berne (1972) argued that the implicit morals in fairy tales help children develop unconscious "scripts" that influence their behavior later in life. Children who are told about Little Red Riding Hood, for example, may be wary of self-disclosure because they unconsciously view others as wolves. Finally, communication practitioners use these interpretive insights to inform people about appropriate courses of action, such as advising parents about which tales they should teach their children. Content analysis is thus a powerful method for analyzing texts that is useful to theorists, researchers, practitioners, and consumers alike.

CONVERSATION ANALYSIS

People typically view conversation as something they know how to do instinctively. We ordinarily don't pay much attention to routine, everyday activities, although we probably pay more attention to talking than walking. From time to time, however, all of us engage in interactions that lead us to pay more conscious attention to conversation, perhaps because our apprehension is increased. You probably pay more attention to what you say, for example, when you are interviewed for a job, plan how to confront someone about something that is bothering you, or talk to a parent while waiting for your date to come downstairs.

Scholars pay a great deal of attention to conversation, believing that much can be learned from what we seem to take for granted (Hopper, 1981). They view conversation as a complex *accomplishment* that requires much knowledge on the part of individual communicators and the ability to coordinate behavior with others. For example, even asking someone the simple question "Can you pass the salt, please?" requires not only rules of grammar and syntax but also a shared understanding that the question is not meant as a request about the person's ability to pass the salt.

Conversation analysis examines messages exchanged during dyadic and small group interactions in order to discover the "systematic and orderly properties which are meaningful to conversants [and researchers]" (Heritage, 1989, p. 23). These systematic properties include the content, function, structure, and effects of conversation. Conversation analysts thus seek to discover how conversants accomplish individual and relational goals as they produce, sequence, and interpret conversational messages.

Scholars who study conversation have many philosophical, theoretical, and methodological differences. Our purpose is not to debate these issues but to provide a broad overview of some research directions pursued by conversation analysts and to explain some of the methods used to conduct this research.

Conversation Content

We have just discussed ways in which the content of communication can be studied. Some conversation analysts also study the content of conversation by examining the topics people talk about.

Sometimes researchers want to know what general topics are discussed. Moore (1922), for example, eavesdropped on people in public on the streets of Manhattan and noted the topics they talked about in same-gender and mixed-gender dyads. Moore's study found that the topics talked about most frequently by men (money or business, amusement) and by women (men, clothing or interior decorating) were the topics talked about the least by the opposite gender. Moore also found that women adapted more to men within mixed-gender dyads by talking about the topics that interested men. A follow-up study by Deakins, Osterink, and Hoey (1987) 65 years later found no change for male and male-female dyads, as money or business and amusement still were the topics talked about most frequently. Female dyads, however, showed some change, as women now talked most frequently about women, clothing, interior decoration, and men.

Other researchers study how particular topics affect conversations. Socha (1988), for example, was interested in how married couples converse about joint decisions, topics that neither is free to decide alone. He first had couples rate how much they wanted a say in, how likely they were to talk about, and how easy it was to reach agreement on 50 decision topics. He then asked couples to carry on a conversation about a topic that both partners wanted a strong say in but had never discussed. These conversations were analyzed using Rogers and Farace's (1975) relational control scheme (to be explained shortly) to describe partners' patterns of control and support messages.

Conversation analysts recognize that topic selection influences conversation significantly. A conversation between a supervisor and a subordinate about a work-related problem will contain different types of messages and lead to different outcomes than a conversation between two friends about how much they liked a movie. Topic selection provides a meaningful boundary within which a conversation can be understood by both conversants and researchers.

Functions of Conversational Messages

Conversation analysts are also interested in identifying the purposes of specific actions and utterances in a conversation. Interactants have general goals in mind when communicating, such as conveying information to others ("There will be an election Tuesday") and persuading them ("You should vote for candidate X on Tuesday"). Researchers want to know what *functions* conversational messages serve.

One of the earliest and most influential functional analysis of communication is Bales's (1950) Interaction process analysis (IPA) scheme, which examines the communication that characterizes decision-making group interaction. The basic purpose of the IPA scheme is to categorize the purpose, or function, of each person's communicative acts in a group setting into 12 categories, 6 of which correspond to task (job-related) messages and 6 to socioemotional (person-related) messages (see Figure 10.1). For example, a comment such as "I think we should vote now" would be coded using this scheme as "giving suggestions."

By studying many decision-making groups, Bales determined a relative range of acts that typically characterize an effective group in each category, and these norms are applied both to individual group members and to the group as a whole. By comparing the interactional patterns of a group and its members to these norms, researchers and practitioners can infer whether a group is effective and what particular problems members are experiencing.

Conversation analysts view functional messages that are designed to accomplish personal and relational goals as *moves* or *strategies.* For example, Bellack, Kliebard, Hyman, and Smith (1966) identified four types of moves associated with teacher-student classroom conversation: (1) *structuring,* moves that focus attention

Figure 10.1   Bales interaction process analysis

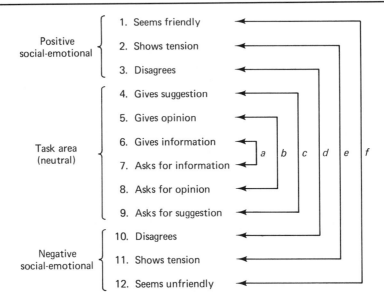

Key

a. Problems of orientation
b. Problems of evaluation
c. Problems of control
d. Problems of decision
e. Problems of tension management
f. Problems of integration

Source: Robert Freed Bales, *Interaction Process Analysis: A Method for the Study of Small Groups*, p. 59, copyright © 1950 by Addison-Wesley Publishing Company. Reprinted by permission of The University of Chicago Press.

(such as "This is very important material"), (2) *soliciting,* questions and requests (such as "Do we have to know this material for the test?"), (3) *responding,* moves that occur only after soliciting moves (such as answering a question), and (4) *reacting,* moves that evaluate other messages (such as "What a great idea!"). The functional communication behaviors identified in Chapter 3, such as how we comfort others, get others to comply with our requests, resist compliance-gaining attempts, and deceive others, are examples of conversational message strategies.

The Structure of Conversation

Researchers interested in the functional nature of conversational messages focus on the purpose of each communicator's moves. Other researchers analyze the *structure* of conversation by studying the relationship between conversants' moves. Jacobs and Jackson (1983) argue that "as in chess, the current position of each player affects the moves that can be appropriately and effectively performed" (p. 55). Each person's moves shape and constrain what the next person's moves might be. For example, if a person asks a question about your car, the content of your answer should refer to your car and not something else, if your answer is to make sense. Moves that are designed intentionally to be recognized by another as requiring a response or uptake are called *illocutionary acts* (Austin, 1962). Obvious examples are "Thank you" followed by "You're welcome" and "How are you?" followed by "Fine, thank you."

The combination of an illocutionary act with a meaningful response is called an *adjacency pair.* Adjacency pairs consist of (1) two utterances in length, (2) occurring one after the other, (3) produced by different speakers, made up of (4) a first pair part (such as a question, "What time is it?") that calls out for (5) a second pair part (in this case the answer, "It's ten o'clock"), which has some discernible relationship to the first pair part (McLaughlin, 1984). Examples of adjacency pairs include request–grant or deny, greeting–greeting, compliment–accept or reject, insult–response, and accuse–deny or confess.

The adjacency pair is used to understand the types of sequences that characterize conversation. For example, researchers have studied the sequences of moves associated with conversational openings (Krivonos & Knapp, 1975; Nofsinger, 1975; Schiffrin, 1977), conversational closings (Knapp, Hart, Friedrich, & Shulman, 1973), and retelling sequences of events stories (Jefferson, 1978).

One of the most interesting and most useful lines of research is the nature of troublesome interactional sequences, such as arguments. Conversation analysts recognize that when two people argue, they not only advance individual propositions (such as competing proposals) but also engage in a particular type of interaction. The cliché "It takes two to argue" recognizes the reciprocal and interactional nature of arguing.

Using the concept of adjacency pairs, researchers argue that generally people prefer agreement in conversation (Brown & Levinson, 1978; Pomerantz, 1978). Therefore, they typically respond to a first-pair part (such as a request) with the preferred second-pair part (granting the request). Jackson and Jacobs (1980) explain that an argument occurs, however, when a person gives a dispreferred second-pair part. For example, consider the following exchange (McLaughlin, 1984, p. 183):

A: I want to get a new suit for my interview, OK?
B: We can't afford it this month.

Speaker B obviously has not responded with the preferred second-pair part, the granting of the request. Hence we have the basic sequence that constitutes an argument. Of course, the argument will continue and escalate if person A's next statement is a dispreferred response that challenges B's statement (for example, "We could afford it if you wouldn't spend so much on other things").

At a more general level, scholars believe that conversational sequences are organized by the use of *rules*. A conversational rule is a "followable prescription" that helps people decide what move is "obligated, preferred, or prohibited" within a particular communication situation (Shimanoff, 1980, p. 57). Conversational rules take this form: In circumstance X, Y is required or permitted (McLaughlin, 1984, p. 17). These rules help people explain, predict, and evaluate how they and others behaved, should have behaved, and will behave within a given interaction.

The origins of these conversational rules include conversants' cultures, relevant referent groups, and the particular communication situation. Some of these rules apply to virtually every conversation regardless of context. Grice (1975), for example, argued that people follow a "cooperative principle," the mutual belief between communicators that a contribution to a conversation will be appropriate and necessary, given the purpose of the interaction. A person is not being cooperative, therefore, if he or she answers the question about passing the salt with, "I can."

Other rules are appropriate only for particular interactions. Raising your hand in class to request permission to speak may be proper, but this rule usually isn't followed when you talk with your best friend. Professors also ordinarily don't invite their friends over and lecture to them from behind a podium!

Researchers sometimes study conversational rules by asking people to articulate them. For example, most students are aware of the rule that you do not call a professor by his or her first name unless you are invited to do so. At other times, however, people are not consciously aware of the conversational rules they follow. How many of us know enough about linguistics or English to articulate all the grammatical and syntactical rules we use to construct sentences? In such cases, researchers infer the existence of rules from recurring sequences of conversational moves.

Once conversational rules have been identified, researchers study how communicators use them to coordinate interaction. For example, people take turns speaking and listening in conversations (although sometimes they talk simultaneously), and this turn taking is regulated by shared rules (such as "When one person talks, the other listens" or "It's rude to interrupt someone"). Researchers also recognize, however, that conversational rules are broken, and much can be learned from rule violations, including the existence of the rule itself as well as how interactants repair a "damaged" conversation.

Effects of Conversation

Many conversation analysts restrict their focus to describing the topics, functions, or structure of conversation; other researchers want to know how these aspects of conversation relate to important outcomes. Fisher (1970), for example, studied how the functional nature of communication characterized the development of decision-making groups. By coding individual group members' functional comments, he identified four primary phases of communication that typify the development of decision-making groups: (1) *orientation,* interaction that enables the group to focus on the nature of the decision-making topic; (2) *conflict,* interaction that enables group members to argue about the issues concerning the decision-making topic and work out competing group roles; (3) *emergence,* interaction that identifies the best solutions to a problem; and (4) *reinforcement,* interaction that directs group members to implement the solutions.

Other researchers study how the sequential nature of conversation leads to important outcomes. Alderton and Frey (1983), for example, showed how argumentative acts and positive and negative reactions to them relate to group polarization, the tendency for a group to make a more extreme decision than its individual members would if they were making the same decision on their own. They found that group polarization decreased when members responded positively to minority arguments but increased when members negated them. They suggest that people who take on a devil's advocate role in a group will restrain a group from making an extreme decision only if most members are willing to listen to and consider their minority arguments. Simply presenting a minority argument is not sufficient in and of itself.

The sequential nature of conversation has also been shown to lead to important relational outcomes. Ruesch and Bateson (1951) argued that all messages contain two types of meaning, content and relational. The relational meaning of messages recognizes that all communication says something about the nature of the relationship between interactants. Watzlawick, Beavin, and Jackson (1967) argued, therefore, that *relational control* is an ever-present element in conversation. They distinguished between *complementary relationships,* in which one person usually controls the other, and *symmetrical relationships,* where both relational partners share control equally.

Rogers and Farace (1975) designed a coding scheme to assess how relational control characterizes the exchange of paired sequential messages over time. The coding scheme involves three steps. First, messages are characterized by speaker, grammatical form (assertion, question, talk-over, noncomplete, or other), and response mode (support, nonsupport, extension, answer, instruction, order, disconfirmation, topic change, initiation-termination, or other). Second, each person's messages are assigned one of three control directions: *one-up messages,* which assert definitional rights (such as an assertion that does not support a previous statement); *one-down messages,* which accept or request the other's definition of the relationship (such as a question that asks for support from the other person); or *one-across messages,* leveling messages that minimize asserting or accepting definitions (such as an assertion that extends a previous point). Third, by looking at paired sequential messages, researchers can characterize the transactional nature of a conversation or an interpersonal relationship as *symmetrical* (such as two consecutive one-up or one-down messages), *complementary* (such as a one-up message followed by a one-down message, or vice versa), or *transitional* (such as a one-up or a one-down message followed by a one-across message, or vice versa).

Many important outcomes are associated with communication in general and conversation in particular. For each outcome, the central question being addressed by researchers is how communication functions as an independent variable to influence important dependent variables.

Conducting Conversation Analysis

Procedures for conducting conversation-analytic research include (1) obtaining samples of conversation; (2) transcribing recorded conversation into a written text; (3) categorizing the messages in the written transcript using coding schemes; (4) analyzing the codings to describe and draw inferences about the content, functions, structure, or effects of conversation; and (5) reporting the findings in written form and explaining how they help develop new or existing views about conversation.

First, a number of ways of obtaining conversational messages were explained earlier in this chapter. In gathering samples of conversation, researchers make choices that affect both the type and the quality of the data obtained. These choices include the type of conversational data required, the desired location of the conversation, and the appropriate means for gathering the data.

At the most general level, conversation analysts study dyadic and small group interactions, since mass-mediated and public messages are analyzed through the use of content analysis and rhetorical criticism. An important consideration, however, is whether any conversation may be studied or whether specific conversations are required. For example, researchers can study turn taking in any conversation. Researchers interested in how status differences affect conversation, however, must study interactions in which status differs, such as superior-subordinate conversations. Finally, some researchers are interested only in particular conversations, such as doctor-patient or spousal interactions.

Another consideration is whether the conversation is to be *natural and unstructured* or whether people are asked to engage in a *structured conversational activity* or task. For example, Moore (1922) studied natural conversations to determine what topics were talked about in same-gender and opposite-gender dyads. Socha (1988), however, was interested in how married couples manage relational control as they discuss controversial decisions, so he asked couples to discuss a particular topic they considered important but disagreed about.

Another consideration is whether the conversation needs to be *real* or can be *hypothetical*. For example, if an actual conversation between married couples about purchasing a home is desired, couples who have contacted real estate agents could be asked to tape their conversations whenever they talk about their impending house purchase. However, if researchers are interested in the functional messages husbands and wives use to persuade their spouse to buy a house, people could be told to imagine themselves engaged in a conversation with their spouse and asked to construct a persuasive message. This procedure, however, does not necessarily capture what occurs in actual conversation because it allows people more time to think about their message choices than they would have in real conversations, and it does not account for interactional sequences of actual conversation.

The location in which the conversation is studied also affects the nature of the data. Three locations that differ in terms of the control provided to researchers and the naturalness of the setting for participants are in a laboratory, in interactants' homes or offices, or in some publicly accessible place, such as a mall or on public transportation. Using a laboratory to study conversation certainly provides researchers with the most control, since they can structure the environment according to their needs (including the use of experimental manipulations), and it makes videotaping easy. Studying conversation in a laboratory, however, may make interactants feel uneasy or overly aware that they are being watched. People may feel more at ease and comfortable in their homes or offices, but researchers have less control over those environments than in a laboratory. Studying conversations overheard in public affords researchers the least amount of control but is the most natural of these three locations.

Researchers must also consider the means for gathering the conversational data. The current available options include audiotaping, videotaping, observational notes taken by researchers, and questionnaires answered by respondents. Audiotape recorders are readily available, and video cameras are becoming smaller and less expensive. In a laboratory setting, a camera can be set up so it cannot be seen by subjects (with their permission, of course). Researchers can even set up cameras on tripods in people's homes and leave them simple instructions on recording their conversations. Taking notes while observing conversation is also possible for certain tasks, such as noting the topics discussed or the types of functional messages constructed. This procedure, however, is open to many problems and biases, since it is very difficult to keep track of all the sequential messages exchanged. Finally, questionnaires can be used with hypothetical situations. For example, researchers can ask people to indicate on a questionnaire which compliance-gaining strategy they would use in a hypothetical instance, or they could ask people to write out what they would say in this situation and then code the message as a particular type of compliance-gaining strategy.

Second, transcribing the conversation means producing a written record of it that can be analyzed. Researchers need to decide how much detail is needed in a transcript in order to answer their research questions. Labov and Fanshel (1977), for example, have one of the most detailed transcription procedures, which includes pictures of electronic spectographic analysis of the pitch waves of the voices of the conversants, times pauses to $\frac{1}{100}$ second, and a detailed system to categorize audible breaths. Their analysis of 15 minutes of a conversation between a therapist and a client took nine years to transcribe and analyze! At the other extreme is a simple counting of the number or types of topics people talk about or the verbal moves they make. The rule of thumb is not to include any more detail in a transcript than is needed to answer the research questions.

Third, once a written text is generated, the types of messages are unitized and categorized by coders, as in content analysis. Sometimes unitizing is relatively easy, such as determining the different topics that are discussed. At other times it is very difficult to determine where each conversational unit begins and ends, as in determining meaningful adjacency pairs in a group discussion. To unitize in a reliable manner, researchers use coders and assess interobserver reliability. Once reliable units are bracketed, the coders use coding schemes to categorize the topics, functions, structure, or effects of conversation, and reliability coefficients are computed.

Fourth, the coded units are analyzed through appropriate data analysis procedures. The analysis may involve counting and summarizing the codes for each participant, such as the type and number of compliance-gaining strategies each person used. The analysis may also involve studying paired sequential messages, such as determining symmetrical, complementary, and transitional relationships based on paired one-up, one-down, and one-across messages. Researchers also often analyze differences between groups, such as J. B. Miller's (1987) study of the different relational control moves used by men and women, or relationships between variables, such as Alderton and Frey's (1983) study of how minority arguments and reactions to them relate to group polarization. Finally, researchers write reports that explain the purpose of the research, the literature reviewed, the methods used, the results obtained, and the significance of the findings.

Conversation analysts thus study what people normally take for granted, that conversation is a complex and organized accomplishment that affects people. By studying the topics, functions, structure, and effects of conversation, researchers make sense out of this very complex art and skill.

UNOBTRUSIVE MEASURES

Detectives often rely on physical forms of evidence for drawing conclusions. Sherlock Holmes, for example, was a master at inferring what had happened from observing physical evidence. He used physical traces left behind, such as footprints, fingerprints, or strands of hair, to identify and track criminals.

Communication researchers are also interested in physical forms of evidence. **Unobtrusive measures** examine physical traces or artifacts to describe people and their communication behavior (Webb, Campbell, Schwartz, & Sechrest, 1973). As the name implies, researchers use unobtrusive measures to study people's behavior without their realizing that they are being studied. When people know that they are being observed or when they are asked questions directly, they may not react in a normal and honest manner (the Hawthorne effect). People may also recognize the purposes of the research, which can influence their behavior (the researcher expectancy effect). Unobtrusive measures are very "clean" ways to gather data because they eliminate much of the reactivity by not asking people to participate in the research. Instead, researchers examine the traces and artifacts of people's behavior.

Three primary techniques are used to gather data unobtrusively: archival research, bibliometrics, and trace measures.

Archival Research

Archival research involves describing and evaluating communication embedded in existing records of human behavior. It is the most frequently used unobtrusive measurement technique because lots of public and private records are available. Webb and colleagues (1973) identify at least four types of public records that are available:

(1) actuarial reports, such as births and deaths; (2) political and judicial records, such as the *Congressional Record* and transcripts of court trials; (3) other government records, such as weather reports, city budgets, and traffic accident reports; and (4) the mass media, such as newspapers and films. Three sources of private records might also be available to researchers: sales records, industrial and institutional records, and personal written documents.

Examining archival records often provides researchers with information more accurate than can be obtained from questionnaires or interviews. For example, the markings on an employee's timecard, the withdrawals marked on a bank customer's monthly statement, or a phone customer's telephone bills reveal how often they are late or absent from work, how often and how much they withdraw from their bank accounts, and how often they call special sex-talk lines, respectively. How accurate do you think people's responses to questions about these topics might be? Of course, these records may not necessarily be accurate. Fellow employees may punch in timecards for workers who are habitually late, friends or family may have access to a person's bank card and make withdrawals, and others in the home may be calling the sex-talk numbers.

Communication researchers have used archival records in some intriguing ways. Rashkis and Wallace (1959), for example, measured the amount of attention paid to particular patients by nurses based on the number of notes they wrote and filed about each patient. Parker (1963), wanting to know the effects of television on reading, found that the withdrawal of nonfiction books from a public library increased after television was introduced in a town.

Archival records can be an excellent source of information for communication researchers. Because many archival records are maintained consistently over a long period of time, they are useful for conducting longitudinal research. However, Webb and colleagues (1973) point out that although archival records are a nonreactive form of research, they are susceptible to the problems of selective deposit and selective survival. Not all records are kept, and not all survive over the course of time.

Bibliometrics

Researchers often use statistical techniques that cluster, or group together, data to study such things as family ties, bureaucratic or organizational structures, professional relationships, or economic dependencies. One important area of research where clustering techniques have proved particularly useful is the study of scholarship itself. These techniques are used to organize the relationships among communication artifacts (typically, research articles published in scholarly journals) and to represent that organization in a meaningful way (Paisley, 1965; Chubin, 1983; Lievrouw, 1988). The use of clustering techniques to study the scholarly literature is referred to as **bibliometrics.**

Bibliometrics has been defined by Pritchard (1969) as "the application of mathematics and statistical methods to books and other media of communication"

(p. 349) and more recently by Broadus (1987) as "the quantitative study of physical published units, or of bibliographic units, or of the surrogates for either" (p. 376). The unit of analysis used in bibliometric studies may be links among authors, sources, publications, or article contents, but most often it is the *citation,* a reference an author makes to another article.

Analyzing citations informs scholars about the general usefulness or impact of a document. The analysis may be as simple as counting the number of citations to a particular document. Another type of citation analysis is *bibliographic coupling,* which studies references to the same document in two other documents. However, the dominant type of citation analysis used today is *cocitation analysis,* which is the consistent reference to a *pair* of documents together in subsequent documents (Small, 1973). Analyzing how the patterns of cocitation change over time provides an interesting and dynamic view not only about which articles are considered most important in a field but also about which articles seem to be associated most closely with each other (Garfield, Malin, & Small, 1978). In recent years, the same technique has been applied to the cocitation of authors as well as documents (White, 1981; White & Griffith, 1981).

Bibliometric studies are of interest to communication researchers because the artifacts being studied result directly from communication among scholars. Communication researchers use the published patterns of references as an operationalization of authors' interpersonal interaction, and bibliometric analysis clarifies those patterns. Clusters or maps of research articles can be interpreted as networks of interpersonal contacts, so citation analysis can be viewed as a type of network analysis, and relevant network concepts are employed in the analysis (Lievrouw, 1989). For example, Parker, Paisley, and Garrett (1967) and Paisley (1984) found that journals in the same field often form a clique by citing each other frequently. Rice, Borgman, and Reeves (1988) found that the scholarly literature in the communication discipline consisted of two primary cliques that demonstrated extreme inbreeding, interpersonal journals and mass media journals.

Because bibliometric techniques analyze the distribution of the research literature, they inform communication scholars about the growth and status of the communication discipline. Wispe and Osborn (1982), for example, found that communication scholars rely extensively on psychology and other social scientific journals for their grounding, while Reeves and Borgman (1983) showed that the reverse was not true. These findings were replicated by So (1988), who reached the following conclusion:

> In comparison with other social science fields, communication is still less developed and occupies only a peripheral position in the ecology of knowledge. The relative lack of interflow within the field and between communication and other fields is quite prominent. (p. 236)

Given the relative youth of the communication discipline, perhaps bibliometric studies will show significant growth in the dissemination of communication research in the coming decades.

Trace Measures

Trace measures assess behavior by studying physical evidence, such as footprints or hair left behind. There are two types of trace measures: measures of erosion and measures of accretion.

Measures of erosion. **Measures of erosion** show how physical objects are worn down by use. For example, Mosteller (cited in Webb et al., 1973) studied which sections of the *International Encyclopedia of the Social Sciences* were read most often by examining the wear and tear on the pages of each section. Similarly, the wearing down of the fabric on easy chairs and couches might be a good measure of which furniture in a student lounge was used most. However, researchers would not know whether this was because the furniture was comfortable or because it was situated in the best locations in the room.

Measures of erosion can be *natural* or *controlled*. The examples just mentioned are natural, occurring normally over the course of time. In contrast, controlled erosion measures are set up by people to identify certain behaviors. For example, tickets numbered consecutively indicating customers' turn in a busy take-out restaurant is a good unobtrusive measure of controlled erosion. Knowing how many customers are served within a specified time period can be used to plan employee staffing around the highest and lowest customer volume shifts and to plan when to cook food ahead of time in preparation for high-volume periods. Sometimes researchers even can speed up the process of erosion by using special materials, such as floor surfaces that wear easily.

Measures of accretion. **Measures of accretion** show how physical traces build up over time. Whereas measures of erosion look at what has worn down, measures of accretion look at what is added on. For example, Du Bois (1963) analyzed the number of different fingerprints on a page to determine how often a magazine advertisement was read. Kinsey, Pomeroy, Martin, and Gebhard (1953) studied the sexual behavior of men and women, noting a significant difference between the number of erotic inscriptions in men's and women's public toilets!

An interesting (but messy) area of accretion study involves examining refuse, or *garbology*. In garbology, researchers gather, sift through, identify, and categorize garbage as a way of determining people's behavior. For example, researchers can determine from empty bottles, discarded containers and wrappings, smudges on paper plates, and so on, the kinds of food and drinks people ingest. Garbology may actually be one of the most accurate ways of determining some types of behavior, such as alcohol consumption. Respondents typically underestimate their alcohol consumption when asked in survey research. In garbology, however, the number of liquor bottles can be easily observed. If the person had a wild party over the weekend, however, a garbologist might seriously overestimate that person's liquor consumption!

Measures of accretion can also be *natural* or *controlled*, based on whether the artifacts build up naturally or are set up by a person. An example of a controlled measure of accretion might be when a marine sergeant dons white gloves while making an inspection of a platoon's barracks. The dirt on the sergeant's gloves becomes a controlled, unobtrusive measure of accretion. Sometimes researchers can also introduce materials to accelerate the process of accretion, such as special glues that help detect how many pages in a book were handled.

It should be pointed out that measures of erosion and accretion, whether natural or controlled, only provide a measure of a physical trace. It is up to researchers to interpret what that physical trace means. Just because people turn a page in a magazine, for example, doesn't mean they read it. Researchers thus need to be very careful in drawing conclusions from data gathered by unobtrusive measures. For that reason, unobtrusive measures are often used in multimethodological research as validity checks on data gathered by means of another measurement technique. Unobtrusive measures, for example, can provide useful information about the possible reactive effects of self-report measures. In the final analysis, however, ingenious researchers may well discover valuable information by using these unobtrusive measures.

CONCLUSION

A famous industrialist once said, "A man's language, as a rule, is an index of his mind." This suggests that examining word choices can provide insights into people's characters. The essence of his message is also a basic premise of textual analysts. Their mission is understanding how people think, and consequently act, by studying patterns displayed in their discourse, broadly defined.

Embedded in texts are clues to the regularities in human thought and conduct. Those regularities are like the tracks wilderness scouts use to trace the movements of wildlife. One has to be trained and equipped to discern animals' footprints and other signs of activity and from them to infer predictable behavioral patterns. But once key features are decoded, they become evidence, useful guides to tracing and predicting the animals' future behavior. Texts preserve tracks of people's communication behavior. Analysts sift through them to identify and point out to us the patterns underlying how we interact.

chapter 11

Ethnography

How people communicate depends, to a great extent, on the situation they are in. Husbands and wives talk differently when alone together than they do with colleagues at work; drill sergeants address new recruits differently than they do their commanding officer; Japanese managers deal with employees much differently than American managers do. Describing how people communicate in *particular contexts* is the focus of **ethnography.**

GOALS OF ETHNOGRAPHY

Ethnography comes from the Greek *ethnos* ("a tribe, race or nation") and *graphos* ("something written down") and thus refers to a written report about a group of people (Philipsen, 1989). Specifically, ethnography involves examining the patterned interactions and significant symbols of specific cultural groups to identify the cultural norms (rules) that direct their behaviors and the meanings people ascribe to each other's behaviors. As Gephart (1988) explains:

> Ethnography is the use of direct observation and extended field research to produce a thick, naturalistic description of a people and their culture. Ethnography seeks to uncover the symbols and categories members of the given culture use to interpret their

world and ethnography thus preserves the integrity and inherent properties of cultural phenomena. (p. 16)

The goals of ethnographic research, therefore, are to "discover and disclose the socially acquired and shared understandings necessary to be a member of a specified social unit" (Van Maanen, 1982, p. 103). Ethnographers want to understand the implicit assumptions that exist tacitly among people in particular cultural groups that constrain interaction between members.

Communication researchers draw on a rich history of ethnographic research in disciplines such as anthropology and sociology. For example, Whyte (1955), in his classic study, *Street Corner Society*, observed the communication behaviors of members of inner-city street gangs to identify the shared rules that governed their interactions. Roy (1959–1960) studied how communication was used to organize factory workers, and Goffman (1961) studied what communication behavior mental hospital workers expect from patients. Garfinkel (1967) studied how communication was used to comfort suicide-prone individuals in an urban suicide prevention center, and Cicourel (1968) studied the communication rules enforced in a juvenile justice system. The findings from these studies demonstrate the powerful role of human communication in establishing and maintaining order in specific populations, settings, or times.

Ethnographic researchers also seek to understand how people think about communication in particular situations. The nature and significance of what people say and do when communicating depends, in large part, on the meanings people give to those messages. Ethnographic research is associated most closely with the **symbolic interactionist** approach to understanding communication. This orientation stresses, as the name suggests, the symbolic nature of human social life, maintaining that the meaning and function of virtually every human action involving communication is a mutual creation defined by the individuals interacting. The study of communication, therefore, must not be mechanical but must, as Benson and Hughes (1983) assert,

> concern itself with exploring the processes by and through which social actors mutually adjust lines of action on the basis of their interpretations of the world in which they live. Symbolic interactionism . . . commits itself to a method of inquiry that emphasizes the actor's point of view and . . . concerns itself with elucidating the meanings and understandings actors themselves use to construct their social world. (p. 44)

Marrione (1985) provides an example:

> Picture yourself in the common situation of driving along in a car with two other people, turning a corner and seeing a person standing off the curb. . . . Upon seeing your car, [the person] now sticks an arm out and extends a clenched fist with a thumb sticking up. At this moment you experience . . . an "impulse" to act—the gesture of the person calls out in you a response as you perceive the thumb-up on the hand. (p. 165)

What you do next depends on the *meaning* you give to that hand signal, to cues suggesting what sort of person is giving the signal, to the act of picking up hitchhikers, and to your expectations regarding how the other people in the car will react to whatever you do. We can only understand the exchange between hitchhiker and driver, or among any interactants, if we understand how each perceives and interprets or gives meaning to symbolic cues from the other.

Because ethnography captures people's own meanings for their everyday behavior, it also is called *naturalistic* or *qualitative research*. Ethnographic researchers report what is learned in qualitative terms and attempt to provide "well-grounded, rich descriptions and explanations of processes occurring in local contexts" (Miles & Huberman, 1984, p. 15).

USES OF ETHNOGRAPHIC RESEARCH

Ethnographic research is conducted in ways similar to the interpretive processes we use in everyday life, and application of findings is often limited to the specific context in which the data are collected. The ordinariness and local focus of ethnography raises the question "Of what value are ethnographers' efforts?"

One kind of utility relates to the overall progress of communication research. Ethnography emphasizes studying subjective reality over objective fact finding. How experimental researchers analyze and divide communication processes (the variables they identify and measure) often corresponds more to lines of study popular among their academic colleagues rather than to how people actually construe their own experiences. Thus incongruities or gaps may exist between how people think and feel in everyday life and what occurs in the experimental laboratory. The fieldwork emphasis in ethnographic research serves to narrow this gap. Kirk and Miller (1986) explain that ethnographic research is "a particular tradition in social science that fundamentally depends on watching people in their own territory and interacting with them in their own language, on their own terms" (p. 9).

Moreover, ethnographers study the particular rather than the general. Nevertheless, useful theoretical formulations and hypotheses about human communication in general often emerge from close study of human communication in particular, even about how one person operates in one setting. An account of one event, such as how President Kennedy and his staff handled the planning of the ill-fated Bay of Pigs invasion, for example, yields insights into how any group might overlook important information in an effort to maintain goodwill among its members.

Ethnographic research also has some very practical benefits. People in situations have an implicitly ordered social life, a culture of their own, and researchers who learn to appreciate and describe that culture assist outsiders who will be entering those situations to learn how to get along with the people there. For example, Buono, Bowditch, and Lewis (1985) studied the difficulties faced by staff members of two mutual savings banks that merged. Each bank had its own "organizational culture," and when employees of each had to work together, their modes of operation frequently collided, seriously affecting the profitability of the merger. These researchers' descriptions of the culture of each organization and of what occurred when they were merged provide insights regarding what any administrator must learn about another organization's culture when planning to merge operations.

Another practical value applies to people beginning work or life in a company or society who must go through a process of socialization in which they "learn the ropes" regarding the communication norms in that setting. Ethnograhpic research identifies such norms, thereby easing the confusion and stress of socialization. Collinson (1988), for example, studied how joking and horseplay was used to initiate new employees and to manage conflict among men working on the shop floor of an engineering company. This information provides people who enter that culture with some explanation for behavior that could easily be misconstrued.

People traveling or moving abroad may also use ethnographic research findings to understand how people in the new culture interpret communication. Many ethnographic studies describe how people in another culture interact. For example, Sherzer's (1983) study of a Central American Indian tribe provides a description of "language and speech in Kuna life and a presentation of Kuna theories and practices of speaking, both as overtly articulated by members of the community and as practiced by them in many activities from ritual to everyday" (p. 11).

Finally, ethnographic research is useful for studying extreme instances of communication behavior, such as *case studies* of particularly unsuccessful or successful episodes. Sutton, Eisenhardt, and Jucker (1985), for example, studied how the Atari Corporation lost many of its best managers and technical wizards because it botched the process of initiating cutbacks necessitated by the decline of the video game boom. Lessons may be drawn from this single experience by the many companies who face "downsizing."

Machungwa and Schmitt (1983) interviewed 341 employees working in a wide range of organizations in Zambia regarding "incidents that made them work very hard or very little." Their aim was to identify and describe factors that influence work motivation in Zambia and perhaps in other developing countries—findings very useful to managers setting off to work there who wish to nurture high worker performance.

Ethnographic research also informs us about how a particular social issue is manifested in communication. Van Dijk (1987), for example, was concerned that

> most of our "Western" societies have become increasingly multiethnic in the past decades, and the persistence and growth of prejudice, discrimination, and racism against ethnic minorities are threatening not only the rights and well-being of these fellow citizens, but also the human and democratic values and goals of our society as a whole. (p. 383)

He therefore interviewed people in Los Angeles and Amsterdam to learn, "How do majority people talk about the minority groups in their city or country?" His study helps us understand how a cognitive pattern, prejudice, is embedded and spread in everyday talk.

COMMONALITIES IN ETHNOGRAPHIC RESEARCH

Numerous research methodologies are roughly equivalent to, or may be incorporated under, the general heading of ethnography, such as naturalistic and qualitative research. Virtually all of these approaches, however, have the following characteristics in common.

Inductive Reasoning

Ethnographic research begins by gathering data from the arena of social life being studied. Only then are patterns or theories sought to explain those data. Generalizations are built from the ground up. The term *presuppositionless research* is often used to describe this characteristic. Anderson (1987) explains:

> This term does not mean that the researcher is somehow a cultural blank without norms, values, and ideology. It means that the researcher makes his or her own norms, values and ideology apparent and does not assume that they are those of the members. (p. 242).

Ethnographic researchers "bracket," or acknowledge and then set aside temporarily, their hypotheses about what they will find and remain open to what the data reveal.

Whitbourne (1986) provides an example of research using an open-minded, inductive approach in her study of adult identity development. She interviewed 94 adults regarding the question "Who am I?" To draw conclusions from what she heard, Whitbourne writes:

> Countless attempts at numerically based rating systems were tried and discarded progressively, until finally I decided to read all the transcripts in sequence, person by person rather than question by question. What I found . . . flew in the face of my previous ideas about developmental changes in adulthood. (p. 1)

Whitbourne had to set aside her assumptions about what she expected to find before she could understand fully the data she had gathered.

Proximity and Interaction

Ethnographic researchers usually deal directly with the people being studied. They observe, interview, or participate with them in the target communication events. Some investigators study contexts with which they themselves are intimately familiar. Rosecrance (1986), for example, studied the nature of "buddy relations" among 67 men who regularly frequent Harrah's Lake Tahoe Race Book, an off-track betting establishment for horse race gamblers in Nevada. His choice of and knowledge about that context was influenced, he says, by my 30-year participation in horse-race gambling. I have gambled at Harrah's for the last 15 years and have developed a rapport with most of the regular participants. As a longstanding member of the group, I was in a unique position to report on the prevailing relationship patterns. (p. 444)

Rosecrance's approach is an example of **autoethnography,** or a study of one's own group.

Shuman (1986) entered a domain where she was an outsider. Her goal was to study how adolescents of junior high school age tell each other stories about fights in their social milieu. To do so, she spent three years investigating their social interaction, staying close to the action. As she explains:

In the school I spent most of my time with students. I attended classes, went to lunch in the student lunchroom, participated in after-school activities and special interest clubs, and spent time in the hallways. . . . I gradually became friendly with students of all races and was invited to their homes after school. (p. 7)

Of course, not all ethnographers invest as much time and effort as Shuman did. Owen (1984), for example, studied teacher-student communication by observing 10 class sessions taught by one teacher. All ethnographers, however, try to learn about the phenomena they are studying as directly and as fully as is feasible.

Ordinary Behavior

Ethnographic researchers are usually concerned with the natural interactions of the people studied, what they say and do as they go about their usual routines. In fact, they are often interested in ordinary, undramatic communication behavior that is usually taken for granted, messages people exchange almost unconsciously.

Craig, Tracy, and Spisak (1986), for example, looked for underlying patterns in how people ask for favors in everyday situations, such as "requesting a stranger to watch one's luggage, asking a friend for a ride to the airport, borrowing a classmate's notes before an exam, and asking a neighbor to watch one's cat over the weekend." Garner (1985) spent time on several "corners" (outdoor settings where people gather to socialize) in an urban black community near Detroit in order to study the functions served by "boasting" or self-exaggeration comments. Such targets of study are not earthshaking, but they are absolutely essential to understanding how the people in these studies negotiate their everyday social lives. People must perform these social behaviors appropriately, as expected, to be accepted and befriended by others in their social group.

Multiple and Flexible Methods

Ethnographers frequently use a variety of methods to gather data about the phenomena they are studying, and they exercise quite a bit of creativity in doing so. Levin and Arluke (1987) provide an illustration of the variety in research methods employed. They studied the nature of gossip in contemporary American society. To do so, they examined closely the content of several newspaper "gossip columns" over the preceding three decades; interviewed 15 gossip reporters from newspapers, magazines, and tabloids; studied biographies and autobiographies of "legendary gossip columnists"; "spent time observing informally and talking casually with the staff of the *National Enquirer* in its Latana, Florida, headquarters"; and over an eight-week period spent the hours of 11 A.M. to 2 P.M. coding 194 instances of gossip overheard being exchanged between people sitting in a college student lounge (pp. 199–202).

Putnam and Geist (1985) provide another good example of multimethod ethnographic research in their examination of the way argumentation in bargaining, the types of claims and reasoning processes used, shapes the outcomes of negotiation. They studied contract negotiations between teachers and administrators of a school district. They observed approximately 40 hours of negotiating sessions, interspersed with an additional 14 hours of caucus meetings. They took 1300 pages of notes on their observations, including a near-verbatim account of the dialogue among interactants and their own comments on the general atmosphere and overall framework of the event. They also conducted 17 one-hour interviews with members of both bargaining teams. Finally, they analyzed the formal documents used in the negotiations to track specific proposed changes and the evolution of these proposals from one counterproposal to the next. Clearly, ethnography is an inclusive research genre.

To obtain firsthand texts of communication data, ethnographers use some imaginative methods. For example, to study patterns in everyday conversation, Shimanoff (1985) paid college students to carry a recorder with them and audiotape all of their conversations for one complete day. Jones and Yarbrough (1985) trained students to record on checklists characteristics of every instance of interpersonal touch they experienced over a three-day period. Ventola (1987) studied how people speak during encounters with business service producers by obtaining permission from employees of three different post offices, jewelry and gift shops, and travel agencies to keep a recorder on their counters and to audiotape their interactions with customers.

When firsthand data from communication are not available, ethnographers often employ textual analysis by studying *cultural artifacts,* recordings or transcripts of interactions. Kerckel (1981), for example, analyzed interactions with families by studying films of a particular family that had been made to produce a cinéma vérité-type documentary for the British Broadcasting Corporation called *The Family.* To produce this film, a film crew of three lived with the family for six months, two months before filming began and four months during filming.

Ragan and Hopper (1984) studied how couples talk about splitting up by analyzing six excerpts of relationship-exiting dialogue from contemporary British and American fiction, two from novels and four from plays or screenplays. "To qualify for selection," they write, "a passage had to represent the last conversation an intimate couple has, after which events depict the couple as no longer being intimate" (p. 312.)

Shimanoff (1984) studied the implicit rules that guide conversation in our society by analyzing portrayals of conversational ideals in "Cathy" cartoons over a period of several years. Finally, Thomas (1986) examined how editorial photographs in erotic magazines contribute to maintaining current modes of relationship communication.

DATA COLLECTION IN ETHNOGRAPHIC RESEARCH

The plethora of methods used in ethnographic research may be collapsed into two major investigative strategies. Poole, Folger, and Hewes (1987) summarize them as follows: "One approach attempts to *elicit* the shared pragmatic knowledge from participants' reports of their own presuppositions. The second approach rests on the researcher's ability to infer speakers' shared knowledge through the identification of formal properties of interaction" (p. 241). In practice, these two approaches correspond to interviews with cultural informants and the use of direct observation, watching communication phenomena systematically as they occur. Let's first look at observational methods and then see how ethnographers use interviewing.

Use of Observation in Ethnographic Research

Ethnographic observations usually involve researchers investigating a particular communication phenomenon by going out "into the field" to observe people interacting as they ordinarily do while carrying out everyday activities. Ethnographers wishing to observe naturalistic behavior confront a number of important issues, including what to study, how to gain access to the field, what role to assume as an observer, how observation affects the people studied, and how to record observations.

Deciding what to observe.   In the give-and-take of everyday life, all the elements in any situation—the people, the communication activity, and the setting—are interrelated. For example, to study how organizations communicate about change, one could observe the individuals most responsible for change, meetings at which proposed changes are being discussed, or a particular organization undergoing change. If a change project were to succeed (or fail), where would the responsibility lie? With the behavior of individuals? With the group dynamics at meetings? With the culture of the organization? Which is the cause and which is the effect? No one element of a communication event can be singled out and observed in isolation from the others. Nevertheless, researchers must make choices, and observations of communication usually focus on one of these aspects or another.

Sometimes the primary target of ethnographic research is a particular person or group of people, such as Philipsen's (1975) study of "talking like a man in Teamsterville," a study of role enactment in a particular urban neighborhood. Sometimes the primary focus is a particular communication activity, such as Martin, Feldman,

Hatch, and Sitikin's (1983) study of the common types of stories that are told to new organizational employees. Finally, to many ethnographers, the setting is of primary interest. Sigman (1986), for example, studied interaction among patients and staff in a nursing home. He visited a particular nursing home regularly over a 15-month period and observed everyone there in the full range of their communication activities (since neither particular people nor particular activities were his primary concern). In the end, he developed a detailed picture of how newcomers are influenced to fit themselves into the "culture" of a long-term residential facility, exemplified by this nursing home.

Gaining access to observational settings. Once ethnographers have chosen a particular focus, the next task is finding an opportunity to observe the communication they wish to study. Some investigators use what is already available to them; they study communication in settings where they work or socialize. Others must gain entry to an environment they wish to study.

Ritti and Silver (1986), for example, studied a setting in which they were involved for other reasons. Their subject was a public agency (the Bureau of Consumer Services) that serves as a "watchdog" for consumers. They analyzed how the BCS interacts with the larger state government department of which it is a part and whose behavior it is monitoring. The researchers first became involved when BCS contracted with their university, Penn State, to develop a computerized information system. At that time, Silver was a graduate assistant, and he was assigned to work on this project. He later assumed the role of project manager, and he eventually became a full-time employee of the BCS. Thus his job provided an insider role that enabled him to gain full access to the BCS's activities.

Other ethnographic researchers must gain entry to a research site. Some simply visit a site or write and ask for permission to observe. Crawford (1986), for example, wanted to study life in a commune. He learned of one headed by an author of books on an Oriental philosophy, Taoism, that he admired. So Crawford called the commune and was invited to come for a preliminary visit of a few days. After deciding that the commune would be a suitable site for his fieldwork, he wrote to the leader, explained his intentions, and was granted permission to join them for the six-month period needed to conduct his research.

Role of the observer. An ethnographer must decide on the role to assume vis-à-vis the people being observed. Gold (1958) explains that researchers can assume four roles in observing everyday interaction: complete observer, observer as participant, participant as observer, or complete participant. These observer roles are defined by how much researchers participate in the activities being observed, from minimal participation to high participation; by the relative level of objectivity on the part of observers, from fairly objective to fairly subjective, respectively; and by whether the people being studied are aware of being observed.

First, a researcher can be a *complete observer* by observing people without their knowledge and not interacting directly with them. In this role, the researcher is primarily concerned with faithfully gathering observational data about people's behavior and not with fitting into the social context being observed. Researchers who systematically eavesdrop on dyadic conversations in public places, for example, assume the role of a complete observer.

Although this strategy affords researchers the greatest objectivity in recording data, it also tends to reduce their potential insights into the social situation since they do not speak directly with the people to learn their perceptions of the phenomena being observed. Since complete observers do not fit into the environment, they also often distract people, which can potentially bias the data being gathered by increasing reactivity effects and eliciting the Hawthorne effect. Would your behavior in grade school have been influenced by the presence of an older man observing and taking notes in the back of the room?

Second, a researcher can be an *observer-participant* by letting people know that they are being observed and participating partially with them. In this role, the researcher attempts to fit into the social situation, perhaps by dressing similarly to the people being studied and recording field notes as unobtrusively as possible, but does not participate fully in the activities. Fine (1980), for example, studied interactions among boys playing on Little League baseball teams by hanging around during practice and games and chatting with players and their families.

In comparison to the complete observer role, the observer-participant minimizes reactivity effects while increasing the researcher's ability to gather reliable data about people's activities. The objectivity of this type of observation, however, may be less than that of the complete observer since the researcher is involved more intimately with what is being studied. In addition, the observer-participant functions as a marginal member of the culture, neither completely in nor completely out of it.

Third, a researcher can be a *participant-observer* by letting people know they are being observed and becoming fully involved in the social situation being studied. In this role, the researcher attempts to become a full-fledged member of the cultural group in order to understand how it influences its members. As Bogdan and Taylor (1975) explain, participant observation refers to "research characterized by a period of intense social interaction between the researcher and the subjects, in the milieu of the latter" (p. 5). Van Maanen (1982), for example, underwent police academy training himself to learn how police recruits are socialized into the culture of law enforcement.

This participant-observer role is a popular image of ethnography. By being a participant in a particular culture, a researcher learns about it firsthand. The problem, of course, is that researchers may bias people's behavior by their own involvement in the situation and lose the ability to separate themselves objectively from the situation. The last phenomenon is sometimes called "going native," which refers to researchers who become so close to the people they are studying that they begin to ignore or deny unpleasant or unethical aspects of their behavior.

Finally, a researcher can be a *complete participant* by becoming fully involved in the social situation without letting people know that they are being studied. The researcher pretends to be part of the social milieu but does not acknowledge his or her role as a researcher. Gold (1958) gives the example of a researcher who became a taxi driver for many months in order to study big-city cab drivers. During the course of the study, the other taxi drivers were not aware that they were being observed.

The complete participant role provides researchers with firsthand knowledge about the social context being studied while minimizing reactivity effects since the people do not know that they are being studied. Gold (1958) points out, however, that researchers often find it difficult to continue assuming this role because they become intimately involved with the people they are studying but must continue to deceive them about the true purpose of their involvement. It is also easy for researchers to become so subjectively involved that they lose the ability to report findings objectively.

Reactive effects of observation.   The roles of observer as participant and participant as observer are obtrusive, since people know that their behavior is being assessed. People may also become aware that they are being observed even when researchers try to be complete observers or complete participants. When people are aware of being observed, they may well change their behavior (the Hawthorne effect).

Besides awareness of being observed, specifically who the observers are and why the people being studied think they are being observed may also influence reactivity. Martin, Gelfand, and Hartmann (1971), for example, studied the aggressive behavior of children. They found that the presence in the room of a same-sex peer was associated with higher levels of aggression than the presence of an adult or of an opposite-sex peer. Kazdin (1982) warns that if people believe that an obtrusive observation will have particular consequences, such as affecting their psychological adjustment or influencing their grade or job status, they will skew their behavior in socially desirable directions.

Because the presence of others may evoke reactivity, ethnographers do several things to minimize their obtrusiveness. One method is to observe the artifacts or "traces" of peoples' behavior, rather than the people themselves, through the use of the unobtrusive measures discussed in Chapter 10. For example, Levine, Reis, and West (1980) did a cross-cultural study of people's perceptions of time and punctuality by noting the differential accuracy of clocks and of responses to requests for the time in Brazil and in Fresno, California. While these indications of precision regarding time were observed, the people being studied were unaware of the researchers' intent.

Webb and Weick (1983) lightheartedly offer several traces of people's behavior on which inferences may be based:

1. The quality of food in a restaurant is in inverse proportion to the number of semicolons and exclamation marks on the menu.
2. You can tell how bad a musical is by how many times the chorus yells hooray.

3. The length of a country's national anthem is inversely proportional to the importance of the country.

4. In war, victory goes to those armies whose leaders' uniforms are least impressive. (p. 579)

A second method is observing unobtrusively. Amato (1983), for example, wanted to compare the pace of life (how quickly people walk and conduct simple business transactions) in rural and urban settings. To do so unobtrusively, he used natural landmarks (such as a tree or a storefront) to mark off 20-meter lengths of sidewalk in both a village and a city. Then he measured with a concealed stopwatch the time it took people to traverse that distance. Amato also used a concealed stopwatch to record how long it took shop assistants in stores to give customers their change. His method was unobtrusive because the people in his studies were completely unaware that they were being observed.

Another method used to minimize obtrusiveness is making observations behind a one-way mirror. G. Miller (1987), for example, studied the rhetoric family therapists use to persuade their clients to adopt a "family perspective" when defining and remedying their problems. To do so, he operated as a participant observer over a 12-month period at one particular agency. During that time, Miller observed over 300 therapy sessions from an observation room that was connected to a therapy room by a one-way mirror and a speaker system that transmitted what the clients and therapist were saying. At the end of the 12-month period, he pooled his observations to develop some generalizations about the therapists' behavior.

Although unobtrusive measures circumvent the problems associated with reactivity, they raise a difficult ethical question: Is it appropriate to study people without their knowledge? Most institutions whose members conduct research (such as universities) insist that people being studied be informed that they are being observed, as well as how and why.

A third way to reduce reactivity, and one that permits informing people of a researcher's presence, is conducting sustained observations. The assumption is that over time, people pay decreasing attention to observers, become acclimated to being observed, and begin acting as they would if the observers weren't there. Rumelhart (1983), for example, studied what people do when they are confused in conversations, when they don't understand the content of a conversation well enough to contribute appropriately to it, but feel impelled to continue participating anyway. She did so by spending two years as a participant-observer (serving as a volunteer social worker) for an organization serving mildly to moderately retarded adults. These clients frequently find themselves in the predicament of not understanding fully conversations in which they must participate. Rumelhart openly acknowledged her research intentions, but she believed that over time the people became accustomed to her presence, so her observations did not cause reactivity.

Van Maanen (1983) identifies another criterion for observation that helps reduce reactivity: "People should be observed engaged in activites that matter to them, the performance of which is, to them, of more importance than the fact that they are performing in front of the researcher" (p. 255). For example, Hollihan,

Riley, and Freadhoff (1986) studied argumentation in a small claims court. For two weeks they sat in the jury box of a court observing a series of litigants argue their cases. Their position was obtrusive, since their presence was obvious. Yet the litigants probably did not alter their oral performance substantially, since they had so much at stake in the proceedings.

Recording observations. Another major decision ethnographers face involves what to observe and record. Observers want to take down a fair representation of the communication behavior being studied. At the start of ethnographic research, many investigators just *observe impressionistically*. Rosenblum (1978) suggests:

> It is best to begin in the most unstructured fashion possible. There is great advantage to beginning such observations with only a pencil and blank pad for recording, putting aside the . . . rigidifying constraints that must be imposed in separating wheat from chaff later on in the development of the research program; it is vital to begin by using the incredible synthesizing and integrating functions of the human mind. (p. 16)

Soon these initial notes are made more selectively, taking the form of **field notes.** Anderson (1987) says:

> Field notes are the researcher's record of what was meaningful. . . . The goal is not to record everything—that simply creates chaos—but to carefully note those critical moments when some meaning of the social action was revealed, however imperfectly, to the researcher. (pp. 257–258)

For example, Barley (1986) wanted to study how the sophisticated new technology being used in hospitals influences communication among the medical staff. To do so, he observed radiologists and radiological technicians before and after a CT scanner was introduced to their department. Barley first made extensive notes on how they interacted when examining patients using traditional X-ray and fluoroscope equipment. Then he did the same after the CT scanners were acquired. Finally, Barley went back over his notes to extract, and then compare, how the staff communicated in examinations made with each type of equipment. He didn't know what communication behavior would be most important when he started out, so he took down everything that seemed meaningful. At the end, he was able to identify from his notes the communication behaviors most affected by the new equipment.

The common goal of all ethnographic observations is inferring patterns in people's communication. But there is little agreement among ethnographers regarding the form that field notes should take. The nature of the behavior being observed influences what is recorded. Standardized observations might be unsuited to the particular nature of the culture being studied. Ethnographers strive to construct in-depth field notes so that they and others can later make sense of what was recorded. From these field notes, conclusions about the context are drawn.

Use of Interviews in Ethnographic Research

When used as a survey instrument, the interview is highly structured. All respondents are asked the same questions in the same order. The investigator's purpose is testing research hypotheses or making generalizations about the population being studied.

Ethnographers, by contrast, use interviews to understand *particular* social phenomena *inductively* by developing "intimate familiarity" (Brenner, 1985, p. 148) or a "detailed, dense acquaintanceship" (Lofland, 1976, p. 8) with the people involved. They want to understand each individual's viewpoint in depth by achieving "empathy, the ability to 'identify' with another person, to appreciate or understand another person's feelings, attitudes, or point of view" (Lewin, 1979, p. 228). For these purposes, they often use a nondirective, or unstructured, interview. In the purest form of an unstructured interview:

> the interviewer does not know in advance which questions are appropriate to ask, how they should be worded so as to be nonthreatening or unambiguous, which questions to include or exclude to best learn about the topic under study, or what constitutes an answer (what the range of answers to any question might be). The answers to these problems are seen to emerge from the interviews themselves, the social context in which they occurred, and the degree of rapport that the interviewer was able to establish during the interview. (Schwartz & Jacobs, 1979, p. 40)

Such an interview is highly exploratory—researchers learn gradually about the participants and events, and they modify their interviewing strategy as they proceed.

Whom to interview. Ethnographic interviews rely on purposive samples. They intentionally select people, called "informants," to interview. Many ethnographic interviewers begin with a **key informant,** someone particularly willing and able to fill them in on what and whom they should know. A key informant can usually "judge the reliability of potential interviewees, suggest people to talk with, make introductions, propose tactics for collecting information, and react to collected data and tentative interpretations" (Murphy, 1980, p. 78). Whyte (1955), for example, was unable to make much headway studying a group of street-corner boys until he explained his research to Doc, a leader of the Norton Street gang, and asked for his help. Doc replied:

> Well, any nights you want to see anything, I'll take you around. I can take you to the joints—gambling joints—I can take you around to the street corners. Just remember that you're my friend. That's all you need to know. I know these places, and if I tell them that you're my friend, nobody will bother you. You just tell me what you want to see and we'll arrange it. (p. 291)

Obtaining cooperation from people in the designated group is sometimes difficult. When contacting people to interview about a sensitive personal topic, a **net-**

work, or **snowball,** sampling technique is used. That is, the first people interviewed who fit the criteria are asked to refer the researcher to other qualified people, and the list of respondents grows, or "snowballs," as they go along. For example, Karp (1986) studied people who moved up in social status during the course of their careers. He wrote:

> After each interview, the respondent was asked for additional names of persons "whom it would be useful for me to interview." This process generated a list of well over 100 names. From these names I chose a compilation of individuals that would reflect variation of gender and professions. (p. 22)

After identifying the people to be interviewed, ethnographers must decide whether to interview them alone or together. Each approach has advantages and disadvantages. Shared interviews help establish common facts and trigger latent memories. For example, Surra, Chandler, and Asmussen (1987) studied the effects of premarital pregnancy on the relationships of 36 newlywed couples. They began their interviews with both spouses together. They asked the couples to

> come to an agreement about if and when these events occurred during their courtship: the wedding date; the first date or 'first time paired off'; times they were physically separated for a month or more; times they lived together; the times each partner first met the other's parents; the time they announced their engagement; the first sexual intercourse; and the occurrence of a pregnancy. For the remainder of the interview, the partners were separated. (pp. 128–129)

The time together clarified some facts and jogged their memories, while the time apart allowed the respondents to speak more freely about their private thoughts and feelings.

Interview locale. Ethnographic interviews are conducted wherever it is most convenient and most comfortable for respondents, usually in people's natural environment. Bowen (1986), for example, studied how mentor-protégé pairs at work communicate. He visited people in such pairs at their place of employment and interviewed them there. Suitor (1987) interviewed most of the women (married mothers returning to school) who participated in her study at their homes.

Ethnographers must sometimes be aggressive to obtain their interviews. For example, Caspi (1984) wanted to know how politicians themselves use various mass media to understand social phenomena. The subjects for his study were representatives in the Israeli parliament, the Knesset. One day, a group of students he had pretrained "swooped down" on the Knesset cafeteria during the lunch hour and interviewed in that setting 91 of the 120 people who were members of the Knesset at that time.

Interview format. Ethnographic interviews usually use a funnel format, proceeding from general to specific levels of inquiry. Ethnographers start with one or

more open-ended questions and then pose a series of more narrow, precise, sometimes closed-ended questions. Weiss and Delbecq (1987), for example, compared
the cultures in high-technology companies in California and Massachusetts by interviewing executives of firms in both places. They began their interviews with a standard request: "Describe the way high-tech business operates around Route 128 as
compared to Silicon Valley. Use your experiences and observations to explain any
differences and why they exist, if they do" (p. 45). Then they asked follow-up questions about possible differences regarding a list of particular management practices
derived from the literature on corporate culture, such as "workplace communication."

Some ethnographers develop interview questions on the basis of their theoretical orientation. Phenomenologists, for example, believe it essential to understand
how people experience important life processes without imposing any of their own
preconceptions on them. Becker (1987) used a *phenomenological interview* to study
friendship between women. She interviewed two sets of women friends separately
for a total of 8 to 10 hours over a four-month period. The initial interview began
with this request: "Please describe as completely as possible your friendship with
(friend's name)" (p. 61). Each woman was encouraged to speak about her everyday
experiences of this particular friendship and to avoid talking abstractly about it.
Subsequent questions followed the structure of her initial remarks and asked for
further descriptions of situations already mentioned. Each additional interview began by asking the woman to describe experiences of the friendship that she had
become aware of since the last interview. In later interviews, Becker pursued unclear
aspects of previous interviews to obtain richer descriptions of these areas. Interviews
were discontinued when each woman felt that she had communicated a thorough
and complete description of that particular friendship.

Burgoyne and Hodgson (1984) take an "action theory" approach—they believe that all human activity is intentional. Therefore, they conduct interviews to
study people's perceptions using *protocol analysis*. Respondents are asked to verbalize their intentions, thoughts, and feelings as they engage in whatever activity is
being studied. People watching television, for example, are asked to "think aloud"
as they choose a program and react to what is being shown on the screen.

To assist protocol analysis, researchers use *stimulated recall,* in which a conversation is first recorded and then the tape is played back for one or more of the
participants (to stimulate their recall of that episode). Listeners are asked to describe
more fully what they were thinking and feeling at points throughout the activity.
Burgoyne and Hodgson provide, as an example, a transcript of a conversation between an executive and a manager who works for him. Then they provide an additional transcript of an interview with the manager after his recall of that incident
has been stimulated by listening to a recording of it. In the second transcript, the
manager's reactions to the original conversation are probed more fully than if he
had been interviewed about it without the aid of the recording.

Flanagan (1954) studied communication in the context of significant events.
He asked people to describe *critical incidents,* events occurring in a particular con-

text (at work, for example) that were "critical" or exceptional by some criterion (unusually important, difficult, successful, unsuccessful, satisfying, unsatisfying, etc.).

A related approach, the *dramaturgical model,* maintains that understanding communication in context involves learning how people view their own and others' roles in that situation. Masheter and Harris (1986) used this model as a basis for an *episode analysis* approach to ethnographic interviewing. Respondents are asked to reconstruct a scene, complete with lines of dialogue, that represents a recurring pattern in their relationship. They interviewed a couple, for example, who had been married and divorced yet now maintain a close friendship. In joint interviews, this couple was asked to reconstruct three scenes from their relationship, one from their marriage (past), one from their postdivorce relationship (present), and one depicting how they would resolve conflict should it arise (future). For every line of dialogue, Masheter and Harris asked the speaker, "What were you trying to do when you said that?" Then they asked the other person, "Was the speaker effective in carrying off this intention?"

Some ethnographers employ *memory aids* and *projective devices* to elicit desired information from their respondents. Zimmerman and Weider (1982), for example, used *diaries* as memory prompts. They asked respondents to record their activities in a semistructured diary over the course of seven days. Then the researchers used these diary entries to generate interview questions that elicited more details regarding the events they were investigating.

Analyzing and reporting the interview.   Many ethnographers, like other researchers, tape their interviews (using audio or video recordings), and many have the recordings transcribed. The transcriptions are then analyzed to develop generalizations about the communication processes being studied. The process of transferring dialogue from an oral to a written medium is a crucial step in the research process. Rawlins and Holl (1987), who interviewed eleventh-graders about their friendships, handled this process particularly well. They read each transcript repeatedly while the tape was played. Doing so served several functions: (1) It ensured accurate transcription, (2) it familiarized them with each respondent as an individual, and (3) it enabled them to note special emphases or prosodic cues that might help them to interpret the written transcript more appropriately.

Some ethnographers approach the interview data *deductively,* by determining the extent to which respondents' comments fit a preexisting theory or category system. Stohl (1986), for example, interviewed people to elicit a "memorable message" they had received at work, "something somebody said to them which had an important effect on their work life" (p. 240). Their responses were then classified and coded according to categories established in previous research on the same topic conducted by Knapp, Stohl, and Reardon (1981). Thus Stohl's data analysis, by using the earlier category system, continued and extended the initial work on this topic.

Other researchers analyze interview data *inductively.* Generalizations are grounded in or inferred from the data collected, rather than being imposed on the data from another source. This approach is based on the **grounded theory method** for analyzing qualitative data developed by Glaser and Strauss (1967) and refined by Strauss (1987). Data are used primarily for theory generation rather than theory testing.

Developing grounded theory from interview data involves several stages. First, of course, the phenomenon of interest—the communication process being studied— is identified, and data are collected as naturalistically as possible (that is, with minimal influence by researchers). Then all interview responses are recorded and included in the data analysis, often by writing each response on a card. The analysis begins by searching for commonalities among responses. When the content of several cards appears to belong together, those responses are presumed to constitute a category, and a word or phrase is selected to title it—in terms used by the respondents, whenever possible. Gradually, all the data (response cards) are sorted into categories. Each card is copied and placed in as many categories as it fits, to preserve the conceptual richness of the phenomenon being studied.

Lederman (1985), who interviewed "communication-apprehensive" students, for example, listened to taped conversations and coded all responses as "I—individual/idiosyncratic" (topics mentioned by only one person), "C—consensus" (topics on which everyone agreed), or "A—areas of agreement/disagreement" (topics on which opinion differed). Then she divided the comments further into several content categories, such as "feelings about talking" and "the relationship between feelings about talking and behaviors." Finally, she developed some generalizations about the students' perceptions within each category.

Throughout the analysis, the researcher's hunches and theoretical ideas about the structure underlying the phenomenon being studied are recorded as "memoranda" kept separate from the data. This recording of preliminary and tentative inferences is intended to reduce drift away from the grounding of the categories in the data gathered from the research participants. As the conceptual scheme develops, new respondents are interviewed who promise to provide further insights into the phenomenon. The initial cycle of data gathering and data analysis is followed by wider-ranging data gathering and refined data analysis.

Karp (1986), for example, studied what occurs when people change their social status by interviewing 72 socially mobile people. As he went along, he wrote "numerous theoretical memos on emerging themes in the data" (p. 22). In other words, as he reviewed his interview tapes and notes, he made initial inferences about his respondents' careers. In fact, Karp changed his interview guide as he went along to probe more deeply into the issues he uncovered along the way. As he explained, "Unproductive questions have been deleted and other questions have been included in order to obtain systematic data on important themes unanticipated at the outset of the project" (p. 22). Karp also developed his own set of coding categories after approximately 30 interviews. This enabled him to "stay close to the data and clarify areas of greatest substantive richness" (p. 22).

Eventually new data (interview responses from additional respondents) add little to the development of new descriptive categories. At this point the categories are considered "saturated." The researcher then reviews the theoretical memoranda and conceptualizes high-level (more abstract) generalizations that subsume the initial set of categories yet are grounded in them. If possible, a "core" category is conceptualized that incorporates all others. The conceptual structure is usually hierarchical: lower-order categories serve as properties of broader categories, which in turn comprise the core category. The resulting grounded theory is a description of this hierarchical category structure, including the relationships among them and the relationships among the categories and the data.

Rawlins and Holl (1987) conducted grounded theory research to identify the conceptual structures underpinning teenagers' descriptions of how they managed their friendships. As they examined the transcripts, they developed conceptual categories on the basis of similar words and phrases used, such as references to "trust, backstabbing, someone you can talk to, keeping a confidence, etc." (p. 348). They also put into a single category statements about friends that seemed similar, even though different words were used. For example, some respondents described what others called "school friends" without exactly using that phrase. The classification scheme was continally revised as analysis proceeded. At the end, the researchers recategorized the transcripts using their final category system to ensure accuracy and consistency. They went so far as to develop a core concept encapsulating the most specific categories developed. They point out that "an overarching concern for these adolescents was the preservation or violation of trust in their friendships" (p. 348).

Grounded theory should meet four criteria. The results from such a study should be *believable,* in that they should seem plausible to the reader. They should be *comprehensive* or account for all (or most) of the data. They should be *grounded* or tied clearly to the data. Finally, they should be *applicable* and lead to testable hypotheses and additional investigation.

To report the findings from ethnographic interviews more fully, researchers often provide verbatim quotes. For example, Kelly (1985) interviewed employees at high-tech companies in Northern California's Silicon Valley to elicit stories that would reveal their organization's "culture," by asking them, "Tell me a story of what it's like to work here." She reported her results quantitatively in terms of the frequency of story themes, but she also provided qualitative results, samples of the stories collected. For example, Kelly found that 10 of the 58 stories centered around the issue "How will the organization deal with obstacles?" Here is one story under this heading reported verbatim:

> For six months we had no product. The Sales and Marketing staff was out there selling like crazy. They were selling an idea that was just on the drawing board. Finally, they produced their first boards and all the employees (including the President) spent the day in the warehouse packing and addressing them. (p. 54)

The fact that 18 percent of the stories were about dealing with obstacles is worth knowing, but so is the example itself, if the researcher's purpose is describing this company's culture.

RELIABILITY AND VALIDITY IN ETHNOGRAPHIC RESEARCH

Like all research, ethnography must be concerned with issues of reliability and validity. If the data obtained from observations and interviews are to be useful, they must be both consistent and accurate.

Reliability

In ethnographic research, the data acquired from observations and interviews, and the conclusions drawn from them, are particularly susceptible to the problem of low reliability. Kirk and Miller (1986) point out that the way ethnographers conduct research threatens reliability.

First, because much in the way of time, effort, and skill is needed to develop rapport with informants, ethnographic researchers usually operate as sole observers or interviewers. By contrast, in experimental, survey, and textual research, multiple observers and interviewers are often used, and their data can be compared to assess reliability. Second, in addition to collecting the data, ethnographic researchers also analyze them, relying on their own field notes. At each stage, researcher bias may distort what is found. Since consumers of ethnographic research see only the finished product, not the actual field notes, ethnographers must be careful to document their research fully (this is called "leaving a paper trail") and to allow other researchers to see their data upon request.

Third, the nature of qualitative data makes them less reliable than quantitative data. It is far easier to obtain consistent responses to structured questionnaires than to open-ended interviews. If asked whether you think President Bush is doing a good job today and one week from today, for example, you might reliably say yes both times. But if asked, "What do you think of President Bush's performance?" on both occasions, your answer might be quite different each time. Nevertheless, qualitative data are particularly appropriate for capturing the complexity of the world in people's own words.

Finally, ethnographers using participant observation are likely to react subjectively to the people being studied, perhaps caring deeply about them or feeling upset if they are treated badly. Objectivity is necessary for establishing reliability, and ethnographers are particularly susceptible to very "human" responses.

Validity

In spite of these potential difficulties with reliability, ethnographic research provides some advantages in terms of validity. Ethnographic research tends to maximize validity because people are studied communicating in a relatively natural context.

The type of data collected in ethnography also increases the validity of the research. First, researchers can record what people actually do rather than what those people (or the researchers) think or wish they would do, as they might respond on a survey. Second, ethnographic research allows the recording of things people do unconsciously, and consequently might never mention in an interview. Third, such research permits long-term contact with subjects. People are usually willing to give experimental researchers only an hour or two of their time. But ethnographers observe people engaging in their natural, everyday activities for days or weeks on end, which allows for thorough data gathering. Goetz and Le Compte (1984) claim that "collecting data for long periods provides opportunities for continual data analysis and comparison to refine constructs and to ensure the match between scientific categories and participant reality" (p. 221).

During longer observation periods, people also become less self-conscious about the researcher's presence. In naturalistic settings, over time subjects become acclimated to a researcher's presence, and the genuine demands of the situation are likely to be more important to them than the fact that they are being studied.

Ethnographers' claim to validity is thus bolstered in part by their "capacity to convince us that what they say is a result of their having actually penetrated (or, if you prefer, been penetrated by) another form of life, of having, one way or another, truly 'been there'" (Geertz, 1988, pp. 4–5). Their methods of observing and interviewing people generates "thick," or richly detailed, accounts of the phenomena being studied. So ethnographers are unlikely to omit an important variable that other researchers might neglect to measure. In short, ethnographers maximize validity by incorporating in the written report (the article or book describing what was learned) sufficient rich detail about the social events observed that the reader credits them with objective, firsthand, comprehensive coverage of what was studied.

Of course, simply gathering data in the field doesn't ensure valid research. Several threats to validity exist. As mentioned, naturalistic research may involve close contact with subjects being studied. Researchers, being human themselves, may become involved emotionally in ways that influence their data. They might get angry at their subjects, for example, or in some way violate their trust. Jacobs (1974) painstakingly established trust with white inmates while observing at a maximum-security prison, for example. But that trust was shattered when they suspected him of aiding their rivals, the blacks, and they would no longer speak openly to him.

Ethnographers may also be limited in their ability to witness all relevant aspects of the phenomena they are studying. Sometimes they are denied access to relevant events, perhaps because people prefer that those events remain private. Or researchers may be excluded from certain events because of associations with particular people. For example, the researchers may have been granted access to the field by an authority (such as a teacher, a warden, a police officer, a manager, or a government official) whom the people resent or suspect or whose approval they want. Both attitudes encourage them to be wary and secretive with the researcher.

Finally, since data are so plentiful in the field, researchers must select what they will collect. Their own backgrounds may bias what they believe to be important. As Agar (1988) points out, "Descriptions of child rearing, for example, might vary depending on the professional training of the ethnographer—Freudian psychology, learning theory, or an interest in kinship would all lead to different descriptions" (p. 13).

To minimize these potential threats to validity, ethnographers frequently triangulate their findings by using various methods to collect data. Kirk and Miller (1986) contend, "The more diffuse and less focused the method, the wider net it casts" (p. 30). So researchers often combine methods to check on the validity of what was learned from each source. Crawford (1986), for example, checked out data recorded in his field notes regarding the commune in which he was a participant observer during informal interviews he conducted with commune residents.

Some ethnographers use multiple observational or interview methods to check for validity. Mehan (1983), for example, used two approaches to observation to study how decisions are made among teams of educators about placing students into special-education classes or retaining them in regular classrooms. Mehan based his findings on his own observations of the meetings and on transcripts of videotapes made of several meetings. His own observing of meetings, he reports,

> provided us [with] information about the routine conduct and order of activities in the meetings we did videotape . . . [and] gave us a way to measure the so-called reactive effect of videotaping. By observing committee members' actions when we did not tape, we had a way to gauge the committee members when we did videotape. (p. 193)

In other ethnographic studies, interviews with research participants and data from archival documents are used to check the validity of observations. Ritti and Silver (1986), for example, who studied the activities of a consumer agency in a state government, wrote up and then presented their observations

> to the principal actors in the agency to verify the accuracy of the observations and to uncover . . . members' interpretive framework for these key events. Finally, substantiation of observations and interview reports came from correspondence files, memoranda, agency reports, and newspaper accounts associated with the key events. (p. 29)

Some ethnographers relate their observations to quantitative data obtained from questionnaires. Earley (1984), for example, did a cross-cultural study of social interaction in the workplace. He observed about 70 employees of tire factories in the United States, England, and Ghana. He stood about 8 feet behind each individual for one hour a day over a 14-week period recording observations of their behavior. At the end of the fourteenth observation period, each worker was asked to fill out a brief questionnaire concerning his opinions about various work factors, including social interaction. These ratings were compared to the observations to assess their validity.

Some ethnographers improvise behavioral methods for assessing the external validity of their findings. Johnson (1975), for example, describes a researcher who observed a number of "psychiatric screening interviews" and then developed a list of likely outcomes he predicted would occur given certain contingencies in the context. He used this list to predict the outcome of future screening interviews prior to the actual decisions of the psychiatric workers who conducted them. The researcher then used the accuracy of his predictions as a measure of the external validity of his findings.

Ethnographers can even use background information about the situation being observed to check the validity of their data. Whyte (1984) gives as an example the 1982 national election held in El Salvador during the nation's civil war. Leaders of the guerrilla rebellion declined to offer themselves as candidates and urged citizens to boycott the election. The election was carried out, nevertheless, and voter turnout was over 80 percent. Government observers hailed this high turnout as reflecting the people's desire for democracy and their rejection of the rebels' boycott. But observers with a deeper understanding of the context point out that in El Salvador at the time, voting was compulsory. To enforce this law, each adult was required to carry a *cedula,* a document to be stamped by election officials when the person voted. Everyone in El Salvador must always carry the *cedula,* and government and military officials have the right and power to inspect a person's *cedula* at any time. Government officials let it be known that they considered failure to vote an act of treason. Death squads were known to have murdered hundreds of people on the basis of less evidence than this. Thus the observed voting behavior of the people of El Salvador may have been due more to their fear of reprisal than to their rejection of the rebels' call for a boycott.

The importance of background information for understanding a particular context cannot be underestimated. Background information would certainly have helped two Eskimos visiting Florida for the first time when they observed a water-skier winding and cavorting his way around a lake. One asked, "Why is the boat going so fast?" The second answered, "That's obvious. It is being chased by a madman on a string!"

CONCLUSION

In the final analysis, ethnography is a powerful methodology for describing and understanding the world of the social actor. It is a "tale" told by a member of one culture about another culture to the members of his or her own culture. The crucial problem in such a description is "to balance, harmonize, mediate, or otherwise negotiate a tale of two cultures (the fieldworkers' and the others')" (Van Maanen, 1988, p. 138).

When such a balance is achieved, ethnographic research expands its readers' horizons. The ethnographer's tale relates how communication creates social order and is constricted by it, either in a foreign community or at home.

As ethnographies are combined, we gradually gain a composite overview, much the way a jigsaw puzzle is put together, of communication commonalities and differences in various human communities. That is, we learn more about how human communication influences and is influenced by the context in which it occurs.

part IV

ANALYZING AND INTERPRETING QUANTITATIVE DATA

chapter **12**

Theory of Statistics

Each research methodology we have examined relies on various measurement techniques (questionnaires, interviews, and observations) to acquire data. Once data are collected, they need to be analyzed. As Carl Sagan might say, "Every day we are exposed to billions and billions of pieces of data." Those data are not very useful, however, without some interpretation of what they mean.

Data analysis is the method researchers use to infer meaning from data, to determine what conclusions are justified. Data analysis transforms numbers or verbal accounts into information, usable knowledge that can be shared with others. This knowledge is used by people to operate more effectively in the world. Success in our society comes largely to people and organizations who have, and can use, more information than their "competitors." Perhaps this is why our whole society now is called an "information society."

But a set of data does not necessarily yield a single conclusion. People must interpret, and can easily misinterpret, the implications of the data they gather. Here are some humorous examples:

1. "Very few auto accidents occur when one is driving over 90 miles an hour. So driving this fast is actually quite safe."
2. "On all my birthdays so far, I've been less than 21 years old. So by induction, on all my future birthdays, I'll be less than 21 years old."

3. "Statistics indicate that one out of four babies born is Chinese. We have three children now, so we expect our next child to be Chinese."

In each of these instances, the quantitative information is accurate, but common sense is clearly violated in the conclusions drawn. In many other instances, however, inaccurate conclusions purported to be based on statistics are not as easy to discover. Huff and Geis (1954) suggest that statistics is a way of lying with numbers. Few researchers deliberately lie. But when research is published, especially in advertisements, the data are presented in ways that support what the author wants you to believe. Consumers of research must be able to detect distorted conclusions. This chapter explains the reasoning behind the process of drawing conclusions from statistics.

QUANTITATIVE DATA ANALYSIS

In this chapter we examine the process of analyzing quantitative, or numerical, data. Qualitative data are also analyzed, of course, and presented in the form of case studies, critiques, and sometimes verbal reports. Analyses of qualitative data are often conducted by ethnographers and textual analysts who review and carefully examine the data they have gathered, infer tentative conclusions from them, and describe in prose how these generalizations serve to explain the phenomena they are studying.

Making sense of numbers, however, is often complex. Many articles in scholarly communication journals contain complicated analyses of quantitative data. Statistical formulas are employed and technical jargon is used to describe them. Quantitative data are also common in reports circulated in many professions (such as ratings research reports, sales charts and graphs, and the results from evaluation research), and the reports are used to make important policy decisions. Quantitative information also appears frequently in newspapers and on television. Examples are political polls and graphs reflecting trends in the stock market. To be a competent and critical consumer of this information, one needs to understand the ways in which quantitative data are analyzed.

Quantitative data lend themselves to data analysis procedures associated closely with the applied branch of mathematics known as statistics. The word *statistics* comes from the Latin root *status*, which implies that these analyses are performed in order to understand the status or characteristics of data. **Statistics** today is a field of science concerned with "the theories and techniques (both descriptive and inferential) that have been developed to manipulate [quantitative] data" (Labovitz & Hagedorn, 1971, p. 65). The word *statistic* also means, however, any "calculated value" that represents some characteristic of data (such as the mean or the arithmetic average), as well as any measurement obtained from a sample of a population.

Statistics are generally esteemed in our culture. We value science and technology, and progress in these domains is based on precise calculations. Scholars recognize, however, that cultural norms influence how statistics are produced, perceived, and used. They now study "ethnostatistics," the everyday behavior of producers and users of statistics (Gephart, 1988). Our goal here is to make some sense out of this culture for you. Too often, all you see are equations that synthesize the end results of data analyses, their meaning encapsulated in one or two letters in the results section of a scholarly journal article (e.g., F, t, r). Statistical terms are intimidating at first to consumers unfamiliar with them, but they become less frightening once they are explained and the procedures used to reach them are understood. The conclusions drawn from data analyses, such as whether there is a significant difference between groups or a significant relationship between variables, then make more sense.

Two general purposes are associated with quantitative data analysis: description and inference. **Descriptive data analysis** is used to summarize the information in the data, often by tabulating and graphing data. **Inferential data analysis** serves two purposes: estimating the characteristics of a population from data gathered on a sample and testing for significant differences between groups and significant relationships between variables.

DESCRIPTIVE DATA ANALYSIS

The most basic quantitative data analysis starts by constructing simple generalizations about data. Descriptive data analysis provides clear generalizations about data. Descriptive data analysis provides a clear understanding of several characteristics of a particular array of measurements. Several important procedures are used, including frequency distributions, measures of central tendency, and measures of dispersion.

Frequency Distributions

Descriptive data analysis may involve merely counting and then reporting how often different categories or points on a measurement scale occur. This is called a **frequency distribution.** A list of the frequency of responses for each category or measurement point is called a **frequency table.** For example, a table listing how many As, Bs, Cs, Ds, and Fs you received in college would be a frequency distribution of your grades.

Frequency tables are used most often to describe the distribution of scores for the categories of a variable measured by a nominal scale. For example, say a researcher interested in knowing why children watch television asked 85 children to indicate the primary reason they watch television. The reasons given might then be classified into the following six categories used by Rubin (1979) (see Chapter 3): (1) to learn about the world, (2) to pass time or out of habit, (3) for companionship, (4) to forget about things, (5) to become aroused, or (6) to relax. These results could be reported in a frequency table (see Figure 12.1). Frequency tables usually include the actual count for each category and the relative or percentage count for each category (found by dividing the actual count for any particular category, such as 10 for learning, by the total count for all categories combined, 85 in this case, which equals 11.8 percent).

Frequency counts of categories serve several useful purposes. First, they can inform researchers about *common communication practices of people and institutions*. For example, Baxter and Bullis (1986) studied turning points in romantic relationships and whether they involved talking about the relationship. They asked respondents to identify all the important events that had changed their joint commitment level from the time they met their partner until the time of the interview. The total frequency of turning points (758) was divided into 13 major categories, ranging from get-to-know time (constituting 19 percent of all the turning points mentioned) to negotiating romantic exclusivity (4.5 percent of all turning points). Respondents were then asked to indicate whether these turning points involved talk about the relationship, and the results were reported in a frequency table. The turning points of romantic exclusivity, making up, disengagement, serious commitment, and passion were most likely to involve relationship talk, while the turning points of get-to-know time, physical separation, and sacrifice (providing assistance or granting favors) were least likely to involve relationship talk.

Frequency counts of categories can also be used to *assess predictions derived from theory*. Herman (1985), for example, studied bias in newspaper reports of political events. He compared the various topics mentioned in the *New York Times* articles from February 1 to March 30, 1984, about the El Salvador election of March 25, 1984, with the topics mentioned in articles from September 5 to November 6, 1984, about the Nicaragua election of November 4, 1984. Using a propaganda

Figure 12.1 A frequency table

The following hypothetical data could result from a study in which a researcher asks 85 children to indicate the primary reason why they watch television. After categorizing the hypothesized data into the categories used by Rubin (1979) and counting the number of responses in each category, the following frequency table could be constructed.

Type of Reason	Number of Responses	Percentage
To learn about the world	10	11.8
To pass time or out of habit	15	17.6
For companionship	22	25.9
To forget about things	18	21.2
To become aroused	8	9.4
To relax	12	14.1
	85	100.0

framework, he predicted that supportive topics would be associated with the U.S.-sponsored elections in El Salvador but nonsupportive topics would be linked with the elections in the nonfavored country of Nicaragua. After categorizing the specific topics discussed in the articles, the frequency counts for the categories confirmed this prediction. For example, whereas 21.4 percent of all the articles linked democratic purposes and hopes with the election in El Salvador, only 4.8 percent of the articles expressed the same opinion about the election in Nicaragua. And whereas 33.3 percent of all articles discussed the elections in Nicaragua as a public relations effort, only 10.7 percent expressed the same view about the election in El Salvador.

Frequency counts of categories can also *show changes over time.* For example, Bogart (1985) wanted to know whether the topics covered in U.S. newspaper articles changed over a 20-year period. He conducted a longitudinal content analysis, comparing the percentage of newspapers carrying particular types of features (70 topics in all) at least once a week in 1963, 1974, 1979, and 1983. The findings, reported in a frequency table, showed that the percentage of articles on business and automotive themes stayed relatively stable across time. However, articles on etiquette and home repair decreased considerably, while articles on people and the environment increased considerably.

Researchers often find that illustrating frequency counts *visually* allows readers to see the "big picture." **Bar graphs,** for example, use "blocks" (rectangles and squares) to show the frequency counts for a variable measured on a nominal or ordinal scale. For example, Mulac, Studley, Wiemann, and Bradac (1987) studied eye contact in conversation by videotaping 54 men and 54 women interacting for eight minutes in same-gender and mixed-gender problem-solving dyads. Trained observers coded the percentage of time interactants gazed at the other person or averted their gaze and the percentage of time they talked or were silent. The researchers used a bar graph to show the frequency counts for each category (see Figure 12.2). This visual display makes it easy to "eyeball" differences among the four categories. In addition, notice how these researchers actually combined what are three separate bar graphs (male-male dyads, female-female dyads, and male-female dyads) into one. Shading the blocks in this bar graph makes it easy to see the differences between same-gender and opposite-gender dyads for the four categories.

Researchers also use *pie charts* to illustrate the frequency counts of categories. **Pie charts** are circles divided into segments proportional to the percentage of the circle that represents the frequency count for each category. For example, Berger (1985), editor of the journal, *Human Communication Research,* classified the themes of 269 manuscripts submitted and accepted between June 1982 and February 1985 into eight categories representing each of the eight divisions of the International Communication Association. He found the following percentages: Information systems, 3 percent submittted, 22 percent accepted; Interpersonal, 62, 24; Mass, 15, 20; Organizational, 13, 17; Intercultural, 2, 25; Political, 0, 0; Instructional, 3, 0; Health, 2, 0.

To illustrate how pie charts assist in understanding quantitative data, we display that data on two pie charts, making it easy to see which types of manuscripts

Figure 12.2 A bar graph

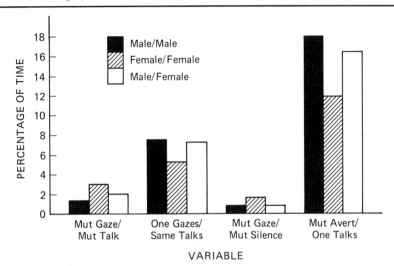

Figure 1. Mean Percentage of Time by the Three Dyad Types for the Four Significant Dependent Variables

Source: Anthony Mulac, Lisa B. Studley, John M. Wiemann, and James J. Bradac," Male/female Gaze in Same-sex and Mixed-sex Dyads: Gender-linked Differences and Mutual Influence," *Human Communication Research, 13*(3), p. 333, copyright © 1987 by Sage Publications, Inc. Reprinted by permission of Sage Publications, Inc.

are and are not represented and in what proportion (see Figure 12.3). Note that although pie charts are used quite often in business, newspaper, and television reports, they are used infrequently in academic journals.

Researchers also use *line graphs* to illustrate the frequency counts of categories. **Line graphs** use a single point to represent the frequency count (usually the mean frequency score) for each of the categories and then connect these points with a single line. Sparks and Spirek (1988), for example, studied how two types of people respond to stress. They argued that "blunters," people who prefer a low amount of information in the face of a stressful situation, should show less negative affect while processing a stressful stimulus (a frightening film) than "monitors," people who prefer a lot of information in the face of a stressful event. They first measured 59 subjects' tendencies toward monitoring and blunting and divided them into two groups: high monitors/low blunters and high blunters/low monitors. Each group of subjects was then shown a segment from the movie *Nightmare on Elm Street.* The segment included four different scenes: a girl telling her father she was going to bed ("Begin"), watching her have a nightmare that involved setting booby traps for the child murderer Krueger ("Booby trap"), descending the staircase into the basement ("Stairs"), and Krueger chasing the girl ("Chase"). To assess negative affect, two small Velcro bands that held electrodes to measure skin conductance (in micromhos) were attached to subjects' index and middle fingers of the nonwriting hand. Subjects' skin conductance was measured prior to the segment (to establish

Figure 12.3 Pie charts

The following pie charts reflect the type and percentage of manuscripts submitted to and published by *Human Communication Research* between June 1982 and February 1985 (based on Berger, 1985).

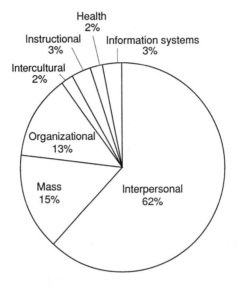

(a) Manuscipts submitted

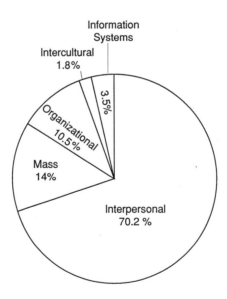

(b) Manuscripts published (computed based on submission and acceptance percentages).

Figure 12.4 A line graph

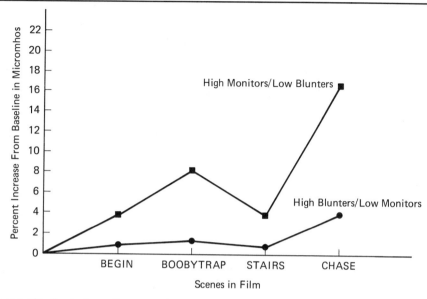

Figure 1. Skin Conductance Responses for High Monitors/Low Blunters and High Blunters/Low Monitors During *Nightmare on Elm Street*

Source: Glenn G. Sparks and Melissa M. Spirek, "Individual Differences in Coping With Stressful Mass Media: An Activation-arousal View," *Human Communication Research, 15*(2), p. 208, copyright © 1988 by Sage Publications, Inc. Reprinted by permission of Sage Publications, Inc.

a baseline reading) as well as every 20 seconds during the film. The scores were averaged for subjects of each type during each of the four scenes, and the percentage of change from the baseline to each average was calculated. The researchers used a line graph to show that the percentage of change for each of these scenes supported their hypothesis (see Figure 12.4). The line graph shows that high monitors/low blunters had a higher percentage increase during all scenes than high blunters/low monitors.

When a variable is measured using an *interval* or *ratio* scale, tables can be constructed to show the frequency counts for each of the measurement points. Typically, however, researchers illustrate these frequency distributions visually. Two procedures used to show frequency distributions for interval or ratio data are *histograms* and *frequency polygons*.

Histograms, like bar graphs, use blocks to show how frequently each point on a measurement scale occurs. Because interval or ratio scales are ordered, however, the blocks touch. For example, suppose that a researcher wanted to know how much information people recall from a public health commercial about AIDS that uses a fear appeal. The researcher shows 100 subjects a commercial containing 10 pieces of information and then asks them one hour later to recall that information. The distribution of subjects' scores on the measurement scale might be as follows:

Pieces of information recalled	0	1	2	3	4	5	6	7	8	9	10
Number of subjects recalling	4	15	0	10	17	5	25	1	8	9	6

Such data can be illustrated visually through the use of a histogram (see Figure 12.5). Notice that even when there are no occurrences at one point on the scale (2 responses), the point is included in the histogram but no bar is drawn, whereas a bar chart includes only categories with observed frequencies. In addition, a histogram can easily combine several points on an ordered measurement scale. For example, showing the frequency counts for every age represented in a sample might be unwieldy. However, a histogram could combine the mean frequency counts for different age groups: 10–19, 20–29, and so on. Bar charts, by contrast, do not group categories because they are assumed to be mutually exclusive, although sometimes several categories can be combined to form a new category (for example, data about England, Germany, and France can be combined in the category "Europe").

Figure 12.5 A histogram

The following hypothetical histogram reflects the number of correct pieces of information (10 in all) that were recalled by 100 subjects after seeing a film.

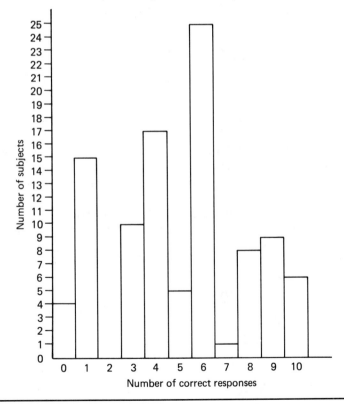

Researchers also show frequency counts for interval and ratio data by using frequency polygons. **Frequency polygons** are similar to line graphs, except a line connects the points representing the frequency count for each point on the measurement scale rather than each category. Figure 12.6 shows a frequency polygon for the data used to construct the histogram in Figure 12.5. The choice between a histogram and a frequency polygon is usually a matter of aesthetics.

Measures of Central Tendency

Researchers often want to condense their report of the distribution of scores further, to a single numerical indicator called a **summary statistic.** One important type of summary statistic, the **measure of central tendency,** describes the one score that best represents the entire distribution, the most characteristic score. The most characteristic score is that which describes the center point of a distribution of scores.

Three different measures of central tendency are the mode, median, and mean.

Figure 12.6   A frequency polygon

The following hypothetical frequency polygon reflects the number of correct pieces of information (10 in all) that were recalled by 100 subjects after seeing a film.

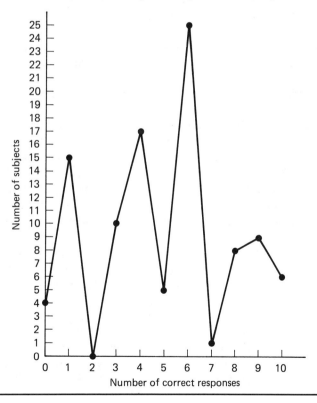

Each is a summary statistic that identifies the most characteristic score for an array of nominal, ordinal, and interval or ratio data, respectively.

Mode. The **mode** (*Mo*), the simplest measure of central tendency, is the number that occurs most frequently. Consider the following distribution of numbers:

$$15 \quad 12 \quad 10 \quad 9 \quad 7 \quad 7 \quad 3$$

In this distribution, the mode is 7 because it occurs twice, whereas the other numbers occur only once.

The mode is considered a weak expression of the central tendency of a distribution. If either extreme score (in this case 15 or 3) occurred three times, that would be the mode, even though it would not be very descriptive of the center point of the data.

The mode can be used to describe the central tendency of any distribution, regardless of the level of measurement. However, only the mode can be used with a nominal scale (on which categories are considered mutually exclusive and are not arranged in any numerical order) to describe the central tendency in terms of the category that occurs most frequently. For example, look back at the distribution presented in Figure 12.1 concerning the reasons given by children for watching television. The mode in this distribution is the category labeled "For companionship," since it occurred most frequently. Sometimes two categories are tied for the highest frequency, in which case the distribution is called **bimodal;** if three or more categories are tied for the highest frequency, the distribution is called **multimodal.**

Median. The **median** (*Md* or *Mdn*) divides the distribution at the 50th percentile, or exactly in half. It is the number above which and below which half the observations fall. In the distribution discussed under the mode, the median is the number 9 because half of the numbers fall above and half below this number. The median is a number occurring in the distribution when an odd number of scores is involved. When there are an even number of observations, the median is found by taking the two middle numbers, adding them together, and dividing by 2. For example, if the number 9 is removed from this distribution, the median is found by taking the two middle numbers (10 and 7), adding them together (17), and dividing by 2 (which equals 8.5).

The median's primary strength as a summary statistic is its insensitivity to extreme scores. If the high score in the distribution just discussed were 80 instead of 15, the median would remain the same. Researchers therefore prefer to use the median to describe the central tendency of a distribution of interval or ratio data that contain very extreme scores. For example, U.S. government officials use the median as a summary statistic to describe "average" income because the few billionaires and millionaires in the population would drive the mean (the arithmetic average) up and thus not describe accurately the average living standards of the majority of the people in this country. Similarly, researchers typically use the median to report the "average" age of the people they study when a wide range of ages is represented.

This strength of the median is also its primary weakness. Because it is not sensitive to how scores are scattered across a distribution, it does not necessarily provide the best indicator of the center point of the data. For example, if the scores in a distribution were 2, 3, 4, 30, 40, the median (4) does not seem to describe the center point of these data accurately.

The median can be used to describe the central point of distributions containing ordinal, interval, or ratio measurements because the numbers on these scales are arranged in a meaningful order from highest to lowest. However, the median is the summary statistic used most frequently to describe the central tendency for variables measured on an *ordinal* scale. Because the distances between the numbers on an ordinal scale are not equal, a mean cannot be calculated. Therefore, the median is the appropriate measure of central tendency.

Mean.   The **mean** ($\overline{X}$; sample mean, M; population mean, μ) is the arithmetic average, and it is computed by adding up all the scores in a distribution of interval or ratio measurements and dividing by the total number of scores. The equal distance between the points on these scales allows these numbers to be added and divided. For example, for the distribution of scores discussed earlier (15, 12, 10, 9, 7, 7, 3), the mean is found by adding up all the scores (63) and dividing by the total number of scores (7), which equals 9.

The mean is the most useful summary statistic for describing the center point of a distribution because it is sensitive to *every* change in the data. The other measures of central tendency don't have this advantage. For example, any number in the distribution just given except 7 could be changed, and if every other number appeared only once, the mode still would be the same. Because the mode is not sensitive to changes in other numbers, it remains the same unless such changes create a new mode. Similarly, the number 15 could be changed to 50 or 500 and the median would still be 9, although now this would be describing the center point of a much different distribution. In contrast, the mean will change if *any* number in this distribution is changed.

The strength of the mean, however, is also its primary weakness. Because the mean *is* sensitive to every score, one or two extreme scores can render it virtually useless, as the example of median income showed. Therefore, the mean is a useful summary statistic to describe the central tendency of a distribution of interval or ratio measurements whenever there are few extreme scores at one or both ends of the measurement scale.

Measures of Dispersion

The measures of central tendency describe only the central point of a distribution, not how scores differ. Consider, for example, the following two groups of scores: 5, 6, 4, 5, 5; and 1, 9, 8, 2, 5. Both groups of scores have the same mean (5), but they are very different in terms of how much the individual scores vary from their respective mean. In essence, the scores in the first group are relatively similar, whereas the scores in the second group are widely dispersed.

Thus researchers want to summarize not only the central tendency of a distribution of scores but also the extent to which the scores in a set vary from the center point of the data. To report how much scores vary from each other or how far they are spread around the center point of the data and across the distribution, researchers need **measures of dispersion,** also called **measures of variability.**

Measures of dispersion are applied to ordinal, interval, and ratio data because these scales used ordered numbers that vary. There is no appropriate measure of dispersion for nominal data since nominal scales use categories instead of meaningful numbers. Three measures of dispersion are used most frequently by researchers: range, variance, and standard deviation.

Range.   The **range,** the simplest measure of dispersion, reports the distance between the highest and lowest scores in a distribution. The range is calculated simply by subtracting the lowest number from the highest number in a distribution. For example, the range for the distribution discussed earlier (15, 12, 10, 9, 7, 7, 3) is found by subtracting 3 from 15, which equals 12. This range can also be expressed as "a range from 3 to 15."

The range gives researchers some sense of how widely the data are spread out across a distribution. For example, researchers often report the age range of the people studied because this summary statistic gives some indication of the variability of the sample. A sample of people aged 18–21 (range = 3) is certainly not as diverse as a sample of people aged 12–60 (range = 48).

Knowing the range, and hence how much scores vary, provides a general understanding of how two groups of people differ. For example, two groups of employees might have mean scores of 7 on a 10-point scale measuring how satisfied they are with the quality of the communication between themselves and their boss. If group A's scores ranged from 1 to 10, however, and group B's scores ranged from 6 to 8, the means are the same, but the two groups of employees are not equally satisfied.

The problem with the range is that it is sensitive to extreme scores, so one or two extreme scores makes a distribution look more dispersed than it is. Furthermore, the range is not sensitive to differences between scores within a distribution. Any number other than the highest and lowest numbers can change without changing the range. To compensate, researchers often divide the distribution at the 25th percentile (the point below which 25 percent of the scores fall) and at the 75th percentile (the point below which 75 percent of the scores fall). They then calculate the **interquartile range,** which is the distance between the 25th percentile point and the 75th percentile point. This summary statistic represents the range of scores for the middle half of a distribution.

Thus the range gives researchers only a global picture of the dispersion of a set of measurement scores. Consequently, researchers typically use the range in combination with other measures of dispersion.

Variance.   **Variance** (sample variance, s^2; population variance, σ^2) is a mathematical index of the average distance of the scores on an interval or ratio scale from the mean in squared units. Figure 12.7 shows how sample variance is calculated, using both the definitional formula and an easier computational formula, for the distribution of scores used in our earlier examples.

A high variance tells researchers that most scores are far away from the mean, and a low variance indicates that most scores cluster tightly about the mean. This is important when one wants to know how two groups of scores differ. For example, if a researcher found that two married couples' scores on a 10-point satisfaction scale (with 1 being low and 10 being high) were 1 and 9, and 5 and 5, the mean would be the same for both couples (5). But that summary statistic hides an important difference between these two couples, revealed by how the two sets of scores are dispersed. The first couple are at odds (one being extremely satisfied and the other extremely dissatisfied), whereas the second couple feel the same moderate amount of satisfaction. Thus to understand how well the mean summarizes a distribution of interval or ratio measurements, researchers also need to know how much scores vary from the mean.

The variance score can be confusing, however, because it is expressed in units of *squared deviations about the mean,* which are not the same as the original units of measurement. For example, if the scores in Figure 12.7 represent the number of minutes each person took to give a persuasive speech, the variance equals 12.86 squared minutes. But "squared minutes" makes little sense. What is needed is a measure of dispersion that is expressed in the same units as the original measurements.

Standard deviation.   **Standard deviation** (SD; sample SD, *s;* population SD, σ) is a summary statistic of how much scores on an interval or ratio scale vary from the mean, expressed in the original units of measurement. The standard deviation of a distribution is found simply by taking the square root of the variance. In the preceding example, the square root of the variance (12.86) equals a standard deviation of 3.59 minutes. The standard deviation can be thought of as the average amount of dispersion within a distribution, just as the mean is the average score in a distribution. (Most people gave their speech within a range of 5–13 minutes.)

The mean and the standard deviation are the measures of central tendency and dispersion reported most frequently by researchers for a distribution of interval or ratio measurements. They are often reported in a table, particularly when scores for different groups of people are being compared. For example, Höijer (1989) studied how people respond to science programs on television. She showed a 40-minute program to 62 people selected randomly from the population of Stockholm, Sweden. After watching the program, they were asked questions about the content of

Figure 12.7 Calculating sample variance

(a) Definitional Formula $s^2 = \dfrac{\Sigma (X - \bar{X})^2}{N}$

Steps:

1. Find the mean for the group of scores (9).
2. Subtract the mean from each score. This yields the *deviation score.*
3. Square each deviation score and add the squares up to get the *sum of squares score* (90).
4. Divide the sum of squares score by the number of scores to get the *variance* (12.86).

Scores (X)	Score − mean ($X - \bar{X}$) **(Deviation Scores)**	(Score − mean)^2 $(X - \bar{X})^2$
15	6	36
12	3	9
10	1	1
9	0	0
7	−2	4
7	−2	4
3	−6	36

$\bar{X} = 9$ $\Sigma (X - \bar{X})^2 = 90$ (Sum of Squares Score)

Variance $= 90 \div 7 = \underline{\underline{12.86}}$

(b) Computational Formula $s^2 = \dfrac{\Sigma X^2}{N} - \left(\dfrac{\Sigma X}{N}\right)^2$

Steps:

1. Find the mean for the group of scores, and square this mean score (81).
2. Square each score and add up the squared scores to get the sum of squares score. Divide the sum of square score by the number of scores (93.86).
3. Subtract the value obtained from step 1 from the value obtained from step 2. This yields the *variance* (12.86).

Scores (X)	Squared Scores (X)^2
15	225
12	144
10	100
9	81
7	49
7	49
3	9
$\Sigma X = 63$	$\Sigma X^2 = 657$ (Sum of Squares Score)

$\dfrac{\Sigma X}{N} = 63 \div 7 = 9$ $\dfrac{\Sigma X^2}{N} = 93.86$

$\left(\dfrac{\Sigma X}{N}\right)^2 = 9 \cdot 9 = 81$

Variance $= 93.86 - 81 = \underline{\underline{12.86}}$

the program, including descriptive content (what the two men bending arms were doing), facts and figures (how many light years out in space scientists can see with their most advanced instruments), and idea content (scientific methods of work). The number of correct answers was tallied, and subjects were divided into three groups based on their level of comprehension: high (19–24 correct answers), medium (13–18), and low (2–12). In addition, Höijer assessed whether subjects had formed any thoughts about each of seven different themes discussed in the program by asking, "Did you think anything when you saw that part? What?" Subjects' topic-relevant previous knowledge was also measured by asking a number of questions about general scientific concepts. The means and standard deviations for these three groups with regard to type of content, thoughts, and previous knowledge were reported in a table (see Figure 12.8). This table makes it easy to see some of the differences among the three levels of comprehension.

Standard Scores

Calculating the mean and standard deviation for a set of interval or ratio measurements allows for an interesting manipulation of data. Researchers often report how many standard deviation units a particular score is above or below the mean, which is called a **standard score.** Standard scores provide a common unit of measurement indicating how far away any particular score is from the mean. Researchers can then compare standard scores from different distributions.

Figure 12.8 A table of means and standard deviations

	Level of Comprehension					
	High (19–24) $n = 23$		Medium (13–18) $n = 23$		Low (2–12) $n = 15$	
Variable	M	SD	M	SD	M	SD
Type of content[a]						
Descriptive	7.70	.56	6.70	1.15	3.87	2.06
Facts and figures	6.78	.73	5.43	1.10	2.80	1.01
Ideas	5.83	1.19	3.78	1.17	2.00	1.25
Thoughts[b]	3.94	1.60	3.22	1.70	1.73	1.66
Previous knowledge[c]	5.58	2.12	3.04	1.40	0.87	0.99

[a] Maximum score on each type = 8.00.
[b] Maximum number of thoughts = 7.00.
[c] Maximum score = 10.00.

Source: Birgitta Höijer, "Television-evoked Thoughts and Their Relation to Comprehension," *Communication Research, 16*(2), p. 196, copyright © 1989 by Sage Publications, Inc. Reprinted by permission of Sage Publications, Inc.

The standard score used most frequently by researchers is the z score. The formula for z scores is:

$$\frac{(Y - \overline{Y})}{\text{SD}}$$

The formula says that a z score can be computed for any score in a distribution by dividing the deviation score (how much an individual score differs from the mean) $(Y - \overline{Y})$ by the standard deviation for the distribution (SD). Using the distribution from our earlier example (15, 12, 10, 9, 7, 7, 3), dividing the deviation scores (6, 3, 1, 0, -2, -2, -6, respectively) by the standard deviation (3.59) produces the following z scores: $+1.67$, $+.83$, $+.29$, $.00$, $-.56$, $-.56$, and -1.67.

Standard scores allow researchers to interpret an individual score meaningfully by showing by how many standard deviation units it differs from the mean of comparable scores. For example, a standard score of $+2.00$ tells researchers that the individual score in question is two standard deviations above the mean. One of the best-known examples of standard scores is IQ tests. Modern IQ tests are designed to have a mean of 100 and a standard deviation of 15. So a person who scores 120 has a standard score of $+1.33$, and a person who scores 85 has a standard score of -1.00.

Standard scores also allow researchers to compare scores on different measurement scales for two different people or for the same individual. Suppose that a sports agent wants to know whether a baseball pitcher is doing relatively better in his sport than a football quarterback. Because the different scales used to measure performance will produce two distributions with different means and standard deviations, the agent must standardize both athletes' performance scores (assuming all the necessary information for doing so is available). These standard scores then indicate how far away the two athletes are from the mean of their own sport in standard deviation units. For example, the number of strikeouts for the baseball pitcher and the number of completions for the quarterback could be converted into z scores. The athlete with the higher z score is doing better than the athlete with the lower z score. Of course, to compare these two athletes accurately, many variables other than strikeouts and completions need to be taken into account.

INFERENTIAL STATISTICS

The descriptive statistics discussed so far explain how scores in a distribution behave. The descriptions they provide are analogous to how we portray human behavior. For example, take a person who consistently arrives late for appointments. To describe this behavior, we could keep track of the number of minutes he or she arrives before or after the designated meeting time, form a distribution of these minutes, and calculate the mean and the standard deviation.

However, we usually don't stop just with describing people's behavior. Typically we use these descriptions to make inferences about them. To infer simply means to conclude or judge from premises or evidence. For example, we infer personality traits from people's behavior, and vice versa. Someone who consistently arrives late is labeled "irresponsible," and we might also believe that irresponsible people can't be trusted not to reveal secrets. Furthermore, we compare people to one another. Based on their consistent differences in arrival time, for example, we might infer that one person is irresponsible but another is conscientious. The process of inference in person perception, then, is a matter of drawing conclusions about people based on their own and others' behaviors.

Researchers also don't stop with describing distributions of data. They often go beyond descriptions to infer conclusions from the data. To do so, they use inferential statistics. **Inferential statistics** are the "set of statistical procedures that allows a researcher to go beyond the group that has been measured, and make statements about the characteristics of a much larger group" (Jaeger, 1983, p. 12).

Inferential statistics generally accomplish two purposes: **estimation,** which generalizes the results obtained from a sample to its parent population, and **significance testing,** which examines the *importance* of the differences between groups or the relationships between variables. The rest of this chapter examines the process of estimation; Chapter 13 explains how researchers test for significant differences between groups, and Chapter 14 explores testing for significant relationships between variables.

Estimation

Because it is too difficult or impossible to conduct a census of every member of a population, researchers rely on samples drawn from a population. The ultimate purpose for many researchers is to generalize from the findings about a sample to the population from which it is drawn. Survey research, in fact, is usually conducted specifically for the purpose of inferring characteristics of a large population from characteristics found in a small sample. Experimental researchers and textual analysts also hope to generalize from the subjects or texts studied to the population or the universe they represent. Researchers *estimate* the characteristics of a population, called **parameters,** based on the characteristics found in a sample, called **statistics.** The procedures used to do this are therefore referred to as **parametric statistics.** Procedures that are used only to describe a sample are sometimes referred to as **nonparametric statistics.**

Estimations of population parameters from sample statistics are based on two assumptions. First, estimation procedures assume that the characteristic of interest is measured on an interval or ratio scale and that the characteristics are distributed "normally" in a population. Second, estimation procedures assume that a sample has been selected randomly so that it reflects the population. We shall explain these two assumptions before proceeding.

Normal curve. Estimation procedures presume that the scores for a variable are distributed in a population in the shape of a *normal curve*. *A* **normal curve** is one in which the distribution of scores is shaped like a symmetrical bell, which is why it is often called a **bell-shaped curve** (see Figure 12.9).

In a normal curve, the distribution is equal on the right and left of the center, so the mean, median, and mode all occur at the same point. That point is exactly in the middle of the distribution and is the highest point of the curve. Because of its shape, researchers also know the proportion of scores that will fall within any particular area of the curve. In a normal curve, 68.3 percent of the scores will fall within the area between one standard deviation (SD) greater than the mean and one SD less than the mean, 95.5 percent of the scores will fall within the area represented by two standard deviations on both sides of the mean, and 99.7 percent of the scores will fall within the area represented by three standard deviations on both sides of the mean. A random sample from a normally distributed population should also have this same general shape.

Figure 12.9 A normal curve

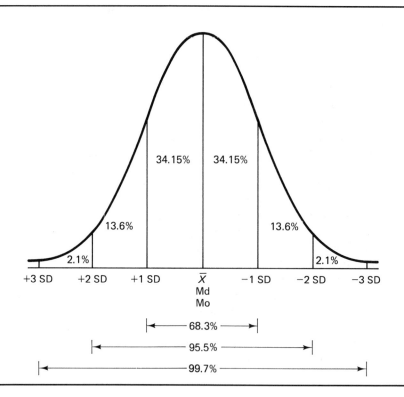

If the data collected are *not* distributed normally, accurate estimations cannot be made. For this reason, researchers must first look at the shape of the frequency distribution of their data to make sure that they are distributed normally, or nearly so, before proceeding with estimation procedures.

Distributions not shaped as a normal curve can demonstrate two characteristics: skewness and kurtosis (see Figure 12.10). **Skewness** means that the majority of scores are toward one end of a distribution, which makes the curve tail off in that direction. **Positive skew** occurs when the tail runs to the right side of the curve, and **negative skew** occurs when the tail runs to the left side of the curve.

Kurtosis refers to how pointed or flat the shape of a distribution is when it is not a normal curve. If the curve is narrow and sharply pointed, it is said to be **peaked,** which means that the scores are clustered around the middle. If the scores do not cluster around the middle but are dispersed rather evenly across the distribution, the curve is said to be **flat.**

Researchers assume that any particular characteristic is distributed normally within a population unless shown otherwise. Kerlinger (1973) argues that "many

Figure 12.10   Shapes of nonnormal distributions

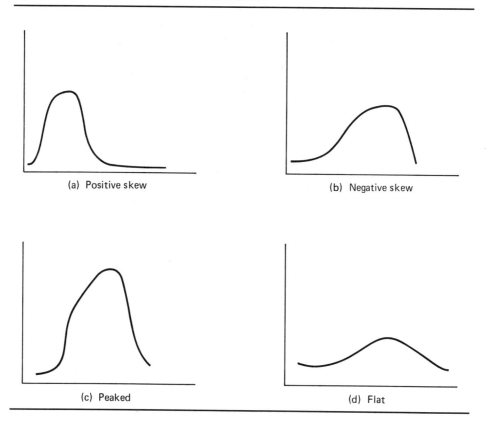

(a) Positive skew   (b) Negative skew

(c) Peaked   (d) Flat

natural phenomena, physical and psychological, distribute themselves in approximately normal form" (p. 191). Communication variables measured on interval or ratio scales are no exception to this rule; they are also assumed to be distributed normally throughout a population.

Use of random sampling. The second assumption on which estimation procedures are based is the use of a random sample. Remember from Chapter 6 that in order for researchers to infer the results from a sample to a population, the sample must be representative of the population. The best assurance of a representative sample is random selection of members from a population. The theory behind using a random sample to infer a population parameter is rather complicated, but we will try to keep it as simple as possible.

Sampling Distribution. Suppose that a researcher is interested in knowing the mean level of communication apprehension in a student population at a particular university. Imagine that a large number of random samples of 100 students (say 1000 samples) were drawn from this population. If the mean communication apprehension score was computed for each sample, only some of these sample means would be the same as the population mean. The majority of the sample means would undoubtedly deviate from the true population mean.

Next, imagine that a distribution of these 1000 random sample means was formed, which is called a **sampling distribution.** The mean of this hypothetical sampling distribution (the mean of these sample means) could then be calculated, as could its standard deviation, referred to as the **standard error** (SE). The standard error tells researchers how much these random sample means are likely to differ from the mean of the sampling distribution.

Remember that researchers assume that a characteristic (scores on a communication apprehension measure in this case) that is distributed normally in the population will also be distributed normally in the random samples. The sampling distribution of the means of these 1000 random samples thus forms a normal curve. Because these random sample means form a normal curve, researchers can estimate the probability of obtaining any particular sample mean. They know that 68 percent of the sample means will fall within one standard error on either side of the mean and that 95 percent will fall within two standard errors on either side of the mean (actually ± 1.96 SE).

Inferring from a Random Sample. It isn't likely that a researcher will draw a large number of random samples as we just did. Indeed, most researchers don't even draw more than *one* random sample. So how can they estimate the population parameter with only one random sample?

Let's assume that a researcher starts by selecting a random sample of 2000 students from a population of 10,000. The researcher's goal is to make an educated guess at the population mean, which is why this whole procedure is called estimation. The researcher knows, however, that a sample mean contains some degree of sampling error. How much error?

The mean and standard deviation computed from this one random sample are used to calculate what would be the standard error for the hypothetical sampling distribution. If researchers use the scores that are two standard errors on either side of the sample mean, they can be 95 percent confident that the true population mean falls somewhere within this range. The degree of assurance that a sample statistic can be used to infer a population parameter is called the *confidence level*. The range of scores associated with this confidence level is called the *confidence interval*.

For example, suppose that a researcher found that the mean communication apprehension score of a random sample was 17.0 and that the standard error was 2.0. By moving two standard errors above and below the mean, the researcher can be 95 percent confident that the true population mean falls somewhere between the confidence interval 13.0–21.0.

The confidence level of 95 percent is an arbitrary level accepted by researchers in the human sciences. In other disciplines, different confidence level rules apply. A 95 percent confidence level may not be acceptable in pharmaceutical research, for example. If researchers were estimating the effect of a new drug on a population based on findings from a random sample, a 95 percent confidence level could mean that the new drug might kill 5 percent of the people taking it, or 1 out of every 20!

Note too that the confidence interval depends partly on the size of a random sample. The smaller the size of a random sample, the less accurately it will approximate a true population parameter. Thus the general rule is that the larger the size of the random sample, the smaller the standard error and the more it approximates the true population parameter. However, after about 2000 people are drawn randomly, the reduction in standard error is too small to justify additional people. For this reason, national random samples drawn by pollsters, such as Gallup and Harris, or by ratings companies, such as Arbitron and Nielsen, use approximately 2000 people. Most researchers, however, must rely on much smaller samples and accept more error in their research findings. (Review the articles you read in the journals to see how many people were studied.)

You should now be able to interpret population parameter estimates the next time you see them. Here's a recent example. Jesse Jackson argued that the term *African-American* should be used instead of *black*. To assess public opinion on this matter, Galloway (1989) reports that the *Chicago Tribune* asked a group of randomly selected black registered voters in Chicago, "Which of these terms do you prefer, *black* or *African-American?*" Results showed that 40 percent preferred to be called "black," 26 percent preferred "African-American," and 31 percent were undecided. The newspaper also published the following short explanation about how the poll was conducted. You should be able to understand this explanation. By the way, if the confidence level associated with a poll is not reported, assume that it is 95 percent.

> The findings of the *Tribune* poll are based on telephone interviews with a random sampling of 512 blacks in Chicago.
>
> In a sample of this size, one can say with 95 percent certainty that results will vary by no more than plus or minus 4 percentage points from results that would have been obtained if all blacks in Chicago had been polled. (Galloway, 1989, p. 5).

A Word of Caution. We have just examined estimation theory and recommended practices. Sometimes scientists and pollsters practice what is preached. But sometimes they violate the assumptions on which estimation is based.

For example, many researchers don't sample randomly from a population of interest. In some cases this may be because they can't afford the time and expense. In other cases researchers may not be able to get a complete list of everyone in a population, such as all people who watch a particular television show or people who give lots of public speeches. In addition, many researchers in university settings use college students to represent the general population, a shaky assumption at best.

Technically, if the assumptions underlying estimations are violated, inferences about a population should not be made. In practice, however, researchers often violate these assumptions by using a small, nonrandom sample, for example, and then in scholarly articles engage in lofty generalizations about the population. Next time you read research, you should be able to judge for yourself whether the results obtained from a sample can be generalized to the population or not.

CONCLUSION

What conclusions can be drawn from a set of data? This chapter has provided several procedures and criteria to apply when making this conceptual leap. Of course, caution and common sense must always be applied. For example, on July 18, 1989, the *Wall Street Journal* reported in an editorial that single men are five times more likely to commit violent crimes than married men, implying that marriage is more effective than most publicly funded programs for containing violent crime. Do you agree? One reader did not. He wrote a letter to the editor saying that this statistic might merely be the result of a propensity for violent men not to marry. Perhaps, the reader added, entering marriage distinguishes violent and peaceable men, and further pressure for men to marry might obscure this indicator. The same statistic led to two different conclusions and two different recommendations—a common phenomenon. So we must continue in our exploration of data analysis to a discussion of how data are analyzed to determine whether and what differences and relationships exist among communicators and communication behaviors.

chapter 13

Analyzing Differences between Groups

In 1986 the *New York Times* published an article reporting that the New York City Transit Authority was at a loss to explain a recent decline in riders using buses. Within a few days, the newspaper received a number of letters from readers posing possible explanations, including these:

> Rear [exit] doors are so heavy that even weight lifters cannot open them.

> Drivers at route starting points refuse to allow passengers on until they are scheduled to leave, even if it is raining, snowing, or freezing cold.

> More competition is being provided by jitney operations, gypsy cabs, car services, and commuter vans. At certain places the operations are overwhelming in scope, but since they are largely illegal, they appear not to be officially visible.

> Very few people have exactly $1.00 in change or extra tokens. Officials need to provide more outlets for tokens and fare boxes.

> It is the rule now for buses to travel their routes in packs, with long delays between the herds' appearance. The drivers seem to band together on purpose, disregarding passenger needs.

Each of these letter writers purports to know what explains, causes, or influences New Yorkers' decisions about bus riding. How might a researcher discover whether or not any of these explanations are correct? We are not directly interested in this particular topic, of course, but the *form* in which the issue is posed is analogous to issues communication researchers confront.

Researchers in our field try to discover what's important or what "makes a difference" in human communication. Researchers begin with a hunch or hypothesis about what factors influence communication. They study those factors and, if they measure them with methods that yield quantitative data, use statistics to determine the extent to which the results found are important, or significant, enough to help explain why or how that communication process works. In this chapter we first explore the general nature of significance testing, which applies to analyzing both differences between groups and relationships between variables. We then show how researchers test for significant differences between groups.

SIGNIFICANCE TESTING

Parts I and II of this book explained how researchers ask questions about communication and how they design studies to answer them. In many studies, researchers pose a **research hypothesis** (H_1), a formal prediction about the expected outcome of the research. Remember that there are two types of research hypotheses: one-tailed and two-tailed hypotheses. A **one-tailed hypothesis** predicts the direction of the difference or relationship, such as "Men are taller on the average than women." A **two-tailed hypothesis** only predicts that there is a difference or relationship but does not specify its direction, such as "Men and women differ with respect to height."

Say researchers believe that employees work harder for bosses who praise rather than criticize them. You might think that in their research they would try to prove this "hypothesis." But this is not so because researchers cannot "prove" an idea by testing *all* possible instances in which it might apply—there might be millions. Rather, if researchers find a situation in which the idea does *not* work, they know the hypothesis is incorrect. If the hypothesis is supported, researchers only have more indication that it may be correct.

Researchers therefore actually test a **null hypothesis** (H_0), a statement indicating that there is *no* difference or relationship. **Significance testing** is the process of analyzing data for the purpose of testing whether a null hypothesis is *probably* either *correct* or *false*. The null hypothesis actually represents chance operating in an unrestricted manner. Researchers need to reject chance differences or relationships before assuming patterned or real ones. Thus if a null hypothesis is probably correct, researchers accept that there is no significant difference or relationship. If, however, a null hypothesis is probably false, researchers reject it and accept its logical alternative, the research hypothesis of a significant difference or relationship. In our example, they would test the null hypothesis that praise or criticism makes no difference in how hard employees work.

Note that on rare occasions, a null hypothesis can serve as a research hypothesis if researchers predict that there will be no significant difference or relationship.

Significance testing, technically, is appropriate *only* when researchers pose a hypothesis, not a research question. In actual practice, however, researchers often treat research questions as two-tailed hypotheses and then employ tests of significance.

Overview of Significance Testing Procedures

The best way to explain how researchers test for significance is through a hypothetical example. Suppose that a researcher wants to know whether people learn more from a multi-image presentation, one that uses several projectors and screens, or from a single-image presentation, one that uses a single projector and a single screen.

Posing a research hypothesis. The first step is for the researcher to pose a hypothesis about the differences between multi-image and single-image presentations with respect to learning. Based on a review of the literature and perhaps interviews with practitioners who use multi-image and single-image presentations, the researcher poses the following one-tailed research hypothesis:

▷ H_1: People learn more from a multi-image presentation than from a single-image presentation.

The corresponding null hypothesis is:

▷ H_0: There is no difference in the amount people learn from multi-image and single-image presentations.

Conducting the study. Say the researcher conducts a posttest-only full laboratory experiment. Subjects are first assigned randomly to either a multi-image or a single-image presentation condition. After watching the presentation, subjects are asked a series of questions that measure how much of the information that was presented they have learned. The researcher could pose, for example, 10 true-or-false questions about the material presented and count up how many answers each subject got correct.

Testing the null hypothesis. The researcher now analyzes the data to determine whether the group that was exposed to the multi-image presentation has more correct answers than the group exposed to the single-image presentation. To do so, the researcher uses an appropriate statistical technique to test whether the null hypothesis of no difference between the two groups is probably correct or incorrect. Testing the null hypothesis entails three things: (1) setting the significance level, (2) computing the calculated value, and (3) comparing the calculated value to the critical value needed for rejecting the null hypothesis.

Setting the Significance Level. The probability level researchers set for rejecting the null hypothesis is called the **significance level,** which corresponds to the confidence level used in estimation procedures. The significance level is, of course, arbitrary, but communication researchers typically use the .05 level of probability. If a significant difference or relationship is found at the .05 level of probability, researchers are 95 percent confident that the relationship or the difference is not due to chance or error. Put another way, this means that the result is only likely to happen by chance 5 times out of 100.

A .05 significance level is stringent. It is set that high to minimize reporting a significant difference or relationship that occurs due to chance. Researchers want to ensure that the result is due to a difference or relationship that would occur so rarely due to chance that it must be due to a difference or relationship that actually exists. This "burden of proof" is analogous to how prosecutors prove guilt in criminal trials. In our criminal justice system, a defendant is assumed to be innocent until proved guilty "beyond a reasonable doubt." In significance testing, groups and variables are assumed to be "innocent" of differences and relationships, respectively (the null hypothesis), until "proved" otherwise "beyond a reasonable doubt" (the research hypothesis). The .05 significance level thus represents the point at which researchers are willing to assume beyond a reasonable doubt that groups are different or variables are related.

Researchers thus always begin by assuming that there are no differences between groups or no relationships between variables (the null hypothesis). The question simply is: When is a difference or relationship judged to be significant? Communication researchers deem a .05 significance level (a difference or relationship that would occur less than 5 percent of the time due to chance or error) as indicating that an actual difference or relationship exists. Thus the null hypothesis is rejected and its antithesis, the research hypothesis, is accepted.

Computing the Calculated Value.   The specific procedures for calculating a critical value are discussed later in this chapter. Each significance-testing procedure, however, yields a numerical value, called the **calculated value.** Researchers can then evaluate this figure to assess the probability that the results indicate a significant difference or relationship, or whether the results were due to chance or error. The possible values and their probability of occurrence for each significance test are listed on separate tables (see Appendixes B through E).

Comparing the Calculated Value to the Critical Value.   Once the significance level is set and the calculated value is determined, researchers consult the table for the particular significance test being used to assess how likely the calculated value occurs by chance. These tables provide the particular value, called the **critical value,** that corresponds to the .05 significance level needed to reject the null hypothesis.

The critical value also depends on the **degrees of freedom,** the number of scores that are "free to vary." For example, if we know that combining three scores equals 10, the first two are free to vary, but the third is not. Thus if the first two numbers are 4 and 3, the third is not free to vary because it *must be* 3.

In research, the degrees of freedom are usually based on sample size (and sometimes on the number of categories employed). When more people are studied, more confidence can be placed in comparable results—you would be less sure of a finding that held true for 4 out of 5 people than you would of a finding that held true for 80 out of 100 people. The degrees of freedom figure generally equals $N - 1$, the number of people sampled minus 1 or the number of categories employed minus 1. When the degrees of freedom are tied to sample size, the larger the degrees of freedom, the smaller the critical value needed for rejecting the null hypothesis. The more people sampled, the easier it is to detect a significant relationship or difference.

Researchers now determine how likely the calculated value is due to chance or error by comparing it to the critical value. If the calculated value does not reach the critical value (a significance level greater than .05), it falls into the **region of acceptance,** and the null hypothesis of no difference or relationship must be accepted. If, however, the calculated value reaches or exceeds the critical value (it is lower than .05, say .03), it falls into the **region of rejection,** which means that the null hypothesis must be rejected. If the null hypothesis is rejected, researchers accept the alternative, the research hypothesis that the difference or relationship is not due to chance or error.

The critical value needed for accepting or rejecting a null hypothesis also depends on whether researchers advance a one-tailed or a two-tailed test. If researchers advance a one-tailed test, they are interested in knowing only whether the calculated value reaches the critical value on one side of the normal curve. In our hypothetical study, a one-tailed hypothesis was advanced that predicted that a multi-image presentation would be more effective than a single-image presentation. The researcher therefore determines whether the calculated value of the significance-testing procedure reaches or exceeds the critical value (.05 significance level) on one side of the normal curve, the side indicating that the multi-image presentation was more effective than the single-image presentation (see Figure 13.1).

When researchers advance a two-tailed hypothesis, however, they must consider both sides of the normal curve. If, for example, a two-tailed hypothesis had been posed for the hypothetical study that predicted only that multi-image and single-image presentations were different with respect to amount learned but didn't specify in which direction, it might be that the multi-image presentation was significantly better or significantly worse than the single-image presentation. For two-tailed hypotheses, researchers must consult both sides of the normal curve, so they divide the .05 significance level in half (.025 on each side; see Figure 13.1). Thus when researchers advance two-tailed hypotheses and divide the .05 significance level in half, they need a higher calculated value for rejecting the null hypothesis.

Type I and Type II Error

There are two kinds of errors researchers wish to avoid when employing significance testing. A **Type I error** (alpha, or α) occurs when researchers reject a null hypothesis and accept a research hypothesis when in fact the null hypothesis is true and should have been accepted. A **Type II error** (beta, or β) occurs when researchers accept a

Figure 13.1 Critical values needed for rejecting the null hypotheses associated with one-tailed and two-tailed research hypotheses

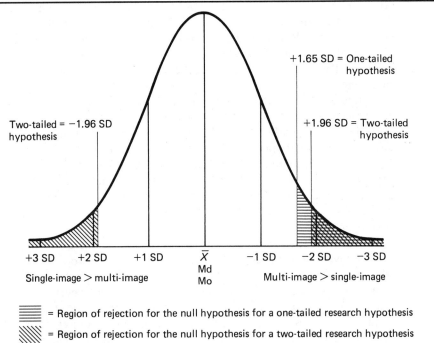

= Region of rejection for the null hypothesis for a one-tailed research hypothesis

= Region of rejection for the null hypothesis for a two-tailed research hypothesis

null hypothesis when it is in fact false, leading them to reject a perfectly sound research hypothesis.

In our hypothetical example, if the subjects in the multi-image and the single-image presentation conditions do not differ significantly on their learning scores but the researcher reports that they do (called a "false positive"), a Type I error has been committed. If the two groups do differ significantly on their scores but the researcher reports that they do not (called a "false negative"), a Type II error has been committed.

Type I error (rejecting a null hypothesis that is true) means that researchers believe that a difference or relationship is significant when it is not. The chance of committing a Type I error is equal to the significance level. So if researchers use a .05 significance level to reject a null hypothesis, the chance of committing a Type I error is 5 percent.

A study can be made more stringent or more conservative by lowering the alpha level and adopting a lower significance level. A .01 significance level, for example, yields a 1 percent chance of committing a Type I error. Researchers using a .01 significance level know that a significant finding means that if the same study were run 100 times, the same type of relationship or difference would likely be found 99 times.

Type II error (accepting a null hypothesis that is false) means that researchers believe that a difference or relationship is not significant when in fact it is. The chance of making a Type II error is not as easy to see. Kashigan (1986) explains that Type II error

> depends on a number of factors, including (1) the true value of the parameter in question, (2) the significance level α we use to evaluate our working hypothesis H_1 and whether we use a one-tailed or two-tailed test, (3) the standard deviation s of the sample population, and (4) the size of our sample n, where the latter two factors combine to determine the standard error of the sampling distribution of the statistic in question. (pp. 169–170)

Though Type II error is complex, a couple of general observations may help. First, increasing sample size decreases the chance of committing a Type II error, so studying more people helps avoid Type II errors. Second, Type I and Type II errors are related inversely, which means that when researchers use a more stringent significance level (such as .01 or .005), the chance of committing a Type I error decreases but the chance of committing a Type II error increases. Likewise, if researchers use a more liberal significance level (such as .10), the risk of committing a Type II error decreases but the chance of committing a Type I error increases.

DIFFERENCE ANALYSIS

Tests of significant difference in communication research serve to determine whether people (or texts) differ with regard to their use of categories or whether two or more groups of people differ on a variable. Metts (1989), for example, studied the most frequent reasons for why people deceive others in close relationships (cognitions) and the content of their deceptive communication (behaviors). Her study examined whether there were significant differences between the number of instances for each category studied.

The second, and more common, purpose is to see whether two or more groups of people (or texts) differ on some variable. Consider the following examples of communication research. Ray (1986) studied how differences in speaker rate, pitch, and loudness affect listeners' judgments of those speakers' competence. Burleson, Levine, and Samter (1984) investigated whether the quality of groups' decisions was different depending on the type of decision-making procedure the groups used. Camden and Kennedy (1986) studied whether differences existed in the morale of nurses who worked for female managers who displayed either stereotypical feminine or stereotypical masculine communication behaviors. Dunning and Lange (1989) investigated whether male and female dental students' interpersonal behaviors differed when they dealt with patients. Bergen and Weaver (1988) studied whether newspaper journalists who worked for small, medium, and large-sized papers had different levels of job satisfaction. Linz, Donnerstein, and Adams (1989) studied subjects exposed to a film portraying violence against women and subjects exposed to an exciting, nonviolent film to assess whether perceptions of violence and emotional reactions and arousal in response to violence decreased when viewing subsequent films.

Each of these studies investigated differences between groups. These differences may be biological (males versus females), situational (newspaper size), or experimental (exposure to violent or nonviolent films).

Types of Difference Analysis

Difference analysis is employed whenever an independent variable is measured on a *nominal* scale, including an interval level variable (such as age) that is broken down into categories (such as young and old). The specific type of difference analysis researchers use, however, depends on how the dependent variable is measured. Here we examine some common procedures researchers use to test for differences between groups when the dependent variable is measured using a nominal, ordinal, or interval or ratio scale.

Differences in nominal-level data.   The **chi-square** (X^2) **test** for signific .nt difference is used whenever a dependent variable is measured on a nominal scale, one that classifies a variable into qualitative categories. Chi-square tests analyze differences between scores in two ways: *a single-sample chi-square* is used to analyze differences within a *single* group (or variable) with respect to a set of categories, while a *contingency table analysis* is used to analyze differences within a single group (or variable) with respect to *two* sets of categories or differences between two or more groups with respect to a set of categories. We will explain both tests.

Single-Sample Chi-Square.   A **single-sample chi-square test** assesses differences in category usage for a single sample. Stewart, Gudykunst, Ting-Toomey, and Nishida (1986), for example, studied the effects of four types of management decision-making styles (authoritative, persuasive, consultative, and participative) on openness and satisfaction of employees in Japanese organizations.

One purpose of their study was to discover which management decision-making style Japanese employees prefer. They had 292 employees of Japanese organizations in Tokyo complete a questionnaire that asked them to indicate which of the following descriptions, taken from Tannenbaum and Schmidt (1958), best described the manager they preferred to work for:

Decision-making style 1: Usually makes his/her decisions promptly and communicates them to his/her subordinates clearly and firmly. Expects them to carry out the decisions loyally without raising difficulties. [*Authoritative*]

Decision-making style 2: Usually makes his/her decisions promptly, but, before going ahead, tries to explain them fully to his/her subordinates. Gives them the reasons for the decisions and answers whatever questions they may have. [*Persuasive*]

Decision-making style 3: Usually consults with his/her subordinates before he/she reaches his/her decision. Listens to their advice, considers it, and then announces his/her decision. He/she then expects all to work loyally to implement it whether or not it is in accordance with the advice they gave. [*Consultative*]

Decision-making style 4: Usually calls a meeting of his/her subordinates when there is an important decision to be made. Puts the problem before the group and invites discussion. Accepts the majority viewpoint as the decision. [*Participative*] (pp. 240–241)

The results showed that Japanese employees preferred a persuasive management style ($n = 117$), followed by a consultative style ($n = 100$), followed by a participative style ($n = 57$), followed by an authoritarian style ($n = 18$). A single-sample chi-square test shows whether the differences in these reported preferences is significant (see Figure 13.2).

A single-sample chi-square begins by noting the frequencies of occurrence for each category, called the "observed" frequencies. Researchers then calculate the "expected" frequencies for each category. These are the frequency to which they will compare their findings. This comparison is made in one of two ways. If researchers know in advance what frequencies to expect, those frequencies are used. For example, if researchers want to know whether the number of viewers who watch particular television shows in a certain year differs significantly from the number of viewers who watched the same shows the previous year, the figures from the previous year serve as the expected frequencies.

Most of the time, however, researchers do not know what frequencies to expect. So they assume that there are no differences between the categories (which reflects the null hypothesis). Therefore, the expected frequencies are found simply by dividing the total number of observations (292 in this example) by the number of categories (4; this comes to 73 per category).

The chi-square calculated value is found by subtracting the expected frequency for each category from the observed frequency, squaring this figure, dividing by the expected frequency, and then adding up these figures. To test whether this calculated value is significant, the researcher consults a chi-square table (see Appendix B). The researcher reads across to the column corresponding to the .05 significance level. The researcher then reads down that column to the row representing the appropriate degrees of freedom. For a single-sample chi-square, the degrees of freedom are always equal to the number of categories minus 1 (in this example, $4 - 1 = 3$). The critical value needed to reject the null hypothesis of no difference between the categories with 3 degrees of freedom at the .05 significance level is 7.815.

The calculated value of 81.46 exceeds this critical value. In fact, it exceeds the critical value of 12.838 for a .005 significance level and the critical value of 16.266 for a .001 significance level. This means that there is about 1 chance in 1000 that the results are due to chance. Thus the null hypothesis can be rejected and its alternative, the research hypothesis that Japanese employees prefer certain types of management decision-making styles, can be accepted. Stewart and colleagues (1986) conclude:

Figure 13.2   Single-sample chi-square

Steps:

1. List the *observed frequency* for each category.
2. Calculate the *expected frequency* for each category by dividing the total number of observations (292) by the total number of categories (4) (equals 73).
3. For each category, subtract the expected frequency from the observed frequency. Square this figure and divide by the expected frequency.
4. Add up the resulting figures for each category to get the *chi-square* (χ^2) *calculated value.*
5. Calculate the *degrees of freedom,* which equal the number of categories (4) minus 1 (equals 3).
6. Look up the *critical value* needed for rejecting the null hypothesis at the .05 significance level with the appropriate degrees of freedom on the chi-square table (see Appendix B) (equals 7.815).
7. If the calculated value meets or exceeds the critical value, the null hypothesis is rejected and the research hypothesis is accepted. If the calculated value does not meet the critical value, the null hypothesis must be accepted.

	Preferred Style				
	Authoritative	Persuasive	Consultative	Participative	Total
Observed frequency	18	117	100	57	292
Expected frequency	73	73	73	73	292

$$\chi^2 = \Sigma \ \frac{(O - E)^2}{E}$$

$$= \Sigma \ \frac{(18 - 73)^2}{73} + \frac{(117 - 73)^2}{73} + \frac{(100 - 73)^2}{73} + \frac{(57 - 73)^2}{73}$$

$$= \quad 41.44 \ + \ 26.52 \ + \ 9.99 \ + \ 3.51$$

$$= 81.46 \text{ with 3 degrees of freedom, } p < .001$$

Data from Stewart, Gudykunst, Ting-Toomey, and Nishida (1986).

Japanese workers in our sample expressed a preference for a more passive mode of decision making than one might expect from the current literature on Japanese management. They preferred to be persuaded of the value of a decision by their supervisors or desired to be approached by their supervisors and asked their opinions. Takezawa and Whitehill (1983) term this mode of decision making "delegating upward." The more passive stance on the part of subordinates is in contrast to the highly active involvement advocated by proponents of participative decision making in North American organizations. (p. 248).

Contingency Table Analysis. **Contingency table analysis,** also called **multiple-sample chi-square** or **crosstabs,** is used whenever researchers compare two or more groups with respect to a set of categories or the same group of people with respect to two different sets of categories.

In the study cited earlier, Japanese employees were asked to indicate not only the management decision-making style they preferred but also which style best described their present manager. The researchers thus studied employees' responses with respect to two nominal variables: preferred style and perceived style.

Essentially, a contingency table analysis (see Figure 13.3) is computed the same as a single-sample chi-square. One difference, however, is in how the expected frequencies are determined. The expected frequency for any particular cell in a contingency table analysis is found by multiplying the total frequency count for the respective row by the total frequency count for the respective column and dividing by the grand sum. For example, the expected frequency for the first cell (authoritative-authoritative) is found by multiplying the total for the authoritative row (18) by the total for the authoritative column (65) and dividing by the grand sum (292; this comes to 4.01).

The calculated value is then compared to the critical value needed for rejecting the null hypothesis, using the same chi-square table (see Appendix B). Degrees of freedom for a contingency table analysis are always equal to the number of rows minus 1 ($r - 1$) multiplied by the number of columns minus 1 ($c - 1$). For this example, degrees of freedom equal 9:$(4 - 1) \times (4 - 1)$. So using the .05 significance level with 9 degrees of freedom, a critical value of 16.19 was needed to reject the null hypothesis.

The results indicate that the calculated value of 28.44 exceeds this critical value. There are thus significant differences between Japanese employees' preferred and perceived management decision-making style. A contingency table analysis, however, tells researchers only that a general significant difference exists, not the specific differences. Researchers must examine the data to detect the specific differences. Note, for example, that although the consultative style is perceived as being used most often, Japanese employees prefer the persuasive style. Also, although employees perceive the authoritative style being used fairly frequently, they prefer it the least.

This example assesses differences within a single group (Japanese employees) with respect to two variables (perceived style and preferred style). Contingency table analysis is also used to test for differences between groups with respect to a set of categories. For example, if researchers compared differences in Japanese, American, and English employees' preferred management decision-making styles or compared Japanese male and female employees' preferences, contingency table analysis would show whether these groups differ significantly.

Differences in ordinal-level data. Recall that ordinal-level scales measure not only categorize variables but also rank them along a dimension. Most analyses of differences between groups with respect to an ordinally measured dependent vari-

Figure 13.3 Contingency table analysis

Steps:

1. List the *observed frequency* for each category.
2. Calculate the *expected frequency* for each category by multiplying the appropriate column total and dividing it by the grand total.
3. For each category, subtract the expected frequency from the observed frequency. Square this figure and divide by the expected frequency.
4. Add up the resulting figures for each category to get the *chi-square* (χ^2) *calculated value.*
5. Calculate the *degrees of freedom*, which equal the number of rows minus 1 ($r - 1$) multiplied by the number of columns minus 1 ($c - 1$) (equals 9).
6. Look up the *critical value* needed for rejecting the null hypothesis at the .05 significance level with the appropriate degrees of freedom on the chi-square table (see Appendix B) (equals 16.919).
7. If the calculated value meets or exceeds the critical value, the null hypothesis is rejected and the research hypothesis is accepted. If the calculated value does not meet the critical value, the null hypothesis must be accepted.

	Perceived Style				
Preferred Style	*Authoritative*	*Persuasive*	*Consultative*	*Participative*	*Row Total*
Authoritative					
Observed frequency	5	5	5	3	18
Expected frequency	4.01	4.93	6.04	3.02	

Persuasive					
Observed frequency	26	40	39	12	117
Expected frequency	26.04	32.05	39.26	19.63	
Consultative					
Observed frequency	19	26	42	13	100
Expected frequency	22.26	27.40	33.56	16.78	
Participative					
Observed frequency	15	9	12	21	57
Expected frequency	12.69	15.61	19.13	9.56	
Column Total	65	80	98	49	292
					Grand Total

$$\chi^2 = \Sigma \frac{(O - E)^2}{E}$$

$$= \Sigma \frac{(5 - 4.01)^2}{4.01} + \frac{(5 - 4.93)^2}{4.93} + \frac{(5 - 6.04)^2}{6.04} + \frac{(3 - 3.02)^2}{3.02} + \frac{(26 - 26.04)^2}{26.04} + \ldots + \frac{(21 - 9.56)^2}{9.56}$$

$$= .24 + 0 + .18 + 0 + 0 + \ldots + 13.69$$

$$= 28.44, \text{ with 9 degrees of freedom, } p < .001$$

Data from Stewart, Gudykunst, Ting-Toomey, and Nishida.

able rely on relationship analysis (see Chapter 14). These analyses show whether one group of ordinal measurements (such as women's class rank) are related to another group of ordinal measurements (such as men's class rank). If there is no significant relationship between the two sets, the groups are different.

Sometimes researchers also examine whether there are significant differences between two groups with respect to how they rank a particular variable. For example, suppose that researchers want to know if male and female Japanese employees differ in their preference for a persuasive management decision-making style. The researchers would advance the following one-tailed research hypothesis and its corresponding null hypothesis:

▷ H_1: Japanese male employees prefer a persuasive management decision-making style more than Japanese female employees.

▷ H_0: There is no difference between male and female Japanese employees' preference for a persuasive management decision-making style.

Suppose, however, that rather than asking the 292 employees (let's assume equal numbers of males and females, 146 each) to choose the one style they preferred, they asked them to rank the four styles in terms of preference. The dependent variable, preferred style, would now be measured on an ordinal scale.

Differences between two groups with respect to an ordinal measurement of a variable would be assessed using the *median test* (see Figure 13.4). The test itself is quite simple. Researchers would first list the rank scores for the persuasive style for all employees and then determine the grand median, the point at which half the scores fall above and half fall below. The number of rank scores for the female group that fall above and below the grand median and the number of rank scores for the male group that fall above and below the grand median would then be computed. They would put these data into a contingency table and use a contingency table analysis to analyze whether there are significant differences between the ranks for these two groups. The expected frequencies are determined as in a single-sample chi-square—by dividing the total number of subjects (292 in this case) by the number of categories (4; the result is 73).

Differences in interval or ratio-level data.   When the dependent variable is measured on an interval or ratio scale, the significance tests assess differences between group means and variances. These tests essentially compare the *between-group variance* (the differences between the group means) to the *within-group variance* (how the scores cluster around the mean within each group). A significant difference exists when there is both a large difference between groups (high between-group variance) *and* comparatively little variation between subjects within each group (low within-group variance). For example, say researchers want to learn whether there is a significant difference in the quality of communication (measured on an interval scale) between married and unmarried couples. A significant difference exists if they find a relatively large difference between the means of these two

Figure 13.4 Median test

Steps:

1. List all the rank scores for both groups.
2. Calculate the *grand median,* the point at which half the rank scores fall above and half the scores fall below.
3. Determine how many of the rank scores for the first group (males in this case) fall above and below the grand median. Determine how many of the rank scores for the second group (females in this case) fall above and below the grand median.
4. Put these data into a contingency table as the *observed frequencies.*
5. Calculate the *expected frequency* for each category by dividing the total number of subjects (292 in this case) by the total number of categories (4) (equals 73).
6. Perform a contingency table analysis as explained in Figure 13.3.

	Above Grand Median	*Below Grand Median*	Total
Males			
Observed frequency	100	46	146
Expected frequency	73	73	
Females			
Observed frequency	46	100	146
Expected frequency	73	73	

$$\chi^2 = \frac{\Sigma(O - E)^2}{E}$$

$$= \Sigma \quad \frac{(100 - 73)^2}{73} \quad + \quad \frac{(46 - 73)^2}{73} \quad + \quad \frac{(46 - 73)^2}{73} \quad + \quad \frac{(100 - 73)^2}{73}$$

$$= \quad 9.986 \quad + \quad 9.986 \quad + \quad 9.986 \quad + \quad 9.986$$

$$= 39.944, \text{ with 1 degree of freedom, } p < .001$$

groups *and* relatively similar scores among both the married and unmarried couples.

Two types of difference analysis are commonly employed to assess differences between group means and variance: the *t* test and the analysis of variance.

t **test.** Researchers use a *t* **test** to examine differences between *two* groups measured on an interval or ratio dependent variable. There are two types of *t* tests, one for comparing two independent samples and one for comparing matched samples.

Independent-Sample t Test. An **independent-sample** *t* **test** examines differences between two unrelated groups. These groups may be natural ones or ones created by researchers. For example, Heeter (1985) investigated how cable television viewers choose programs to watch. As part of the research, she asked viewers who used a remote control whether "during channel searches, they stopped at the first show that looked good (a terminating search) or finished checking their usual channels and went back (an exhaustive search)" (p. 140). An independent-sample *t* test revealed that terminating-search viewers checked fewer channels than exhaustive searchers.

To illustrate further how an independent *t* test is used, suppose that a researcher believes that there are differences between male and female Japanese employees' preference for a persuasive management decision-making style. The researcher advances the same one-tailed hypothesis and corresponding null hypothesis used in the example of a median test:

▷ H_1: Male Japanese employees prefer a persuasive management decision-making style more than female employees.

▷ H_0: There is no difference between male and female Japanese employees' preference for a persuasive management decision-making style.

This time the researcher conducts a study by asking 20 male and 20 female Japanese employees to answer 10 questions using a 5-point agree-disagree style. Responses are added together to get an overall score that represents the respondents' preference for a persuasive management decision-making style. The data are now measured on a Likert scale, which researchers in the human sciences assume to represent an interval scale with equal distances between the points. An independent-sample *t* test could therefore be used to examine the differences between males' and females' ratings of the persuasive management decision-making style (see Figure 13.5).

Figure 13.5   An independent-sample *t*-test

Steps:

1. Find the mean for each group (35 for males; 33 for females).
2. For each group, subtract the mean from each of the scores to get the *deviation scores.*
3. For each group, square the deviation scores and add them up to get the *sum-of-squares scores* (2100 for males; 3020 for females).
4. Subtract the mean of group 2 from the mean of group 1 (equals 2).
5. (a) Add the sum-of-squares scores for both groups (equals 5120) and divide by the total number of subjects minus 2 (38) (equals 134.74). (b) Divide the total number of subjects (40) by the number of subjects in group 1 (20) multiplied by the number of subjects in group 2 (20) (20 × 20 = 400) (40 ÷ 400 = .1) (c) Multiply the result of step 5a (134.74) by the result of step 5b (.1) (equals 13.47). (d) Take the square root of step 5c (equals 3.67).
6. Divide step 4 (2) by step 5d (3.67) to get the *calculated t value* (equals .54).
7. Calculate the *degrees of freedom,* which equal the total number of subjects minus 2 for independent samples (equals 38).

8. Look up the *critical value* needed for rejecting the null hypothesis at the .05 significance level with the appropriate degrees of freedom on the t table (see Appendix C) (equals 1.684 for a one-tailed hypothesis).

9. If the calculated value meets or exceeds the critical value, the null hypothesis is rejected and the research hypothesis is accepted. If the calculated value does not meet the critical value, the null hypothesis must be accepted.

	Males			**Females**	
Score	$(X - \bar{X})$ Deviation	$(X - \bar{X})^2$ Squared Deviation	Score	$(X - \bar{X})$ Deviation	$(X - \bar{X})^2$ Squared Deviation
40	5	25	30	-3	9
30	-5	25	40	7	49
20	-15	225	50	17	289
40	5	25	50	17	289
30	-5	25	40	7	49
10	-25	625	30	-3	9
40	5	25	40	7	49
30	-5	25	30	-3	9
50	15	225	40	7	49
20	-15	225	50	17	289
50	15	225	10	-23	529
40	5	25	40	7	49
30	-5	25	30	-3	9
50	15	225	40	7	49
40	5	25	40	7	49
30	-5	25	30	-3	9
40	5	25	30	3	9
40	5	25	20	-13	169
40	5	25	10	-23	529
30	-5	25	10	-23	529
$M = 35$		$\Sigma d_1^2 = 2100$ (sum of squares)	$M = 33$		$\Sigma d_2^2 = 3020$ (sum of squares)

$$t = \frac{M_1 - M_2}{\sqrt{\frac{(\Sigma d_1^2 + d_2^2)}{(n_1 + n_2 - 2)} \cdot \frac{(n_1 + n_2)}{(n_1 n_2)}}}$$

$$= \frac{35 - 33}{\sqrt{\frac{(2100 + 3020)}{(20 + 20 - 2)} \cdot \frac{(20 + 20)}{(20 \cdot 20)}}}$$

(continued)

Figure 13.5 An independent-sample test (continued)

$$= \frac{2}{\sqrt{\left(\frac{5120}{38}\right)\left(\frac{40}{400}\right)}} = \frac{2}{\sqrt{(134.74)(.1)}} = \frac{2}{\sqrt{13.47}} = \frac{2}{3.67}$$

$= .54$, with 38 degrees of freedom, N.S.

The calculated t value of .54 is compared with the critical value needed for rejecting the null hypothesis (see Appendix C). The .05 significance level is used because the researcher advanced a one-tailed research hypothesis. Degrees of freedom for an independent-sample t test are equal to the number of people in the first group minus 1 plus the number of people in the second group minus 1, or the total number of subjects minus 2 ($40 - 2 = 38$ in this example). The critical value of 1.686 needed to reject the null hypothesis is higher than the calculated value. Therefore, the researcher would have to accept the null hypothesis that there is no difference betwen male and female Japanese employees' preference for the persuasive management decision-making style.

Matched-Sample t Test.   A **matched-sample t test,** also called a **paired t test,** examines differences between two measurements from the same group of subjects. For example, Babbitt and Jablin (1985) studied the types of questions a group of applicants asked during employment screening interviews. The researchers counted up the number of open and closed questions asked and used a matched-sample t test to analyze the differences between these kinds of questions. Their analysis revealed that interviewees asked significantly more closed than open questions.

A matched-sample t test is also used to see whether there is a significant difference in subjects' scores when they are measured before and after experimental manipulation. For example, Burgoon, Cohen, Miller, and Montgomery (1978) wanted to know what makes people resist persuasive attempts. They designed an experiment to study whether people induced to evaluate sources negatively and those induced to evaluate arguments negatively demonstrate a different level of attitude change after receiving a second persuasive message. Subjects were assigned randomly to conditions in which they were told to focus on the negative characteristics of either the speaker or the arguments advanced. Both groups then received two persuasive messages that urged the legalization of heroin in the United States. Matched-sample t tests were used to analyze changes in each group's attitudes from the first persuasive message to the second. The results supported the research hypothesis: Subjects in the negative source condition demonstrated a more positive attitude toward legalization of heroin after receiving the second message. Subjects in the negative argument condition demonstrated no significant attitudinal change.

Analysis of variance. A *t* test is appropriate *only* when researchers analyze differences between two groups or two measurements for a single group. An **analysis of variance (ANOVA,** or *F* **test)** procedure is used when researchers examine differences between two or more groups on an interval dependent variable or two or more measurements for a single group. There are two types of analysis-of-variance procedures: one-way and factorial.

One-Way Analysis of Variance. **One-way ANOVA** is used to examine differences between two or more groups created from *a single independent variable* (such as nationality) on a single dependent variable (such as income level) or to examine differences between two or more measurements for a single group. A one-way ANOVA thus has only *one* independent variable, although that variable can have any number of levels. A one-way ANOVA with only two levels of an independent variable (such as males and females) is simply an alternative to a *t* test.

The more common use of one-way ANOVA is to examine differences among three or more groups. For example, Glasser, Zamanou, and Hacker (1987) used one-way ANOVA to assess differences among governmental employees at four different organizational levels (line workers, clerical, supervisors, and managers) with respect to the dependent variable of how satisfied they were with the flow of communication within their organization.

To illustrate a one-way ANOVA further, suppose that a researcher wants to know whether there are differences in Japanese, American, and Polish employees' preferences for a persuasive management decision-making style. The researcher advances the following two-tailed research hypothesis and its corresponding null hypothesis:

▷ H$_1$: Japanese, American, and Polish employees differ in their preference for a persuasive management decision-making style.

▷ H$_0$: There are no differences in Japanese, American, and Polish employees' preferences for a persuasive management decision-making style.

To conduct the research, the researcher asks five Japanese, American, and Polish employees to answer the same 10 questions using a 5-point agree-disagree scale as discussed for the independent-sample *t* test. The researcher would now use a one-way ANOVA to see whether there are differences among these three groups.

Computing a one-way ANOVA is fairly simple (see Figure 13.6). The formula for a one-way ANOVA is:

$$F \text{ value} = \frac{\text{MS}_b}{\text{MS}_w}$$

Figure 13.6 One-way ANOVA

Steps:

1. Calculate the mean for each group. Sum these group means and divide by the number of groups to get the *grand mean* (31.33).
2. (a) Subtract the grand mean from each score to get the deviation scores ($d_g = X - \bar{X}$). (b) Square these deviation scores (d_g^2). (c) Add these squared deviation scores to get the sum of squared deviations (Σd_g^2) for each group. (d) Add these sums of group-squared deviations to get the *total sum of squares* ($\Sigma d_g^2 = 873.35$).
3. (a) Subtract the group mean from each score to get the deviation within scores (d_w). (b) Square these deviations within (d_w^2). (c) Sum for each group. (d) Add the group sums of squares to get the *within-group sum of squares* ($\Sigma d_w^2 = 730$).
4. (a) Subtract the grand mean from each group mean to get the deviation between scores (d_b). (b) Square these scores (d_b^2). (c) Multiply by the number in each group (n) (5) to get the between-group deviations squared for each group (nd_b^2). (d) Sum these to get the *between-group sum of squares* ($\Sigma nd_b^2 = 143.35$).
5. The total sum-of-squares score, the within-group sum-of-squares score, and the between-group sum-of-squares scores go into the summary table. (Note that the between-group and within-group sum of squares must add up to the total sum of squares.)
6. The between-group degrees of freedom equal the number of groups minus 1 (3 − 1 = 2). The within-group degrees of freedom equal the number of subjects in each group minus 1, added together [(5 − 1) + (5 + 1) + (5 + 1) = 12].
7. Divide the between-group sum of squares by the between-group degrees of freedom to get the between-group mean square (MS) (71.68).
8. Divide the within-group sum of squares by the within-group degrees of freedom to get the within-group mean square (60.83).
9. Divide the between-group mean square by the within-group mean square to get the F value (1.178).
10. Look up the critical F value with 2 (top row) and 12 (left margin) degrees of freedom in the F table in Appendix D to find the critical F value needed to reject the null hypothesis at the .05 significance level (3.89).
11. If the calculated value meets or exceeds the critical value, the null hypothesis is rejected and the research hypothesis is accepted. If the calculated value does not meet the critical value, the null hypothesis must be accepted.

	Group 1			Group 2			Group 3	
	X Score	$(X - \bar{X})$ d_g	$(X - \bar{X})^2$ d_g^2	X Score	$(X - \bar{X})$ d_g	$(X - \bar{X})^2$ d_g^2	X Score	$(X - \bar{X})$ d_g	$(X - \bar{X})^2$ d_g^2
	20	−11.33	128.37	35	3.67	13.47	45	13.67	186.87
	25	−6.33	40.07	35	3.67	13.47	45	13.67	186.87
	30	−1.33	1.77	30	−1.33	1.77	20	−11.33	128.37
Total									

Group 1 (M = 27)

	d_g	d_g^2
35	3.67	13.47
25	− 6.33	40.07
$M = 27$		$\Sigma d_g^2 = 223.75$

Grand mean = 31.33
Total sum of squares (Σd_g^2) = 873.35

Within

d_w	d_w^2
−7	49
−2	4
3	9
8	64
−2	4
	$\Sigma d_w^2 = 130$

Group 2 (M = 34)

	d_g	d_g^2
40	8.67	75.17
30	−1.33	1.77
$M = 34$		$\Sigma d_g^2 = 105.65$

Within

d_w	d_w^2
−1	1
−1	1
−4	16
−6	36
−4	16
	$\Sigma d_w^2 = 70$

Group 3 (M = 33)

	d_g	d_g^2
25	− 6.33	40.07
30	− 1.33	1.77
$M = 33$		$\Sigma d_g^2 = 543.95$

Within

d_w	d_w^2
12	144
12	144
−13	169
−8	64
−3	9
	$\Sigma d_w^2 = 530$

Sum of squares within (Σd_w^2) = 730

Between

	Group 1	Group 2	Group 3
Group mean	27	34	33
Group mean deviation from grand mean (d_b)	−4.33	2.67	1.67
Squared deviation (d_b^2)	18.75	7.13	2.79
Group n × squared deviation	93.75	35.65	13.95

Sum of squares between (Σd_b^2) = 143.35

Summary

Source	SS	df	MS	F	p
Total	873.35				
Between groups	143.35	2	71.68	1.178	N.S.
Within groups	730.00	12	60.83		

(continued)

This formula is a ratio of the variance between groups (MS_b), which represents systematic variance, to the variance within groups (MS_w), which represents random variance. Put another way, an ANOVA tells researchers if the amount of difference between groups is sufficiently greater than the differences within the groups to warrant a claim of a statistically significant difference between the groups. In fact, most of the advanced statistical procedures are based on this notion of "partitioning" variance.

The calculated value ANOVA yields is called an F value and is compared to the critical value needed for rejecting the null hypothesis by consulting an F table (see Appendix D). Degrees of freedom are calculated in two ways. Numerator degrees of freedom (between-group variance) are the number of groups minus 1 and run across the top of the F table. Denominator degrees of freedom (within-group variance) are the sum of the number of subjects in each group minus 1 and run down the side of the F table. Since the calculated F value does not meet or exceed the critical value, the null hypothesis must be accepted.

When an F value is significant, it tells researchers only that differences exist *somewhere* among the groups. It does not reveal which specific groups differ. For example, when a study involves three groups, a significant F value can mean one of four things: (1) that all three groups are significantly different from one another, (2) that group A is different from group B but not from group C, (3) that group A is different from group C but not from group B, or (4) that group B is different from group C but not from group A.

To solve this puzzle, researchers use a **multiple comparison test** as a follow-up, or post hoc, procedure to learn what specific differences exist. Many comparison tests are available. All pinpoint the specific significant differences by comparing all possible two-group combinations. For example, follow-up tests for the Glasser et al. (1987) study described earlier revealed that top management perceived communication to be significantly stronger than the other three groups did (line workers, clerical, and supervisors).

Factorial Analysis of Variance. **Factorial analysis of variance** is used when researchers examine differences between two or more groups created from *two or more independent variables* on a single dependent variable. For example, Reeves and Garramone (1983) designed an experiment to learn whether a television program activating, or "priming," a trait influences how children think. They first selected children from second, fourth, and sixth grades. Children from each grade in the treatment condition watched a 10-minute television show that emphasized the trait "funny," while children in the control group did not. All children then read a paragraph about a real child and rated the child on 25 traits (such as "funny," "attractive," and "strong"). This experiment thus had a 3 × 2 factorial design: One independent variable was grade (with three levels) and the other independent variable was treatment (with two levels). Factorial analysis of variance then was used to examine the differences among the ratings made by these six groups.

Computing a factorial ANOVA is too complicated to be explained here. All factorial ANOVAs, however, yield two types of F values. One type of F value corresponds to the overall effects of each independent variable, which are called **main effects.** The second type of F value corresponds to the unique combination of the independent variables, called the **interaction effects.**

It is possible that a factorial ANOVA may reveal significant main effects but no significant interaction effect. It also is possible that there are no significant main effects but a significant interaction effect. Reeves and Garramone (1983), for example, found no significant main effects for either treatment or grade for any of the children's ratings of a new child. Children who saw the television program did not rate the new child differently from children in the control group. There were also no overall differences among the ratings made by second, fourth, and sixth graders. There was, however, a significant interaction effect, the *combination* of treatment and age affected ratings of "funny," "attractive," and "strong." Follow-up tests showed that second-grade children in the experimental group judged the target child to be significantly less funny, attractive, and strong than the control group. The authors conclude that "presentations of television people can influence children's use of personality traits in the evaluations of unrelated real-life people. However, the type of effect is dependent upon the child's age" (p. 264). Finally, when there are both significant main and interaction effects, only the interaction effects are considered important while the main effects are dismissed.

ADVANCED DIFFERENCE ANALYSES

The difference analyses discussed so far are some of the most common techniques employed by researchers. There are, however, many additional, and more complex, significance tests for analyzing differences between groups. Some of these advanced procedures assess differences between groups with respect to multiple dependent variables, which are called **multivariate tests.**

Although these advanced difference analyses are too complex to examine within the scope of this text, researchers use them quite frequently. For that reason, in Figure 13.7 we explain the purpose of some of these advanced difference analyses and illustrate how each has been used to study communication behavior.

CONCLUSION

Significance testing is an inferential technique that researchers use to accept or reject a null hypothesis about differences between groups or relationships between variables. Significance testing tells researchers how important the observed differences or relationships are. That is, all significance testing results in a numerical value indicating how often the difference or relationship is likely to occur by chance or

Figure 13.7   Advanced difference analyses

Researchers use the following advanced difference analyses when they are appropriate. We present a summary of the purpose of each procedure and an example of how it has been used in communication research.

---

1. **LOG-LINEAR ANALYSIS.**   **Log-linear analysis** is an advanced chi-square test used to analyze the "goodness of fit" between observed and expected frequencies of three or more nominal variables. For example, Metts (1989) studied the nature of deception in close relationships. She used log-linear analysis to assess the interactions among antecedent conditions (prompted or unprompted deception; that is, whether or not a person had been questioned or confronted about a lie by his or her partner), type of information the lie contained (factual or emotional), type of lie ([a] falsification, asserting information contradictory to the true information; [b] distortion, manipulation of true information through exaggeration, minimization, and equivocation; or [c] omission, withholding all references to relevant information), and relationship status (friends, dating, engaged, or married). Results of the log-linear analysis showed that falsification was most likely to occur when it was prompted, distortion was most likely to involve emotional information and be used by married couples, and omission was most likely to involve factual information and be used by married couples.

2. **ANALYSIS OF COVARIANCE.**   **Analysis of covariance (ANCOVA)** is used to analyze differences between groups on a dependent interval variable while controlling for the effects of a potentially confounding variable. For example, Zillman and Bhatia (1989) used ANCOVA to examine differences between male and female college students' perceptions of the desirability of a potential date as a function of the date's musical preference (classical, country, soft rock, heavy metal, or none). The ANCOVA results showed that preference for country music diminished the appeal of a date for both men and women. The results also showed that less appeal was expressed for college women who prefer heavy metal. In contrast, the appeal of college men increased when they prefer heavy metal but decreased when they prefer classical music or soft rock.

3. **MULTIPLE ANALYSIS OF VARIANCE.**   **Multiple analysis of variance (MANOVA)** is used to analyze differences between groups measured on multiple, and related, interval dependent variables. For example, Botan and Frey (1983) used MANOVA to examine differences between workers' trust of their labor union and its messages with respect to three interrelated dependent measures of trust (character, expertness, and dynamism). The results showed that the labor union was perceived as significantly more trustworthy than the union's messages with respect to character and dynamism. The authors conclude, "If unions and other organizations fail to understand that organization in part grows from communication, they may tend to use communication only as a means to an end, thereby contributing to their messages being seen as significantly less trustworthy than the organization itself" (p. 242).

4. **MULTIPLE ANALYSIS OF COVARIANCE.**   **Multiple analysis of covariance (MANCOVA)** is used to analyze differences between groups on multiple, and related, interval dependent variables while controlling for the effects of a potentially confounding variable. For example, Linz, Donnerstein, and Adams (1989) examined whether exposure to filmed violence against women leads to decreased perceptions of violence. Subjects first completed a rape myth acceptance (RMA) scale that measured their hostility toward victims of sexual

assault and their endorsement of negative stereotypes about rape and rape victims. The researchers then showed an experimental group a violent film and a control group a nonviolent film. Finally, they exposed both groups to a violent film and measured subjects on eight related scales assessing beliefs and feelings about the men and women in the films. The researchers used MANCOVA to examine differences between the experimental and control groups on eight dependent attitude measures. The results showed that differences between the groups on three of the dependent variables were related to their RMA scores. Specifically, the greater the rape myth acceptance, the less subjects expressed sympathy for the victim, the less they attributed responsibility to the perpetrator, and the more they attributed responsibility to the victim.

---

error. A finding that is very unlikely to occur by chance is assumed to be due to the actual difference or relationship that exists.

In this chapter we examined some of the most common techniques for assessing differences between groups. In Chapter 14 we examine the nature of relationship analysis and some of the more common techniques for assessing relationships.

chapter 14

Analyzing Relationships between Variables

Two variables are related if one changes when the other does. Some research suggests, for example, that our self-disclosure is related to trust because it increases or decreases depending on how much we trust people. Likewise, employees' job satisfaction may be related to how much praise they receive from their employer. And watching violent cartoon programs may be related to aggressive behavior in children.

This chapter examines how two or more variables may be related. We examine the types of possible relationships, explain how relationships are analyzed statistically, show how relationship analysis is used to make predictions, and introduce some advanced statistical relationship analyses used frequently in communication research.

TYPES OF RELATIONSHIPS

Two variables can be associated in one of three ways: They can be *unrelated, linear,* or *nonlinear.* Imagine that we want to know whether time spent doing assignments for the course you are taking is related to performance on an examination testing mastery of the material covered. This is a question about the relationship between two variables, defined operationally as work hours (x) and test scores (y). Say we measured both variables for everyone in the class and plotted each person's position on a matrix (called a **scattergram**) showing the relationship between them (see Figure 14.1). **Unrelated** variables (also called **orthogonal** or **independent** variables) have no systematic relationship (Figure 14.1a). **Linear** relationships between variables are distributions of data that can generally be represented and explained by a straight line (Figures 14.1b and 14.1c). **Nonlinear** relationships between variables are distributions of data that can be represented and explained by a curved line (Figures 14.1d and 14.1e).

Unrelated Variables

Two variables are unrelated when they vary independently of each other (see Figure 14.1a). This means that there is no systematic relationship between the variables. Changes in variable x are simply not related to changes in variable y, and vice versa. In this case, test scores don't seem influenced by or related to hours of work. When two variables are unrelated, knowing how one changes does not give researchers any understanding of changes in the other.

For example, Gudykunst (1985) wanted to learn whether diverse cultural contacts influence communication attitudes. He investigated the relationship between two kinds of variables: (1) the number of friendships international students form with members of their own culture in the United States and with U.S. nationals and (2) how similar they perceived themselves and their best friend in the United States (labeled "intercultural homogeneity"). Respondents were 83 international students who had developed a close friendship with a U.S. national. They were asked to indicate the number of friendships formed with members of their own culture in the United States and with U.S. nationals. They also rated their best friend in the United States on an instrument that measured four dimensions of perceived intercultural homogeneity: attitude, morality, background, and appearance. Gudykunst found no significant relationship between the number of same-culture friends in the United States and intercultural homogeneity or between the number of U.S. national friends and intercultural homogeneity. Perceived intercultural similarity therefore seems unrelated to these particular friendships that international students form. This study is illustrative of findings that inform us that two variables are not significantly related.

Linear Relationships between Variables

Linear relationships between two variables generally follow a consistent pattern that can be illustrated graphically by a straight line. There are two types of linear relationships: *positive* and *negative* relationships.

A **positive relationship** means that two variables move, or change, in the *same* direction (see Figure 14.1b). If variable x goes up, variable y goes up; if variable x goes down, variable y goes down. A positive relationship tells researchers that changes in one variable are associated with similar changes in another variable. If

Figure 14.1 Types of relationships

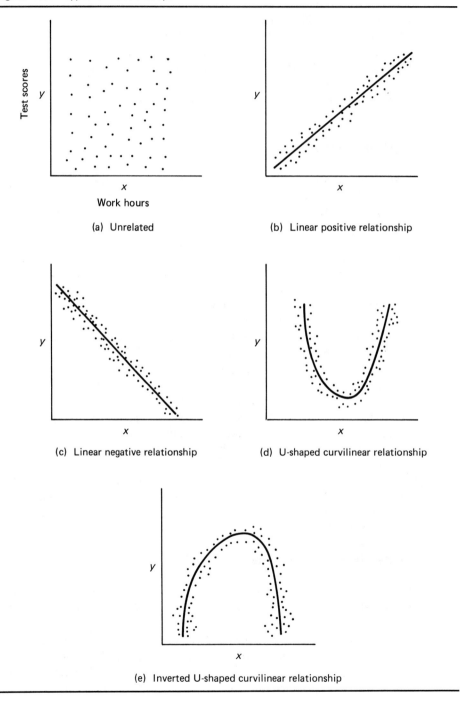

(a) Unrelated

(b) Linear positive relationship

(c) Linear negative relationship

(d) U-shaped curvilinear relationship

(e) Inverted U-shaped curvilinear relationship

people who invest more work time get higher test scores and people who work fewer hours get lower test scores, these two variables are related positively.

A **negative relationship** means that two variables move, or change, in *opposite* directions (see Figure 14.1c). If variable x goes up, variable y goes down; if variable x goes down, variable y goes up. A negative relationship means that changes in one variable are associated with opposite changes in another variable. If people who work more hours get lower test scores and people who work fewer hours get higher scores, these two variables are related negatively.

To illustrate positive and negative relationships further, consider a study by Street (1989), who examined the relationship between dentists' communicative style and their patients' satisfaction. After receiving dental treatment, 572 patients of 17 dentists completed a mailed questionnaire that measured perceptions of their dentists' *communicative involvement* (the degree to which the dentist appeared attentive, perceptive, and responsive to patients' comments and needs) and *communicative dominance* (the degree to which the dentist controlled the nature and topics of the encounter) and satisfaction with their dentist. The results showed that there was a strong *positive* relationship between dentists' communicative involvement and patients' satisfaction. The more attentive, perceptive, and responsive to patients' needs dentists seemed, the more satisfied patients were. The results also showed a *negative* relationship between dentists' communicative dominance and patients' satisfaction. The more dentists argued with patients and took charge of the interaction, the less satisfied patients felt.

Nonlinear Relationships between Variables

Nonlinear relationships between variables follow a pattern, but that pattern is not simple and direct enough to be illustrated by a straight line. Instead, there is at least one curve, or "hump," in the line (see Figures 14.1d and 14.1e). Let's take the relationship between amount of talk and having friends as an example. Certainly, most people who talk very little have few friends. People who talk a moderate amount probably have more friends. So the two variables seem positively related. But people who talk a lot aren't likely to have even more friends—probably fewer. So the relationship isn't consistently positive. It's more complex and curved.

A **curvilinear relationship,** also called a **quadratic trend,** means that two variables are related in a positive or a negative way up to a certain point, at which the relationship reverses. There are two types of curvilinear relationships. A **U-shaped curvilinear relationship** means that two variables are related negatively up to a point but then are related positively (see Figure 14.1d). An **inverted U-shaped curvilinear relationship** means that two variables are related positively up to a point and then are related negatively (see Figure 14.1e).

Our example, relating talk and friendships, describes an inverted U-shaped curvilinear relationship. This relationship is particularly interesting because it reflects the fact that it is indeed possible to have "too much of a good thing," as well as the idea that at some point returns begin to diminish.

Variables are also related in more complex ways. Curvilinear relationships have only one hump, but in cubic relationships there are two humps, and in quartic relationships there are three humps. These complex relationships are thus defined by the number of humps or curves, and the statistical procedure used to determine the number of humps is referred to as **trend analysis.**

CORRELATIONS

Researchers use statistical procedures to assess the relationship between two variables. A statistical relationship between two variables is referred to as a **correlation.** To determine the statistical correlation between two variables, researchers calculate two things: a *correlation coefficient,* which indicates the type and strength of the relationship between the variables, and a *coefficient of determination,* which indicates how much one variable can be explained by the other variable.

Correlation Coefficients

A **correlation coefficient** is a numerical summary of the type and strength of a relationship between two variables. A correlation coefficient takes the form $r_{ab} = \pm x$, where r stands for the correlation coefficient, a and b represent the two variables being correlated, the sign indicates the direction of the relationship between the two variables, and x stands for some numerical value.

A correlation coefficient thus has two separate parts. The first part is the sign, which indicates the *direction* of a relationship between two variables. A plus sign ($+$) means a positive relationship, and a negative sign ($-$) means a negative relationship.

The second part is a numerical value that indicates the *strength* of a relationship between two variables. This number is expressed as a decimal value that ranges from $+1.00$ to -1.00. A correlation coefficient of $+1.00$ is a perfect positive relationship, which means that as one variable moves up one unit, the other variables increases one unit (although the units of measurement do not have to be the same). Say a company started all new hires at the same salary and then gave everyone an equal annual raise. The correlation coefficient between seniority and pay would be $+1.00$. The correlation coefficient between pay and ability, however, would probably be much lower. A correlation coefficient of 0.00 means that two variables are unrelated. For example, the correlation coefficient between the size of people's tongues and their ability to speak or the size of their ears and their ability to listen probably is almost certainly 0.00. A perfect negative correlation coefficient of -1.00 means that as one variable increases one unit, the other variable decreases one unit. The farther apart people move from each other, for example, the less they can hear, if their volume stays constant.

Interpreting correlation coefficients. Two variables are rarely related perfectly to one another, so researchers need to assess the significance of a correlation

hypothesis of no relationship and a research hypothesis, either predicting a relationship but not specifying its direction (a two-tailed hypothesis) or predicting a positive or negative relationship (a one-tailed hypothesis).

Once data are collected and a correlation coefficient has been computed, researchers test whether that correlation coefficient is significant, usually by employing a modified form of a t test. The degrees of freedom for this t test are equal to the number of subjects minus 2 ($n - 2$). The calculated value derived from the t test is compared to the critical value to see how likely it is that the correlation coefficient occurs by chance. If the calculated value equals or exceeds the critical value for the .05 significance level used in communication research, researchers reject the null hypothesis of no relationship and accept its alternative, the research hypothesis.

Just because a relationship between two variables is significant statistically, however, does not mean that it is an *important* relationship. Researchers have to be careful not to report significant but trivial results. Interpreting the importance or strength of a correlation coefficient depends on many things, including the purpose and use of the research and the sample size. There are no universal guidelines for interpreting the strength of a significant correlation coefficient, but Guilford (1956) proposes that when sample size is fairly large, the following criteria can be used:

    $< .20$ Slight, almost negligible relationship

  .20–.40 Low correlation, definite but small relationship

  .40–.70 Moderate correlation, substantial relationship

  .70–.90 High correlation, marked relationship

    $> .90$ Very high correlation, very dependable relationship (p. 145)

Calculating correlation coefficients. Researchers use a variety of statistical procedures to calculate correlation coefficients between two variables. Which statistical procedure is used depends on how the two variables are measured. Here we explain three procedures that are appropriate when both variables are measured at the interval/ratio, ordinal, and nominal level.

Relationships between Interval-Level Data. The most popular correlational procedure is probably the **Pearson product-moment correlation.** This procedure calculates a correlation coefficient for two variables that are measured on interval/ratio scales.

For example, suppose that a researcher is interested in the relationship between the amount of time supervisors spend talking face to face with their employees and employee satisfaction. Based on a review of the literature, the researcher advances the following one-tailed research hypothesis and corresponding null hypothesis:

▷ H_1: There is a positive relationship between the amount of time supervisors spend talking face to face with their employees and employee satisfaction.

▷ H_0: There is no relationship between the amount of time supervisors spend talking face to face with their employees and employee satisfaction.

To test the null hypothesis of no relationship between these two variables, the researcher draws a random sample of 10 employees from various companies (the sample would, of course, be larger, but we want to keep the computations simple) and asks them to keep track for one week of how many minutes per day their employer spends talking with them face to face. The researcher then computes the average number of minutes per day for each employee. The researcher also asks the employees to answer 20 questions about their satisfaction with their supervisor using a 5-point agree-disagree scale that can be summed to produce a total satisfaction score (ranging from 20 to 100).

Since both variables are measured on an interval scale, the researcher uses the Pearson product-moment correlation to calculate the correlation coefficient (see Figure 14.2). The resulting correlation coefficient of $r = +.97$ shows that there is a very strong positive relationship between these two variables. The researcher then calculates the significance of this correlation coefficient using the modified t test (see Figure 14.2). The calculated value of 11.85 exceeds the critical value of 1.86 needed to reach the .05 significance level with 8 degrees of freedom ($n - 2 = 10 - 2 = 8$; see Appendix C). The researcher thus rejects the null hypothesis of no relationship and accepts its alternative, the research hypothesis of a positive relationship between these two variables.

Relationships between Ordinal-Level Data.   When two variables are measured on an ordinal (or ranked) scale, researchers can calculate the correlation coefficient by using the **Spearman rho (ρ) correlation.**

Suppose, for example, that a researcher is interested in the relationship between argumentativeness and leadership emergence within a small group. Based on a review of the small group communication literature, the researcher advances the following one-tailed research hypothesis and its corresponding null hypothesis:

▷ H_1: There is a positive relationship between argumentativeness and small group leadership emergence.

▷ H_0: There is no relationship between argumentativeness and small group leadership emergence.

To test the null hypothesis of no relationship between these two variables, the researcher might put 10 people in a group and ask them to engage in a decision-making task. The researcher might also ask one observer to rank the members of the group on argumentativeness and another observer to rank them on leadership behavior.

Because both of these variables are measured on an ordinal scale, the researcher would use the Spearman rho correlation procedure to calculate the correlation coefficient (see Figure 14.3). In our sample, this procedure yields a non-statistically significant coefficient of $\rho = +.012$, indicating almost no correlation between argumentativeness and leadership emergence. The researcher must thus accept the null hypothesis of no relationship between these two variables.

Figure 14.2   Pearson product-moment correlation

Steps:

1. Calculate the mean for each set of scores (18 for minutes; 60 for satisfaction).
2. For each set of scores, subtract the mean from each score to get the *deviation scores* (columns x and y).
3. Square the deviation scores for column x and add these squared deviation scores to get the x^2 score (equals 1320). Square the deviation scores for column y and add these squared deviation scores to get the y^2 score (equals 7400).
4. Multiply each score in column x by its respective score in column y, and add these scores together to get the xy score (equals 3040).
5. Multiply the x^2 score (1320) by the y^2 score (7400) (equals 9,768,000), and take the square root of this value (equals 3125.38).
6. Divide the xy score (3040) by the result of step 5 (3125.38) to get the *Pearson product-moment correlation* (equals +.97).
7. Use the modified form of the t test to test for the significance of the Pearson product-moment correlation. Degrees of freedom for this t test are equal to the number of subjects minus 2 (equals 8).
8. If the calculated t value meets or exceeds the critical value, the null hypothesis is rejected and the research hypothesis is accepted. If the calculated value does not meet the critical value, the null hypothesis must be accepted.

Subject	Minutes	Satisfaction	x	y	x^2	y^2	xy
1	40	100	22	40	484	1600	880
2	35	100	17	40	289	1600	680
3	20	60	2	0	4	0	0
4	5	20	−13	−40	169	1600	520
5	5	20	−13	−40	169	1600	520
6	9	40	−9	−20	81	400	180
7	13	50	−5	−10	25	100	50
8	15	60	−3	0	9	0	0
9	27	80	9	20	81	400	180
10	21	70	3	10	9	100	30
	$M = 18$	$M = 60$			$\Sigma x^2 = 1320$	$\Sigma y^2 = 7400$	$\Sigma xy = 3040$

$$r = \frac{\Sigma\, xy}{\sqrt{\Sigma\, x^2 \cdot \Sigma\, y^2}}$$

$$= \frac{3040}{\sqrt{(1320)(7400)}} = \frac{3040}{\sqrt{9,768,000}} = \frac{3040}{3125.38} = \underline{+.973}$$

Testing the significance of the Pearson product-moment correlation:

$$t = \frac{r\sqrt{n-2}}{\sqrt{1-r^2}} = \frac{.973\sqrt{8}}{\sqrt{1-.946}} = \frac{2.75}{.232} = \underline{11.85,\ 8\ df,\ p < .001}$$

Figure 14.3 Spearman Rho correlation

Steps:

1. Take the *difference* between the two rankings for each subject.
2. Square each difference score, and add these squared difference scores to get the Σd^2 score (equals 163).
3. Multiply the Σd^2 score by 6 (equals 978).
4. Multiply the number of subjects by itself twice and subtract the number of subjects from this figure (equals 990).
5. Divide step 3 (978) by step 4 (990) (equals .988). Subtract this figure (.988) from 1 to get the *Spearman rho correlation* (equals .02).
6. Test the significance of the Spearman rho correlation using the appropriate procedure.
7. If the calculated value for the significance test exceeds the critical value, the null hypothesis is rejected and the research hypothesis is accepted. If the calculated value does not meet the critical value, the null hypothesis must be accepted.

Subject	Rank on Argumentation	Rank on Leadership	Difference	Squared Difference
1	4	9	−5	25
2	8	5	3	9
3	2	8	−6	36
4	1	1	0	0
5	9	7	2	4
6	10	2	8	64
7	3	5	−2	4
8	5	6	−1	1
9	7	3	4	16
10	6	4	2	4
				$\Sigma D^2 = 163$

$$\rho = 1 - \frac{6\,\Sigma D^2}{N^3 - N} = 1 - \frac{6(163)}{1000 - 10} = 1 - \frac{978}{990} = 1 - .988 = \underline{\underline{.012}}$$

Testing the significance of the Spearman rho correlation:

If N is between 10 and 30:

$$t = \rho \sqrt{\frac{N - 2}{1 - \rho^2}}$$

If N is 30 or greater:

$$z = \rho \sqrt{N - 1}$$

(If $z \geq \pm 1.96$, ρ is significant at the .05 level using a two-tailed test. If $z \geq \pm 1.65$, ρ is significant at the .05 level using a one-tailed test.)

At times researchers measure one variable using a nominal scale and another variable on an ordinal scale. Say a researcher wants to know whether observers rank males and females differently with regard to argumentativeness or leadership displayed. In such cases they can use the **point biserial correlation** to analyze the relationship between the two genders' ordinal scores. If there is no relationship between the scores, the groups are significantly different.

Relationships between Nominal Data.   Finally, researchers can assess the relationship between two variables that are both measured on a nominal scale. For example, a researcher might want to assess the relationship between gender and the types of strategies used to comfort others.

The procedures for computing a correlation coefficient between two nominal variables are based on the chi-square value associated with the contingency table analysis discussed in Chapter 13. For instance, a procedure used commonly for this purpose is Cramer's V coefficient. The formula for Cramer's V coefficient is:

$$V = \frac{X^2}{N}$$

where X^2 is the chi-square calculated value and N is the number of observations summed across all the categories.

For example, look back at the contingency table analysis in Chapter 13 performed on Japanese employees' perceived and preferred management decision-making styles (Figure 13.3). Computing Cramer's V coefficient for the chi-square value of 28.44 with 292 total observations yields a correlation coefficient of .31. This is a relatively low correlation, which confirms the contingency table analysis of a significant difference between perceived and preferred management decision-making styles.

Correlation matrices.   Researchers often study the relationships of numerous variables. In such cases they compute correlation coefficients for all the possible pairs of variables. They often report these multiple correlation coefficients by depicting them visually on a *correlation matrix*. A **correlation matrix** lists all the relevant variables both across the top and down the left side of a matrix. Where the respective rows and columns meet, researchers indicate the correlation coefficient for those two variables and whether it is significant. The diagonal line from the top left to the bottom right of the matrix is usually left blank, since the relationship between a variable and itself is $+1.00$. The bottom left half of the matrix is also typically left blank because it would merely be the same as the top right half.

Baxter and Wilmot (1983), for example, studied several communication characteristics associated with friendships at different stages of development. They asked 58 subjects to keep track of two relationships (one same-sex relationship and one opposite-sex relationship) for two weeks. After each face-to-face or telephone encounter, subjects were asked to indicate in a diary such things as the topics they discussed, the overall importance of the encounter, and the perceived effect of the encounter on the overall relationship. From these diary entries, the researchers computed interval scores for the following variables: (1) *talk embeddedness,* the proportion of conversations in which they talked for talk's sake, as opposed to carrying out a recognized social activity (such as playing a game); (2) *number of encounters;* (3) *topic breadth,* the mean number of different topics discussed per encounter; (4) *encounter satisfaction;* (5) *encounter importance;* (6) *interaction effectiveness,* a score computed by combining responses on three 7-point bipolar scales (attentive versus poor listening, great deal of understanding versus misunderstanding, and frequent communication breakdowns versus none); and (7) *personalness,* a score computed by combining responses on three 7-point bipolar scales (impersonal versus personal, deep versus superficial, and guarded versus open).

As part of the analysis, the researchers reported the correlation coefficients for each of the possible pairs of variables using a correlation matrix (see Figure 14.4). The correlation matrix shows clearly the degree to which the variables are correlated and whether these correlations are significant. Note, for instance, that topic breadth and encounter satisfaction are positively, and significantly, related: The more topics discussed, the greater the satisfaction with the conversations. The researchers then went on to show how relationships at various stages of development differed with respect to these variables.

Causation and correlation.   A correlation coefficient only indicates whether two variables are related and if so, how much. It does not tell researchers how changes in one variable produce changes in another. Causation thus cannot be inferred from a correlation coefficient. Correlations are extremely susceptible to alternate causality arguments—multiple explanations for why change occurs. For example, two variables may vary together not because one causes the other but because a third variable causes both of them to vary.

Figure 14.4   A correlation matrix

	1.	2.	3.	4.	5.	6.	7.
1. Talk-embeddedness	—	−.11	.05	.09	.07	.05	.12
2. Number of encounters		—	−.01	.13	.18*	.19*	.20*
3. Topic breadth			—	.19*	.12	.14	.14
4. Encounter satisfaction				—	.64*	.57*	.56*
5. Encounter importance					—	.21*	.49*
6. Interaction effectiveness						—	.49*
7. Interaction personalness							—

*Significant beyond the .05 level for all 116 relationships

Source: Leslie A. Baxter and William W. Wilmot, "Communication Characteristics of Relationships With Differential Growth Rates," *Communication Monographs, 50*(3), p. 268, copyright © 1983 by the Speech Communication Association. Reprinted by permission of the Speech Communication Association.

The following Chinese fable illustrates that even in ancient times, people recognized the danger of confusing correlation with causation.

> While hunting for prey, a tiger caught a fox. The fox thought quickly and said, "You can't eat me! The Emperor of Heaven appointed me king of the beasts. If you eat me, you'll be disobeying his orders. If you don't believe me, follow me. You'll soon see whether the other animals run away at the sight of me or not."
>
> Agreeing to this, the tiger accompanied him. Every beast who saw them coming dashed away. Not realizing they were afraid of him, the tiger believed they were afraid of the fox.

Researchers must therefore refrain from inferring causation from correlation. For example, suppose that researchers found a very high positive correlation between increased advertising and increased sales of a particular product. Would it be safe to assume that increasing advertising *causes* the increased sales? Maybe, maybe not. What if the increased advertising and the increased sales were both due to a once-a-year clearance sale during which prices were cut in half and two-thirds of the year's advertising budget was spent to promote that sale?

Although a correlation coefficient does not indicate whether one variable causes a change in another variable, researchers can use the sequencing of events in time to infer causation. It wouldn't make much sense, for example, to suggest that dying causes heart attacks!

Another problem with interpreting correlation coefficients is assuming that just because two variables are correlated, they are related meaningfully. *Mad* magazine once "proved" that baseball causes juvenile delinquency because more than 90 percent of juvenile delinquents played baseball! Similarly, suppose that people's height correlates positively with how much television they watch. Does any theoretical or logical rationale suggest that a meaningful relationship exists between these two variables? It seems safe to assume that this correlation occurs because of chance and is therefore not meaningful. Situations in which variables are correlated but are not related meaningfully are referred to as **spurious relationships.**

Coefficient of Determination

A correlation coefficient tells researchers how two variables are related and how strongly. It does not indicate, however, how much changes in one variable can be explained by changes in the other variable. For example, say studying hard correlates positively with grades on final examinations at $r = +.91$. This is obviously a significant and very strong positive correlation.

This correlation, however, does not tell researchers how much of the differences between students' grades can be explained by the amount of studying they do. To know this, researchers calculate a **coefficient of determination,** a numerical indicator that tells how much of the variance in one variable can be explained by knowledge of another variable.

The coefficient of determination (r^2) is a decimal value ranging from 0.00 to 1.00 computed simply by squaring the correlation coefficient. For the example of the relationship between grades and studying, squaring the correlation coefficient of $+.91$ yields a coefficient of determination of .83.

Venn diagrams are useful for illustrating graphically the information contained in a coefficient of determination (see Figure 14.5). The two circles represent the amount of time spent studying and grades on final examinations. The shaded area of overlap shows that the two variables share 83 percent of their variance. Put another way, about 83 percent of the variance in final exam scores is explained by the amount of time spent studying. This does not mean that studying necessarily *causes* higher grades, but this sequence certainly makes sense since studying precedes the examinations.

Multiple Correlations

Because communication processes are complex, researchers are often interested in the relationships of more than two variables. For example, a researcher might want to know how trust is related to liking and friendliness. Computing the relationships of each of the possible pairs of variables (trust and liking, trust and friendliness, and liking and friendliness) would not reveal how trust is related to the *combination* of liking and friendliness working together.

Researchers compute **multiple correlations** when they want to assess the relationship between the variable they wish to explain, the **criterion variable,** and two

Figure 14.5 Variance explained by a coefficient of determination

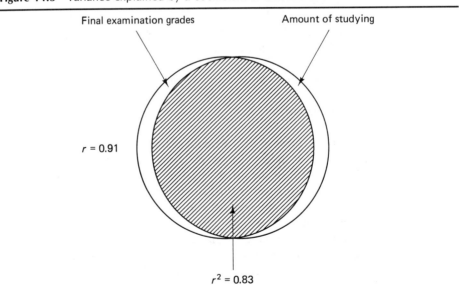

Final examination grades   Amount of studying

$r = 0.91$

$r^2 = 0.83$

or more other variables working together. Multiple correlations yield two types of statistics: a multiple correlation coefficient and a multiple coefficient of determination.

Multiple correlation coefficient.   A **multiple correlation coefficient** (R) is just like a correlation coefficient, except that it tells researchers how two or more variables *working together* are related to the criterion variable. A multiple correlation, for example, shows how liking and friendliness working together are related to trust.

A multiple correlation coefficient indicates both the direction and the strength of the relationship between a criterion variable and the other variables. A multiple correlation coefficient takes the form $R_{a.bc} = \pm x$, read, "The multiple correlation of variables b and c with variable a is . . ." For example, an observed multiple correlation coefficient of $+.98$ might mean that the amount of trust (a) we have for people is related positively with how much we like them (b) combined with how friendly they are (c).

Researchers can relate as many variables to the criterion variable as they deem important, and any of the variables can be considered the criterion variable. For example, trust (b) and liking (c) could be related to the criterion variable of friendliness (a).

Coefficient of multiple determination.   A **coefficient of multiple determination** (R^2) expresses the amount of variance in the criterion variable that can be explained by the other variables acting together. A coefficient of multiple determination is computed simply by squaring the multiple correlation coefficient.

In the hypothetical example of the relationship of trust, liking, and friendliness, $R^2_{a.bc} = .98^2 = .96$. If this correlation were actually true, it would mean that 96 percent of the variance in trust could be explained by liking and friendliness working together. Consequently, only 4 percent of trust would be left unexplained by these two variables.

Partial Correlations

A multiple correlation assesses the relationship of more than two variables, but it does not inform researchers about the relationship between two variables when the effects of another variable are removed. A **partial correlation** explains the relationship between two variables while controlling for or ruling out the influence of one or more other variables. A partial correlation coefficient takes the form $r_{ab.c} = \pm x$, read, "The partial correlation coefficient of variable a and variable b with variable c controlled for is . . ."

For example, researchers differentiate among three types of conflict strategies: *integrative,* which promote both parties' objectives; *distributive,* which pursue one individual's goals over another's; and *avoidant,* which attempt to avert direct conflict altogether. A number of studies report that the type of conflict strategy used affects relational outcomes. For example, participants are more satisfied with the outcome of a conflict episode when integrative strategies are used. Canary and Spitzberg (1989), however, hypothesized that perceptions of a communicator's competence (a general impression of communication quality associated especially with perceptions of appropriateness and effectiveness) would mediate the effects of these conflict strategies on relational outcomes (including trust, control mutuality, intimacy, and satisfaction). After measuring people on all three variables (communicator competence, conflict strategies used, and relational outcomes), they computed correlations between every combination of two variables (conflict strategies and relational outcomes, conflict strategies and communicator competence, and communicator comptence and relational outcomes). They "partialed out" the effects due to the third variable in each case. The partial correlations demonstrated support for their hypothesis. None of the partial correlations between integrative or distributive strategies and relational outcomes, for example, were significant when controlling for perceptions of a partner's communication competence. Attributions of communication competence, therefore, explain the relationship between conflict strategies and relational outcomes. Canary and Spitzberg conclude that "conflict messages are assessed as more or less appropriate, effective, and globally competent, and these assessments then affect relational features of trust, control mutuality, intimacy, and relational satisfaction" (p. 644).

Partial correlations also allow researchers to assess a relationship between variables while eliminating the influence of a potentially confounding variable. For example, say a $100,000 study was conducted to find out whether the voters of a state are willing to elect a particular candidate. The researcher might compute multiple correlations to relate voters' willingness to support the candidate to their favorability ratings of the candidate's stance on some major issues and their belief in a recent accusation of illegal campaign contributions. Suppose that after the study is completed, the accusations are found to be false, and the researcher suspects that they may have biased the survey results. Not having a spare $100,000 around, the researcher can reexamine the data to partial out the effects due to the false charges. The partial correlations will show which issues crucially affect people's support for the candidate once the effects due to the confounding variable are removed.

REGRESSION ANALYSES

Besides investigating whether two variables are associated, researchers may also wish to *predict* or *explain* how people are likely to score on a criterion, or outcome, variable based on their scores on another variable, called a **predictor variable.** Statistical procedures used for prediction are referred to as **regression analyses.**

Linear Regression

Linear regression is used to predict or explain scores on a criterion variable on the basis of scores on a predictor variable and knowledge of the relationship between the two variables. For example, universities often use a linear regression to evaluate applicants. They use the known relationship between SAT or ACT scores and college cumulative grade point averages to predict a particular high school applicant's future cumulative college GPA based on his or her particular SAT or ACT score. Some organizations use known relationships between certain screening instruments and employee success to predict the likelihood that a particular applicant will be successful. In each case, a person's score on one variable is used to predict or explain scores on another variable based on the known relationship between the two variables.

To understand linear regression, suppose that a researcher wants to predict a person's knowledge of current events (the criterion variable) based on the number of minutes he or she spends watching television news per day (the predictor variable). The researcher collects data on the number of minutes people spend watching television news per day and how much knowledge they have of current events (measured on an interval scale from 0 to 100). The researcher then plots these data on a scattergram (see Figure 14.6). The researcher then draws a straight line that minimizes the distance between each observed score and the line. In regression analysis, this straight line is referred to as the **line of best fit** or the **regression line.** The researcher can then locate a person's score on the horizontal or X-axis of the line of best fit (the number of minutes spent watching television news per day) and find the corresponding point on the vertical or Y-axis (knowledge of current events) to predict the score on that variable. For example, if a person watched 50 minutes of television news per day, the researcher would find this point on the x-axis, move up

Figure 14.6 Linear regression

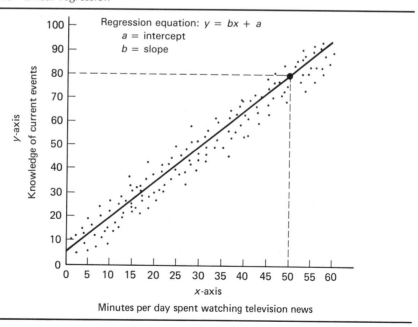

Minutes per day spent watching television news

to the line of best fit, and then follow a straight line across to the *y*-axis to predict the person's knowledge-of-current-events score. So if a person watched 50 minutes of television news per day, the best prediction of his or her knowledge of current affairs would be 80 on a scale from 0 to 100.

Now let's formalize the procedure a bit. Regression analysis is actually accomplished by constructing a **regression equation,** which is a mathematical description of the line of best fit (see Figure 14.6). We won't worry about the math, but two properties of a regression equation are important.

First, the **intercept** is how far up the *y*-axis the regression line begins, somewhere about 5 in this example. Second, the **slope** is how steeply the regression line is angled, which really depends on the correlation between the two variables. A regression analysis thus uses a known score and the slope and intercept of the regression line to predict what another score is likely to be without having to measure the other score.

It should be pointed out that the stronger the correlation between two variables, the more accurate the prediction. In addition, significance tests can be applied to a regression equation to determine whether the predicted variance is significant. One common procedure, for example, is to use an *F* test to see whether the predicted variance is significantly greater than the unpredicted variance.

Multiple Regression

A **multiple regression** allows researchers to predict or explain scores on a criterion variable on the basis of scores on two or more predictor variables and knowledge of the relationships between all the variables. For example, a multiple regression could be used to predict a person's knowledge-of-current-events score from knowing how much time he or she spends reading the newspaper, listening to the radio, and watching television news *combined,* if the relationships between these variables are known.

A multiple regression provides researchers with three pieces of information. First, a multiple regression yields a multiple correlation coefficient (*R*) that tells researchers the relationship between the criterion variable and all the predictor variables. Second, a multiple regression yields a coefficient of multiple determination (R^2) that expresses the amount of *variance* in the criterion variable that can be explained by the predictor variables acting together. Third, a multiple regression tells researchers how much *each* of the predictor variables contributes toward explaining the criterion variable. It does this by providing a relative weighting, called a **beta weight,** that indicates the extent to which each predictor variable explains the scores on the criterion variable.

To illustrate the use of a multiple regression analysis, consider the Desmond, Singer, Singer, Calam, and Colimore (1985) study of the extent to which family communication mediates children's comprehension of television. They showed kindergarten and first-grade children a 15-minute edited version of an episode of the

to recall what happened in the show—a measure of their comprehension of what they saw. The children also completed a series of questionnaires that measured such things as their general television knowledge and their knowledge of their parents' specific rules about watching television. Finally, the researchers asked the children's parents to complete a number of questionnaires that measured how they communicated with their children in general and about television in particular.

The researchers used a multiple regression procedure to show how the criterion variable of television comprehension could be explained by the various communication predictor variables. The regression analysis showed that comprehension could be predicted by three variables ($R = .367$, $R^2 = .135$), listed in order of their predictive strength. As the researchers explain:

> When television comprehension is examined as a function of family variables, television-specific rules, a report of positive communication between mother and child, and a pattern of explanation of television content by parents are associated with children who gain knowledge from a television plot. (p. 476)

The multiple regression analysis thus showed how television comprehension could be explained by these three predictor variables.

Explaining and predicting communication behavior often demands taking numerous variables into account. Because multiple regression assesses the relationships between numerous predictor variables and a criterion variable, researchers frequently use this procedure to capture the complexity of communication processes.

ADVANCED RELATIONSHIP ANALYSES

The relationship analyses discussed so far are among the most common techniques employed by researchers. There are, however, more complex, *multivariate* correlational procedures that assess relationships between two *groups* of variables.

These advanced relational analyses, too complex to examine within the scope of this text, are used quite frequently by researchers. For that reason, in Figure 14.7 we explain the purpose of these advanced relationship analyses and illustrate how each has been used to study communication behavior.

CONCLUSION

Like the relationship between husband and wife, boss and employee, and parent and child, the relationships between variables measured in a research study are important for understanding but are not easy to decipher. When people quarrel, each

Figure 14.7   Advanced relationship analyses

Researchers use the following advanced relationship analyses when they are appropriate. We give a summary of the purpose of each procedure and an example of how it has been used in communication research.

1. CANONICAL CORRELATION: **Canonical correlation** is used to examine the relationships between a set of independent variables and a set of dependent variables. For example, Chen (1989) used canonical correlation to study the relationships between 7 communication qualities (such as empathy and tolerance of ambiguity) and 13 components of intercultural communication competence (such as amount of disclosure and communication adaptability). Canonical correlation showed that there was a significant positive relationship between a set of variables defined by a display of respect and a second set of variables defined by communication competence. Chen concludes that "appropriateness and effectiveness are the two indispensible elements for conceptualizing intercultural communication competence" (p. 129).

2. CLUSTER ANALYSIS: **Cluster analysis** is used to explain how scores on multiple variables can be grouped together, or clustered, into meaningful subgroups that have not been predetermined by researchers. For example, Poole (1981) used cluster analysis to isolate sets of "interacts" (act-response pairs in conversation) that occur together regularly during group decision-making discussions. Cluster analysis revealed 36 theoretically meaningful clusters of interacts that could be grouped into four general sets related to proprosal development, socioemotional concerns, conflict, and expression of ambiguity.

3. DISCRIMINANT ANALYSIS: **Discriminant analysis** is used to predict membership in predetermined groups based on responses to a set of variables. For example, Andersen and Kibler (1978) used discriminant analysis to predict voter preference for two Democratic candidates eight days prior to a primary for the United States Senate in Florida. They analyzed voters' evaluations of the candidates' source credibility (competence, extroversion, sociability, and composure), attraction (social and physical attraction), and homophily (attitude and background similarity between candidate and voter). Discriminant analysis revealed that 61.6 percent of voters could be assigned correctly to the actual voter preference group based on their evaluations of a candidate on these variables. Attitude homophily, in particular, was found to be the best predictor of voter preference.

4. FACTOR ANALYSIS: **Factor analysis** is used to reduce scores on multiple variables to a few common underlying dimensions, called *factors*. For example, Babrow (1989) used factor analysis to understand the reasons for college students' high interest in television soap operas. Factor analysis revealed that students' ratings of 18 perceived outcomes from watching soap operas (such as relaxation and reinforcement of reality) could be reduced to three primary factors: social-pleasure (perceived opportunities for social interaction combined with general immediate pleasures such as amusement), anticipated learning, and expected opportunity for romantic fantasy.

5. MULTIDIMENSIONAL SCALING ANALYSIS: **Multidimensional scaling analysis** is used to plot scores on variables in two or more dimensions to see the similarity between variables. For example, Livingstone (1987) used multidimensional scaling analysis to discover the main themes viewers use to describe the characters in the television show *Dallas*. She asked subjects who watched *Dallas* regularly to rate 13 characters (such as J. R. Ewing and Sue Ellen Ewing) on 14 seven-point bipolar scales (such as sociable/unsociable and

warm/cold). Multidimensional scaling analysis revealed that viewers' descriptions of the characters could be plotted on two dimensions: morality and power. These dimensions were also shown to account generally for perceptions of male and female characters. Livingstone concludes, "*Dallas* is thus perceived as presenting the contrast between a (mainly female) world of pleasure, weakness, and femininity and a (mainly male) world of organizational power and hard-headed business" (pp. 416–417).

---

presumes to know who "started it." Actually, one can usually say with certainty only that the two parties were in each other's presence throughout the argument and that their behaviors are related. Likewise, researchers and readers of research must be careful interpreting statistical relationships between variables. Remember that variables must be related meaningfully and that correlation does not equal causation.

part V

RECONCEPTUALIZING COMMUNICATION
RESEARCH

chapter **15**

*Epilogue:
Concluding Research*

This excerpt from a poem by T. S. Eliot expresses the process of research well:

> We shall not cease from our exploration
> And the end of all our exploring
> Will be to arrive where we started
> And know the place for the first time

Research studies are indeed cyclical: Each ends by returning to the issues introduced at the start, ideally with greater understanding.

Reports of research are usually structured in an "hourglass" shape. Researchers begin by addressing a broad issue, by posing a major question about the communication process. At the core of each study their perspective is narrowed; precise questions are answered or hypotheses are tested with a particular population in a specific context. At the end, their perspective widens again as they relate what they have done to other research literature and to social issues to which their findings might apply. This chapter deals with the expansive phase that completes the research process, the concluding "so what?" portion of a research project, the return to broader issues.

DISCUSSING RESEARCH FINDINGS

The "Results" section of a research article is a straightforward report about what researchers found. Authors are usually careful here to relate only what the data examined in that study revealed. In the final section of a research article, however, often headed "Discussion," researchers are free to place what they found in a larger context. They typically examine three things in this section: the meaning or significance of the findings, the limitations of the study, and suggestions for future research.

Interpreting the Meaning of the Findings

Researchers first examine the meaning or significance of the findings in the discussion section. To do so, researchers will relate findings to theory, previous research, and expectations, provide alternative explanations for findings, or explain how the findings may be applied.

Relating findings to theory. Many research studies are *theory-based.* That is, they are attempts to disprove a concise statement (a theory) that purports to explain a wide range of human behavior. (Yes, we said "disprove," not "prove." Theories are valid only if they hold up despite scholars' attempts to disprove them.) After the findings of a particular study have been determined, researchers must relate them to the theory being tested. If the findings are consistent with the theory, the validity of that theory is strengthened. If the findings are inconsistent, the theory must be modified or replaced with an alternative theoretical explanation for what occurred.

In most cases, the theory being tested is essentially supported. Researchers usually start out with good reasons to believe that a theory is valid, and their predictions, as expected, are borne out. Occasionally, however, the underlying theory is disconfirmed. Such an outcome places an explanatory burden on the researcher. Why would a reasonable prediction not be fulfilled; what other explanation applies? The unsupported theory must be reconceptualized.

For example, the Yerkes-Dodson theory predicts that learning is an inverse curvilinear (an inverted U-shaped) function of anxiety (or drive or motivation). That is, people at either extreme—those either very low or very high in anxiety—learn less well than people with moderate levels of anxiety. Booth-Butterfield (1988) found that the greater the communication apprehension of students he studied, the less they recalled what a teacher said—a *linear* relationship. At the end of his study, he explained the inconsistency between his findings and the Yerkes-Dodson theory by suggesting that the theory relates primarily to "state" anxiety, the assumption that anxiety is context-specific, that is, we are anxious in some situations but not others. Booth-Butterfield argued that he measured "trait" anxiety, the assumption that anxiety is personality-based; that is, some people are more anxious than others regardless of situation. So he reconceptualized the theory in relation to communication behavior by identifying a limitation in the range it explained. Revising a theory by redefining its range of application is a common way in which unexpected findings are explained.

Sometimes researchers are comparing two theories that appear to be contradictory or mutually exclusive. Their findings are used to lend support to one theory or the other. For example, some personality theories, such as Freud's, presume that all people are fundamentally alike. Others, such as Jung's, posit that people differ in fundamental ways and, moreover, that those ways can be condensed into four basic types. If the latter theory is true, people should perceive and communicate with people of their own type better than they do with people of different types. Motley and Smith (1989) found that after a job interview, employers are more likely to offer positions to candidates of their own type than they are to candidates of different types. They argue that this finding lends support to Jung's theory. Using findings to argue for the greater validity of one theory over another is another common way in which research results are tied to theory development.

Relating findings to previous research. Researchers also compare their findings to those from *other research*. Research is a cooperative enterprise; researchers attempt to interrelate and build on each others' work. If the findings from two or more studies are consistent, the strength of both studies is bolstered. That consistency suggests that the findings were meaningful and not due to idiosyncrasies in the research methods or the phenomena being studied.

Comparisons to findings from other studies may also help researchers to explain their own findings. For example, O'Hair, Cody, Goss, and Krayer (1988) asked people to judge the honesty of candidates they observed in videotaped job interviews. They found that the candidates' attentiveness affected observers' judgments—attentive people seemed honest; inattentive people seemed dishonest. Their results don't explain, however, *why* the observers made these inferences. The authors provide this explanation by relating their finding to other research studies reporting that deception takes more "cognitive processing" time. They refer to this finding to explain their results—presumably their subjects inferred that inattentive interviewees were conjuring up, or "cognitively processing," deceptive answers.

Researchers don't always obtain findings harmonious with what was learned in other studies. On occasion, their results are *inconsistent* with what others have found. The discrepancy must be explained: Was one finding inaccurate, or does a variable that was previously overlooked account for the difference?

Harper and Hirokawa (1988), for example, found that the female managers they studied tended to use different methods to influence female and male employees. This finding contradicts an earlier study reporting that female managers treat male and female employees alike. The authors attribute the discrepancy to differences in social conditions that prevailed when the two studies were conducted, five years apart. They maintain that during the intervening years, "increased numbers of women in management . . . reduce any tendency women managers may have had to avoid 'male' behaviors and to bring to the ranks of women in management the same range of diversity that exists among men in management" (p. 166).

Relating findings to expectations. When analyzing the data for a study, researchers occasionally obtain results that are *surprising* or that *contradict their own expectations*. In everyday life, people often let their prior beliefs influence how they draw inferences from data, even data that contradict their expectations. The following humorous story illustrates the point.

> A baseball manager wanted to convince some hard-drinking team members of the dangers of alcohol. He called them into his office and placed on a table two glasses filled with a clear liquid and a plate of live worms. The manager dropped a worm into one glass, containing water. It wriggled about happily. Next, he plunged the same worm into the other glass, filled with vodka. It stiffened and died.
>
> A murmur ran through the room, and some of the players were obviously impressed. One particularly heavy drinker just smiled. The manager prodded, "What does that mean to you, Smith?"
>
> Smith replied, "It proves that if you drink vodka, you'll never have worms."

When findings contradict expectations, conscientious researchers develop an explanation or a rationale that takes these unanticipated findings into account. For example, Booth-Butterfield and Jordan (1988) studied how people of different races change their behavior when communicating with people of their own race and with people of other racial groups. They found that blacks smile more than whites when in racially similar groups but less than whites in mixed-race groups. The researchers did not anticipate this finding, so they were obliged to explain it. To do so, they point out first that people are usually less comfortable in mixed-race groups. Therefore, they suggest that whites use smiling to cover uncertainty and anxiety, while blacks use nonsmiling for that purpose. This generalization, of course, is mere conjecture, so the authors add, "This finding deserves further attention from researchers" (p. 266). This example illustrates how researchers use unexpected findings to generate hypotheses for future investigation.

Providing alternative explanations. Even if the findings of a study are as expected and consistent with other research, more than one conclusion may be drawn from them. Researchers can legitimately interpret the same research findings differently. Researchers must therefore consider *alternative explanations* for their results.

For example, Alberts (1988) studied how couples voice complaints and found that compared to unhappy couples, happy couples phrase their complaints more in behavioral terms, express more positive feelings when discussing complaints, and respond to spouses' complaints more often by agreeing. She concludes, "The implications of this study seem clear: Couples' feelings about their relationship are connected to their complaint behavior." But she wisely adds, "What is not clear is whether the differences in complaint behavior preceded or followed the couples' feelings about their partners" (p. 193). That is, did their level of satisfaction influence how they talked about problems, or vice versa—which came first? Again, further research will be needed to determine which of these alternative explanations applies.

Applying findings.   Researchers attempt to abstract knowledge from their particular study that may be applied to other people and situations. Another responsibility they have, therefore, is commenting on *how broadly to apply their findings;* that is, the extent to which the findings fit people other than the research participants.

In the study just mentioned, Alberts (1988) concludes by acknowledging that her findings may apply only to the "normal" or just moderately troubled couples she studied. She recommends that further research be done with couples experiencing more severe relational problems before applying her findings to describing or treating couples of that type.

In their conclusions, researchers address most suggestions to other researchers "for further study." Despite the limitations in most research studies, however, the work of the world must go on. So many researchers also propose implications that their results may have for how practitioners can operate more effectively—they suggest *practical uses* for their findings. For example, Pfau and Burgoon (1988) studied "inoculation" in political campaign communication—how messages from candidates can minimize the effect of later attacks on their qualifications by their political foes. The researchers found that the inoculation messages they tested had a slight effect on their subjects' later responses. They conclude their study by suggesting, "In close political contests, the variance accounted for in this investigation could prove sufficient to put one candidate over the top" (p. 108). So they recommend that campaign planners use inoculation messages to influence voters—a practical-use suggestion.

Identifying the Limitations of Research

Besides commenting on the content of their findings, researchers discuss the *limitations or flaws* in their studies. Ethical researchers make a point of explaining all aspects of the study that limit generalization of the findings. Research findings have limited utility when studies are compromised by too many threats to internal and external validity.

Limitations due to internal validity threats.   Remember that criteria of internal validity must be met for a study to obtain accurate conclusions. When research is plagued by the internal validity threats discussed in Chapter 6, little confidence in the conclusions is warranted.

Researchers assess the internal validity of their findings by reporting any limitations or flaws in the study's design or execution. They will point out, for example, how *unobserved variables* may have confounded the results. Street and Buller (1988) examined the impact of various patients' characteristics (age, sex, education, anxiety, and relational history with physicians) on patterns of nonverbal communication exhibited in physician-patient interactions at a family practice clinic. Although patients' age and anxiety level affected the type of nonverbal behavior physicians used, the researchers point out in the discussion section that they did not account for physicians' characteristics (such as cultural background, patient load, sex, and age), which may also have a significant impact on the structure of medical interactions.

Researchers also point out shortcomings in the *measurement techniques* used to gather data for their study and how these might limit the findings. For example, Poole and Roth (1989) tested a model of the factors that influence groups to follow various paths as they make decisions. They employed three judges to rate group discussions on such task-related variables as openness, goal clarity, expertise, and novelty. At first there was relatively low interobserver reliability. So they allowed the observers to discuss disagreements on codings to increase the reliability of the ratings. The researchers point out in the discussion section, however, that this low reliability renders questionable the reported relationships between the independent and dependent variables studied.

Measurement techniques sometimes need to be *modified* to compensate for shortcomings, and in the discussion these modifications are also pointed out by researchers. For example, Darling (1989) did ethnographic research in several classrooms using an already established category system to record how students signal to their teachers that they don't understand something being explained. She found that only 88 percent of the relevant comments could be classified into one of the system's categories. So she created an additional category that covered the other 12 percent of the comments. Thus part of her findings included assessing and improving a measuring instrument.

Yet another element discussed in the conclusion of a research study are any *time-bound limitations* to the findings. For example, Ayers (1988) studied the degree to which positive visualizations (mentally picturing success) reduce communication apprehension. After reporting the improvement his treatment achieved, Ayers acknowledged that his investigation was limited to a relatively short-term effect (about six weeks). He appropriately states, "Consequently, we have very little information on whether the reductions . . . are maintained over the long term" (p. 4).

Limitations due to external validity threats. Remember that external validity asks whether the findings from a particular research study can be generalized to other people and situations. Researchers sometimes discuss the generalizability of their research based on the people or texts sampled, the ecological validity of the study, and the need to replicate the research findings before they are accepted fully.

Much published communication research is weak in external validity because researchers pay more attention to meeting standards of internal validity. Research methodology experts, such as Campbell and Stanley (1963) and Cook and Campbell (1979), argue that internal validity is more important than external validity. This makes sense; after all, if results are not internally valid, generalizing them to other people is a moot point.

Many internally valid conclusions in communication studies, however, are not necessarily generalizable. The primary reason is use of *nonrandom samples* drawn from the college population. Convenience sampling of college students, in particular, is used frequently in communication research. McNemar (1960) argued that social science research was becoming "a science of the behavior of sophomores." Rosenthal and Rosnow (1969) contend that what we really have is "a science of just those sophomores who volunteer to participate in research and who also keep their appointment with the investigator" (p. 110).

Little has changed over the years concerning the use of college students as research subjects. Rossiter (1976) and Applebaum and Phillips (1977) found, respectively, that 75 and 77 percent of the subjects used in communication research were college students. By 1985, Applebaum found that 65.5 percent of published communication research still used samples drawn from the college population. Similarly, Frey (1988) found in a review of small group communication research published during the 1980s that 72 percent of studies relied solely on student groups.

Significant differences exist, however, between college and noncollege populations on such variables as intelligence, age, and social-class background (Applebaum & Phillips, 1977). College students majoring in different disciplines also vary in their patterns of attitudes, values, and interests (Jung, 1969). Generalizing findings from student samples or from majors in any one department or area of study to the general population is therefore questionable.

At the very least, researchers should draw random samples from the college population. More important, the generalizability of research findings would be increased if researchers sampled from noncollege populations. Smart (1966) recommends, for example, that researchers establish large groups of volunteers from surrounding areas, local industries, and churches who could serve as research subjects.

A second way to increase the generalizability of communication research findings is by conducting more *replications.* Replication is at the heart of disciplinary research because it means that the core research findings of the field have been verified independently. This increases the confidence that experts in that field have when applying the knowledge of that discipline to people and situations.

Exact replications in the human sciences are rare, however (Denzin, 1970; Sterling, 1959). One reason may be that researchers don't always provide clear and detailed information regarding their procedures. Applebaum's (1985) survey of the communication literature found that the majority of articles provided no information regarding subject selection procedures. Reinard (1988) reviewed the literature regarding the persuasive effects of evidence. One of his conclusions was that "the failure of many researchers to describe the types of evidence they have used (testimonial assertion, factual evidence, statistics, abstracts and summaries, and the like) had made interpretation of findings difficult at best" (p. 47). How can a study be reproduced or accepted as internally valid if we don't know all the details of how it was done?

Lack of replication may also be due to the way in which articles are selected for publication. Kelly, Chase, and Tucker (1979) found that the leading reason given for rejecting manuscripts for publication in communication journals was that they were "mere replications" (p. 341). Interestingly, these authors also found that as many as 28 percent of the studies in their sample of journals actually were replications. Only 3 percent, however, were openly called replications by their authors, probably due to editors' tendency to reject replication studies submitted for publication.

Suggesting Future Research Directions

The final element discussed in concluding a study is an agenda for future research. Most studies end with what's known familiarly as MRNTBD, "more research needs to be done." Researchers point out new questions worth asking and new *procedures* worth trying.

Many researchers propose follow-up research questions. For example, Reeves, Lang, Thorson, and Rothschild (1989) studied how positive and negative television scenes influenced hemispheric differences in cortical arousal. In line with their predictions, they found greater cortical arousal for negative than positive scenes. They go on to suggest in the discussion section that future researchers should investigate three features of television scenes: luminance, movement, and picture complexity. They suspect that negative scenes cause more emotional responses than positive scenes because they are darker, show less movement, and use more simple visual patterns, and they encourage researchers to test this hypothesis.

Researchers also suggest *methodological* considerations for future research. For example, Stafford, Waldron, and Infield (1989) studied differences between participants and observers on the quantity and quality of information recalled from conversations. They found that observers when recalling conversations produce more errors and elaborations than participants. In their discussion section they point out that the common practice of using observers in studies of conversation may be questionable.

One frequent call for future research is to *transfer findings* from laboratory experiments to the "real world." For example, Bavelas, Black, Chovil, Lemery, and Mullett (1988) conducted a laboratory experiment to study motor mimicry behavior during dyadic conversations by having a confederate manipulate her leaning behavior and observing whether subjects mimicked the behavior. The results from three separate experiments showed that motor mimicry functions primarily as a nonverbal message that indicates that the observer is aware of and concerned about the situation rather than as a way of taking the role of the other or of "feeling oneself into" the other person. The researchers caution, however, that "we cannot know about the communicative function of a nonverbal behavior unless we study it in a communicative setting rather than in experimentally isolated individuals" (p. 297).

This discussion of future research truly completes the research cycle. The mission of research is fulfilled in two essential steps: (1) making a contribution to the reservoir of knowledge communication professionals can call on to explain and influence communication events and (2) raising meaningful new questions for future communication researchers to pursue. This final phase of research thus serves a *heuristic function* of encouraging future investigation.

CONCLUSION

Researchers are like pioneers venturing into unexplored territory. When they begin their investigations, what is to be investigated is unknown yet intriguing. Setting off down "the road less traveled by" involves entering an area of life where clear paths have yet to be charted. To do research requires a restless spirit and a willingness to devote oneself to a long-term, demanding journey.

Biologist Albert Szent-Gyorgyi (1971) wrote:

> Research means going out into the unknown with the hope of finding something new to bring home. If you know in advance what you are going to do, or even to find there, then it is not research at all. (p. 1)

Doing research is a challenging endeavor—to succeed seems at times to require taking it on as a way of life. Indeed, we might say the process of research takes a practitioner through a full life cycle.

Researchers when they begin must call on the curiosity, creativity, and love of adventure they had as children, for when they operate on the cutting edge of knowledge, they are in the same frightening yet exhilirating position children are in when first exposed to new experiences. They must comprehend for themselves something unfamiliar, something no one else can explain to them.

At first they may explore simply in an impromptu fashion, as children do, playfully feeling their way around in the new domain. Once they believe they sense intuitively the lay of the land and know with some precision what they want to map, they must bring out their scientific instruments and measure the territory. We have tried to provide some of those instruments, in the form of ideas, skills, and tools, in this book.

The number of instruments needed may appear overwhelming. Because there are so many approaches to doing research, few people are equally adept at them all. In fact, one of the hardest aspects of being a researcher—an aspect we can't teach *to* you—is making choices: What topic will I study? What questions will I investigate? In what context will I work? What method will I use? How will I gather data? How can I infer conclusions from my data? and so on through innumerable questions. Research involves a long series of decisions.

So researchers must quickly lose their innocence and assume the very adult position of making difficult personal and professional choices. And they must carry out their work thoroughly and responsibly if what they do is to be worthwhile.

Moreover, when they have something to report about the object of their study, they age once again. They become elders or teachers to their peers and the general public. Their task becomes providing a full description of their explorations and what they have found so that others may share their discoveries.

Yet sociologist Thorstein Veblen (1919) suggests that the outcome of research can only be to generate more research questions. No sooner do researchers shed some light on what they have studied than the next areas of darkness—which they might never have known existed had they not done their research—call out for exploration. And the life cycle is resumed.

Research is a spiral, looping endlessly, evading full resolution. Yet knowledge grows continually. More and more of human life is understood; problems can be addressed more skillfully; people can treat each other more compassionately—*nam et ipsa scientia potestas est:* For knowledge itself is power.

The researchers of one generation pass on what they learned to the next so that they may live with greater understanding and may fulfill their intentions in life. What you have learned in your communication courses, and in most of your formal education, is knowledge contributed by the efforts of researchers.

Recall a moment when you felt increased insight or personal power from an idea encountered when reading or listening in class. After reading this book, you have a much better idea of the activities from which that idea was derived—and consequently a greater appreciation of the industry and intelligence of the people who did the research.

You also have a better ability to eliminate the middlemen—the teachers and textbook authors who have paraphrased researchers' writings for you. Now you can read, understand, and enjoy researchers' reports in their original form, "hot off the presses" in the journals in which they are published. Finally, you can make an informed choice regarding whether to incorporate the practice of research into your own life. If you wish, you can experience the excitement of exploration firsthand. You can discover, and pass along to the generation of students that will follow yours, new information about what now is unknown about communication, thereby enriching their lives as countless researchers have enriched yours. We hope you will.

appendix A

Table of Random Numbers

	00-04	05-09	10-14	15-19	20-24	25-29	30-34	35-39	40-44	45-49
00	22808	04391	45529	53968	57136	98228	85485	13801	68194	56382
01	49305	36965	44849	64987	59501	35141	50159	57369	76913	75739
02	81934	19920	73316	69243	69605	17022	53264	83417	55193	92929
03	10840	13508	48120	22467	54505	70536	91206	81038	22418	34800
04	99555	73289	59605	37105	24621	44100	72832	12268	97089	68112
05	32677	45709	62337	35132	45128	96761	08745	53388	98353	46724
06	09401	75407	27704	11569	52842	83543	44750	03177	50511	15301
07	73424	31711	65519	74869	56744	40864	75315	89866	96563	75142
08	37075	81378	59472	71858	86903	66860	03757	32723	54273	45477
09	02060	37158	55244	44812	45369	78939	08048	28036	40946	03898
10	94719	43565	40028	79866	43137	28063	52513	66405	71511	66135
11	70234	48272	59621	88778	16536	36505	41724	24776	63971	01685
12	07972	71752	92745	86465	01845	27416	50519	48458	68460	63113
13	58521	64882	26993	48104	61307	73933	17214	44827	88306	78177
14	32580	45202	21148	09684	39411	04892	02055	75276	51831	85686
15	88796	30829	35009	22695	23694	11220	71006	26720	39476	60538
16	31525	82746	78935	82980	61236	28940	96341	13790	66247	33839
17	02747	35989	70387	89571	34570	17002	79223	96817	31681	15207
18	46651	28987	20625	61347	63981	41085	67412	29053	00724	14841
19	43598	14436	33521	55637	39789	26560	66404	71802	18763	80560
20	30596	92319	11474	64546	60030	73795	60809	24016	29166	36059
21	56198	64370	85771	62633	78240	05766	32419	35769	14057	80674
22	68266	67544	06464	84956	18431	04015	89049	15098	12018	89338
23	31107	28597	65102	75599	17496	87590	68848	33021	69855	54015
24	37555	05069	38680	87274	55152	21792	77219	48732	03377	01160
25	90463	27249	43845	94391	12145	36882	48906	52336	00780	74407
26	99189	88731	93531	52638	54989	04237	32978	59902	05463	09245
27	37631	74016	89072	59598	55356	27346	80856	80875	52850	36548
28	73829	21651	50141	76142	72303	06694	61697	76662	23745	96282
29	15634	89428	47090	12094	42134	62381	87236	90118	53463	46969
30	00571	45172	78532	63863	98597	15742	41967	11821	91389	07476
31	83374	10184	56384	27050	77700	13875	96607	76479	80535	17454
32	78666	85645	13181	08700	08289	62956	64439	39150	95690	18555
33	47890	88197	21368	65254	35917	54035	83028	84636	38186	50581
34	56238	13559	79344	83198	94642	35165	40188	21456	67024	62771
35	36369	32234	38129	59963	99237	72648	66504	99065	61161	16186
36	42934	34578	28968	74028	42164	56647	76806	61023	33099	48293
37	09010	15226	43474	30174	26727	39317	48508	55438	85336	40762
38	83897	90073	72941	85613	85569	24183	08247	15946	02957	68504
39	82206	01230	93252	89045	25141	91943	75531	87420	99012	80751
40	14175	32992	49046	41272	94040	44929	98531	27712	05106	35242
41	58968	88367	70927	74765	18635	85122	27722	95388	61523	91745
42	62601	04595	76926	11007	67631	64641	07994	04639	39314	83126
43	97030	71165	47032	85021	65554	66774	21560	04121	57297	85415
44	89074	31587	21360	41673	71192	85795	82757	52928	62586	02179
45	07806	81312	81215	99858	26762	28993	74951	64680	50934	32011
46	91540	86466	13229	76624	44092	96604	08590	89705	03424	48033
47	99279	27334	33804	77988	93592	90708	56780	70097	39907	51006
48	63224	05074	83941	25034	43516	22840	35230	66048	80754	46302
49	98361	97513	27529	66419	35328	19738	82366	38573	50967	72754

Source: Jerrold H. Zar, *Biostatistical Analysis* (2nd ed.), p. 653, copyright © 1984 by Prentice Hall. Reprinted by permission of Prentice Hall.

appendix B

Table of Critical Values
for the Chi-Square Statistic

Directions: Find the degrees of freedom (df $= [r - 1] [c - 1]$). Read across to the appropriate row (.05) to find the critical value. If the calculated value meets or exceeds the critical value, the null hypothesis is rejected and the research hypothesis is accepted.

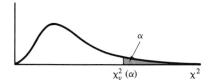

d.f. ν	α								
	.990	.950	.900	.500	.100	.050	.025	.010	.005
1	.0002	.004	.02	.45	2.71	3.84	5.02	6.63	7.88
2	.02	.10	.21	1.39	4.61	5.99	7.38	9.21	10.60
3	.11	.35	.58	2.37	6.25	7.81	9.35	11.34	12.84
4	.30	.71	1.06	3.36	7.78	9.49	11.14	13.28	14.86
5	.55	1.15	1.61	4.35	9.24	11.07	12.83	15.09	16.75
6	.87	1.64	2.20	5.35	10.64	12.59	14.45	16.81	18.55
7	1.24	2.17	2.83	6.35	12.02	14.07	16.01	18.48	20.28
8	1.65	2.73	3.49	7.34	13.36	15.51	17.53	20.09	21.95
9	2.09	3.33	4.17	8.34	14.68	16.92	19.02	21.67	23.59
10	2.56	3.94	4.87	9.34	15.99	18.31	20.48	23.21	25.19
11	3.05	4.57	5.58	10.34	17.28	19.68	21.92	24.72	26.76
12	3.57	5.23	6.30	11.34	18.55	21.03	23.34	26.22	28.30
13	4.11	5.89	7.04	12.34	19.81	22.36	24.74	27.69	29.82
14	4.66	6.57	7.79	13.34	21.06	23.68	26.12	29.14	31.32
15	5.23	7.26	8.55	14.34	22.31	25.00	27.49	30.58	32.80
16	5.81	7.96	9.31	15.34	23.54	26.30	28.85	32.00	34.27
17	6.41	8.67	10.09	16.34	24.77	27.59	30.19	33.41	35.72
18	7.01	9.39	10.86	17.34	25.99	28.87	31.53	34.81	37.16
19	7.63	10.12	11.65	18.34	27.20	30.14	32.85	36.19	38.58
20	8.26	10.85	12.44	19.34	28.41	31.41	34.17	37.57	40.00
21	8.90	11.59	13.24	20.34	29.62	32.67	35.48	38.93	41.40
22	9.54	12.34	14.04	21.34	30.81	33.92	36.78	40.29	42.80
23	10.20	13.09	14.85	22.34	32.01	35.17	38.08	41.64	44.18
24	10.86	13.85	15.66	23.34	33.20	36.42	39.36	42.98	45.56
25	11.52	14.61	16.47	24.34	34.38	37.65	40.65	44.31	46.93
26	12.20	15.38	17.29	25.34	35.56	38.89	41.92	45.64	48.29
27	12.88	16.15	18.11	26.34	36.74	40.11	43.19	46.96	49.64
28	13.56	16.93	18.94	27.34	37.92	41.34	44.46	48.28	50.99
29	14.26	17.71	19.77	28.34	39.09	42.56	45.72	49.59	52.34
30	14.95	18.49	20.60	29.34	40.26	43.77	46.98	50.89	53.67
40	22.16	26.51	29.05	39.34	51.81	55.76	59.34	63.69	66.77
50	29.71	34.76	37.69	49.33	63.17	67.50	71.42	76.15	79.49
60	37.48	43.19	46.46	59.33	74.40	79.08	83.30	88.38	91.95
70	45.44	51.74	55.33	69.33	85.53	90.53	95.02	100.43	104.21
80	53.54	60.39	64.28	79.33	96.58	101.88	106.63	112.33	116.32
90	61.75	69.13	73.29	89.33	107.57	113.15	118.14	124.12	128.30
100	70.06	77.93	82.36	99.33	118.50	124.34	129.56	135.81	140.17

Source: Richard A. Johnson and Dean W. Wichern, *Applied Multivariate Statistical Analysis* (2nd ed.), p. 583, copyright © 1988 by Prentice Hall. Reprinted by permission of Prentice Hall.

appendix C

Table of Critical Values for the t Statistic

Directions: Find the degrees of freedom (df $= n - 2$). Read across to the appropriate row (.05 for a one-tailed hypothesis, .025 for a two-tailed hypothesis) to find the critical value. If the calculated value meets or exceeds the critical value, the null hypothesis is rejected and the research hypothesis is accepted.

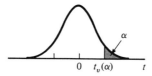

d.f. ν	α							
	.250	.100	.050	.025	.010	.00833	.00625	.005
1	1.000	3.078	6.314	12.706	31.821	38.190	50.923	63.657
2	.816	1.886	2.920	4.303	6.965	7.649	8.860	9.925
3	.765	1.638	2.353	3.182	4.541	4.857	5.392	5.841
4	.741	1.533	2.132	2.776	3.747	3.961	4.315	4.604
5	.727	1.476	2.015	2.571	3.365	3.534	3.810	4.032
6	.718	1.440	1.943	2.447	3.143	3.287	3.521	3.707
7	.711	1.415	1.895	2.365	2.998	3.128	3.335	3.499
8	.706	1.397	1.860	2.306	2.896	3.016	3.206	3.355
9	.703	1.383	1.833	2.262	2.821	2.933	3.111	3.250
10	.700	1.372	1.812	2.228	2.764	2.870	3.038	3.169
11	.697	1.363	1.796	2.201	2.718	2.820	2.981	3.106
12	.695	1.356	1.782	2.179	2.681	2.779	2.934	3.055
13	.694	1.350	1.771	2.160	2.650	2.746	2.896	3.012
14	.692	1.345	1.761	2.145	2.624	2.718	2.864	2.977
15	.691	1.341	1.753	2.131	2.602	2.694	2.837	2.947
16	.690	1.337	1.746	2.120	2.583	2.673	2.813	2.921
17	.689	1.333	1.740	2.110	2.567	2.655	2.793	2.898
18	.688	1.330	1.734	2.101	2.552	2.639	2.775	2.878
19	.688	1.328	1.729	2.093	2.539	2.625	2.759	2.861
20	.687	1.325	1.725	2.086	2.528	2.613	2.744	2.845
21	.686	1.323	1.721	2.080	2.518	2.601	2.732	2.831
22	.686	1.321	1.717	2.074	2.508	2.591	2.720	2.819
23	.685	1.319	1.714	2.069	2.500	2.582	2.710	2.807
24	.685	1.318	1.711	2.064	2.492	2.574	2.700	2.797
25	.684	1.316	1.708	2.060	2.485	2.566	2.692	2.787
26	.684	1.315	1.706	2.056	2.479	2.559	2.684	2.779
27	.684	1.314	1.703	2.052	2.473	2.552	2.676	2.771
28	.683	1.313	1.701	2.048	2.467	2.546	2.669	2.763
29	.683	1.311	1.699	2.045	2.462	2.541	2.663	2.756
30	.683	1.310	1.697	2.042	2.457	2.536	2.657	2.750
40	.681	1.303	1.684	2.021	2.423	2.499	2.616	2.704
60	.679	1.296	1.671	2.000	2.390	2.463	2.575	2.660
120	.677	1.289	1.658	1.980	2.358	2.428	2.536	2.617
∞	.674	1.282	1.645	1.960	2.326	2.394	2.498	2.576

Source: Richard A. Johnson and Dean W. Wichern, *Applied Multivariate Statistical Analysis* (2nd ed.), p. 582, copyright © 1988 by Prentice Hall. Reprinted by permission of Prentice Hall.

appendix D

Table of Critical Values (p = .05) for the F Statistic

Directions: Use the degrees of freedom for the denominator mean square (within groups) (v_2) and for the numerator mean square (between groups) (v_1) to find the critical value at the .05 level of probability. If the calculated value meets or exceeds the critical value, the null hypothesis is rejected and the research hypothesis is accepted.

$F_{v_1, v_2}(.05)$

v_2 \ v_1	1	2	3	4	5	6	7	8	9	10	12	15	20	25	30	40	60
1	161.5	199.5	215.7	224.6	230.2	234.0	236.8	238.9	240.5	241.9	243.9	246.0	248.0	249.3	250.1	251.1	252.2
2	18.51	19.00	19.16	19.25	19.30	19.33	19.35	19.37	19.38	19.40	19.41	19.43	19.45	19.46	19.46	19.47	19.48
3	10.13	9.55	9.28	9.12	9.01	8.94	8.89	8.85	8.81	8.79	8.74	8.70	8.66	8.63	8.62	8.59	8.57
4	7.71	6.94	6.59	6.39	6.26	6.16	6.09	6.04	6.00	5.96	5.91	5.86	5.80	5.77	5.75	5.72	5.69
5	6.61	5.79	5.41	5.19	5.05	4.95	4.88	4.82	4.77	4.74	4.68	4.62	4.56	4.52	4.50	4.46	4.43
6	5.99	5.14	4.76	4.53	4.39	4.28	4.21	4.15	4.10	4.06	4.00	3.94	3.87	3.83	3.81	3.77	3.74
7	5.59	4.74	4.35	4.12	3.97	3.87	3.79	3.73	3.68	3.64	3.57	3.51	3.44	3.40	3.38	3.34	3.30
8	5.32	4.46	4.07	3.84	3.69	3.58	3.50	3.44	3.39	3.35	3.28	3.22	3.15	3.11	3.08	3.04	3.01
9	5.12	4.26	3.86	3.63	3.48	3.37	3.29	3.23	3.18	3.14	3.07	3.01	2.94	2.89	2.86	2.83	2.79
10	4.96	4.10	3.71	3.48	3.33	3.22	3.14	3.07	3.02	2.98	2.91	2.85	2.77	2.73	2.70	2.66	2.62
11	4.84	3.98	3.59	3.36	3.20	3.09	3.01	2.95	2.90	2.85	2.79	2.72	2.65	2.60	2.57	2.53	2.49
12	4.75	3.89	3.49	3.26	3.11	3.00	2.91	2.85	2.80	2.75	2.69	2.62	2.54	2.50	2.47	2.43	2.38
13	4.67	3.81	3.41	3.18	3.03	2.92	2.83	2.77	2.71	2.67	2.60	2.53	2.46	2.41	2.38	2.34	2.30
14	4.60	3.74	3.34	3.11	2.96	2.85	2.76	2.70	2.65	2.60	2.53	2.46	2.39	2.34	2.31	2.27	2.22

(continued)

ν_1 / ν_2	1	2	3	4	5	6	7	8	9	10	12	15	20	25	30	40	60
15	4.54	3.68	3.29	3.06	2.90	2.79	2.71	2.64	2.59	2.54	2.48	2.40	2.33	2.28	2.25	2.20	2.16
16	4.49	3.63	3.24	3.01	2.85	2.74	2.66	2.59	2.54	2.49	2.42	2.35	2.28	2.23	2.19	2.15	2.11
17	4.45	3.59	3.20	2.96	2.81	2.70	2.61	2.55	2.49	2.45	2.38	2.31	2.23	2.18	2.15	2.10	2.06
18	4.41	3.55	3.16	2.93	2.77	2.66	2.58	2.51	2.46	2.41	2.34	2.27	2.19	2.14	2.11	2.06	2.02
19	4.38	3.52	3.13	2.90	2.74	2.63	2.54	2.48	2.42	2.38	2.31	2.23	2.16	2.11	2.07	2.03	1.98
20	4.35	3.49	3.10	2.87	2.71	2.60	2.51	2.45	2.39	2.35	2.28	2.20	2.12	2.07	2.04	1.99	1.95
21	4.32	3.47	3.07	2.84	2.68	2.57	2.49	2.42	2.37	2.32	2.25	2.18	2.10	2.05	2.01	1.96	1.92
22	4.30	3.44	3.05	2.82	2.66	2.55	2.46	2.40	2.34	2.30	2.23	2.15	2.07	2.02	1.98	1.94	1.89
23	4.28	3.42	3.03	2.80	2.64	2.53	2.44	2.37	2.32	2.27	2.20	2.13	2.05	2.00	1.96	1.91	1.86
24	4.26	3.40	3.01	2.78	2.62	2.51	2.42	2.36	2.30	2.25	2.18	2.11	2.03	1.97	1.94	1.89	1.84
25	4.24	3.39	2.99	2.76	2.60	2.49	2.40	2.34	2.28	2.24	2.16	2.09	2.01	1.96	1.92	1.87	1.82
26	4.23	3.37	2.98	2.74	2.59	2.47	2.39	2.32	2.27	2.22	2.15	2.07	1.99	1.94	1.90	1.85	1.80
27	4.21	3.35	2.96	2.73	2.57	2.46	2.37	2.31	2.25	2.20	2.13	2.06	1.97	1.92	1.88	1.84	1.79
28	4.20	3.34	2.95	2.71	2.56	2.45	2.36	2.29	2.24	2.19	2.12	2.04	1.96	1.91	1.87	1.82	1.77
29	4.18	3.33	2.93	2.70	2.55	2.43	2.35	2.28	2.22	2.18	2.10	2.03	1.94	1.89	1.85	1.81	1.75
30	4.17	3.32	2.92	2.69	2.53	2.42	2.33	2.27	2.21	2.16	2.09	2.01	1.93	1.88	1.84	1.79	1.74
40	4.08	3.23	2.84	2.61	2.45	2.34	2.25	2.18	2.12	2.08	2.00	1.92	1.84	1.78	1.74	1.69	1.64
60	4.00	3.15	2.76	2.53	2.37	2.25	2.17	2.10	2.04	1.99	1.92	1.84	1.75	1.69	1.65	1.59	1.53
120	3.92	3.07	2.68	2.45	2.29	2.18	2.09	2.02	1.96	1.91	1.83	1.75	1.66	1.60	1.55	1.50	1.43
∞	3.84	3.00	2.61	2.37	2.21	2.10	2.01	1.94	1.88	1.83	1.75	1.67	1.57	1.51	1.46	1.39	1.32

Source: Richard A. Johnson and Dean W. Wichern, *Applied Multivariate Statistical Analysis* (2nd ed.), pp. 586–587, copyright © 1988 by Prentice Hall. Reprinted by permission of Prentice Hall.

Table of Critical Values (p = .01) for the F Statistic

Directions: Use the degrees of freedom for the denominator mean square (within groups) (v_2) and for the numerator mean square (between groups) (v_1) to find the critical value at the .01 level of probability. If the calculated value meets or exceeds the critical value, the null hypothesis is rejected at the .01 significance level and the research hypothesis is accepted.

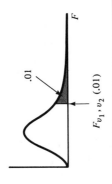

$$F_{v_1, v_2}(.01)$$

v_2 \ v_1	1	2	3	4	5	6	7	8	9	10	12	15	20	25	30	40	60
1	4052.	5000.	5403.	5625.	5764.	5859.	5928.	5981.	6023.	6056.	6106.	6157.	6209.	6240.	6261.	6287.	6313.
2	98.50	99.00	99.17	99.25	99.30	99.33	99.36	99.37	99.39	99.40	99.42	99.43	99.45	99.46	99.47	99.47	99.48
3	34.12	30.82	29.46	28.71	28.24	27.91	27.67	27.49	27.35	27.23	27.05	26.87	26.69	26.58	26.50	26.41	26.32
4	21.20	18.00	16.69	15.98	15.52	15.21	14.98	14.80	14.66	14.55	14.37	14.20	14.02	13.91	13.84	13.75	13.65
5	16.26	13.27	12.06	11.39	10.97	10.67	10.46	10.29	10.16	10.05	9.89	9.72	9.55	9.45	9.38	9.29	9.20
6	13.75	10.92	9.78	9.15	8.75	8.47	8.26	8.10	7.98	7.87	7.72	7.56	7.40	7.30	7.23	7.14	7.06
7	12.25	9.55	8.45	7.85	7.46	7.19	6.99	6.84	6.72	6.62	6.47	6.31	6.16	6.06	5.99	5.91	5.82
8	11.26	8.65	7.59	7.01	6.63	6.37	6.18	6.03	5.91	5.81	5.67	5.52	5.36	5.26	5.20	5.12	5.03
9	10.56	8.02	6.99	6.42	6.06	5.80	5.61	5.47	5.35	5.26	5.11	4.96	4.81	4.71	4.65	4.57	4.48
10	10.04	7.56	6.55	5.99	5.64	5.39	5.20	5.06	4.94	4.85	4.71	4.56	4.41	4.31	4.25	4.17	4.08
11	9.65	7.21	6.22	5.67	5.32	5.07	4.89	4.74	4.63	4.54	4.40	4.25	4.10	4.01	3.94	3.86	3.78

ν_1 / ν_2	1	2	3	4	5	6	7	8	9	10	12	15	20	25	30	40	60
12	9.33	6.93	5.95	5.41	5.06	4.82	4.64	4.50	4.39	4.30	4.16	4.01	3.86	3.76	3.70	3.62	3.54
13	9.07	6.70	5.74	5.21	4.86	4.62	4.44	4.30	4.19	4.10	3.96	3.82	3.66	3.57	3.51	3.43	3.34
14	8.86	6.51	5.56	5.04	4.69	4.46	4.28	4.14	4.03	3.94	3.80	3.66	3.51	3.41	3.35	3.27	3.18
15	8.68	6.36	5.42	4.89	4.56	4.32	4.14	4.00	3.89	3.80	3.67	3.52	3.37	3.28	3.21	3.13	3.05
16	8.53	6.23	5.29	4.77	4.44	4.20	4.03	3.89	3.78	3.69	3.55	3.41	3.26	3.16	3.10	3.02	2.93
17	8.40	6.11	5.19	4.67	4.34	4.10	3.93	3.79	3.68	3.59	3.46	3.31	3.16	3.07	3.00	2.92	2.83
18	8.29	6.01	5.09	4.58	4.25	4.01	3.84	3.71	3.60	3.51	3.37	3.23	3.08	2.98	2.92	2.84	2.75
19	8.18	5.93	5.01	4.50	4.17	3.94	3.77	3.63	3.52	3.43	3.30	3.15	3.00	2.91	2.84	2.76	2.67
20	8.10	5.85	4.94	4.43	4.10	3.87	3.70	3.56	3.46	3.37	3.23	3.09	2.94	2.84	2.78	2.69	2.61
21	8.02	5.78	4.87	4.37	4.04	3.81	3.64	3.51	3.40	3.31	3.17	3.03	2.88	2.79	2.72	2.64	2.55
22	7.95	5.72	4.82	4.31	3.99	3.76	3.59	3.45	3.35	3.26	3.12	2.98	2.83	2.73	2.67	2.58	2.50
23	7.88	5.66	4.76	4.26	3.94	3.71	3.54	3.41	3.30	3.21	3.07	2.93	2.78	2.69	2.62	2.54	2.45
24	7.82	5.61	4.72	4.22	3.90	3.67	3.50	3.36	3.26	3.17	3.03	2.89	2.74	2.64	2.58	2.49	2.40
25	7.77	5.57	4.68	4.18	3.85	3.63	3.46	3.32	3.22	3.13	2.99	2.85	2.70	2.60	2.54	2.45	2.36
26	7.72	5.53	4.64	4.14	3.82	3.59	3.42	3.29	3.18	3.09	2.96	2.81	2.66	2.57	2.50	2.42	2.33
27	7.68	5.49	4.60	4.11	3.78	3.56	3.39	3.26	3.15	3.06	2.93	2.78	2.63	2.54	2.47	2.38	2.29
28	7.64	5.45	4.57	4.07	3.75	3.53	3.36	3.23	3.12	3.03	2.90	2.75	2.60	2.51	2.44	2.35	2.26
29	7.60	5.42	4.54	4.04	3.73	3.50	3.33	3.20	3.09	3.00	2.87	2.73	2.57	2.48	2.41	2.33	2.23
30	7.56	5.39	4.51	4.02	3.70	3.47	3.30	3.17	3.07	2.98	2.84	2.70	2.55	2.45	2.39	2.30	2.21
40	7.31	5.18	4.31	3.83	3.51	3.29	3.12	2.99	2.89	2.80	2.66	2.52	2.37	2.27	2.20	2.11	2.02
60	7.08	4.98	4.13	3.65	3.34	3.12	2.95	2.82	2.72	2.63	2.50	2.35	2.20	2.10	2.03	1.94	1.84
120	6.85	4.79	3.95	3.48	3.17	2.96	2.79	2.66	2.56	2.47	2.34	2.19	2.03	1.93	1.86	1.76	1.66
∞	6.63	4.61	3.78	3.32	3.02	2.80	2.64	2.51	2.41	2.32	2.18	2.04	1.88	1.78	1.70	1.59	1.47

Source: Richard A. Johnson and Dean W. Wichern, *Applied Multivariate Statistical Analysis* (2nd ed.), pp. 588–589, copyright © 1988 by Prentice Hall. Reprinted by permission of Prentice Hall.

Glossary

ABSTRACT A brief summary of important points in an article or conference paper that generally appears at the beginning of the manuscript.

ACADEMIC FREEDOM The right that scholars at universities have to teach and research topics that they consider important.

ACTIVE VARIABLE An independent variable that is manipulated by a researcher.

ADJACENCY PAIR The combination of an illocutionary act with a meaningful response that is analyzed in conversational analysis.

ADVANCED RELATIONSHIP ANALYSES Complex multivariate correlational statistical tests that assess relationships between two groups of variables. These tests include canonical correlation, cluster analysis, discriminant analysis, factor analysis, and multidimensional scaling analysis.

AGENDA SETTING The media's ability to structure people's thinking.

AGGREGATE DATA (GROUPED DATA) Results reported for groups rather than for individuals in order to maintain subject confidentiality.

ALTERNATE PROCEDURE METHOD Test of the reliability of a measurement instrument whereby the results of an administration of the instrument are compared to the results of another, equivalent, instrument.

ALTERNATIVE CAUSALITY ARGUMENT An explanation other than the research hypothesis that accounts for changes in the dependent variable.

ANALYSIS OF VARIANCE (ANOVA, *F* TEST)   A statistical procedure used when researchers examine differences between two or more groups on an interval/ratio dependent variable or two or more measurements for a single group.

> ***One-Way Analysis of Variance (One-Way ANOVA)***   A statistical procedure used to examine differences between two or more groups created from a single independent variable on a single dependent variable or to examine differences between two or more measurements for a single group.

> ***Factorial Analysis of Variance***   A statistical procedure that is used when researchers examine differences between two or more groups created from two or more independent variables on a single dependent variable.

ANDROCENTRICITY   Viewing the world from a male perspective.

ANONYMITY   The condition wherein researchers cannot connect responses to the individuals who provided them.

BAR GRAPH   A visual depiction of data that uses blocks (rectangles and squares) to show the frequency counts for a variable measured on a nominal or ordinal scale.

BEHAVIORISM   The use of careful and systematic observation and measurement of what people do to generate objective knowledge.

BETWEEN-GROUP VARIANCE   The differences between groups.

BIMODAL   Having two modes; having two categories tied for greatest frequency in a distribution.

BLIND REVIEW   Review of manuscripts submitted to scholarly journals or academic conferences by experts in the particular field, to whom the authors are not identified, to decide on publishability and to suggest possible improvements.

CARD CATALOG   A centralized file that lists all of a library's holdings.

> ***Electronic Card Files***   Card catalogs that are accessible to library users through a computer terminal.

CATALOGING SYSTEM   An organizational strategy used in libraries to determine where any given data record can be found, such as the Dewey Decimal System or the Library of Congress system.

CAUSAL RELATIONSHIP   The relationship whereby one variable produces changes in another variable.

CENSUS   Data collection from all members of a population.

CHI-SQUARE   A statistical test for the significance of a difference that is used whenever an independent and a dependent variable is measured on a nominal scale.

CLASSICAL PERIOD OF COMMUNICATION INQUIRY   The earliest study of communication, traced back as far as the fifth century B.C., when philosophers like Plato and Aristotle studied the public speaking strategies of Greek orators, calling this area of inquiry *rhetoric*.

CLUSTER SAMPLE   A sample assembled by means of a procedure that selects units (clusters) of subjects randomly.

> ***Multistage Cluster Sample***   A cluster sample wherein successively smaller random samples of clusters are selected from a very large population.

CODER A trained observer who observes and classifies units and/or the categories to which they belong in textual analysis and observational research.

CODING The process of assigning meaning, whether numerical (quantitative) or verbal (qualitative), to survey answers or observations.

CODING SCHEMES A classification system that describes the nature or quantifies the frequency of particular communication behaviors, either before or after research observations have taken place.

COEFFICIENT OF DETERMINATION A numerical indicator that tells how much of the variance of one variable can be explained by knowledge of another variable.

COEFFICIENT OF MULTIPLE DETERMINATION A statistic that expresses the amount of variance in a criterion variable that can be explained by other variables acting together.

COGNITIVE CONSERVATISM The tendency to hold on to conclusions even when presented with contradictory evidence.

COMMUNICATION The management of messages for the purpose of creating meaning.

Communication and Aging The effect of age on communication. Researchers in this area are interested in the communication abilities of the elderly and whether their communication needs are being met.

Communication and Children The effect of communication on the young. Researchers in this area are interested in how children acquire language; how they develop communication competence; how they communicate with their parents, teachers, and friends; and how the media influence children.

Communication Campaigns Communication used by change agents to influence audience behavior. Researchers in this area are interested in political, informational, and preventive (health) communication campaigns.

Communication Education The role of communication in the educational system. Researchers in this area are interested in teacher-student communication patterns and the use of communication strategies to influence learning.

Family Communication Communication within the family. Researchers in this area are interested in how communication is used in spousal, parenting, and sibling subsystems to affect such outcomes as role relationships and satisfaction.

Group Communication Communication among three or more people who are interacting to achieve commonly recognized goals.

Health Communication Communication in the health care system. Researchers in this area are interested in how patients talk about their illnesses, communication between health care providers and patients, message flow in health care organizations, and public health care campaigns.

Intercultural Communication Communication phenomena in which participants with different cultural backgrounds come into direct or indirect contact.

Intracultural Communication (Interethnic Communication)   Communication that takes place between members of the same dominant culture who have slightly different values.

Mediated Communication   Communication via mass media. Researchers in this area are interested in the media's uses of and influences on communication.

Political Communication   Using communication to negotiate the allocation of limited resources.

COMPACT DISK READ-ONLY MEMORY (CD-ROM)   A computer disk capable of storing about 275,000 printed pages of data.

COMPLEMENTARY RELATIONSHIP   A relationship in which one person usually controls the other.

COMPUTER-ASSISTED TELEPHONE INTERVIEWING (CATI)   The use of specialized computer-assisted telecommunication equipment to streamline administration and coding of interviews. The computerized equipment randomly dials telephone numbers, feeds interviewers specific questions to be asked via a computer terminal, and enables the interviewers to enter responses to questions as they are being given by touching a few keys on the computer keyboard or even by touching the computer terminal screen. The computer also analyzes the data quickly by adding the respondents' answers to the existing data set.

COMSERVE   An online database, sponsored by the Rensselaer Polytechnic Institute's Department of Language, Literature, and Communication, that provides up-to-date information about communication research, including grants, and provides a job advertising service called COMJOBS.

CONCEPTUAL DEFINITION   A statement that describes what a concept means by relating it to similar concepts.

CONCEPTUALIZATION   Forming an idea about what is to be studied by identifying a topic worthy of study, defining the primary concepts of the research topic, reviewing the relevant literature to learn what is already known about the topic, and phrasing the topic as a formal research question or a hypothesis.

CONFEDERATE   A person whom researchers employ to play a role in an experimental manipulation.

CONFIDENCE INTERVAL   The range of scores associated with the confidence level.

CONFIDENCE LEVEL   The degree of assurance that a sample statistic can be used to infer a population parameter. Also known as the *alpha level*, this statistic reflects the probability of rejecting a null hypothesis that is in fact true.

CONFIDENTIALITY   A condition wherein researchers know who said what but promise not to reveal that information publicly.

CONSTRUCT VALIDITY   The validity of a measurement instrument as inferred from a theoretical framework.

CONSUMER BEHAVIOR   The behavior of the buyers of products and services, often in reaction to communication by sellers or marketers. Researchers in this area are interested in how mass-mediated communication influences consumers' information processing and buying behavior.

CONTENT ANALYSIS   A research technique for making inferences by systematically identifying specified characteristics in a text.

CONTENT INFORMATION   The substantive information present in any message.

CONTENT VALIDITY   The extent to which a measurement instrument reflects the attributes of the concept being investigated.

CONTEXT   The physical and temporal environment in which communication takes place.

CONTINGENCY TABLE ANALYSIS (MULTIPLE-SAMPLE CHI-SQUARE, CROSSTABS)   A statistical test used whenever researchers compare two or more groups with respect to a set of categories or the same group of people with respect to two different sets of categories.

CONTROL   The systematic elimination of variables, other than the independent variables, that are possible causes of the effects being studied.

CONVERSATIONAL ANALYSIS   A textual analysis research technique that examines exchanges during interpersonal and small group interactions to discover systematic and orderly properties that are meaningful to communicators.

CONVERSATIONAL RULE   A prescription that encourages people to decide how to communicate in a particular conversational situation.

CORRELATION   A statistical relationship between two variables.

CORRELATIONAL DESIGN   A research strategy that assesses all of the variables of interest at one point in time in order to describe the relationships among those variables.

CORRELATION COEFFICIENT   A numerical summary of the type and strength of a relationship between two variables.

CORRELATION MATRIX   A depiction of all the relevant variables both across the top and down the left side of a matrix. Where the respective rows and columns meet, researchers indicate the correlation coefficient for those two variables and whether it is significant.

CRAMER'S V CORRELATION   A statistical calculation of the correlation coefficient for two variables that are measured on nominal scales.

CRITERION-RELATED VALIDITY   The validity of a measurement instrument determined by comparing the outcome of the instrument with another technique or outcome (criterion) that is known to be valid. The more the scores from the instrument are positively related to the criterion, the more valid the instrument is determined to be.

Concurrent Validity   A form of criterion-related validity whereby a new measurement technique is tested against an existing criterion known to be valid.

Predictive Validity   A form of criterion-related validity whereby a measurement technique is tested to see how well it forecasts a future criterion.

CRITERION VARIABLE   The variable that researchers want to explain in a correlation.

CRITICAL INCIDENTS   Events occurring in a particular context that are exceptional by some criteria, most often used to inform ethnographic research.

CROSS-SECTIONAL RESEARCH   Gathering and analyzing data at one point in time.

CULTIVATION RESEARCH   The study of the extent to which the mass media influence viewers' beliefs about social reality.

CULTURAL ARTIFACTS   Recordings or physical traces of interactions that are used in ethnographic research to examine different cultures.

CULTURE   The composite of knowledge, experience, beliefs, values, attitudes, meanings, hierarchies, religion, timing, roles, spatial relations, concepts of the universe, and material objects and possessions acquired by a group of people.

CURVILINEAR RELATIONSHIP   The relationship of two variables such that they are related in a positive or a negative way up to a certain point, after which the relationship is reversed.

Inverted U-shaped Curvilinear Relationship   A relationship whereby two variables are related positively up to a point and then are related negatively.

U-shaped Curvilinear Relationship   A relationship whereby two variables are related negatively up to a point and then are related positively.

DATA ANALYSES   Methods researchers use to infer meaning from data, to determine what conclusions are justified by transforming numbers or verbal accounts into information that can be shared with others.

DATABASE   A place where large amounts of data, usually on a specific topic, are stored.

Online Database   A database that can be accessed by a computer via a modem.

DEBRIEFING   A discussion session between researchers and subjects after a study is conducted to explain the full purpose of the study, as well as to learn the subjects' perceptions.

DECODING   Attributing meanings to symbols received.

DEGREES OF FREEDOM (df)   The number of scores that are free to vary in a sample.

DEMOGRAPHIC QUESTIONS   Survey questions that inquire about respondents' personal characteristics, such as name, age, gender, and education.

DESCRIPTIVE DATA ANALYSIS   A method used to summarize data, often by tabulating and graphing them.

DESIGN DIAGRAM   A visual depiction of a factorial design statement, showing all the possible combinations of the independent variables.

DESIGN STATEMENT   A series of numbers, one for each independent variable in a factorial study, separated by a multiplication sign. Each number indicates the total number of levels for the independent variable it represents.

DIALOG   One of the largest popular and scholarly online database vendors, providing over 320 separate databases and more than 175 million records.

DIRECTIVE QUESTIONNAIRES AND INTERVIEWS   Questionnaires and interviews that use mostly closed questions that lead respondents to answer in specific ways by limiting the range of responses available to them.

DIRECT OBSERVATION   A measurement strategy whereby researchers watch and code communication behaviors as they occur.

DISCIPLINARY MODEL OF EDUCATION   A current perspective on education, emphasizing specialized knowledge housed within academic disciplines.

DISSERTATION ABSTRACTS ONLINE   An online database of close to 1 million records including virtually every Ph.D. dissertation submitted in the United States since 1861.

DRAMATURGICAL MODEL   A communication perspective that maintains that understanding communication in context involves learning how people view their own and others' roles in a particular situation.

ECOLOGICAL FALLACY   An error that occurs when researchers attempt to describe a population on the basis of data collected from a sample that does not represent the population accurately.

ECOLOGICAL VALIDITY   Determination of whether the procedures used in a research study mirror real-life conditions.

EDUCATIONAL RESOURCES INFORMATION CENTER (ERIC)   An online and microfiche database started by the U.S. Department of Education in 1966 that specializes in education-related references.

ELECTROENCEPHALOGRAM (EEG)   A measurement tool that enables researchers to record electrical activity in a subject's brain via electrodes attached to the subject's scalp.

ELECTRONIC SPECTROGRAPHIC ANALYSIS   The use of pictures of the pitch waves of voices to categorize vocal cues in conversational analysis.

ELECTRONIC SURVEY   A computer-based questionnaire that is self-administered to respondents through use of a text processing program.

EMBEDDED NATURE OF COMMUNICATION   The concept that different levels of communication influence communication phenomena, making it necessary for communication researchers to use sophisticated multilevel analyses of communication events.

ENCODING   Putting thoughts into symbols that can be transmitted.

EPISODE ANALYSIS   An ethnographic interviewing technique whereby respondents are asked to reconstruct a scene, complete with lines of dialogue, that represents a recurring pattern in their relationship.

ERROR SCORE COMPONENT   The amount of deviation from the true average in a score in a particular study.

ETHICS   Moral principles and recognized rules of conduct regarding a particular class of human behavior.

ETHNOGRAPHIC METHOD   A research method that uses measurement techniques to observe and describe carefully the communication behaviors that occur naturally in a specific population.

EVALUATION RESEARCH   A form of applied survey research used to assess the performance of specific programs, products, or organizations. Examples of eval-

formance of specific programs, products, or organizations. Examples of evaluation research include need analyses, organizational feedback surveys and audits, and network analyses.

Formative Evaluation   Evaluation research conducted while a program or product is in progress to identify ways to refine it.

Need Analysis   The use of surveys to identify both specific problems experienced by a target group, usually by comparing what exists with what would be preferred, and potential solutions to those problems.

Network Analysis   Use of the survey method to examine the patterns of interaction between members of a social system (network); it identifies system roles such as isolates, opinion leaders, gatekeepers, cosmopolites, bridges, and liaisons. Three levels of communication networks can be identified through network analysis: total system networks, clique networks, and personal networks.

Organizational Feedback Surveys and Audits   Uses of the survey method to question organization members and representatives of the organizational environment about current or potential opportunities or constraints the organization faces.

Summative Evaluation   Evaluation research conducted after a program or product is completed to assess its overall effectiveness, usually to determine whether to continue or discontinue it.

EVENTLOG   A computer program by which researchers can easily code and score live or mediated communication events. The computer records the coded data for later analysis.

EXPERIMENTAL CONDITIONS (EXPERIMENTAL GROUPS)   Division of experimental subjects into groups, such as treatment groups and control groups.

Control Group   A group of subjects that does not receive an experimental manipulation. It is compared to the treatment group.

Treatment Group   A group of subjects that receives an experimental manipulation. It is often compared to a control group.

EXPERIMENTAL MANIPULATION   Control of subjects' exposure to an independent variable.

EXPERIMENTAL METHOD   A research method using measurement techniques to assess the causal effects of independent variables on dependent variables.

Field Experiment   An experiment that is conducted in a natural setting.

Full Experiment (True Experiment)   A highly controlled experiment wherein the independent variable is manipulated and subjects are assigned randomly to conditions. Examples of full experiment designs include the pretest-posttest control group design, the posttest-only control group design, and the Solomon four-group design.

Laboratory Experiment   An experiment that is conducted in a controlled environment created by a researcher.

Preexperiment   An experiment that manipulates or observes an independent variable and may or may not have two experimental groups. When there is a comparison group, no attempt is made to assess the groups' equivalency. Examples of preexperiment designs include the one-shot case study design, the one-group pretest-posttest design, and the static group comparison design.

Quasi-experiment An experiment that manipulates or observes an independent variable and may or may not have two experimental groups. When there is a comparison group, subjects are not randomly assigned to make the groups equivalent, but pretests are used to determine whether the groups started off equivalent, establishing quasi-equivalent experimental groups. Examples of quasi-experiment designs include the nonequivalent control group design, the time series design, and the multiple time-series design.

EXTERNAL VALIDITY   The generalizability of the findings from a research study based on whether the conclusions from a particular study can be applied to other people and other contexts.

FACTOR   Each of the independent variables in a study (underlying dimensions in multivariate studies).

FACTORIAL STUDY   A study in which there is more than one independent variable.

FIELD NOTES   A researcher's record of what was meaningful in an ethnographic observation, detailing critical moments and activities.

FOCUS GROUP INTERVIEW   A relatively open discussion about a specific product or program among a small group of people (usually five to seven) led by a facilitator, who introduces topics, encourages participation, and probes for information in a flexible, interactive way to elicit subjects' genuine views.

FOLLOW-UP MAILING   A reminder letter and perhaps an additional questionnaire sent to people who haven't responded to the initial mailing of a questionnaire in an attempt to increase the response rate.

FREQUENCY DISTRIBUTION   The tabulation of how often different categories or points on a measurement scale occur.

FREQUENCY TABLE   A list of the frequency of responses for each category or measurement.

GARBOLOGY   An unobtrusive trace measure of accretion whereby researchers gather, sift through, identify, and categorize garbage as a way of determining people's behaviors.

GENDER INSENSITIVITY   Ignoring gender as a variable in research.

GROUNDED THEORY   A method for analyzing data, using them primarily for theory generation rather than theory testing.

HAWTHORNE EFFECT   The fact that people who are aware of being studied often behave differently from when they do not know they are being observed; this can threaten the validity of a research study.

HEURISTIC   Research or a theory that generates more research and theorizing.

HISTOGRAM   A visual depiction of data that uses blocks to show how frequently each point on an interval/ratio measurement scale occurs.

HISTORY   The concept that changes in the environment external to a research study may influence subjects' behaviors; this can threaten the validity of the study.

HORIZONTAL DATA Quantitative data with great breadth, covering a broad range of respondents.

HUMANITIES The creative arts.

HYPOTHESIS (RESEARCH HYPOTHESIS) A tentative statement predicting a relationship between variables or a difference between groups.

Null Hypothesis A hypothesis predicting no relationship between variables or a difference between groups.

One-tailed Hypothesis A hypothesis predicting the specific nature (direction) of the relationship between variables or a difference between groups.

Two-tailed Hypothesis A hypothesis predicting only that there is some significant relationship between variables or a difference between groups.

ICA COMMUNICATION AUDIT A set of research instruments designed to assess communication needs within an organization with respect to two categories, the amount of actual information received versus the amount of information needed.

ILLOCUTIONARY ACTS Verbal messages analyzed in conversational analysis that are intentionally designed to be recognized by another as requiring a response.

INDIRECT OBSERVATION A measurement strategy whereby researchers examine communication artifacts, such as transcripts of discourse or products of communication, rather than observing live communication events.

INFERENTIAL DATA ANALYSIS (INFERENTIAL STATISTICS) Strategies for estimating the characteristics of a population from data gathered on a sample and testing for significant differences between groups and significant relationships between variables by accomplishing estimation and significance testing.

Estimation Generalizing the results obtained from a sample to its parent population.

Significance Testing Examining the importance of the differences between groups or the relationships between variables, for the purpose of testing whether a null hypothesis is probably true or probably false.

INSTITUTIONAL REVIEW BOARD (IRB) A committee that reviews research proposals to ensure the protection of human beings affected in the course of research studies conducted by scholars affiliated with the university or organization that supports the committee.

INTERACTION EFFECTS Effects due to the unique combination of independent variables in a factorial study.

INTERACTION PROCESS ANALYSIS (IPA) A conversational analysis scheme, developed by R. F. Bales, that examines group interaction by categorizing the function of each person's communicative acts into one of 12 categories.

INTERNAL CONSISTENCY METHOD An approach to testing the reliability of a self-report measurement instrument, whereby the results of various items on the instrument are paired and compared. The more consistent the results are, the more reliable the instrument is judged to be.

INTERNAL VALIDITY   The accuracy of the conclusions drawn from a research study as determined by its design and conduct.

INTEROBSERVER RELIABILITY (INTERCODER RELIABILITY)   The trustworthiness of observational research as determined by assessing agreement among observations by independent coders. The greater the agreement among observers, the more reliable the coding scheme is considered to be.

INTERPERSONAL COMMUNICATION   Communication between two people (a dyad), either face to face or through media, characterized by mutual awareness of each other's individuality.

Accounting Behaviors   Interpersonal communication strategies designed to manage failure episodes in interpersonal relationships.

Affinity-seeking Behaviors   Interpersonal communication strategies designed to win the liking of other people.

Comforting Behaviors   Interpersonal communication strategies designed to provide a relational partner with emotional support or assistance.

Compliance-gaining or Compliance-resisting Behaviors   Interpersonal communication strategies designed to get others to behave in accordance with one's wishes or to refuse such compliance.

Conflict Behaviors   Interpersonal communication strategies designed to manage dyadic disagreements.

Deception   An interpersonal communication strategy designed to mislead.

Disengagement   An interpersonal communication strategy designed to terminate interpersonal relationships.

Disqualification and Equivocation   Interpersonal communication strategies designed to answer questions in an evasive manner.

Embarassment-reducing Behaviors   Interpersonal communication strategies designed to reduce the discomfort associated with embarrassment.

Interruption and Silence   Interpersonal communication strategies designed to end discussion of a topic.

Politeness   An interpersonal communication strategy designed to be courteous to others.

Secret Tests   Interpersonal communication strategies designed to acquire knowledge about the state of a person's opposite-gender relationship.

Self-disclosure   An interpersonal communication strategy designed to share information about oneself with others.

Storytelling   An interpersonal communication strategy designed to tell a story.

INTERQUARTILE RANGE   A descriptive statistic of dispersion that describes the distance between the 25th percentile point and the 75th percentile point.

INTERSUBJECT BIAS   The influence that research subjects have on one another; this can threaten the validity of a research study.

INTERVAL MEASUREMENT SCALES   Scales that classify a variable into qualitatively different categories, rank those categories along some dimension, and also

INTERVAL MEASUREMENT SCALES   Scales that classify a variable into qualitatively different categories, rank those categories along some dimension, and also establish standard or equal distances between each of the adjacent points along the scale.

INTERVIEWEE   A person who is interviewed.

INTERVIEWER   A person who conducts an interview.

INTERVIEW SCHEDULE (PROTOCOL)   A list of questions that guide an interview.

Highly Scheduled Interview   An interview conducted according to a list of all the questions the interviewer is supposed to ask.

Moderately Scheduled Interview   An interview in which the specific questions the interviewer is to ask are specified but the interviewer has the freedom to probe for additional information after responses to the primary questions are given.

Unscheduled Interview   An interview in which the interviewer has been told which primary topics to cover, allowing the interviewer maximum freedom in phrasing and ordering questions and in probing for additional information.

INTIMATE COMMUNICATION   The expression and maintenance of intimacy in romantic relationships. The study of sexual communication is representative of this topic area.

INTRAPERSONAL COMMUNICATION   An internal communication process that occurs when a person sends a message to himself or herself and develops messages to send to others.

KEY INFORMANT   A person who provides ethnographic researchers with inside information about a particular culture being studied.

KURTOSIS   Deviance in the amplitude of a distribution from a normal curve. If the curve is narrow and sharply pointed, it is said to be *peaked.* If the scores do not cluster around the middle but are dispersed rather evenly across the distribution, the curve is said to be *flat.*

LEGAL COMMUNICATION   Communication in the criminal and civil justice system. Researchers in this area are interested in communication between lawyers and clients, argumentation in the courtroom setting, and the jury deliberation process.

LIBERAL TRADITION IN EDUCATION   The prevailing perspective on education in the 1800s, which emphasized generalized knowledge.

LIBRARY   An establishment where knowledge is stored in an organized fashion and made available to patrons.

Public Library (General-Use Library)   A library that stocks a broad range of materials to serve its community.

Research Library   A library that has extensive reference materials and a wide selection of books but within a narrower scope than public libraries.

Special-Use Library   A library that serves a special population of users and provides specialized information functions, such as archives.

LIKERT SCALE   A measurement scale developed by psychologist Rensis Likert which identifies the extent of a person's feelings or attitudes toward a referent.

LINEAR RELATIONSHIP   A relationship between measured variables that can be represented and explained by a straight line on a scattergram.

LINE GRAPH   A visual depiction of data that uses a single point to represent the frequency count for each category and then connects these points with a single line.

LONGITUDINAL RESEARCH   Gathering and analyzing data at multiple points over time.

> *Cohort Study*   Longitudinal research in which responses from specific subgroups of a population are identified and compared over time.
>
> *Panel Study*   Longitudinal research in which responses are obtained from the same people over time to learn whether and how they change.
>
> *Trend Study*   Longitudinal research in which a measurement is administered at two or more points in time to identify changes (trends).

MAIN EFFECTS   The effects due to each of the independent variables in a factorial study.

MARKET RESEARCH   A form of applied survey research in which consumer attitudes and product preferences are described.

> *Audience Ratings*   Market research that identifies the size and composition of the audience that different programs, networks, and stations reach.
>
> *Readership Surveys*   Market research conducted with subscribers to periodicals to determine how often these subscribers read the publication, which articles they like and don't like, and what topics they would like to see covered in future issues.

MASS COMMUNICATION   The transmission of messages from a small number of people to a large, anonymous, and usually heterogeneous audience through the use of specialized communication media.

MATURATION   The concept that internal changes that occur in subjects over the course of the study might influence their behaviors; this can threaten the validity of a research study.

MEANING   A mental image people create to interpret and understand a stimulus.

MEASUREMENT   The process of determining the existence, characteristics, size, or quantity of some variable through systematic recording and organization of observations.

MEASUREMENT ERROR   The amount of error in a measurement that can be attributed to weaknesses in research instrumentation and administration.

MEASUREMENT RELIABILITY   The extent to which measurements of a variable are consistent and trustworthy.

MEASUREMENT TECHNIQUES   Strategies for measuring research concepts. The three general techniques used are interviews, observations, and questionnaires.

> *Interview*   A presentation of spoken questions to evoke spoken responses from subjects.

Questionnaire A list of written questions intended to evoke written responses from subjects.

MEASUREMENT VALIDITY The extent to which researchers are actually measuring the concepts they intend to measure.

MEASURES OF CENTRAL TENDENCY Descriptive statistics that describe the center point of a distribution.

Mean A descriptive statistic that is the arithmetic average of a distribution.

Median A descriptive statistic that divides the distribution at the 50th percentile (exactly in half). It is the number above which and below which half the observations fall.

Mode A descriptive statistic that is the number that occurs most often in a distribution.

MEASURES OF DISPERSION (MEASURES OF VARIABILITY) Descriptive statistics that describe the extent to which scores in a distribution differ.

Range A descriptive statistic that reports the distance between the highest and lowest scores in a distribution.

Standard Deviation A descriptive statistic that describes the extent to which scores on an interval or ratio scale vary from the mean, expressed in the original units of measurement.

Variance A descriptive statistic that is a mathematical index of the average distance of the scores on an interval or ratio scale from the mean, in squared units.

MESSAGES The symbols that people attend to and for which they create meanings.

External Messages The messages that people react to from others and from the environment.

Internal Messages The messages that people send to themselves.

Nonverbal Messages Symbols that are neither words nor language.

Verbal Messages Symbols composed of words and language, both spoken and written.

MORTALITY The loss of subjects during the course of a research study; this can threaten the validity of the study.

MULTIDIMENSIONAL CONCEPTS Research concepts composed of a number of sub-concepts (factors).

MULTIMODAL Having three or more modes; having three or more categories tied for greatest frequency in a distribution.

MULTIPLE CORRELATION A statistical procedure that assesses the relationship between a variable that a researcher wishes to explain, the criterion variable, and two or more other variables working together. This procedure yields two statistics, a multiple correlation coefficient and a multiple coefficient of determination.

MULTIPLE CORRELATION COEFFICIENT A statistic that tells researchers how two or more variables working together are related.

MULTIVARIATE TESTS Advanced statistical procedures used to assess differences between groups with respect to multiple dependent variables. These tests include log-linear analysis, analysis of covariance, multiple analysis of variance, and multiple analysis of covariance.

NEGATIVE RELATIONSHIP Situation that exists when increases in one variable are associated with decreases in another variable.

NOMINAL MEASUREMENT SCALES (CLASSIFICATORY MEASURES) Scales that classify variables into qualitatively different categories.

NONCAUSAL RELATIONSHIP Situation that exists when variables are associated, or go together, without one necessarily causing changes in the other.

NONDIRECTIVE QUESTIONNAIRES AND INTERVIEWS Questionnaires and interviews that use mostly open questions that expand the range of answers available to respondents.

NONEQUIVALENT EXPERIMENTAL GROUPS Experimental groups in which there is no assurance that changes observed in a dependent variable are the result of changes in an independent variable, resulting from the researchers' failure to check on initial differences between the groups.

NONLINEAR RELATIONSHIP A relationship between measured variables that can only be represented and explained by a curved line on a scattergram.

NONPARAMETRIC STATISTICS Statistics used only to describe the characteristics of a sample, without being able to generalize back to its population.

NONRANDOM SAMPLE A sample that does not use procedures to ensure that each subject has an equal chance of selection from the overall population.

Convenience Sample (Accidental Sample) A nonrandom sample in which subjects are selected simply because they are available.

Network Sample (Snowball Sample) A nonrandom sample in which subjects are asked to refer researchers to other people who could serve as subjects.

Purposive Sample A nonrandom sample in which subjects are chosen because they possess a particular characteristic.

Quota Sample A nonrandom sample in which subjects are chosen on the basis of their known representation in the population.

Volunteer Sample A nonrandom sample in which subjects choose purposely to participate in a study, usually due to rewards offered.

NONVERBAL COMMUNICATION All communication that does not include the use of words, yet surrounds verbal messages.

Artifacts Nonverbal messages related to personal appearance and decorative objects.

Chronemics Nonverbal messages related to time and its effects on communication.

Kinesics Nonverbal messages related to the way people move their bodies and position themselves.

Paralanguage Nonverbal messages related to the sounds people make, especially the nonverbal aspects of verbal communication, including speech rate, pauses and silence sequences, vocal intensity, vocal pitch, volume, talk duration, breathiness, throatiness, nasality, flatness, and disfluent speech.

Proxemics   Nonverbal messages related to the nature and effects of space or distance between people or objects.

Tactilics   Nonverbal messages related to touching behaviors, including skin-to-skin touching (haptics) and the touching of objects.

NORMAL CURVE (BELL-SHAPED CURVE)   The plot of a distribution of scores that is equally divided on the left and the right, so that the mean, median, and mode all occur at the same point and specific percentages of responses fall within specified numbers of standard deviations from the mean.

OBSERVED VARIABLE   An independent variable that is not manipulated directly by a researcher.

OPERATIONAL DEFINITION   A statement that describes the observable characteristics of a concept being investigated in a study, specifying how researchers may observe the concept in actual practice.

Experimental Observational Definitions   Observational definitions that specify the behaviors researchers use to manipulate a variable.

Measured Operational Definitions   Observational definitions that specify how researchers ascertain the existence or quantity of a concept, generally using behavioral observations, observers' ratings, or self-reports.

OPERATIONALIZATION   Determining the observable attributes or characteristics of the concepts to be studied by developing strategies for their measurement.

ORAL TRADITION IN COMMUNICATION INQUIRY   The emphasis on the central role of spoken public communication in developing and maintaining government and society, as established by the classical period of communication inquiry.

ORDINAL MEASUREMENT SCALES   Scales that classify a variable into qualitatively different categories and rank those categories along some dimension.

ORGANIZATIONAL COMMUNICATION   Communication within a particular social system composed of interdependent groups attempting to achieve commonly recognized goals.

OUTPUTS OF COMMUNICATION   Messages produced by communicators themselves, including written artifacts, works of art, and other symbolic outputs.

PANEL ATTRITION   Mortality as it affects panel studies.

PARAMETER   A characteristic of a population or a universe.

PARAMETRIC STATISTICS   Statistics used to estimate the characteristics of a population based on the characteristics of a sample.

PARSIMONIOUS THEORY   A simply stated theory that explains a complex phenomenon.

PARTIAL CORRELATION   The relationship between two variables while controlling for or ruling out the influence of one or more other variables.

PARTICIPANT OBSERVATIONAL ROLES   An ethnographic technique for observing communication in different cultural groups.

Complete Observer   A researcher who observes people without their knowledge and without interacting with them directly.

Complete Participant   A researcher who participates fully in a social situation without letting people know that they are being studied.

Observer as Participant   A researcher who informs people that they are being observed and participates partially with them.

Participant-Observer   A researcher who informs people that they are being observed and participates fully in the social situation being studied.

PEARSON PRODUCT-MOMENT CORRELATION   A correlation coefficient calculated for two variables that are measured on interval scales.

PERIODICALS   Regularly appearing publications including newspapers, magazines, government reports, and documents.

PERSONALITY PREDISPOSITIONS   Traits that relate directly to a person's tendencies toward particular communication behaviors.

Communicator Style   A communication personality predisposition that influences the way a person interacts verbally, nonverbally, and paraverbally to signal how literal meanings should be interpreted, filtered, or understood. Ten types of communicator style have been identified: animated, attentive, contentious or argumentative, dominant, dramatic, friendly, impression-leaving, precise, open, and relaxed.

Interaction Involvement   A communication personality predisposition that influences the extent to which a person partakes in a social environment.

Rhetorical Sensitivity   A communication personality predisposition that influences whether a person characterizes himself or herself as an undulating, fluctuating entity, always unsure, always guessing, and continually weighing potential communicative decisions.

Self-monitoring   A communication personality predisposition that influences the degree to which a person pays attention to his or her verbal and nonverbal behaviors and adapts them to the requirements of social situations.

Verbal Aggressiveness   A communication personality predisposition that influences how bold, assertive, or hostile a person's communication behaviors are.

Willingness to Communicate   A communication personality predisposition that influences the degree to which a person is oriented psychologically toward talking, made up of a person's unwillingness to communicate, predispositions toward verbal behavior, and shyness.

PHENOMENOLOGY   The examination of how internal, psychological meanings guide behavior to determine how individuals construct meaning, generating subjective knowledge.

PHONOLOGY (PHONEMICS)   The study of the performance of spoken language, focusing on the sounds and pronunciations of words.

PHYSICAL SCIENCES   Studies of the physical or natural world.

PIE CHART   A visual depiction of data that uses a circle divided into segments showing the percentage of the circle that represents the frequency count for each category.

POLITICAL POLLS   Applied survey research conducted to describe public opinion on political issues and potential voting patterns.

POPULATION   All the people that possess a characteristic (parameter) of interest to a researcher.

POSITIVE RELATIONSHIP   Situation that exists when increases in one variable are associated with increases in another variable.

PRAGMATICS   The study of the intended and unintended effects and behavioral functions of language use by people in different situations.

PRETEST   Assesses whether some initial differences exist between subjects who have not been assigned randomly to experimental groups, creating quasi-equivalent groups. Researchers often measure these subjects on relevant variables that need to be accounted for before exposing the treatment groups to the manipulation of the independent variable.

PRIOR GENERAL CONSENT PLUS PROXY CONSENT   A technique whereby a researcher first obtains the consent of a subject to participate in a study that may involve extreme procedures. The potential subject then empowers a friend to serve as a proxy, to examine the details of the specific procedures in advance and to make a judgment as to whether the subject would have consented to participate if made aware of the procedures.

PRIVATE GRANTS   Financial awards given by individuals and organizations.

PROCEDURE VALIDITY AND RELIABILITY   Assessments of how accurately and consistently a research study is conducted.

PROCEEDINGS   Written and polished versions of conference papers presented at scholarly meetings that are compiled in a book.

PROJECTIVE DEVICES   Memory aids, such as diaries, used in ethnographic research to help elicit information from respondents.

PROTOCOL ANALYSIS   An ethnographic research technique whereby respondents are asked to verbalize their intentions, thoughts, and feelings as they engage in whatever activity is being studied.

PUBLIC COMMUNICATION   Situation in which a small number of people (usually one person) address a larger group of people.

PUBLIC GRANTS   Financial awards given by government bodies.

PUBLIC OPINION PROCESSES   The methods whereby communication influences public opinion. Researchers in this area are interested in the formation of, measurement of, and strategies for changing public opinion.

PUBLIC OPINION RESEARCH   An applied use of survey research to measure public opinion.

PUBLIC RELATIONS   The management of communication between an organization and its publics.

QUALITATIVE DATA   Data reported as symbols (words or diagrams) that indicate the presence or absence of something or categorize an object into different types.

QUALITATIVE OBSERVATIONS   Observations that use symbols (words or diagrams) to indicate the presence or absence of something or categorize an object into different types.

QUANTITATIVE DATA   Data reported as numerical indicators that describe relative size.

QUANTITATIVE OBSERVATIONS   Observations that use numerical indicators to describe relative size.

QUASI-EQUIVALENT EXPERIMENTAL GROUPS   Experimental groups that result when a researcher attempts to make them somewhat equivalent, often by means of pretests.

QUESTION FORMAT   The strategic sequence of queries on a questionnaire or in an interview.

> *Funnel Question Format*   Format wherein broad, open questions are used to introduce the questionnaire or interview, followed by narrower, closed questions that seek more specific information from the respondents.

> *Inverted Funnel Question Format*   Format wherein narrow, closed questions are used to introduce the questionnaire or interview, followed by broad, open questions about a topic.

> *Tunnel Question Format*   Format wherein a straight series of similarly organized questions are posed to respondents.

RANDOM ASSIGNMENT (RANDOMIZATION)   A procedure used in experimental research that employs a random method to assign subjects to experimental groups, thus giving each subject an equal chance of being assigned to any particular group and hence creating equivalent experimental groups.

RANDOM DIGIT DIALING   A computer program that generates and dials telephone numbers randomly selected from all the possible combinations of telephone numbers within a given range of phone numbers.

RANDOM ERROR   An inevitable loss of accuracy in measurement that is not under the control of the researcher.

RANDOM SAMPLE   A group of subjects selected in such a way that each member of the population or universe of interest has an equal chance of being selected.

RAPPORT   Sense of harmony achieved by putting interviewees at ease through personal identification and comfortable interaction to encourage interviewees to provide full and accurate information.

RATIO MEASUREMENT SCALES   Scales that classify variables into qualitatively different categories, rank those categories along some dimension, establish standard or equal distances between each of the adjacent points along the measurement scale, and also establish a true or absolute zero point where the variable measured ceases to exist.

RECONCEPTUALIZATION   Reevaluation of a topic of inquiry based on the results of research efforts. This process often leads to new research questions.

REFERENCE NOTES   Notes included either at the bottom of the page or at the end of a manuscript that provide explanations about material in the body of a manuscript but do not belong in the body itself.

REFERENCES A complete and accurate list of all sources used in a research report.

REGRESSION ANALYSES Statistical procedures used to predict an outcome on the basis of scores on another variable (a predictor variable).

Linear Regression A statistical procedure used to explain scores on a criterion variable on the basis of scores on a predictor variable.

Multiple Regression A statistical procedure used to explain scores on a criterion variable on the basis of scores on two or more predictor variables.

RELATIONSHIP INFORMATION Information describing how a message defines the nature of the relationship between communicators.

REPEATED-MEASURES FACTORIAL DESIGN An experimental approach that exposes the same subjects to different experimental treatments to minimize the number of subjects needed for factorial design studies with several different independent variables.

REPLICATION Conducting a study on a particular topic that repeats a previous study exactly or varies from it in some systematic way.

Constructive Replication Using entirely different procedures, measurement instruments, sampling procedures, and data analysis techniques to study the same topic.

Instrumental Replication Measuring the dependent variable in the same way as the original study but changing the independent variable to see if a different operationalization will give the same results.

Literal Replication Duplicating a previous study as closely as possible.

Operational Replication Duplicating the sampling and procedures from a previous study but applying different measurement and analytic techniques.

REPRESENTATIVENESS The extent to which a sample can accurately stand for or approximate a population or universe.

RESEARCH A form of disciplined inquiry, studying something in a planned manner and reporting it so that other inquirers can replicate the process if they choose to.

Applied Research Studies conducted to solve practical problems.

Basic (Pure) Research Studies conducted to test or refine theory.

Deductive Research Studies conducted to uncover data to suport a predetermined theory.

Inductive Research Studies conducted to gather data, from which a theory will be developed.

Proprietary Research Studies conducted for a specific audience and not shared beyond that audience.

Scholarly Research Studies conducted to increase knowledge and to promote public access to knowledge.

RESEARCHER-ADMINISTERED QUESTIONNAIRES Questionnaires administered in person by researchers.

RESEARCHER EFFECT The influence of the researcher on the subjects being studied.

Personal Attribute Effect A researcher effect that occurs when particular characteristics of the researcher affect subjects' behaviors.

Unintentional Expectancy Effect   A researcher effect that occurs when researchers affect subjects' responses by inadvertently letting the subjects know the results they desire from the study.

RESEARCH QUESTION   Any explicit question researchers ask about the variables of interest to them.

Directional Research Question   A closed-ended question.

Nondirectional Research Question   An open-ended question.

RESEARCH METHODS   The particular strategies that researchers use to collect the evidence necessary for building and testing theories.

RESEARCH PROCESS CYCLE MODEL   A five-phase cyclic model of research consisting of (1) conceptualization, (2) planning and designing research, (3) methodologies for conducting research, (4) analyzing and interpreting data, and (5) reconceptualization.

RESEARCH TOPICS   The ideas that communication researchers consider worth studying.

RESPONSE BIAS   A tendency for survey respondents to answer a series of questions in the same way automatically.

RESPONSE RATE   The percentage of individuals who complete and return surveys out of the total number of people contacted to participate.

REVIEW OF THE LITERATURE   The process whereby a researcher identifies and examines research done by scholars that is relevant to the topic under investigation.

RHETORICAL CRITICISM   Research involving the description, analysis, interpretation, and evaluation of persuasive uses of communication.

Biographical Studies   Rhetorical research that examines the public and private communication of prominent, influential, or otherwise remarkable individuals.

Case Studies   Rhetorical research that examines a single, salient social situation to interpret the role played by communication.

Classical Rhetoric   Rhetorical research emphasizing the central role of public communication in developing and maintaining government and society.

Contemporary Rhetorical Criticism   Rhetorical research incorporating a wide range of philosophical, theoretical, and methodological perspectives, used to examine a broad spectrum of persuasive messages.

Dramatistic Criticism   Rhetorical research, based on the work of Kenneth Burke, that analyzes social events as dramas, often using Burke's pentad model (act, purpose, agent, agency, scene) to isolate essential elements of symbolic acts and differences between them.

Fantasy Theme Analysis   Rhetorical research, a form of dramatistic criticism based on the work of Ernest Bormann, that examines the influence on people's interpretations of social reality of embedded narrative dramatizations in four symbolic categories: fantasy themes, fantasy types, rhetorical visions, and rhetorical communities.

Genre Criticism   Rhetorical analysis of certain types (genres) of texts that are similar in function and form, including forensic, epidectic, deliberative, apologia, campaign, eulogies, inaugural, and jeremiad.

Historical Criticism   Rhetorical research that describes and evaluates important past events by compiling and analyzing relevant documents.

Neo-Aristotelian Criticism   Rhetorical research, based on the classical rhetorical tradition, that evaluates the means of persuasion used by a speaker according to a specific set of criteria (five canons) cited in Aristotle's *Rhetoric:* invention, disposition, elocution, delivery, and memory.

Oral Histories   Rhetorical research that examines spoken accounts of past experiences.

Social Movement Studies   Rhetorical research that examines the historical development of a movement and the rhetorical strategies used to unite people in a common cause.

SAMPLE   A subgroup of a population or universe.

SAMPLING   The process of selecting subjects from a population for a research study.

SAMPLING ERROR   The amount by which the characteristics of a sample differ from the parameters of the poulation or universe.

SAMPLING FRAME   As complete a list as possible of the membership of a population or universe from which subjects for a sample can be selected.

Biased Sampling Frame   An incomplete list of people in a population.

SAMPLING RATE   The interval used in a systematic sampling to choose every *n*th subject.

SCATTERGRAM   A graphic depiction of a set of scores plotted on a grid.

SCHOLARLY CONFERENCE PAPERS   Reports of research presented at meetings of scholars.

SCHOLARLY JOURNAL   A regular periodical, often appearing quarterly, that publishes scholarly essays and sometimes book reviews.

SELECTION   The process of choosing people or texts for a research study; flawed selection can threaten the validity of a study.

SELF-ADMINISTERED QUESTIONNAIRE   A questionnaire that can be completed independently at the individual's discretion.

SEMANTIC DIFFERENTIAL SCALE   A scale developed by Osgood, Suci, and Tannenbaum (1957) that measures the meanings people create in response to specific stimuli.

SEMANTICS   The study of word meanings.

SENSITIVITY   The tendency for an initial measurement or procedure to influence a subsequent measurement or procedure; this can threaten the validity of a research study.

SIMPLE RANDOM SAMPLE   A representative sample obtained when each element in a population or universe is assigned a consecutive number and is then selected randomly according to assigned number until the desired sample size is obtained.

SKEWNESS   The asymmetry that occurs when the majority of scores fall toward one end of a distribution, making the curve tail off in that direction. Positive skew occurs when the tail runs to the right side of the curve; negative skew occurs when the tail runs to the left side of the curve.

SOCIAL SCIENCES   Human behavior studies.

SOCIAL SUPPORT   Being aided or assisted by others.

SOCIETAL COMMUNICATION   Communication within and between social systems composed of interdependent organizations attempting to achieve commonly recognized goals.

SPEARMAN RHO CORRELATION   A correlation coefficient calculated for two variables that are measured on ordinal scales.

SPLIT-HALF METHOD   An approach to the single-administration testing of the reliability of a measurement instrument, whereby the instrument is administered and then the results are separated into two parts and compared to determine the consistency of results between the two parts. The more consistent the results, the more reliable the instrument is judged to be.

STANDARD ERROR   The standard deviation of a sampling distribution.

STATISTIC   A measurement of a sample with respect to a variable.

STATISTICAL REGRESSION   The tendency for subjects selected on the basis of extreme scores to move toward the mean on subsequent measurements; this can threaten the validity of a research study.

STIMULATED RECALL   A technique in which a conversation is first recorded and is then played back for one or more participants to stimulate their memory of the particular incident.

STRATIFICATION VARIABLE   The characteristic used in a stratified sample to categorize a population.

STRATIFIED SAMPLE   A random sample that categorizes a population along a characteristic considered important to the research.

SUBJECT   A person who participates in a study or a text selected for examination in a study.

SUBJECT SELECTION   Choosing participants for a research study; if experimental groups are not selected to be equivalent, the validity of the study is jeopardized.

SURVEY METHOD   A research method that uses measurement techniques to gather information about the attitudes and behaviors of a defined population on the basis of answers to questions posed to samples drawn from the population.

SYMBOLIC INTERACTIONISM   An approach to understanding communication that stresses the symbolic nature of human social life.

SYMMETRICAL RELATIONSHIP   A relationship wherein both partners share control of their relationship equally.

SYNTACTICS   The study of the meanings derived from word order, emphasizing the grammar of verbal messages.

SYSTEMATIC SAMPLE   A representative sample obtained when every nth subject from a complete list of a population or universe is selected after starting at a random point.

TEST-RETEST METHOD   Checking the reliability of a measurement instrument by administering it to the same group at different times to determine the consistency of results.

TEXTUAL ANALYSIS METHOD   A research method that uses measurement techniques to classify and evaluate the characteristics of spoken, written, artistic, and electronic documents.

THEORY   A generalization about a phenomenon that explains how or why the phenomenon occurs.

THURSTONE SCALE   A measurement scale developed by L. L. Thurstone that attempts to ensure that the distances between adjacent points on the scale are of equal distance by using an elaborate process of refining the scale. First, many judges (often 50 to 300) categorize a large list of statements (usually several hundred) into 18 categories ranging from extremely favorable to extremely unfavorable. Then the researcher selects those statements (usually about 20) that have been consistently coded into a particular category by the judges. Each of these statements is assigned a value based on the mean rating by all the judges and is used in the scale. The resulting instrument incorporating these statements is then assumed to provide interval-level data.

TIME-LAPSE FILMING   An observational measurement technique whereby a communication event is filmed frame by frame so that the event can be slowed down for careful analysis.

TRANSACTIONAL COMMUNICATION   A process containing many interrelated components of human interaction, including such elements as messages, meanings, context, personalities, past experiences, and relationships established between communicators.

TRANSCRIPTS OF COMMUNICATION   Verbatim recordings of actual communication, such as written transcripts and audio or video recordings.

TREATMENT VALIDITY AND RELIABILITY   Assessments of the conceptual accuracy of treatment conditions and the consistency of administration of the experimental manipulations.

TRIANGULATION   The coordination of various research techniques producing consistent results to provide a more effective base for describing, explaining, understanding, interpreting, predicting, controlling, and critiquing a research topic than a single research method producing a single result could provide.

t **TEST**   A statistical test used to examine differences between two groups measured on an interval or ratio dependent variable.

  Independent-Sample t Test   A statistical test that examines differences between two unrelated groups.

  Matched-Sample t Test (Paired t Test)   A statistical test that examines differences between two measurements from the same group of subjects.

TYPE I ERROR   Rejecting a null hypothesis and accepting a research hypothesis when in fact the null hypothesis is true and should have been accepted.

TYPE II ERROR   Accepting a null hypothesis and rejecting a research hypothesis when in fact the null hypothesis is false and should have been rejected.

UNIDIMENSIONAL CONCEPTS   Concepts composed of multiple indicators that can be added equally to derive an overall score on a measurement instrument.

UNITS OF ANALYSIS   The message units that will be coded in content analysis.

Physical Units   The actual communication texts that are analyzed in content analysis.

Propositional Units   The messages that convey specific proposals that are analyzed in content analysis.

Referential Units   The symbols that describe specific referents that are analyzed in content analysis.

Syntactical Units   The individual symbols, such as words, that are analyzed in content analysis.

Thematic Units   The messages that convey specific topics that are analyzed in content analysis.

UNIVERSE   All of the inanimate subjects (generally texts in communication research) that share a characteristic of interest to a researcher.

UNOBTRUSIVE MEASURES   Analyses of physical traces or artifacts to describe people and their communication behavior.

Archival Research   An unobtrusive approach that involves describing and evaluating communication embedded in existing records of human behavior.

Bibliometrics   The examination of books and other publications to quantify such aspects as authorship, sources, publication, article content, or citation patterns, including bibliographic coupling and cocitation analysis.

Trace Measures   Measures of erosion (wearing down of traces) and accretion (building up of traces) used to analyze people's behavior.

UNRELATED VARIABLES (ORTHOGONAL VARIABLES)   Variables that have no systematic relationship.

USES AND GRATIFICATION RESEARCH   The study of how audiences use the mass media to meet particular needs.

VARIABLE   Any research concept that takes on two or more values.

Confounding Variable   A variable that explains the changes in the dependent variable but was not controlled or measured.

Dependent Variable   A variable that is thought to be changed by another (independent) variable.

Independent Variable   A variable that is thought to influence changes in another (dependent) variable.

Nominal Variable   A variable that can only be differentiated on the basis of type.

Ordered Variable   A variable that can be assigned meaningful numerical values.

VERBAL COMMUNICATION   The use of words and language.

VERTICAL DATA   Qualitative data with great depth, describing the perspectives of respondents fully.

WITHIN-GROUP VARIANCE   A description of how the scores cluster around the mean within a group.

z **SCORE**   A standard score that describes how many standard deviation units a particular score is above or below the mean.

Bibliography

AGAR, M. H. (1988). *Speaking of ethnography*. Newbury Park, CA: Sage.

ALBERTS, J. K. (1988). An analysis of couples' conversational complaints. *Communication Monographs, 55,* 184–197.

ALBRECHT, T. L., & ADELMAN, M. B. (1987). *Communicating social support*. Newbury Park, CA: Sage.

ALDERTON, S. M., & FREY, L. R. (1983). Effects of reactions to arguments on group outcome: The case of group polarization. *Central States Speech Journal, 34,* 88–95.

AMATO, P. R. (1983). The effects of urbanization on interpersonal behavior: Field studies in Papua New Guinea. *Journal of Cross-cultural Psychology, 13,* 353–367.

American Psychological Association. (1983). *Publication manual of the American Psychological Association* (3rd ed.). Washington, DC: Author.

ANDERSEN, P. A. (1989). Philosophy of science. In P. Emmert & L. L. Barker (Eds.), *Measurement of communication behavior* (pp. 3–17). White Plains, NY: Longman.

ANDERSEN, P. A., & KIBLER, R. J. (1978). Candidate valence as a predictor of voter preference. *Human Communication Research, 5,* 4–14.

ANDERSON, J. A. (1987). *Communication research: Issues and methods*. New York: McGraw-Hill.

ANDRESKI, S. (1972). *Social science as sorcery*. London: Andre Deutsch.

ANDREWS, J. R. (1983). *The practice of rhetorical criticism*. New York: Macmillan.

ANDREWS, P. H. (1987). Gender differences in persuasive communication and attribution of success and failure. *Human Communication Research, 13,* 372–385.

APPLEBAUM, R. L. (1985). Subject selection in speech communication research: A reexamination. *Communication Quarterly, 33,* 227–235.

ARMSTRONG, J. S., & LUSK, E. J. (1987). Return postage in mail surveys: A meta-analysis. *Public Opinion Quarterly, 51,* 233–248.

ARNSTON, P., & TURNER, L. H. (1987). Sex role socializations: Children's enactments of their parents' behaviors in a regulative and interpersonal context. *Western Journal of Speech Communication, 51,* 304–316.

ARONSON, E., & CARLSMITH, J. M. (1968). Experimentation in social psychology. In G. Lindzey & E. Aronson (Eds.), *Handbook of social psychology: Vol. 2. Research methods* (2nd ed., pp. 1–79). Reading, MA: Addison-Wesley.

ASANTE, M., & GUDYKUNST, W. B. (Eds.). (1989). *Handbook of international and intercultural communication.* Newbury Park, CA: Sage.

AUSTIN, J. L. (1962). *How to do things with words.* Oxford: Oxford University Press.

AYERS, J. (1988). Coping with speech anxiety: The power of positive thinking. *Communication Education, 37,* 289–296.

AZRIN, N. H., HOLTZ, W., ULRICH, R., & GOLDIAMOND, I. (1961). The control of the content of conversation through reinforcement. *Journal of the Experimental Analysis of Behavior, 4,* 25–30.

BABBIE, E. (1973). *The practice of social research.* Belmont, CA: Wadsworth.

BABBIE, E. (1986). *The practice of social research* (4th ed.). Belmont, CA: Wadsworth.

BABBIE, E. (1989). *The practice of social research* (5th ed.). Belmont, CA: Wadsworth.

BABBITT, L. V., & JABLIN, F. M. (1985). Characteristics of applicants' questions and employment screening interview outcomes. *Human Communication Research, 11,* 507–535.

BABROW, A. S. (1989). An expectancy-value analysis of the student soap opera audience. *Communication Research, 16,* 155–178.

BALES, R. F. (1950). *Interaction process analysis: A method for the study of small groups.* Reading, MA: Addison-Wesley.

BALES, R. F. (1970). *Personality and interpersonal behavior.* New York: Holt, Rinehart and Winston.

BANDURA, A. (1977). *Social learning theory.* Englewood Cliffs, NJ: Prentice-Hall.

BANTZ, C. R., & SMITH, D. H. (1977). A critique and experimental test of Weick's model of organizing. *Communication Monographs, 44,* 171–184.

BARBER, T. X. (1976). *Pitfalls in human research: Ten pivotal points.* Elmsford, NY: Pergamon Press.

BARGE, J. K., SCHLUETER, D. W., & PRITCHARD, A. (1989). The effects of nonverbal communication and gender on impression formation in opening statements. *Southern Communication Journal, 54,* 330–349.

BARKER, L. L. (1989). Evaluating research. In P. Emmert & L. L. Barker (Eds.), *Measurement of communication behavior* (pp. 68–83). White Plains, NY: Longman.

BARLEY, S. R. (1986). Technology as an occasion for structuring: Evidence from observation of CT scanners and the social order of radiology departments. *Administrative Science Quarterly, 31,* 78–108.

BARNLUND, D. C. (1968). *Interpersonal communication: Survey and Studies.* Boston: Houghton Mifflin.

BARNLUND, D. C. (1988). Communication in a global village. In L. A. Samovar & R. E. Porter (Eds.), *Intercultural communication: A reader* (5th ed.) (pp. 5–14). Belmont, CA: Wadsworth.

BAUMRIN, B. H. (1970). The immortality of irrelevance: The social role of science. In F. F. Korten, S. W. Cook, & J. I. Lacey (Eds.), *Psychology and the problems of society* (pp. 73–83). Washington, DC: American Psychological Association.

BAUMRIND, D. (1979). IRBs and social science research: The costs of deception. *IRB: A Review of Human Subjects Research, 1,* 1–4.

BAVELAS, J. B. (1983). Situations that lead to disqualification. *Human Communication Research, 9,* 130–145.

BAVELAS, J. B., BLACK, A., CHOVIL, N., LEMERY, C. R., & MULLETT, J. (1988). Form and function in motor mimicry: Topographic evidence that the primary function is communicative. *Human Communication Research, 14,* 275–300.

BAVELAS, J. B., & CHOVIL, N. (1986). How people disqualify: Experimental studies of spontaneous written disqualification. *Communication Monographs, 53,* 70–74.

BAVELAS, J. B., & SMITH, B. J. (1982). A method for scaling verbal disqualification. *Human Communication Research, 8,* 214–227.

BAXTER, L. A. (1979). Self-disclosure as a relationship disengagement strategy. *Human Communication Research, 5,* 215–222.

BAXTER, L. A. (1982). Strategies for ending relationships: Two studies. *Western Journal of Speech Communication, 46,* 223–241.

BAXTER, L. A. (1984). An investigation of compliance-gaining as politeness. *Human Communication Research, 10,* 427–456.

BAXTER, L. A., & BULLIS, C. (1986). Turning points in developing romantic relationships. *Human Communication Research, 12,* 469–494.

BAXTER, L. A., & WILMOT, W. W. (1983). Communication characteristics of relationships with differential growth rates. *Communication Monographs, 50,* 264–272.

BAXTER, L. A., & WILMOT, W. W. (1984). "Secret tests": Social strategies for acquiring information about the state of the relationship. *Human Communication Research, 11,* 171–201.

BECKER, C. S. (1987). Friendship between women: A phenomenological study of best friends. *Journal of Phenomenological Psychology, 18,* 59–72.

BELL, R. A. (1987). Social involvement. In J. C. McCroskey & J. A. Daly (Eds.), *Personality and interpersonal communication* (pp. 195–242). Newbury Park, CA: Sage.

BELL, R. A., & DALY, J. A. (1986). The affinity-seeking function of communication. *Communication Monographs, 51,* 70–74.

BELL, R. A., TREMBLAY, S. W., & BUERKEL-ROTHFUSS, N. L. (1987). Interpersonal attraction as a communication accomplishment: Development of a measure of affinity-seeking competence. *Western Journal of Speech Communication, 51,* 1–18.

BELLACK, A., KLIEBARD, H., HYMAN, R., & SMITH, F. (1966). *The language of the classroom.* New York: Teacher's College Press.

BEM, S. L. (1979). The measurement of psychological androgeny. *Journal of Consulting and Clinical Psychology, 42,* 155–162.

BENDERLY, B. L. (1981, March). The multilingual mind. *Psychology Today,* pp. 9–12.

BENIGER, J. R. (1987). The future study of public opinion: A symposium. *Public Opinion Quarterly, 51,* S173–S191.

BENSON, T. W. (1974). Rhetoric and autobiography: The case of Malcolm X. *Quarterly Journal of Speech, 60,* 1–13.

BENSON, D. & HUGHES, J. (1983). The perspective of ethnomethodology. New York: Longman.

BERELSON, B. (1952). *Content analysis in communications research.* New York: Free Press.

BERGEN, L. A., & WEAVER, D. (1988). Job satisfaction of daily newspaper journalists and organization size. *Newspaper Research Journal, 9,* 1–13.

BERGER, C. R. (1985). Editor's note. *Human Communication Research, 11,* 459.

BERGER, C. R., & BRADAC, J. J. (1982). *Language and social knowledge: Uncertainty in interpersonal relationships.* London: Edward Arnold.

BERGER, C. R., & CALABRESE, R. J. (1975). Some explorations in initial interaction and beyond: Toward a developmental theory of interpersonal communication. *Human Communication Research, 1,* 99–112.

BERGER, C. R., & CHAFFEE, S. H. (Eds.). (1987a). *Handbook of communication science.* Newbury Park, CA: Sage.

BERGER, C. R., & CHAFFEE, S. H. (1987b). The study of communication as a science. In C. R. Berger & S. H. Chaffee (Eds.), *Handbook of communication science* (pp. 15–19). Newbury Park, CA: Sage.

BERGER, C. R., & KELLERMANN, K. (1989). Personal opacity and social information gathering: Explorations in strategic communication. *Communication Research, 16,* 309–313.

BERLO D. J. (1955). Problems in communication research. *Central States Speech Journal, 7,* 3–7.

BERNE, E. (1972). *What do you say after you say hello? The psychology of human destiny.* New York: Grove Press.

BERRY, S. H., & KANOUSE, D. E. (1987). Physician response to a mailed survey: An experiment in timing of payment. *Public Opinion Quarterly, 51,* 102–114.

BERSCHEID, E., BARON, R. S., DERMER, M., & LEBMAN, M. (1973). Anticipating informed consent: An empirical approach. *American Psychologist, 28,* 913–925.

BERTHOLD, C. A. (1976). Kenneth Burke's cluster-agon method: Its development and an application. *Central States Speech Journal, 27,* 302–309.

BEVILLE, H. M., Jr. (1988). *Audience ratings: Radio, television, and cable.* Hillsdale, NJ: Erlbaum.

BILLIET, J., & LOOSVELDT, G. (1988). Improvement of the quality of responses to factual survey questions by interviewer training. *Public Opinion Quarterly, 52,* 190–211.

BLACK, E. (1965). *Rhetorical criticism: A study in method.* New York: Macmillan.

BLOOMFIELD, L. (1933). *Language.* New York: Holt, Rinehart and Winston.

BOCHNER, S. (1979). Designing unobtrusive field experiments in social psychology. In L. Sechrest (Ed.), *Unobtrusive measurement today* (pp. 33–46). San Francisco: Jossey-Bass.

BOGART, L. (1985). How U.S. newspapers are changing. *Journal of Communication, 35,* 82–90.

BOGDAN, R., & TAYLOR, S. J. (1975). *Introduction to qualitative research methods: A phenomenological approach to the social sciences.* New York: Wiley.

BOOTH-BUTTERFIELD, M., & JORDAN, F. (1989). Communication adaptation among racially homogenous and heterogeneous groups. *Southern Communication Journal, 14,* 253–272.

BOOTH-BUTTERFIELD, S. (1988). Inhibition and student recall of instructional messages. *Communication Education, 37,* 312–324.

BORMANN, E. H. (1972). Fantasy and rhetorical vision: The rhetorical criticism of reality. *Quarterly Journal of Speech, 58,* 396–407.

BORMANN, E. H. (1973). The Eagleton affair: A fantasy theme analysis. *Quarterly Journal of Speech, 59,* 143–159.

BORMANN, E. H. (1982). Colloquy I. Fantasy and rhetorical vision: Ten years later. *Quarterly Journal of Speech, 68,* 288–305.

BOSMAJIAN, H. A. (1974). The sources and nature of Adolph Hitler's techniques of persuasion. *Central States Speech Journal, 25,* 240–248.

BOSTER, F. J., & STIFF, J. B. (1984). Compliance-gaining message selection behavior. *Human Communication Research, 10,* 539–556.

BOTAN, C. H., & FREY, L. R. (1983). Do workers trust labor unions and their messages? *Communication Monographs, 50,* 233–244.

BOUCHARD, T. J. (1976). Field research methods: Interviewing, questionnaires, participant observation, systematic observation, unobtrusive measures. In M. E. Dunnette (Ed.), *Handbook of industrial and organizational psychology* (pp. 363–413). Skokie, IL: Rand McNally.

BOWEN, D. (1986). The role of identification in mentoring female protégées. *Group & Organizational Studies, 11,* 61–74.

BOWERS, J. W., & COURTRIGHT, J. A. (1984). *Communication research methods.* Glenview, IL: Scott, Foresman.

BOWERS, J. W., & OCHS, D. J. (1971). *The rhetoric of agitation and control.* Reading, MA: Addison-Wesley.

BRENNER, M. (1985). Intensive interviewing. In M. Brenner (Ed.), *The research interview* (pp. 147–162). London: Academic Press.

BRIM, O. (1966). Socialization through the life cycle. In O. Brim & S. Wheeler (Eds.), *Socialization after childhood.* New York: Wiley.

BRINBERG, D., & MCGRATH, J. E. (1985). *Validity and the research process.* Newbury Park, CA: Sage.

BROADUS, R. N. (1987). Toward a definition of "bibliometrics." *Sociometrics, 12,* 373–379.

BROCKRIEDE, W. (1974). Rhetorical criticism as argument. *Quarterly Journal of Speech, 60,* 165–174.

BROSS, I. B. J. (1953). *Design for decisions.* New York: Macmillan.

BROWN, B. R. (1970). Face-saving following experimentally induced embarrassment. *Journal of Experimental Social Phycology, 48,* 231–246.

BROWN, M. H. (1985). That reminds me of a story: Speech action in organizational socialization. *Western Journal of Speech Communication, 49,* 27–42.

BROWN, P., & LEVINSON, S. (1978). Universals in language usage: Politeness phenomena. In E. Goody (Ed.), *Questions and politeness: Strategies in social interaction* (pp. 256–289). Cambridge, MA: Harvard University Press.

BROWNLOW, P. C., & DAVIS, B. (1974). A certainty of honor: The eulogies of Adlai Stevenson. *Central States Speech Journal, 21,* 242–247.

BRUMMETT, B. (1975). Presidential substance: The address of August 15, 1973. *Western Speech, 39,* 249–259.

BRUMMETT, B. (1979). Gary Gilmore, power, and the rhetoric of symbolic forms. *Western Speech, 43,* 2–13.

BUDDENBAUM, J. M. (1988). The religion beat at daily newspapers. *Newspaper Research Journal, 9,* 57–70.

BULLIS, C., & BACH, B. W. (1989). Socialization turning points: An examination of change in organizational identification. *Western Journal of Speech Communication, 53,* 273–293.

BUONO, A. F., BOWDITCH, J. L., & LEWIS, J. W., III. (1985). When cultures collide: The anatomy of a merger. *Human Relations, 35,* 477–500.

BURGCHARDT, C. R. (1980). Two faces of American communism: Pamphlet rhetoric of the third period and the popular front. *Quarterly Journal of Speech, 66,* 375–391.

BURKE, K. (1945). *A grammar of motives.* Englewood Cliffs, NJ: Prentice-Hall.

BURKE, K. (1950). *A rhetoric of motives.* Englewood Cliffs, NJ: Prentice-Hall.

BURKE, K. (1966). *Language as symbolic action.* Berkeley: University of California Press.

BURGOON, J. K., & KOPER, R. J. (1984). Nonverbal and relational communication associated with reticence. *Human Communication Research, 10,* 601–626.

BURGOON, M., COHEN, M., MILLER, M. D., & MONTGOMERY, C. L. (1978). An empirical test of a model of resistance to persuasion. *Human Communication Research, 5,* 27–39.

BURGOYNE, J. G., & HODGSON, V. E. (1984). An experimental approach to understanding managerial action. In J. G. Hunt, D. Hosking, C. Schriesheim, & R. Stewart (Eds.), *Leaders and managers: International perspectives on mangerial behavior and leadership* (pp. 163–178). Elmsford, NY: Pergamon Press.

BURLESON, B. R. (1984). Comforting communication. In H. E. Sypher & J. L. Applegate (Eds.), *Communication by children and adults: Social cognitive and strategic processes* (pp. 63–104). Newbury Park, CA: Sage.

BURLESON, B. R., LEVINE, B. J., & SAMTER, W. (1984). Decision-making procedure and decision quality. *Human Communication Research, 10,* 557–574.

BYTWERK, R. L. (1975). Rhetorical aspects of the Nazi meeting, 1926–1933. *Quarterly Journal of Speech, 61,* 307–318.

BYTWERK, R. L. (1978). The rhetoric of defeat: Nazi propoganda in 1945. *Central States Speech Journal, 29,* 44–52.

CAHN, D. D., & HANFORD, J. T. (1984). Perspectives on human communication research: Behaviorism, phenomenology, and an integrated view. *Western Journal of Speech Communication, 48,* 277–292.

CAMDEN, C. T., & KENNEDY, C. W. (1986). Manager communicative style and nurse morale. *Human Communication Research, 12,* 551–563.

CAMPBELL, D. T., & STANLEY, J. C. (1963). *Experimental and quasi-experimental designs for research.* Skokie, IL: Rand McNally.

CAMPBELL, J. A. (1974). Charles Darwin and the crisis of ecology: A rhetorical perspective. *Quarterly Journal of Speech, 60,* 442–449.

CAMPBELL, J. A. (1975). The polemical Mr. Darwin. *Quarterly Journal of Speech, 61,* 375–390.

CAMPBELL, J. P., DAFT, R. L., & HULIN, C. L. (1982). *What to study: Generating and developing research questions.* Newbury Park, CA: Sage.

CAMPBELL, K. K. (1972). *Critiques of contemporary rhetoric.* Belmont, CA: Wadsworth.

CAMPBELL, K. K. (1973). The rhetoric of women's liberation: An oxymoron. *Quarterly Journal of Speech, 59,* 74–86.

CANARY, D. J., & SPITZBERG, B. H. (1989). A model of the perceived competence of conflict strategies. *Human Communication Research, 15,* 630–649.

CANNELL, C. F., & KAHN, R. L. (1968). Interviewing. In G. Lindzey & E. Aronson (Eds.), *Handbook of social psychology: Vol. II. Research methods* (2nd ed., pp. 526–595). Reading, MA: Addison-Wesley.

CAPELLA, J. (1979). Talk-silence sequence in informal conversation (I). *Human Communication Research, 6,* 3–17.

CAPELLA, J. (1980). Talk and silence sequences in informal conversations (II). *Human Communication Research, 6,* 130–145.

CAPELLA, J., & PLANALP, S. (1981). Talk and silence sequences in informal conversations (III): Interspeaker influence. *Human Communication Research, 7,* 117–132.

CAREY, M. S. (1978). Does civil inattention exist in pedestrian passing? *Journal of Personal and Social Psychology, 36,* 1185–1193.

CARMINES, E. G., & ZELLER, R. A. (1979). *Reliability and validity assessment.* Newbury Park, CA: Sage.

CASPI, D. (1984). On the control of media by politicians: A new perspective. *Political Communication and Persuasion, 2,* 263–269.

CEGALA, D. J. (1981). Interaction involvement: A cognitive dimension of communicative competence. *Communication Education, 30,* 109–121.

CEGALA, D. J., SAVAGE, G. T., BRUNNER, C. C., & CONRAD, A. B. (1982). An elaboration of the meaning of interaction involvement: Toward the development of a theoretical concept. *Communication Monographs, 50,* 229–248.

CHAFFEE, S. H., & BERGER, C. R. (1987). What communication scientists do. In C. R. Berger & S. H. Chaffee (Eds.), *Handbook of communication science* (pp. 99–122). Newbury Park, CA: Sage.

CHAPANIS, A. (1963). Engineering psychology. *Annual Review of Psychology, 14,* 285–318.

CHAPEL, W. G. (1975). Christian Science and the nineteenth century women's movement. *Central States Speech Journal, 40,* 191–203.

CHEN, G. (1989). Relationships of the dimensions of intercultural communication competence. *Communication Quarterly, 37,* 118–133.

CHOMSKY, N. (1957). *Syntactic structures.* The Hague: Mouton.

CHOMSKY, N. (1966). *Topics in the theory of generative grammar.* The Hague: Mouton.

CHRISTENSON, P. G., & PETERSON, J. B. (1988). Genre and gender in the structure of music preferences. *Communication Research, 15,* 282–301.

CHUBIN, D. W. (1983). *Sociology of sciences: An annotated bibliography on invisible colleges, 1972–1981.* New York: Garland.

CICOUREL, A. (1968). *The social organization of juvenile justice.* New York: Wiley.

CISSNA, K. N. (1982). Editor's note: What is applied communication research? *Journal of Applied Communication Research, 10,* (Editorial Statement).

CLARK, A. L., & WALLIN, P. (1964). The accuracy of husbands' and wives' reports of the frequency of marital coitus. *Population Studies, 18,* 165–173.

CLINE, R. (1982, May). *Revealing and relating: A review of self-disclosure theory and research.* Paper presented at the meeting of the International Communication Association, Boston.

CODY, M. J. (1982). A typology of disengagement strategies and an examination of the role intimacy, reactions to inequity, and relational problems play in strategy selection. *Communication Monographs, 49,* 148–170.

CODY, M. J., & MCLAUGHLIN, M. L. (1985). The situation as a construct in interpersonal communication research. In M. L. Knapp & G. R. Miller (Eds.), *Handbook of interpersonal communication* (pp. 263–312). Newbury Park, CA: Sage.

COHEN, B. (1963). *The press, the public and foreign policy.* Princeton, NJ: Princeton University Press.

COKER, D. A., & BURGOON, J. K. (1987). The nature of conversational involvement and nonverbal encoding patterns. *Human Communication Research, 13,* 463–494.

COLLINSON, D. L. (1988). "Engineering humour": Masculinity, joking and conflict in shop-floor relations. *Organization Studies, 9,* 181–189.

COMSTOCK, G. (1975). *Television and human behavior: The key studies.* Santa Monica, CA: Rand Corporation.

COOK, T. D., & CAMPBELL, D. T. (1979). *Quasi-experimentation: Design and analysis issues for field settings.* Boston: Houghton Mifflin.

COZBY, P. C. (1973). Self-disclosure: A literature review. *Psychological Bulletin, 79,* 73–91.

CRAGAN, J. F., & SHIELDS, D. C. (1981). *Applied communication research: A dramatistic approach.* Prospect Heights, IL: Waveland Press.

CRAIG, J. R., & REESE, S. C. (1973). Retention of raw data: A problem revisited. *American Psychologist, 28,* 723.

CRAIG, R. T., TRACY, K., & SPISAK, F. (1986). The discourse of requests: Assessment of a politeness approach. *Human Communication Research, 12,* 437–468.

CRAWFORD, L. (1986). Reluctant communitarians: Personal stories and commune behavior. *Communication Quarterly, 34,* 286–305.

CRONBACH, L. J. (1951). Coefficient alpha and the internal structure of tests. *Psychometrika, 16,* 297–334.

CRONBACH, L. J. & MEEHL, P. E. (1955). Construct validity in psychological tests. *Psychological Bulletin, 52,* 281–302.

CUPACH, W. R., & METTS, S. (1986). Accounts of relational dissolution: A comparison of marital and non-marital relationships. *Communication Monographs, 53,* 331–334.

CUPACH, W. R., METTS, S., & HAZELTON, V., Jr. (1986). Coping with embarrassing predicaments: Remedial strategies and their perceived utility. *Journal of Language and Social Psychology, 5,* 181–200.

DALY, J. A. (1987). Personality and interpersonal communication: Issues and directions. In J. C. McCroskey & J. A. Daly (Eds.), *Personality and interpersonal communication* (pp. 13–41). Newbury Park, CA: Sage.

DANCE, F. E. X. (1982). *Essays in human communication theory: A comparative overview.* In F. E. X. Dance (Ed.), *Human communication theory: Comparative essays* (pp. 286–299). New York: Harper & Row.

DANCE, F. E. X., & LARSON, C. E. (1976). *The functions of human communication: A theoretical approach.* New York: Holt, Rinehart and Winston.

DARLING, A. L. (1989). Signalling non-comprehensions in the classroom: Toward a descriptive typology. *Communication Education, 38,* 34–40.

DARNELL, D. K., & BROCKRIEDE, W. (1976). *Persons communicating.* Englewood Cliffs, NJ: Prentice-Hall.

DAWES, R. M., & SMITH, T. L. (1986). Attitude and opinion measurement. In G. Lindzey &

E. Aronson (Eds.), *Handbook of social psychology: Vol. 1. Theory and methods* (3rd ed., pp. 509–566). New York: Random House.

DEAKINS, A. H., OSTERINK, C., & HOEY, T. (1987). Topics in same sex and mixed sex conversations. In L. B. Nadler, M. J. Nadler, & W. R. Todd-Mancillas (Eds.), *Advances in gender and communication research* (pp. 89–108). Lanham, MD: University Press of America.

DENZIN, N. K. (1970). *The research act: A theoretical introduction to sociological methods.* Hawthorne, NY: Aldine.

DESMOND, R. J., SINGER, J. L., SINGER, D. G., CALAM, R., & COLIMORE, K. (1985). Family mediation patterns and television viewing: Young children's use and grasp of the medium. *Human Communication Research, 11,* 461–480.

DETURCK, M. A., & MILLER, G. R. (1985). Deception and arousal: Isolating the behavioral correlates of deception. *Human Communication Research, 12,* 181–202.

Dialog Information Services. (1989). *Dialog database catalog, 1989.* Palo Alto, CA: Author.

DIPBOYE, R. L., & FLANAGAN, M. F. (1979). Research settings in industrial and organizational psychology: Are findings in the field more generalizable than in the laboratory? *American Psychologist, 34,* 141–150.

DOELGER, J. A., HEWES, D. E., & GRAHAM, M. L. (1986). Knowing when to "second guess": The mindful analysis of messages. *Human Communication Research, 12,* 301–338.

DOUGLAS, J. D. (1985). *Creative interviewing.* Newbury Park, CA: Sage.

DOUGLAS, W. (1985). Anticipated interaction and information seeking. *Human Communication Research, 12,* 243–258.

DOUGLAS, W. (1987). Affinity-testing in initial interactions. *Journal of Social and Personal Relationships, 3,* 323–336.

DOVRING, K. (1954–1955). Quantitative semantics in 18th century Sweden. *Public Opinion Quarterly, 18,* 389–394.

DOWNS, C. W., CLAMPITT, P. G., & PFEIFFER, A. L. (1988). Communication and organizational outcomes. In G. M. Goldhaber & G. A. Barnett (Eds.), *Handbook of organizational communication* (pp. 171–212). Norwood, NJ: Ablex.

DU BOIS, C. N. (1963). *Time* magazine's fingerprints study. *Proceedings: 9th Conference, Advertising Research Foundation.* New York: Advertising Research Foundation.

DUNNING, D. G., & LANGE, B. M. (1989). Male and female dental students' interaction with patients: A test of sex differences. *Health Communication, 1,* 155–163.

EARLEY, P. C. (1984). Social interaction: The frequency of use and valuation in the United States, England, and Ghana. *Journal of Cross-cultural Psychology, 15,* 477–485.

EDDY, E. M., & PARTRIDGE, W. L. (1978). Development of applied anthropology in America. In E. M. Eddy & W. L. Partridge (Eds.), *Applied anthropology in America* (pp. 3–45). New York: Columbia University Press.

EICHLER, M. (1988). *Nonsexist research methods: A practical guide.* Boston: Allen & Unwin.

ELMER-DE WITT, P. (1989, April 17). Trying to tame A-bomb power. *Time,* p. 72.

ENOS, R. L. (1975). Cicero's forensic oratory: The manifestation of power in the Roman republic. *Southern Speech Communication Journal, 40,* 377–394.

ERICKSON, B. H., & NOSANCHUK, T. A. (1977). *Understanding data.* Toronto: McGraw-Hill Ryerson.

Ethical principles of psychologists. (1981). *American Psychologist, 36,* 633–638.

FARACE, R. V., MONGE, P. R., & RUSSELL, H. (1977). *Communicating and organizing.* Reading, MA: Addison-Wesley.

FARROW, J. M., FARROW, B. J., LOHSS, W. E., & TAUB, S. I. (1975). Intersubject communication as a contaminating factor in verbal conditioning. *Perceptual and Motor Skills, 40,* 975–982.

FELDMAN, J. J., HYMAN, H., & HART, C. W. (1951). A field study of interviewer effects on the quality of survey data. *Public Opinion Quarterly, 15,* 734–761.

FINE, G. A. (1980). Cracking diamonds: Observer role in Little League baseball settings and the acquisition of social competence. In W. Shaffir, R. A. Stebbins, & A. Turowitz (Eds.), *Fieldwork experience: Qualitative approaches to social research* (pp. 117–132). New York: St. Martin's Press.

FINN, S., & GORE, M. B. (1988). Social isolation and social support as correlates of television viewing motivations. *Communication Research, 15,* 135–158.

FISCHLI, R. (1979). Anita Bryant's stand against "militant homosexuality": Religious fundamentalism and the democratic process. *Central States Speech Journal, 30,* 262–271.

FISHER, B. A. (1970). Decision emergence: Phases in group decision making. *Speech Monographs, 37,* 55–66.

FISHER, B. A., (1978). *Perspectives on human communication.* New York: Macmillan.

FISHER, B. A., & HAWES, L. C. (1971). An interact system model: Generating a grounded theory of small groups. *Quarterly Journal of Speech, 57,* 444–453.

FISHER, D. V. (1986). Decision-making and self-disclosure. *Journal of Social and Personal Relationships, 3,* 323–336.

FISHER, J. Y. (1974). A Burkean analysis of the rhetorical dimensions of a multiple murder and suicide. *Quarterly Journal of Speech, 60,* 175–189.

FITZPATRICK, M. A. (1983). Predicting couples' communication from couples' self-reports. In R. Bostrum (Ed.), *Communication yearbook 7* (pp. 49–82). Newbury Park, CA: Sage.

FITZPATRICK, M. A., & DINDIA, K. (1986). Couples and other strangers: Talk time in spouse-stranger interaction. *Communication Research, 13,* 625–652.

FLANAGAN, J. C. (1954). The critical incident technique. *Psychological Bulletin, 51,* 327–358.

FLESCH, R. (1949). *The art of readable writing.* New York: Collier.

FOSS, S. K. (1979). Equal Rights Admendment controversy: Two worlds in conflict. *Quarterly Journal of Speech, 65,* 275–288.

FOX, R. J., CRASK, M. R., & KIM, J. (1988). Mail survey response rate: A meta-analysis of selected techniques for inducing response. *Public Opinion Quarterly, 52,* 467–491.

FRANKEL, M. R., & FRANKEL, L. R. (1987). Fifty years of survey sampling in the United States. *Public Opinion Quarterly, 51,* S127–S138.

FREY, L. R. (1988, November). *Meeting the challenges posed during the '70s: A critical review of small group communication research during the '80s.* Paper presented at the meeting of the Speech Communication Association, New Orleans.

FREY, L. R., & BOTAN, C. H. (1988). The status of instruction in introductory communication research methods. *Communication Education, 37,* 249–256.

FREY, L. R., & SNIDER, A. C. (1986, April). *The final frontier: The rhetoric of space exploration in President Kennedy's and Reagan's administrations.* Paper presented at the meeting of the Eastern Communication Association convention, Atlantic City, NJ.

FRIEDMAN, P. G., BOTAN, C. H., FREY, L. R., & KREPS, G. L. (1991). *Interpreting communication research.* Englewood Cliffs, NJ: Prentice Hall.

FRIES, C. (1952). *The structure of English.* New York: Humanities Press.

GALLOWAY, P. (1989, April 26). "African-American" or "black"? A poll of cultural identity. *Chicago Tribune,* pp. C1, C5.

GARDNER, P. (1975). Scales and statistics. *Review of Educational Research, 45,* 43–57.

GARFIELD, E., MALIN, M. V., & SMALL, H. G. (1978). Citation data as science indicators. In Y. Elkana, J. Lederberg, R. K. Merton, A. Thachary, & H. Zuckerman (Eds.), *Toward a metric of science: The advent of science indicators* (pp. 179–207). New York: Wiley.

GARFINKEL, H. (1967). *Studies in ethnomethodology.* Englewood Cliffs, NJ: Prentice-Hall.

GARNER, T. (1985). Instrumental interactions: Speech acts in daily life. *Central States Speech Journal, 36,* 229–238.

GEERTZ, C. (1988). *Works and lives: The anthropologist as author.* Stanford, CA: Stanford University Press.

GEPHART, R. P., Jr. (1988). *Ethnostatistics: Qualitative foundations for quantitative research.* Newbury Park, CA: Sage.

GERBNER, G. (1964). Ideological perspectives and political tendencies in news reporting. *Journalism Quarterly, 41,* 495–508.

GERBNER, G., GROSS, L., MORGAN, M., & SIGNORIELLI, N. (1986). Living with television: The dynamics of the cultivation process. In J. Bryant & D. Zillman (Eds.), *Perspectives on media effects* (pp. 17–40). Hillsdale, NJ: Erlbaum.

GERBNER, G., GROSS, L., SIGNORIELLI, N., MORGAN, M., & JACKSON-BEECK, M. (1979). *Violence profile no. 10: Trends in network television drama and view concepts of social reality, 1967–1978.* Philadelphia: University of Pennsylvania, Annenberg School of Communication.

GIFFIN, K. (1968). *The trust differential.* Lawrence: University of Kansas, Communication Research Center.

GIFFIN, K., & PATTON, B. R. (1974). *Personal communication in human relations.* Westerville, OH: Merrill.

GLASER, B. G., & STRAUSS, A. L. (1967). *The discovery of grounded theory: Strategies for qualitative research.* Hawthorne, NY: Aldine.

GLASSER, S. R., ZAMANOU, S., & HACKER, K. (1987). Measuring and interpreting organizational culture. *Management Communication Quarterly, 1,* 173–198.

GOETZ, J. P., & LE COMPTE, M. D. (1984). *Ethnography and qualitative design in educational research.* Orlando, FL: Academic Press.

GOFFMAN, E. (1961). *Asylums: Essays on the social situation of mental patients and other inmates.* Garden City, NY: Anchor/Doubleday.

GOLD, R. L. (1958). Roles in sociological field observations. *Social Forces, 36,* 217–223.

GOLDHABER, G. M., & BARNETT, G. A. (Eds.) (1988). *Handbook of organizational communication.* Norwood, NJ: Ablex.

GOLDHABER, G. M., & ROGERS, D. (1979). *Auditing organizational communication systems: The ICA communication audit.* Dubuque, IA: Kendall/Hunt.

Gorbachev's smile and shoeshine. (1989, June 18). *Chicago Tribune,* p. D2.

GRANOVETTER, M. S. (1976). Network sampling: Some first steps. *American Journal of Sociology, 81,* 1287–1303.

GREENBAUM, H. H., HELLWIG, S. A., & FALCIONE, R. L. (1988). Organizational communication evaluation: An overview, 1950–1981. In G. M. Goldhaber & G. A. Barnett (Eds.), *Handbook of organizational communication* (pp. 275–318). Norwood, NJ: Ablex.

GREENFIELD, P., GERBER, B., BEAGLES-ROOS, J., FARRAR, D., & GAT, I. (1981, April). *Television and radio experimentally compared: Effects of the medium on imagination and transmission of content.* Paper presented at the meeting of the Society for Research in Child Development, Boston.

GREENE, J. O., O'HAIR, H. D., CODY, M. J., & YEN, C. (1985). Planning and control of behavior during deception. *Human Communication Research, 11,* 335–364.

GRICE, H. P. (1975). Logic and conversation. In P. Cole & J. L. Morgan (Eds.), *Syntax and semantics: Vol. 3. Speech acts* (pp. 41–58). Orlando, FL: Academic Press.

GRIMSHAW, A. D. (1974). Data and data use in an analysis of communicative events. In R. Bauman & J. Sherzer (Eds.), *Explorations in the ethnography of speaking* (pp. 419–424). London: Cambridge University Press.

GRONBACH, B. (1975). Rhetorical history and rhetorical criticism. *Speech Teacher, 24,* 309–320.

GROSVERNOR, D., & GROSVERNOR, G. (1966, April). Ceylon. *National Geographic,* pp. 447–497.

GROVES, R. M. (1987). Research on survey data quality. *Public Opinion Quarterly, 51,* S156–S172.

GROVES, R. M. & KAHN, R. L. (1979). *Surveys by telephone: A national comparison with personal interviews.* Orlando, FL: Academic Press.

GRUNIG, J. E., & HUNT, T. (1984). *Managing public relations.* New York: Holt, Rinehart and Winston.

GUDYKUNST, W. B. (1985). An exploratory comparison of close intracultural and intercultural friendships. *Communication Quarterly, 33,* 270–283.

GUEST, L. (1947). A study of interviewer competence. *International Journal of Opinion and Attitude Research, 1,* 17–30.

GUILFORD, J. P. (1956). *Fundamental statistics in psychology and education.* New York: McGraw-Hill.

GUILFORD, J. P. (1959). *Personality.* New York: McGraw-Hill.

HACKMAN, J. D. (1985). Power and centrality in the allocation of resources in colleges and universities. *Administrative Science Quarterly, 30,* 61–77.

HAIMAN, F. S. (1949). An experimental study of the effects of ethos in public speaking. *Speech Monographs, 16,* 190–202.

HALL, C. S., & LINDZEY, G. (1970). *Theories of personality.* New York: Wiley.

HALL, E. (1966). *The hidden dimension.* New York: Random House.

HAMMERBACK, J. C., & JENSEN, R. J. (1980). The rhetorical worlds of César Chávez and Reies Tijerina. *Western Speech, 44,* 176–189.

HANSEN, M. H., HURWITZ, W. N., MARKS, E. S., & MAUDLIN, W. P. (1951). Response errors in surveys. *Journal of the American Statistical Association, 46,* 147–190.

HARPER, N., & HIROKAWA, R. (1988). A comparison of persuasive strategies used by female and male managers: 1. An examination of downward influence. *Communication Quarterly, 36,* 157–168.

HARRIS, Z. (1951). *Structural linguistics.* Chicago: University of Chicago Press.

HART, D., & DAMON, W. (1986). Developmental trends in self-understanding. *Social Cognition, 4,* 388–407.

HART, R. P., CARLSON, R. E., & EADIE, W. F. (1980). Attitudes toward communication and the assessment of rhetorical sensitivity. *Communication Monographs, 47,* 1–22.

HARTMAN, J. J., & HEDBLOM, J. H. (1979). *Methods for the social sciences: A handbook for students and non-specialists.* Westport, CT: Greenwood Press.

HARTMANN, D. P. (1982). Assessing the dependability of observational data. In D. P. Hartmann (Ed.), *Using observers to study behavior* (pp. 51–66). San Francisco: Jossey-Bass.

HAWES, L. C. (1975). *Pragmatics of analoguing: Theory and model construction in communication.* Reading, MA: Addison-Wesley.

HAWKINS, R. P., PINGREE, D., & ADLER, I. (1987). Searching for cognitive processes in the cultivation effect: Adult and adolescent samples in the United States and Australia. *Human Communication Research, 13,* 553–577.

HAYAKAWA, S. I. (1972). *Language in thought and action* (3rd ed.). Orlando, FL: Harcourt Brace Jovanovich.

HEETER, C. (1985). Program selection with abundance of choice: A process model. *Human Communication Research, 12,* 126–152.

HENDERSON, R. W. (1988). EVENTLOG: A tool for observational research. *Academic Computing, 2,* 36, 47.

HERITAGE, J. (1989). Current developments in conversation analysis. In D. Roger & P. Bull (Eds.), *Conversation: An interdisciplinary perspective* (pp. 21–47). Clevedon, England: Multilingual Matters.

HERMAN, E. S. (1985). Diversity of news: "Marginalizing" the opposition. *Journal of Communication, 35,* 135–146.

HILL, F. (1972). Conventional wisdom—traditional form: The president's message of November 3, 1969. *Quarterly Journal of Speech, 58,* 373–386.

HILLBRUNER, A. (1974). Archetype and signature: Nixon and the 1973 inaugural. *Central States Speech Journal, 25,* 169–181.

HILTZ, S. R., JOHNSON, K., & TUROFF, M. (1986). Experiments in group decision making: Communication processes and outcomes in face-to-face versus computerized conferences. *Human Communication Research, 13,* 225–252.

HIROKAWA, R. Y. (1980). A comparative analysis of communication patterns within effective and ineffective decision-making groups. *Communication Monographs, 47,* 312–321.

HIROKAWA, R. Y. (1982). Group communication and problem-solving effectiveness: 1. A critical review of inconsistent findings. *Communication Quarterly, 30,* 134–141.

HIROKAWA, R. Y. (1983). Group communication and problem-solving effectiveness: An investigation of group phases. *Human Communication Research, 9,* 291–305.

HIRSCH, E. D., Jr. (1967). *Validity and interpretation.* New Haven, CT: Yale University Press.

HOCHSTIM, J. R. (1967). A critical comparison of three strategies of collecting data from households. *Journal of the American Statistical Association, 62,* 976–989.

HOFFNER, C., CANTOR, J., & THORSON, E. (1988). Children's understanding of a televised narrative: Developmental differences in processing video and audio content. *Communication Research, 15,* 227–245.

HÖIJER, B. (1989). Television-evoked thoughts and their relation to comprehension. *Communication Research, 16,* 179–203.

HOLLIHAN, T. A., RILEY, P., & FREADHOFF, H. (1986). Arguing for justice: An analysis of arguing in small claims court. *Journal of the American Forensic Association, 22,* 187–195.

HOPE, D. S. (1975). Redefinition of self: A comparison of the rhetoric of the women's liberation and black liberation movements. *Today's Speech, 23,* 17–26.

HOPPER, R. (1981). The taken-for-granted. *Human Communication Research, 7,* 195–211.

HOPPER, R. (1989). Speech in telephone openings: Emergent interactions v. routines. *Western Journal of Speech Communication, 53,* 178–194.

HOUSTON, M. J., & NEVIN, J. R. (1977). The effects of source and appeal on mail survey response patterns. *Journal of Marketing Research, 14,* 374–378.

HSIA, H. J. (1988). *Mass communications research methods: A step-by-step approach.* Hillsdale, NJ: Erlbaum.

HUCK, S. W., CORMIER, W. H., & BOUNDS, W. G., Jr. (1974). *Reading statistics and research.* New York: Harper & Row.

HUFF, D. & GEIS, I. (1954). *How to lie with statistics.* New York: Norton.

HYMAN, H. H. (1954). *Interviewing in social research.* Chicago: University of Chicago Press.

INFANTE, D. A. (1987). Aggressiveness. In J. C. McCroskey & J. A. Daly (Eds.), *Personality and interpersonal communication* (pp. 157–192). Newbury Park, CA: Sage.

International encyclopaedia of communications. (1979). Oxford: Oxford University Press.

IVIE, R. L. (1974). Presidential motives for war. *Quarterly Journal of Speech, 60,* 337–345.

JABLIN, F. M., PUTNAM, L. L., ROBERTS, K. H., & PORTER, L. W. (1987). *Handbook of organizational communication: An interdisciplinary perspective.* Newbury Park, CA: Sage.

JABLONSKI, C. J. (1980). Promoting radical change in the Roman Catholic church: Rhetorical requirements, problems, and strategies of the American bishops. *Central States Speech Journal, 31,* 282–289.

JACKSON, S., & JACOBS, S. (1980). Structure of conversational argument: Pragmatic bases for the enthymeme. *Quarterly Journal of Speech, 66,* 251–265.

JACKSON-BEECK, M., & KRAUS, S. (1980). Political communication theory and research: An overview, 1978–1979. In D. D. Nimmo (Ed.), *Communication yearbook 4* (pp. 449–465). New Brunswick, NJ: Transaction Books.

JACOBS, J. B. (1974). Participant observation in prison. *Urban Life and Culture, 3,* 221–240.

JACOBS, S., & JACKSON, S. (1983). Conversational argument: A discourse analytic approach. In R. Cox & C. A. Willard (Eds.), *Advances in argumentation theory and research* (pp. 205–237). Carbondale: Southern Illinois University Press.

JAEGER, R. M. (1983). *Statistics: A spectator sport.* Newbury Park, CA: Sage.

JEFFERSON, G. (1978). Sequential aspects of storytelling in conversation. In J. Schenkein (Ed.), *Studies in the organization of conversational interaction* (pp. 219–248). Orlando, FL: Academic Press.

JENSEN, K. B. (1987). Qualitative audience research: Toward an integrative approach to reception. *Critical Studies in Mass Communication, 4,* 21-36.

JOHANNESEN, R. L. (1985). Ronald Reagan's economic jeremiad. *Central States Speech Journal, 37,* 79-89.

JOHANNESEN, R. L. (1986). An ethical assessment of the Reagan rhetoric, 1981-1982. In K. R. Sanders, L. L. Kaid, & D. Nimmo (Eds.), *Political communication yearbook 4* (pp. 226-241). Carbondale: Southern Illinois University Press.

JOHNSON, J. M. (1975). *Doing field research.* New York: Free Press.

JOHNSON, R. A., & WICHERN, D. W. (1988). *Applied multivariate statistical analysis* (2nd ed.). Englewood Cliffs, NJ: Prentice Hall.

JOHNSON, R. W., & ADAIR, J. G. (1972). Experimenter expectancy vs. systematic recording errors under automated and nonautomated stimulus presentation. *Journal of Experimental Research in Personality, 6,* 88-94.

JONES, S. E., & YARBROUGH, A. E. (1985). A naturalistic study of the meanings of touch. *Communication Monographs, 52,* 19-35.

JONES, W. H., & LANG, J. R. (1980). Sample composition bias and response bias in a mail survey: A comparison of inducement methods. *Journal of Marketing Research, 17,* 69-76.

JONES, W. H., & LINDA, G. (1978). Multiple criteria effects in a mail survey experiment. *Journal of Marketing Research, 15,* 280-284.

JORGENSEN, D. (1984). Divinatory discourse. *Symbolic interaction, 7,* 135-153.

JOURARD, S. M. (1971). *The transparent self.* New York: Van Nostrand Reinhold.

JUNG, J. (1969). Current practices and problems in the use of college students for psychological research. *Canadian Psychologist, 10,* 280-290.

KACHIGAN, S. K. (1986). *Statistical analysis: An interdisciplinary introduction to univariate and multivariate methods.* New York: Radius Press.

KAHN, R. L. (1979). Aging and social support. In M. W. Riley (Ed.), *Aging from birth to death* (pp. 71-91). Boulder, CO: Westview Press.

KAHNEMAN, D., & TVERSKY, A. (1982). Psychology of preference. *Scientific American, 247,* 161-173.

KAID, L. L., & WADSWORTH, A. J. (1989). Content analysis. In P. Emmert & L. L. Barker (Eds.), *Measurement of communication behavior* (pp. 197-217). White Plains, NY: Longman.

KAPLAN, A. (1964). *The conduct of inquiry.* New York: Harper & Row.

KARP, D. A. (1986). "You can take the boy out of Dorchester, but you can't take Dorchester out of the boy": Toward a psychology of social mobility. *Symbolic Interaction, 9,* 19-36.

KASSARJIAN, H. H. (1977). Content analysis in consumer research. *Journal of Consumer Research, 4,* 8-18.

KATULA, R. A. (1975). The apology of Richard M. Nixon. *Today's Speech, 23,* 1-6.

KAZDIN, A. E. (1982). Observer effects: Reactivity of direct observation. In D. P. Hartmann (Ed.), *Using observers to study behavior* (pp. 5-21). San Francisco: Jossey-Bass.

KELLEY, C. W., CHASE, L. J., & TUCKER, R. K. (1979). Replication in experimental communication research: An analysis. *Human Communication Research, 5,* 338-342.

KELLY, J. W. (1985). Storytelling in high tech organizations: A medium for sharing culture. *Journal of Applied Communication Research, 13,* 45-58.

KELMAN, H. C. (1967). Humane use of human subjects: The problem of deception in social psychological experiments *Psychological Bulletin, 67,* 1-11.

KENDALL, K. E. (1988). *Major directions of research in political communication: An overview.* Unpublished manuscript, State University of New York, Albany.

KENNEDY, C. W., & CAMDEN, C. T. (1983). A new look at interruptions. *Western Journal of Speech Communication, 47,* 45-58.

KENNEDY, J. J. (1952). An evaluation of extra-sensory perception. *Proceedings of the American Philosophical Society, 96,* 513-518.

KERCKEL, M. (1981). Tone units as message blocks in natural discourse: segmentation of face to face interaction by naive, native speakers. *Journal of Pragmatics, 5,* 459-476.

KERLINGER, F. N. (1973). *Foundations of behavioral research* (2nd ed.). New York: Holt, Rinehart and Winston.

KERLINGER, F. N. (1986). *Foundations of behavioral research* (3rd ed.). New York: Holt, Rinehart and Winston.

KIDDER, L. H. (1981). *Selltiz, Wrightsman and Cook's research methods in social relations* (4th ed). New York: Holt, Rinehart and Winston.

KIESLER, S., & SPROULL, L. S. (1986). Response effects in the electronic survey. *Public Opinion Quarterly, 50,* 402–413.

KIM, Y. Y. (1984). Searching for creating integration. In W. B. Gudykunst & Y. Y. Kim (Eds.), *Methods for intercultural communication research* (pp. 13–30). Newbury Park, CA: Sage.

KIMMEL, A. J. (1988). *Ethics and values in applied social research.* Newbury Park, CA: Sage.

KINSEY, A. C., POMEROY, W. B., MARTIN, C. E., & GEBHARD, P. H. (1953). *Sexual behavior in the human female.* Philadelphia: Saunders.

KIRK, J., & MILLER, M. L. (1986). *Reliability and validity in qualitative research.* Newbury Park, CA: Sage.

KISH, L. (1970). Some statistical problems in research design. In D. E. Morrison & R. E. Henkel (Eds.). *The significance test controversy: A reader* (pp. 127–141). Hawthorne, NY: Aldine.

KISH, L., & SLATER, C. W. (1960). Two studies of interviewer variance of socio-psychological variables. *Proceedings of the American Statistical Association, Social Science Section,* 66–70.

KNAPP, M. L., HART, R. P., & DENNIS, H. (1974). An exploration of deception as a communication construct. *Human Communication Research, 1,* 15–29.

KNAPP, M. L., HART, R. P., FRIEDRICH, G. W., & SHULMAN, G. M. (1973). The rhetoric of goodbye: Verbal and nonverbal correlates of human leave-taking. *Speech Monographs, 40,* 182–198.

KNAPP, M. L., HOPPER, R., & BELL, R. A. (1984). Compliments: A descriptive taxonomy. *Journal of Communication, 34,* 19–35.

KNAPP, M. L., & MILLER, G. R. (Eds.). (1985). *Handbook of interpersonal communication.* Newbury Park, CA: Sage.

KNAPP, M. L., STOHL, C., & REARDON, K. K. (1981). "Memorable" messages. *Journal of Communication, 31,* 27–41.

KOESTNER, R., & WHEELER, L. (1988). Self-presentation in personal advertisements: The influence of implicit notions of attraction and role expectations. *Journal of Social and Personal Relationships, 5,* 149–160.

KORZYBSKI, Q. (1948). *Science and sanity: An introduction to non-Aristotelian systems and general semantics* (3rd ed.). Lakeville, CT: International Non-Aristotelian Library Publishing Company.

KOSKI-JANNES, A. (1985). Alcohol and literary creativity: The Finnish experience. *Journal of Creative Behavior, 19,* 120–125.

KREPS, G. L. (1980). A field experimental test and revaluation of Weick's model of organizing. In D. D. Nimmo (Ed.), *Communication yearbook 4* (pp. 389–398). New Brunswick, NJ: Transaction Books.

KREPS, G. L. (1986). *Organizational communication.* White Plains, NY: Longman.

KRIPPENDORF, K. (1980). *Content analysis: An introduction to its methodology.* Newbury Park, CA: Sage.

KRIVONOS, P. D., & KNAPP, M. L. (1975). Initiating communication: What do you say when you say hello? *Central States Speech Journal, 26,* 115–125.

KUHN, T. S. (1970). *The structure of scientific revolutions.* Chicago: University of Chicago Press.

LABOV, W., & FANSHEL, D. (1977). *Therapeutic discourse: Psychotherapy as conversation.* New York: Free Press.

LABOVITZ, S., & HAGEDORN, R. (1971). *Introduction to social research.* New York: McGraw-Hill.

LANSING, J. B., & BLOOD, D. M. (1964). *The changing travel market* (Monograph No. 38). Ann Arbor: University of Michigan Survey Research Center.

LASLO, J. P., & ROSENTHAL, R. (1971). Subject dogmatism, experimenter status and experimenter expectancy effects. *Personality, 1,* 11-23.

LAZARSFELD, P. (1959). Problems in methodology. In R. K. Merton (Ed.), *Sociology today* (pp. 39-78). New York: Basic Books.

LEDERMAN, L. A. (1985). High communication apprehensives talk about communication apprehension and its effects on their behavior. *Communication Quarterly, 31,* 233-237.

LEE, B. S. (1988). Holocaust survivors and internal strengths. *Journal of Humanistic Psychology, 28,* 67-96.

LEFF, M. C., & MOHRMANN, G. P. (1974). Lincoln at Cooper Union: A rhetorical analysis of the test. *Quarterly Journal of Speech, 60,* 346-358.

LEVIN, J., & ARLUKE, A. (1987). *Gossip: The inside scoop.* New York: Plenum.

LEVINE, R. V., REIS, H. T., & WEST, L. J. (1980). Perceptions of time and punctuality in the United States and Brazil. *Journal of Personality and Social Psychology, 38,* 541-550.

LEVY-LEBOYER, C. (1988). Success and failure in applying psychology. *American Psychologist, 43,* 779-785.

LEWIN, K. (1947). Group decision and social change. In T. M. Newcomb & E. L. Hartley (Eds.), *Readings in social psychology.* New York: Holt, Rinehart and Winston.

LEWIN, K. (1951). *Field theory in social science.* Chicago: University of Chicago Press.

LEWIN, M. (1979). *Understanding psychological research.* New York: Wiley.

LEWIS, W. (1989). Readership of buried ads versus ads placed next to editorial copy. *Newspaper Research Journal, 10,* 55-66.

LIEVROUW, L. A. (1988). Four programs of research in scientific communication. *Knowledge in Society, 1,* 6-22.

LIEVROUW, L. A. (1989). *Bibliometrics in communication research.* Unpublished manuscript, Rutgers University.

LIKERT, R. (1932). A technique for the measurement of attitudes. *Archives of Psychology, 140,* 1-55.

LINCOLN, Y. S., & GUBA, E. G. (1985). *Naturalisitc inquiry.* Newbury Park, CA: Sage.

LINDKVIST, K. (1981). Approaches to textual analysis. In K. E. Rosengren (Ed.), *Advances in content analysis* (pp. 23-42). Newbury Park, CA: Sage.

LINZ, D., DONNERSTEIN, E., & ADAMS, S. M. (1989). Physiological desensitization and judgments about female victims of violence. *Human Communication Research, 15,* 509-522.

LIPSET, S. M., TROW, M. A., & COLEMAN, J. S. (1970). Statistical problems. In D. E. Morrison & R. E. Henkel (Eds.), *The significance test controversy: A reader* (pp. 81-86). Hawthorne, NY: Aldine.

LITTLEJOHN, S. W. (1987). *Theories of human communication* (3rd ed.). Belmont, CA: Wadsworth.

LIVINGSTONE, S. M. (1987). The implicit representation of characters in *Dallas:* A multidimensional scaling approach. *Human Communication Research, 13,* 399-420.

LOFLAND, J. (1971). *Analyzing social settings.* Belmont, CA: Wadsworth.

LOFLAND, J. (1976). *Doing social life.* New York: Wiley.

LOFTUS, E. F. (1979). *Eyewitness testimony.* Cambridge, MA: Harvard University Press.

LYKKEN, D. T. (1968). Statistical significance in psychological research. *Psychological Bulletin, 21,* 151-159.

MACHUNGWA, P. D., & SCHMITT, N. (1983). Work motivation in a developing country. *Journal of Applied Psychology, 68,* 31-42.

MACKAY, A. L. (1977). *The harvest of a quiet eye: A selection of scientific quotations.* London: Institute of Physics.

MARKEL, N., LONG, J., & SAINE, T. (1976) Sex effects in conversational interaction: Another look at male dominance. *Human Communication Research, 2,* 356–364.

MARRIONE, T. J. (1985). Situated interaction. In H. A. Farberman & R. S. Perinbanayagam (Eds.), *Studies in symbolic logic* (pp. 161–192). Greenwich, CT: JAI Press.

MARTIN, J., FELDMAN, M. S., HATCH, M. J., & SITIKIN, S. B. (1983). The uniqueness paradox in organizational stories. *Administrative Science Quarterly, 28,* 438–453.

MARTIN, M. F., GELFAND, D. M., & HARTMANN, D. P. (1971). Effects of adult and peer observers on boys' and girls' responses to an aggressive model. *Child Development, 42,* 1271–1275.

MARWELL, G., & SCHMITT, D. R. (1967). Dimensions of compliance-gaining behavior: An empirical analysis. *Sociometry, 30,* 350–364.

MASHETER, C., & HARRIS, L. M. (1986). From divorce to friendship: A study of dialectic relationship development. *Journal of Social and Personal Relationships, 3,* 177–189.

MATLON, R. J. (1987). *Index to journals in communication studies through 1985.* Annandale, VA: Speech Communication Association.

MAYNARD, D. W. (1985). How children start arguments. *Language and Society, 14,* 1–30.

McCROSKEY, J. C. (1977). Oral communication apprehension: A summary of recent theory and research. *Human Communication Research, 4,* 78–96.

McCROSKEY, J. C., & RICHMOND, V. P. (1987). Willingness to communicate. In J. C. McCroskey & J. A. Daly (Eds.), *Personality and interpersonal communication* (pp. 129–156). Newbury Park, CA: Sage.

McDIARMID, J. (1937). Presidential inaugural addresses: A study in verbal symbols. *Public Opinion Quarterly, 1,* 79–82.

McKILLIP, J. (1987). *Need analysis: Tools for the human services and education.* Newbury Park, CA: Sage.

McLAUGHLIN, M. L. (1984). *Conversation: How talk is organized.* Newbury Park, CA: Sage.

McLAUGHLIN, M. L., & CODY, M. J. (1982). Awkward silences: Behavioral antecedents and consequences of the conversational lapse. *Human Communication Research, 8,* 299–316.

McLAUGHLIN, M. L., CODY, M. J., KANE, M. L. & ROBEY, C. S. (1981). Sex differences in story receipt and story sequencing behaviors in dyadic conversations. *Human Communication Research, 7,* 99–116.

McLAUGHLIN, M. L., CODY, M. J., & O'HAIR, H. D. (1983). The management of failure events: Some contextual determinants of accounting behavior. *Human Communication Research, 9,* 208–224.

McLAUGHLIN, M. L., CODY, M. J., & ROBEY, C. S. (1980). Situational influences on the selection of strategies to resist compliance-gaining attempts. *Human Communication Research, 7,* 14–36.

McLAUGHLIN, M. L., CODY, M. J., & ROSENSTEIN, N. E. (1983). Account sequences in conversations between strangers. *Communication Monographs, 50,* 102–125.

McNEMAR, Q. (1960). Opinion-attitude methodology. *Psychological Bulletin, 53,* 289–374.

McQUAIL, D. (1987). Functions of communication: A nonfunctionalist overview. In C. R. Berger & S. H. Chaffee (Eds.), *Handbook of communication science* (pp. 327–349). Newbury Park, CA: Sage.

McQUILLEN, J. S. (1986). The development of listener-adapted compliance-resisting strategies. *Human Communication Research, 12,* 354–375.

MEADOWCROFT, J. M., & REEVES, B. (1989). Influence of story schema development on children's attention to television. *Communication Research, 16,* 314–351.

MEHAN, H. (1983). The role of language and the language of role in institutional decision making. *Language and Society, 12,* 187–211.

MERRILL, J. C. (1987). Governments and press control: Global attitudes on journalistic matters. *Political Communication and Persuasion, 4,* 223–262.

MERTON, R. K., FISKE, M., & KENDALL, P. L. (1956). *The focused interview.* New York: Free Press.

METTS, S. (1989). An exploratory investigation of deception in close relationships. *Journal of Social and Personal Relationships, 6,* 159-179.

MIALL, C. E. (1986). The stigma of involuntary childlessness. *Social Problems, 33,* 268-279.

MILES, M. B., & HUBERMAN, A. M. (1984). *Qualitative data analysis: A sourcebook of new methods.* Newbury Park, CA: Sage.

MILGRAM, S. (1963). Behavioral study of obedience. *Journal of Abnormal and Social Psychology, 69,* 137-143.

MILLAR, F. E., ROGERS, L. E., & BAVELAS, J. B. (1984). Identifying patterns of verbal conflict in interpersonal dynamics. *Western Journal of Speech Communication, 48,* 231-246.

MILLER, B., & HUMPHREYS, L. (1980). Keeping in touch: Maintaining contact with stigmatized subjects. In W. B. Shaffir, R. A. Stebbins, & A. Turowitz (Eds.), *Fieldwork experience: Qualitative approaches to social research* (pp. 212-222). New York: St. Martin's Press.

MILLER, G. (1987). Producing family problems: Organization and uses of the family perspective and rhetoric in family therapy. *Symbolic Interaction, 10,* 245-265.

MILLER, G. R., & BOSTER, F. J. (1989). Data analysis in communication research. In P. Emmert & L. L. Barker (Eds.), *Measurement of communication behavior* (pp. 18-39). White Plains, NY: Longman.

MILLER, J. B. (1987). Sex differences in interaction management and goals. In L. B. Nadler, M. J. Nadler, & W. R. Todd-Mancillas (Eds.), *Advances in gender and communication research* (pp. 109-126). Lanham, MD: University Press of America.

MILLER, K. I., & MONGE, P. R. (1985). Social information and employee anxiety about organizational change. *Human Communication Research, 11,* 365-386.

MOOK, D. G. (1983). In defense of external invalidity. *American Psychologist, 38,* 379-387.

MOONEY, H. W. (1962). *Methodology in two California health surveys* (Public Health Monograph No. 70). Washington, DC: GPO.

MOORE, H. T. (1922). Further data concerning sex differences. *Journal of Abnormal Social Psychology, 17,* 210-214.

MOTLEY, M. T., & SMITH, N. L. (1989). Effects of temperament upon hiring decisions: A preliminary examination of global personality traits and communicator compatibility. *Communication Reports, 2,* 22-29.

MOYLAN, M. J. (1988, August 28). Proposal to use data from Nazi death tests ignites new debate. *Chicago Tribune,* p. A6.

MULAC, A., STUDLEY, L. B., WIEMANN, J. W., & BRADAC, J. J. (1987). Male/female gaze in same-sex and mixed-sex dyads: Gender-linked differences and mutual influence. *Human Communication Research, 13,* 323-344.

MURPHY, E. F. (1978). *Webster's treasury of relevant quotes.* New York: Greenwich House.

MURPHY, J. T. (1980). *Getting the facts: The fieldwork guide for evaluators and policy analysts.* Santa Monica, CA: Goodyear.

NICHOLS, R., & STEVENS, L. (1957). Listening to people. *Harvard Business Review, 35,* 85-92.

NIMMO, D. D., & SANDERS, K. R. (Eds.). (1981). *Handbook of political communication.* Newbury Park, CA: Sage.

NISBETT, R. E., & ROSS, L. (1980). *Human inference: Strategies and shortcomings of social judgment.* Englewood Cliffs, NJ: Prentice-Hall.

NOFSINGER, R. E. (1975). The demand ticket: A conversational device for getting the floor. *Speech Monographs, 42,* 1-9.

NORTON, R. W. (1978). Foundation of a communicator style construct. *Human Communication Research, 4,* 99-112.

NORTON, R. W. (1983). *Communicator style.* Newbury Park, CA: Sage.

NOTARIUS, C. I., & GERRICK, L. R. (1988). Listener response strategies to a distressed other. *Journal of Social and Personal Relationships, 5,* 97-108.

Nunnally, J. C. (1978). *Psychometric theory.* New York: McGraw-Hill.

Ogilvie, J. R., & Haslett, B. (1985). Communicating peer feedback in a task group. *Human Communication Research, 12,* 54–78.

O'Hair, H. D., Cody, M. J., Goss, B., & Krayer, K. (1988). The effect of gender, deceit orientation and communicator style on macro-assessments of honesty. *Communication Quarterly, 36,* 77–93.

O'Hair, H. D., Kreps, G. L., & Frey, L. R. (1990). Conceptual issues. In H. D. O'Hair & G. L. Kreps (Eds.), *Handbook of applied communication* (pp. 3–27). Hillsdale, NJ: Erlbaum.

O'Leary, K. D., & Kent, R. N. (1973). Behavior modification for social action: Research tactics and problems. In L. A. Hamerlynck, L. C. Handy, & E. J. Mash (Eds.) *Behavior change: Methodology, concepts, and practice* (pp. 69–96). Campaign, IL: Research Press.

O'Leary, K. D., Kent, R. N., & Kanowitz, J. (1975). Shaping data collection congruent with experimental hypotheses. *Journal of Applied Behavior Analysis, 8,* 43–51.

Osgood, C. E., Suci, C. J., & Tannenbaum, P. H. (1957). *The measurement of meaning.* Urbana: University of Illinois Press.

Owen, W. F. (1984). Teacher classroom management communication: A qualitative study. *Communication Education, 33,* 127–141.

Paisley, W. J. (1965). *The flow of (behavioral) scientific information: A review of the research literature.* Stanford, CA: Stanford University, Institute for Communication Research.

Paisley, W. J. (1984). Communication in the communication sciences. In B. Dervin & M. J. Voigt (Eds.), *Progress in communication sciences* (pp. 1–43). Norwood, NJ: Ablex.

Papa, M. J., & Natalle, E. J. (1989). Gender, strategy selection, and discussion satisfaction in interpersonal conflict. *Western Journal of Speech Communication, 53,* 260–272.

Parker, E. B. (1963). The effects of television on public library circulation. *Public Opinion Quarterly, 27,* 578–589.

Parker, E. B., Paisley, W. J., & Garrett, R. (1967). *Bibliographic citations as unobtrusive measures of scientific communication.* Stanford, CA: Stanford University, Institute for Communication Research.

Patton, B. R., Giffin, K., & Patton, E. N. (1989). *Decision-making group interaction* (3rd ed.). New York: Harper & Row.

Patton, M. Q. (1980). *Qualitative evaluation methods.* Newbury Park, CA: Sage.

Paulson, S. F. (1980). Speech communication and survival of academic disciplines. *Communication Education, 29,* 319–323.

Peacock, J. L. (1986). *The anthropological lens: Harsh light, soft focus.* Cambridge: Cambridge University Press.

Petersen, C. (1989, August 8). For heaven's sake: Astronomers (don't ask, "what's your sign?") break out their "astrology defense kits." *Chicago Tribune,* pp. E1, E5.

Peterson, R. A. (1975). An experimental investigation of mail-survey responses. *Journal of Business Research, 3,* 199–209.

Petronio, S. A. (1984). Communication strategies to reduce embarrassment. *Western Journal of Speech Communication, 48,* 28–38.

Pettegrew, L. S., & Turkat, I. D. (1986). How patients communicate about their illness. *Human Communication Research, 12,* 376–394.

Pettey, G. R. (1988). The interaction of the individual's social environment, attention and interest, and public affairs media use on political knowledge holding. *Communication Research, 15,* 265–281.

Pfau, M., & Burgoon, M. (1988). Inoculation in political campaign communication. *Human Communication Research, 15,* 91–111.

Philipsen, G. (1975). Speaking "like a man" in Teamsterville: Cultural patterns of role enactment in an urban neighborhood. *Quarterly Journal of Speech, 61,* 13–22.

PHILIPSEN, G. (1989). An ethnographic approach to communication studies. In B. Dervin, L. Grossberg, B. J. O'Keefe, & E. Wartella (Eds.). *Rethinking communication: Vol. 2. Paradigm exemplars* (pp. 258–268). Newbury Park, Ca: Sage.

PILIAVIN, I. M., RODIN, J., & PILIAVIN, J. A. (1969). Good samaritanism: An underground phenomenon? *Journal of Personality and Social Psychology, 13,* 289–299.

PINFIELD, L. T. (1986). A field evaluation of perspectives on organizational decision-making. *Administrative Science Quarterly, 31,* 365–388.

PINGREE, S. (1986). Children's activity and television comprehensibility. *Communication Research, 13,* 239–256.

POLISKY, J. B., & WOLPAW, F. R. (1972). Jewish statehood legitimated: Abba Hiller Silver at the American Jewish Conference. *Quarterly Journal of Speech, 58,* 209–216.

POMERANTZ, A. (1978). Compliment responses: Notes on the co-operations of multiple constraints. In J. Schenkein (Ed.), *Studies in the organization of conversational interaction* (pp. 79–112). Orlando, FL: Academic Press.

POOL, I. de S., FREY, F. W., SCHRAMM, W. L., MACCOBY, N., & PARKER, E. B. (Eds.). (1973). *Handbook of communication.* Skokie, IL: Rand McNally.

POOLE, M. S. (1981). Decision development in small groups (I): A comparison of two models. *Communication Monographs, 48,* 1–24.

POOLE, M. S. (1988, May). *Do we have any theories of group communication?* Paper presented at the meeting of the International Communication Association, New Orleans.

POOLE, M. S., FOLGER, J. P., & HEWES, D. E. (1987). Analyzing interpersonal interaction. In M. E. Roloff & G. R. Miller (Eds.), *Interpersonal processes: New directions in communication research* (pp. 220–256). Newbury Park: CA: Sage.

POOLE, M. S., & McPHEE, R. D. (1985). Methodology in interpersonal communication research. In M. L. Knapp & G. R. Miller (Eds.), *Handbook of interpersonal communication* (pp. 100–170). Newbury Park, CA: Sage.

POOLE, M. S., & ROTH, J. (1989). Decision development in small groups (V): Test of a contingency model. *Human Communication Research, 15,* 549–589.

PORTER, R. E., & SAMOVAR, L. A. (1988). Approaching intercultural communication. In L. A. Samovar & R. E. Porter (Eds.), *Intercultural communication: A reader* (5th ed., pp. 15–30). Belmont, CA: Wadsworth.

POTTER, W. H., & WARE, W. (1987). An analysis of the contexts of antisocial acts on prime-time television. *Communication Research, 14,* 664–686.

PRITCHARD, A. (1969). Statistical bibliography or bibliometrics? *Journal of Documentation, 25,* 358–359.

PUTNAM, L., & GEIST, P. (1985). Argument in bargaining: An analysis of the reasoning process. *Southern Speech Communication Journal, 50,* 225–245.

PUTNAM, L., & SORENSON, R. L. (1982). Equivocal messages in organizations. *Human Communication Research, 8,* 114–132.

RAGAN, S. L., & HOPPER, R. (1984). Ways to leave your lover: A conversational analysis of literature. *Communication Quarterly, 32,* 310–319.

RASHKIS, H., & WALLACE, A. F. C. (1959). The reciprocal effect. *Archives of General Psychiatry, 1,* 489–498.

RAWLINS, W. K., & HOLL, M. (1987). The communicative achievement of friendship during adolescence: Predicaments of trust and violation. *Western Journal of Speech Communication, 51,* 354–363.

RAY, G. B. (1986). Vocally cued personality prototypes: An implicit personality theory approach. *Communication Monographs, 53,* 266–276.

REESE, H. W., & FREMOUW, W. J. (1984). Normal and normative ethics in behavioral sciences. *American Psychologist, 39,* 863–876.

REEVES, B., & BORGMAN, C. L. (1983). A bibliographic evaluation of core journals in communication research. *Human Communication Research, 10,* 119–136.

REEVES, B., & GARRAMONE, G. M. (1983). Television's influence on children's encoding of person information. *Human Communication Research, 10,* 257–268.

REEVES, B., LANG, A. THORSON, E., & ROTHSCHILD, M. (1989). Emotional television scenes and hemispheric specialization. *Human Communication Research, 15,* 493–508.

REID, J. B. (1982). Observer training in naturalistic research. In D. P. Hartmann (Ed.), *Using observers to study behavior* (pp. 37–50). San Francisco: Jossey-Bass.

REINARD, J. C. (1988). The empirical study of the persuasive effects of evidence: The status after fifty years of research. *Human Communication Research, 15,* 3–59.

RICE, R. E., BORGMAN, C. L., & REEVES, B. (1988). Citation networks of communication journals, 1977–1985: Cliques and positions, citations made and citations received. *Human Communication Research, 15,* 256–283.

RICHES, S. V., & SILLARS, M. O. (1980). The status of movement criticism. *Western Speech, 44,* 275–287.

RICHMOND, V. P., DAVIS, L. M., SAYLOR, K., & McCROSKEY, J. C. (1984). Power strategies in organizations: Communication techniques and messages. *Human Communication Research, 11,* 85–108.

RICHMOND, V. P., GORHAM, J. S., & FURIO, B. J. (1987). Affinity-seeking communication in collegiate male-female relationships. *Communication Quarterly, 35,* 334–348.

RITTI, R. R., & SILVER, J. H. (1986). Early processes of institutionalization: The dramaturgy of exchange in interorganizational relations. *Administrative Science Quarterly, 31,* 25–42.

ROETHLISBERGER, F. J., & DICKSON, W. J. (1939). *Management and the worker.* Cambridge, MA: Harvard University Press.

ROGERS, E., & AGARWALA-ROGERS, R. (1976). *Communication in organizations.* New York: Free Press.

ROGERS, L. E., & FARACE, R. V. (1975). Relational communication analysis: New measurement techniques. *Human Communication Research, 1,* 222–239.

ROSCOE, J. T. (1975). *Fundamental research statistics for the behavioral sciences.* New York: Holt, Rinehart and Winston.

ROSECRANCE, J. (1986). Racetrack buddy relations: Compartmentalized and satisfying. *Journal of Social and Personal Relations, 3,* 441–456.

ROSENBLUM, L. A. (1978). Effects of adults on peer interactions. *Genesis of Behavior, 2,* 195–217.

ROSENTHAL, R. (1965). The volunteer subject. *Human Relations, 18,* 403–404.

ROSENTHAL, R. (1966). *Experimenter effects in behavioral research.* Norwalk, CT: Appleton & Lang.

ROSENTHAL, R., & ROSNOW, R. L. (1969). The volunteer subject. In R. Rosenthal & R. L. Rosnow (Eds.), *Artifact in behavioral research* (pp. 59–118). Orlando, FL: Academic Press.

ROSSITER, C. M. (1976). The validity of communication experiments using human subjects: A review. *Human Communication Research, 2,* 197–206.

ROTH, J. A. (1966). Hired hand research. *American Sociologist, 1,* 190–196.

ROTHSCHILD, M. L., THORSEN, E., REEVES, B., HIRSCH, J. E., & GOLDSTEIN, R. (1986). EEG activity and the processing of television commercials. *Communication Research, 13,* 182–220.

ROY, D. (1959-1960). Banana time: Job satisfaction and informal interaction. *Human Organization, 18,* 158–168.

RUBEN, B. D. (1988). *Communication and human behavior* (2nd ed.). New York: Macmillan.

RUBIN, A. M. (1979). Television use by children and adolescents. *Human Communication Research, 5,* 109–120.

RUBIN, A. M., PERSE, E. M., & TAYLOR, D. S. (1988). A methodological examination of cultivation. *Communication Research, 15,* 107–134.

RUBIN, R. B., PERSE, E. M., & BARBATO, C. A. (1988). Conceptualization and measurement of interpersonal communication motives. *Human Communication Research, 14,* 602–628.

RUBIN, R. B., RUBIN, A. M., & PIELE, L. J. (1986). *Communication research: Strategies and sources.* Belmont, CA: Wadsworth.

RUESCH, J., & BATESON, G. (1951). *Communication: The social matrix of society.* New York: Norton.

RUMELHART, M. (1983). When in doubt: Strategies used in response to uncertainty. *Discourse Processes, 6,* 377–402.

RUNCO, M. A., & PEZDEK, K. (1984) The effect of television and radio on children's creativity. *Human Communication Research, 11,* 109–120.

SABLE, A. (1978). Deception in social science research: Is informed consent possible? *Hastings Center Report, 8,* 40–46.

SALANCKI, G. R. (1979). Field stimulation for organizational behavior research. *Administrative Science Quarterly, 24,* 638–649.

SAMTER, W., & BURLESON, B. R. (1984). Cognitive and motivational influences on spontaneous comforting behavior. *Human Communication Research, 11,* 231–260.

SAPIR, E. (1964). *Language and personality.* Berkeley: University of California Press.

SCHATZMAN, L., & STRAUSS, A. L. (1973). *Field research: Strategies for a natural sociology.* Englewood Cliffs, NJ: Prentice-Hall.

SCHENCK-HAMLIN, W. J. (1978). The effects of dialectical similarity, stereotyping, and message agreement on interpersonal perception. *Human Communication Research, 5,* 15–26.

SCHENKLER, B. R. (1985). Introduction: Foundations of the self in social life. In B. R. Schenkler (Ed.), *The self and social life* (pp. 1–21). New York: McGraw-Hill.

SCHIAVONE, N. P. (1984). Guilt by association: The dilemma of phony polls. *Proceedings of the Second Advertising Research Quality Workshop.* New York: Advertising Research Foundation.

SCHIFFRIN, D. (1977). Opening encounters. *American Sociological Review, 42,* 679–691.

SCHILIT, W. K. (1987). Upward influence activity in strategic decision making: An examination of organizational differences. *Group and Organizational Studies, 12,* 343–368.

SCHONBACH, P. (1980). A category system for account phases. *European Journal of Social Psychology, 10,* 195–200.

SCHULTZ, B. (1982). Argumentativeness: Its effect in group decision-making and its role in leadership perception. *Communication Quarterly, 30,* 368–375.

SCHWARTZ, H., & JACOBS, J. (1979). *Qualitative sociology: A method to the madness.* New York: Free Press.

SCOTT, W. A. (1955). Reliability of content analysis: The case for nominal scale coding. *Public Opinion Quarterly, 19,* 321–325.

SELVIN, H. C. (1970). A critique of tests of significance in survey research. In D. E. Morrison & R. E. Henkel (Eds.), *The significance test controversy: A reader* (pp. 94–106). Hawthorne, NY: Aldine.

SHANNON, C., & WEAVER, W. (1949). *The mathematical theory of communication.* Urbana: University of Illinois Press.

SHEATSLEY, P. B. (1947). Some uses of interviewer-report forms. *Public Opinion Quarterly, 11,* 601–611.

SHERZER, J. (1983). *Kuna ways of speaking.* Austin: University of Texas Press.

SHIELDS, E. (1974). The rhetoric of emerging nationalism: A case study in Irish rhetorical failure. *Central States Speech Journal, 25,* 225–232.

SHIMANOFF, S. B. (1980). *Communication rules: Theory and research.* Newbury Park, CA: Sage.

SHIMANOFF, S. B. (1984). The portrayal of conversation in "Cathy" cartoons: A heuristic tool for rules research. In R. N. Bostrum (Ed.), *Communication yearbook 8* (pp. 788–799). Newbury Park, CA: Sage.

SHIMANOFF, S. B. (1985). Expressing emotions in words: Verbal patterns of interaction. *Journal of Communication, 35,* 16–28.

SHUMAN, A. (1986). *Storytelling rights: The use of oral and written texts by urban adolescents.* Cambridge, MA: Harvard University Press.

SIGMAN, S. (1986). Adjustment to the nursing home as a social interactional accomplishment. *Journal of Applied Communication Research, 14,* 37–58.

SILLARS, A. L. (1980). Attribution and communication in roomate conflicts. *Communication Monographs, 47,* 180–200.

SILLARS, A. L., COLETTI, S. F., PARRY, D., & ROGERS, M. A. (1982). Coding verbal conflict tactics: Nonverbal and perceptual correlates of the "avoidance-distributive-integrative" distinction. *Human Communication Research, 9,* 83–95.

SILLARS, A. L., WEISBERG, J., BURGGRAF, C. S., & WILSON, E. A. (1985). Content themes in marital communication. *Human Communication Research, 10,* 427–456.

SILVERMAN, I. (1968). The effects of experimenter outcome expectancy on latency of word association. *Journal of Clinical Psychology, 24,* 718–721.

SITARAM, K. S., & COGDELL, R. T. (1979). *Foundations of intercultural communication.* Websterville, OH: Merrill.

SMALL, H. G. (1973). Co-citation in the scientific literature: A new measure of the relationship between two documents. *Journal of the American Society for Information Science, 24,* 265–269.

SMART, R. G. (1966). Subject selection bias in psychological research. *Canadian Psychologist, 7,* 115–121.

SMITH, A. D., & REID, W. J. (1986). *Role-sharing marriage.* New York: Columbia University Press.

SMITH, K. A. (1988). Effects of coverage on neighborhood and community concerns. *Newspaper Research Journal, 9,* 35–48.

SMITH, M. J. (1988). *Contemporary communication research methods.* Belmont, CA: Wadsworth.

SMITH, N. L. (1985). Introduction: Moral and ethical problems in evaluation. *Evaluation and Program Planning, 8,* 1–3.

SMITH, R. F. (1989). How design and color affect reader judgment of newspapers. *Newspaper Research Journal, 10,* 75–84.

SMITH, T. W. (1987). The art of asking questions, 1936–1985. *Public Opinion Quarterly, 51,* S95–S108.

SNYDER, M. (1974). Self-monitoring of expressive behavior. *Journal of Personality and Social Psychology, 30,* 526–537.

SNYDER, M. (1979). Self-monitoring processes. In L. Berkowitz (Ed.), *Advances in experimental social psychology* (Vol. 12, pp. 85–128). Orlando, FL: Academic Press.

So, C. Y. K. (1988). Citation patterns of core communication journals: An assessment of the developmental status of communication. *Human Communication Research, 15,* 236–255.

SOCHA, T. (1988). *Marital decision conversation: An investigation of spouses' perceptions of decision topics and relational communication control and support structures.* Unpublished doctoral dissertation, University of Iowa.

SOLOMAN, M. (1980). Redemptive rhetoric: The continuity motif in the rhetoric of Right to Life. *Central States Speech Journal, 31,* 52–62.

SOMERS, R. H., MANNHEIMER, D., KELMAN, M., & MELLINGER, G. D. (1982). Structured interviews: Technical and ethical problems. In R. B. Smith & P. K. Manning (Eds.), *Handbook of social science methods: Vol. 2. Qualitative methods* (pp. 145–162). Cambridge, MA: Ballinger.

SPARKS, G. G., & Spirek, M. M. (1988). Individual differences in coping with stressful mass media: An activation-arousal view. *Human Communication Research, 15,* 236–255.

SPITZBERG, B. H., & HECHT, M. L. (1984). A component model of relational competence. *Human Communication Research, 10,* 575–600.

SPRADLEY, J. P. (1980). *Participant observation.* New York: Holt, Rinehart and Winston.

SQUIRE, P. (1988). Why the 1936 *Literary Digest* poll failed. *Public Opinion Quarterly, 52,* 125–133.

STAFFORD, L. (1987). Maternal input to twins and singleton children: Implications for language acquisition. *Human Communication Research, 13,* 429–462.

STAFFORD, L., WALDRON, V. R., & INFIELD, L. L. (1989). Actor-observer differences in conversational memory. *Human Communication Research, 15,* 590–611.

STEPHEN, T., & HARRISON, T. M. (1989). *Comserve user's guide: Version 3.0.* Troy, NY: Rensselaer Polytechnic Institute.

STERLING, T. D. (1959). Publication decisions and their possible effects on inferences drawn from tests of significance—or vice versa. *Journal of the American Statistical Association, 54,* 30–34.

STEVENS, S. S. (1958). Problems and methods of psychophysics. *Psychological Bulletin, 55,* 177–196.

STEWART, C., SMITH, C., & DENTON, R. E. (1984). *Persuasion and social movements.* Prospect Heights, IL: Waveland Press.

STEWART, L. P., GUDYKUNST, W. B., TING-TOOMEY, S., & NISHIDA, T. (1986). The effects of decision-making style on openness and satisfaction within Japanese organizations. *Communication Monographs, 53,* 236–251.

STOHL, C. (1986). The role of memorable messages in the process of organizational socialization. *Communication Quarterly, 34,* 231–249.

STONE, G. (1987). *Examining newspapers: What research reveals about America's newspapers.* Newbury Park, CA: Sage.

STONE, P. J., DUNPHY, D. C., SMITH, M. S., & OGILVIE, D. M. (1966). *The general inquirer: A computer approach to content analysis.* Cambridge, MA: MIT Press.

STRAUSS, A. L. (1987). *Qualitative analysis for social scientists.* Cambridge: Cambridge University Press.

STREET, R. L., Jr. (1989). Patients' satisfaction with dentists' communicative style. *Health Communication, 1,* 137–154.

STREET, R. L., Jr., & BULLER, D. B. (1988). Patients' characteristics affecting physician-patient nonverbal communication. *Human Communication Research, 15,* 60–90.

SUDMAN, S. (1986). Do exit polls influence voting behavior? *Public Opinion Quarterly, 50,* 331–339.

SUITOR, J. J. (1987). Friendship networks in transitions: Married mothers return to school. *Journal of Social and Personal Relationships, 4,* 445–461.

SURRA, C., CHANDLER, M., & ASMUSSEN, L. (1987). Effects of premarital pregnancy on the development of interdependence in relationships. *Journal of Social and Clinical Psychology, 5,* 123–139.

SUTTON, R. I., EISENHARDT, K. M., & JUCKER, J. V. (1985). Managing organizational decline: Lessons from Atari. *Organizational Dynamics, 14,* 17–28.

SZENT-GYORGYI, A. (1971). *Perspectives in biology and medicine.* Orlando, FL: Academic Press.

TAKEZAWA, S., & WHITEHILL, A. M. (1983). *Work ways: Japan and America.* Tokyo: Japanese Institute of Labor.

TAMBORINI, R., STIFF, J., & ZILLMAN, D. (1987). Preference for graphic horror featuring male versus female victimization. *Human Communication Research, 13,* 529–552.

TANNENBAUM, R., & SCHMIDT, W. T. (1958). How to choose a leadership pattern. *Harvard Business Review, 36,* 95–101.

TAYLOR, D. C. (1989). Reference ROMs: Six implications for libraries building CD-ROM database services. *American Libraries, 20,* 452–454.

THOMAS, S. (1986). Gender and social-class coding in popular photographic erotica. *Communication Quarterly, 34,* 103–114.

THURSTONE, L. L. (1929). Theory of attitude measurement. *Psychological Bulletin, 36,* 222–241.

THURSTONE, L. L. (1931). The measurement of social attitudes. *Journal of Abnormal and Social Psychology, 26,* 249–269.

TICHENOR, P. J., DONOHUE, G. C., & OLIEN, C. (1987). Is newspaper reading related to where people shop? *Newspaper Research Journal, 9,* 61–71.

TORRANCE, E. P. (1974). *Torrence tests of creative thinking.* Lexington, MA: Personnel Press.

TRACEY, K., CRIAG, R. T., SMITH, M., & SPISAK, F. (1984). The discourse of requests: Assessment of a compliance-gaining approach. *Human Communication Research, 10,* 513–538.

TROMBETTA, J. J., & ROGERS, D. P. (1988). Communication climate, job satisfaction, and organizational commitment: The effects of information adequacy, communication openness, and decision participation. *Management Communication Quarterly, 1,* 494–514.

TUCKER, R. K., WEAVER, R. L., & BERRYMAN-FINK, C. (1981). *Research in speech communication.* Englewood Cliffs, NJ: Prentice-Hall.

TUKEY, J. W. (1969). Analyzing data: Sanctification or detective work? *American Psychologist, 24,* 83–91.

TUKEY, J. W. (1977). *Exploratory data analysis.* Reading, MA: Addison-Wesley.

VAN DIJK, T. A. (1987). *Communicating racism: Ethnic prejudice in thought and talk.* Newbury Park, CA: Sage.

VAN MAANEN, J. (1982). Fieldwork on the beat. In J. Van Maanen, J. M. Dabbs, Jr., & R. R. Faulkner (Eds.), *Varieties of qualitative research* (pp. 103–151). Newbury Park, CA: Sage.

VAN MAANEN, J. (1983). Epilogue: Qualitative methods reclaimed. In J. Van Maanen (Ed.), *Qualitative methodology* (pp. 247–268). Newbury Park, CA: Sage.

VAN MAANEN, J. (1988). *Tales of the field: On writing ethnography.* Chicago: University of Chicago Press.

VEBLEN, T. (1919). *The place of science in modern civilization and other essays.* New York: Viking Penguin.

VELMANS, L. A. (1984). Public relations—what it is and what it does: An overview. In B. Cantor (Ed.), *Experts in action: Inside public relations* (pp. 1–6). White Plains, NY: Longman.

VENTOLA, E. (1987). *The structure of social interaction: A systemic approach to the semiotics of service encounters.* London: Frances Pinter.

WALLACE, W. (1971). *The logic of science in sociology.* Hawthorne, NY: Aldine.

WALN, V. G. (1984). Questions in interpersonal conflict participant and observer perceptions. *Southern Speech Communication Journal, 49,* 277–288.

WARD, J., & HANSEN, K. (1987). *Search strategies in mass communication.* White Plains, NY: Longman.

WATZLAWICK, P., BEAVIN, J. H., & JACKSON, D. D. (1967). *Pragmatics of human communication.* New York: Norton.

WEAVER, D. H., & GRAY, R. G. (1980). Journalism and mass communication research in the United States. In G. C. Wilhoit & H. de Bock (Eds.), *Mass communication review yearbook 1* (pp. 124–151). Newbury Park, CA: Sage.

WEBB, E. J., CAMPBELL, D. T., SCHWARTZ, R. D., & SECHREST, L. (1973). *Unobtrusive measures: Nonreactive research in the social sciences.* Skokie, IL: Rand McNally.

WEBB, E. J., & WEICK, K. E. (1983). Unobtrusive measures in organizational theory: A reminder. In J. Van Maanen (Ed.), *Qualitative methodology* (pp. 209–224). Newbury Park, CA: Sage.

WEBER, M. (1949). *The methodology of the social sciences* (E. A. Shils & H. A. Finch, Trans. and Eds.). New York: Free Press.

WEICK, K. E. (1969). *The social psychology of organizing.* Reading, MA: Addison-Wesley.

WEICK, K. E. (1985). Systematic observation methods. In G. Lindzey & E. Aronson (Eds.), *Handbook of social psychology: Vol. 1. Theory and research* (3rd ed., pp. 567–634). New York: Random House.

WEIDHORN, M. (1972). Churchill the phrase forger. *Quarterly Journal of Speech, 67,* 57–68.

WEIDHORN, M. (1975). Churchill as orator: Wish and fulfillment. *Southern Speech Communication Journal, 40,* 217–227.

WEISS, J., & DELBECQ, A. (1987). High technology cultures and management. *Group and Organizational Studies, 12,* 39–54.

WENAR, C. (1963). *The reliability of developmental histories: Summary and evaluation of evidence.* Philadelphia: University of Pennsylvania Medical School.

WENNER, L. A. (1983). Political news on television: A reconsideration of audience orientations. *Western Journal of Speech Communication, 47,* 380–395.

WHEELESS, L. R. (1976). Self-disclosure and interpersonal solidarity: Measurement, validation, and relationships. *Human Communication Research, 3,* 47–61.

WHEELESS, L. R., & GROTZ, J. (1976). Conceptualization and measurement of reported self-disclosure. *Human Communication Research, 2,* 338–346.

WHEELESS, L. R., WHEELESS, V. E., & BAUS, R. (1984). Sexual communication, communication satisfaction, and solidarity in the developmental stages of intimate relationships. *Western Journal of Speech Communication, 48,* 217–230.

WHITBOURNE, S. K. (1986). *The me I know: A study of adult identity.* New York: Springer-Verlag.

WHITE, H. D. (1981). Co-cited author retrieval online: An experiment with the social indicators literature. *Journal of the American Society for Information Science, 32,* 16–21.

WHITE, H. D., & GRIFFITH, B. C. (1981). Author co-citation: A literature measure of intellectual structure. *Journal of the American Society for Information Science, 32,* 163–171.

WHORF, B. L. (1956). *Language, thought, and reality.* New York: Wiley.

WHYTE, W. (1955). *Street corner society.* Chicago: University of Chicago Press.

WHYTE, W. (1984). *Learning from the field: A guide from experience.* Newbury Park, CA: Sage.

WICHELNS, H. A. (1925). The literary criticism of oratory. In A. M. Drummond (Ed.), *Studies in rhetoric and public speaking in honor of James A. Wineans* (pp. 181–216). Norwalk, CT: Appleton & Lang.

WIETHOFF, W. E. (1975). Guns or butter: The American Revolution as a parliamentary ploy. *Central States Speech Journal, 26,* 244–253.

WILEY, M. M., & RICE, S. A. (1924). William Jennings Bryan as a social force. *Journal of Social Forces, 2,* 338–344.

WILLIAMS, F. (1986). *Reasoning with statistics: How to read quantitative research* (3rd ed.). New York: Holt, Rinehart and Winston.

WILLIAMS, M. L., & GOSS, B. (1975). Equivocation: Character insurance. *Human Communication Research, 1,* 257–264.

WILMOT, W. W., CARBAUGH, D. A., & BAXTER, L. A. (1985). Communication strategies used to terminate romantic relationships. *Western Journal of Speech Communication, 51,* 1–18.

WIMMER, R. D., & DOMINICK, J. R. (1983). *Mass media research: An introduction.* Belmont, CA: Wadsworth.

WIMMER, R. D., & DOMINICK, J. R. (1987). *Mass media research: An introduction* (2nd ed.). Belmont, CA: Wadsworth.

WISEMAN, R. L., & SCHENCK-HAMLIN, W. (1981). A multidimensional scaling validation of an inductively derived set of compliance-gaining strategies. *Communication Monographs, 48,* 251–270.

WISPE, L., & OSBORN, C. (1982). Citation patterns in communication: A study of interdisciplinary influences. *ACA Bulletin, 42* (10), 32–39.

WOLF, F. A. (1981). *Taking the quantum leap.* New York: Harper & Row.

WOLINS, L. (1962). Responsibility for raw data. *American Psychologist, 17,* 657–658.

WOOLBERT, C. H. (1916). The organization of departments of speech in universities. *Quarterly Journal of Public Speaking, 2,* 64–77.

WRIGHT, S. R. (1979). *Quantitative methods and statistics: A guide to social research*. Newbury Park, CA: Sage.

WUEBBEN, P. L., STRAITS, B. C., & SCHULMAN, G. I. (1974). *The experiment as a social occasion*. Berkeley, CA: Glendessary Press.

WYATT, D. F., & CAMPBELL, D. T. (1950). A study of interviewer bias as related to interviewers' expectations and own opinions. *International Journal of Opinion and Attitude Research, 4*, 77-83.

YAGODA, G., & WOLFSON, W. (1964). Examiner influence on projective test responses. *Journal of Clinical Psychology, 20*, 389.

ZAR, J. H. (1984). *Biostatistical analysis* (2nd ed.). Englewood Cliffs, NJ: Prentice Hall.

ZALESKI, C. (1987). *Otherworld journeys: Accounts of near-death experiences in medieval and modern times*. New York: Oxford University Press.

ZALESNY, M. D., & FARACE, R. V. (1986). A field study of social information processing: Mean differences and variance differences. *Human Communication Research, 13*, 268-290.

ZEGIOB, L. E., & FOREHAND, R. (1978). Parent-child interactions: Observer effects and social class differences. *Behavior Therapy, 9*, 118-123.

ZILLMANN, D., & BHATIA, A. (1989). Effects of associating with musical genres on heterosexual attraction. *Communication Research, 16*, 263-288.

ZIMMERMAN, D. H., & WEIDER, D. L. (1982). The diary-diary interview method. In R. B. Smith & P. K. Manning (Eds.), *Handbook of social science methods: Vol. 2. Qualitative methods* (pp. 145-162). Cambridge, MA: Ballinger.

ZIMMERMAN, D. H., & WEST, C. (1975). Sex roles, interruptions and silences in conversations. In B. Thorne & N. Henley (Eds.), *Language and sex: Differences and dominance* (pp. 105-129). Cambridge, MA: Newbury House.

ZUCKERMAN, M., DE PAULO, B. M., & ROSENTHAL, R. (1981). Verbal and nonverbal communication of deception. In L. Berkowitz (Ed.), *Advances in experimental social psychology* (Vol. 14, pp. 1-59). Orlando, FL: Academic Press.

Index

Subject Index

Abstracts, **84, 86, 88**
Academic freedom, 142
Accidental sample, 134
Active variable, 157
Advertising, 69
Alpha coefficient, 121
Alternate causality arguments, 156
Alternative procedure method, 121
American Psychological Association (APA), 91, 143
Analysis of covariance (ANCOVA), 298
Analysis of variance (ANOVA), 293–97
Analyzing data and findings, 152–53
Anonymity, 147
Apologias, 209
Applied research, 41–43
Arbitron, 185, 273
Archival research, 224–25
Archives, 73
Artifacts, 54
Association for Educational Journalism and Mass Communication (AEJMC), 24
Audience ratings, 185
Audiotaping method of observation, 115
Authority, influence of, 2
Autoethnography, 234

Bar graphs, **256**
Basic research, 40–41, 42–43
Behavioral observations, 98–99
Behaviorism, 8–9, 10
Bell-shaped curve, 270
Beta weight, 316
Between-subjects design, 177
Biased sampling frame, 186
Bibliometrics, 225–26
Bimodal, 262
Biographical studies, 210
Bitnet, 74
"Blind Men and the Elephant, The," (Saxe), 14–15
Blind reviews, 80
Books on communication, 76–78
Business and management journals, 82

Campaign speeches, **209**
Canonical correlation, 318
Card catalogs, 75–76, 77
Case studies, 209–10
Causal relationship, 156
Causation, 310–11
CD-ROM, 74–75
Census, 130
Chi-square statistic, table of critical values for, 332–33
Chi-square test, 282–84
Chronemics, 56
Classificatory measures, 100
Cluster analysis, 318
Cluster samples, 133–34
Coding:
  content analysis and, 215
  survey answers and, 202

Coding observations, 116
Coefficient of determination, 311–12
Coefficient of multiple determination, 313
Coefficients, correlation, 304–11
Coefficients, multiple correlation, 313
Cognitive conservatism, 5
COMJOBS, 74
Communication:
  characteristics of, 29–32
  context of, 32–33
  definitions of, 21–22, 27–32
  functions of, 55
  history of inquiry into, 22–24
  information-based view of, 27, 28
  levels of, 33–36, 56–69
  meaning-based view of, 27, 28
  structure of, 24–25
Communication Abstracts, 84
Communication message systems, research on, 53–56
Communication predispositions, 57, 58
Communication research:
  analyzing and interpreting data, 19–20
  conceptualizing, 16–17
  developmental role of, 23–24
  implications for, 37–38
  methodologies for conducting, 18–19
  need for, 25–27
  planning and designing, 17–18
  reconceptualizing, 20
  what constitutes, 37
  See also Research
Communication Yearbook, 78
Comparison group, 158
Compliance-gaining strategies, 61–62
Computers, use of, 116
Comserve, 74
Conceptual definitions, 44–45, 95
Conceptual fit, 95
Concurrent validity, 123
Confederates, 161
Conference papers, 84–85
Confidentiality, 147
Confounding variables, 47
Connotations, 30
Constructive replication, 138
Construct validity, 123–24
Content analysis:
  definition of, 212–13
  procedures, 213–15
  value of, 213
Content validity, 122–23
Context, 32–33
Contextual nonverbal messages, 56
Contingency table analysis, 285
Control group, 158
Control in experimental research, 156–63
Convenience sample, 134
Conversation analysis:
  conducting, 222–24
  content, 216–17
  description of, 216
  effects of conversation, 220–21

functions of, 217–18
structure of conversation, 218–20
Correlation:
  causation and, 310–11
  coefficient of determination, 311–12
  coefficients, 304–11
  definition of, 304
  matrices, 309–10
  multiple, 312–13
  partial, 313–14
Correlational designs, 180, 182
Cramer's *V* coefficient, 309
Criterion-related validity, 123
Criterion variable, 312
Cross-sectional survey designs, 188–89
Crosstabs, 285
Cultural communication, 67
Curvilinear relationship, 303
Customs, 2

Data analysis:
  definition of, 252
  descriptive, 254–68
  ethics and, 152–53
  in ethnographic research, 236–47
  inferential, 254, 268–74
  quantitative, 253–54
  survey research and, 202
  validity of research and, 127
Databases, online, 74
Debriefing sessions, 149–50
Decoding, 33, 56
Deliberative speeches, 208
Denotations, 30
Dependent variables, 46–47
Descriptive data analysis:
  frequency distributions, 254–61
  measures of central tendency, 261–63
  measures of dispersion, 263–67
  standard scores, 267–68
Design diagrams, 175–76
Design statements, factorial, 175
Dewey Decimal System, 75, 76
Dialogue, 74
Difference analysis:
  advanced, 297, 298–99
  differences in interval/ratio level data, 288–97
  differences in nominal-level data, 282–85
  differences in ordinal-level data, 285–88
  purpose for, 281–82
Directional research questions, 50, 52
Directive questionnaires and interviews, 109
Direct observations, 114
Discriminant analysis, 318
Dissertation Abstracts International, 75
Dissertation Abstracts Online, 74
Double-barreled questions, 192
Dramatistic criticism, 210–11
Dramaturgical model, 245

Libraries:
card catalogs, 75–76, 77
cataloging systems, 75
reference aids, 78–79
types of, 73
Library and Information Science journals, 82
Library of Congress cataloging system, 75
Likert scale, 103–4
Linear regression, 314–16
Linear relationships between variables, 301, 303
Line graphs, 257, 259
Line of best fit, 315
Literal replication, 137–38
Literary Digest, 182
Literature review, writing a, 89–92
Log-linear analysis, 298
Longitudinal survey designs, 188–89

Magic, 2–3
Main effects, 174, 297
Manipulation checks, 162
Market research, 182, 184–85
Mass communication:
description of, 35
journals, 81
research on, 67–69
survey research method in, 181
Mass Communication Review Yearbook, 78
Mass media effects, 67–69
Matched-sample *t* test, 292
Maturation, 129
Mean, 263
Measured operational definitions, 98
Measurement, definition of, 100
Measurement reliability:
advantages of, 124
description of, 119–20
establishing, 120–22
Measurement scales:
interval, 103–5
nominal, 100–102
ordinal, 102–3
ratio, 105
Measurement techniques:
observations, 108, 113–16, 189
questionnaires and interviews, 108–13, 189–201
unobtrusive, 224–28
Measurement validity:
advantages of, 124
description of, 119
establishing, 122–24
Measures of:
accretion, 227–28
central tendency, 261–63
dispersion, 263–67
erosion, 227
variability, 264
Measuring unidimensional and multidimensional concepts, 106–8
Median, 262–63
Memory aids, 245
Messages and meanings, 29
verbal and nonverbal, 30–31
Mode, 262
Moderately scheduled interviews, 110
Modern Language Association, 91
Mortality, 128–29
Multidimensional concepts, 106–8
Multidimensional scaling analysis, 318–19
Multimodal, 262
Multiple-administration techniques, 121

Multiple analysis of covariance (MANCOVA), 298–99
Multiple analysis of variance (MANOVA), 298
Multiple comparison test, 296
Multiple correlations, 312–13
Multiple regression, 316–17
Multiple-sample chi-square, 285
Multiple time series design, 170–71
Multistage cluster sample, 133–34
Multivariate tests, 297

National Association of Academic Teachers of Public Speaking, 22, 24
National Association of Elocutionists, 22
Naturalistic research, 231
Need analysis, 183
Negative relationship, 303
Neo-Aristotelian criticism, 208
Network analysis, 184, 242–43
Network sample, 135
Nielsen, 185, 273
Nominal measurement scale, 100–102
Nominal variables, 45–46
Nondirectional research questions, 50, 52
Nondirective questionnaires and interviews, 109
Nonequivalent control group design, 169–70
Nonlinear relationships between variables, 301, 303–4
Nonparametric statistics, 269
Nonrandom samples, 134–35
Nonreactive research method, 205
Nonverbal communication, research on, 54–56
Nonverbal message systems, 31, 54–56
Normal curve, 270
Null hypothesis, 52–53, 276

Observation(s):
coding, 116
direct, 114
ethnographic research and, 236–41
indirect, 114–15
methods of, 115–16
quantitative and qualitative, 99–100
uses for, 113
Observers' ratings, 97–98
Observing behavior, 98–99
Oculesics, 55
One-group pretest-posttest design, 172–73
One-shot case study design, 171–72
One-tailed research hypothesis, 52, 276
One-way analysis of variance, 293–96
Online databases, 74
Operationalization:
definitions, 95–96
description of, 17, 94–95
procedures for, 96–99
quantitative and qualitative observations, 99–100
Operational replication, 138
Oral histories, 209
Oral tradition, 22
Ordered variables, 45
Ordinal measurement scale, 102–3
Organizational communication:
description of, 34
external, 65
internal, 65
research on, 63–65
Organizational feedback surveys and audits, 183

Orthogonal variables, 301
Outputs of communication, 204–5

Paired *t* test, 292
Panel approach, 123
Paralanguage, 55–56
Parameters, 130, 269
Partial correlations, 313–14
Pearson product-moment correlation, 305–6, 307
Periodicals, 85
Periodicity, 132
Personal experience, 2
Phenomenology, 9–10, 244
Phonology, 53–54
Physical sciences, 8
Pie charts, 256–57
Point biserial correlation, 309
Political communication, 65, 67
Political polls, 182–83
Political science journals, 82–83
Population, 130
Positive relationship, 301, 303
Posttest-only control group design, 166–68
Pragmatics, 54
Predictive validity, 123
Predictor variable, 314
Preexperiments, 164–66, 171–73
Presuppositionless research, 233
Pretest-posttest control group design, 166
Pretests, 160
Print media, 69
Procedure validity and reliability, 126
Proceedings, 85
Proprietary research, 6
Protocol analysis, 244
Proxemics, 56
Psychology journals, 83
Public communication, 34
research on, 65, 67
Public/general-use libraries, 73
Public opinion research, 182–85
Public relations, 69
Public speaking, 22
Pure research, 41, 42–43
Purposive sample, 135

Quadratic trend, 303
Qualitative research, 231
Quantitative and qualitative observations, 99–100
Quantitative data analysis, 253–54
Quasi-equivalent control group design, 170
Quasi-experiments, 164–66, 168–71
Question format, 110
Questionnaires and interviews:
administration of questionnaires, 194–95
advantages of, 111–13
designing questions for survey, 190–93
directive and nondirective, 109
self-report, 190
strategies and formats, 110–11
uses for, 108–9, 193–201
Questions, 47
directional and nondirectional, 50, 52
types of research, 48–51
Quota sample, 135

Random assignment, 159–60
Random-digit dialing, 186
Randomization, 159

397

Author Index

401